Kāvyamīmāṁsā of Rājaśekhara

Kāvyamīmāṁsā of Rājaśekhara

Original text in Sanskrit and Translation with Explanatory Notes

by

Sadhana Parashar

DK®
PRINTWORLD
Publishers of Indian Traditions

Cataloging in Publication Data — DK
[Courtesy: D.K. Agencies (P) Ltd. <docinfo@dkagencies.com>]

Rājaśekhara, approximately 880-approximately 920, author.
Kāvyamīmāṁsā of Rājaśekhara : original text in Sanskrit and translation with explanatory notes / by Sadhana Parashar.
pages cm
English and Sanskrit.
Reprint. Originally published: 2000.
Classical treatise on Sanskrit poetics; Sanskrit text with English translation.
Includes bibliographical references.
ISBN 9788124601402 (HB)
ISBN 9788124606940 (PB)

1. Sanskrit poetry – History and criticism. 2. Poetics. I. Parashar, Sadhana, 1962- editor, translator. II. Rājaśekhara, approximately 880-approximately 920. Kāvyamīmāṃsā. III. Rājaśekhara, approximately 880-approximately 920. Kāvyamīmāṃsā. English. IV. Title.

LCC PK2916.R35 2026 | DDC 891.2109 23

ISBN: 978-81-246-0140-2 (HB)
ISBN: 978-81-246-0694-0 (PB)

First published in India in 2000
Second impression published in 2013
Third impression published in 2026

Printed and published by:
D.K. Printworld (P) Ltd.
Regd. *Office* : "*Vedaśrī*", F-395, Sudarshan Park
ESI Hospital Metro Station, New Delhi - 110015
Phones : (011) 4172 2626, 98713 94815
e-mail : indology@dkprintworld.com
Web : www.dkprintworld.com

Preface

THERE has been an increasing awareness and interest in the study of Sanskrit literary theory and its comparison and contrast with and in the light of Western critical tenets. The concepts and theories propounded by Sanskrit poeticians and critics can be modified and adapted to suit the demands of modern literature. The issues raised by the Indian critics are of universal interest and their relevance can be felt only after a comprehensive study of the works of Sanskrit critics. It is unfortunate that the access to them is restricted because only some works have been translated.

The beginnings of Sanskrit literary theory can be traced to Bharata (first century AD) and his *Rasa* theory (aesthetic appreciation) propounded in his work *Nāṭyaśāstra* though it is a treatise on dramaturgy.

The first work directly related to literary theory was Bhāmaha's *Kāvyālaṁkāra*. He is the oldest exponent of the Alaṁkāra school of poetics and defines poetry as an integration of *śabda* and *artha* (sound and sense) marked with *vakrokti* (archedness of expression) and with *alaṁkāra* as the beautifying principle.

Daṇḍin, probably a contemporary of Bhāmaha in his *Kāvyādarśa* defines poetry as composed of words conveying the *iṣṭa-artha* or desired sense, and *alaṁkāra* as a principle of embellishment and attribute conducive to the beauty of poetry. He also takes up *doṣa*s (literary defects) and poetic-diction or *mārga*.

Lollaṭa and Udbhaṭa follow Daṇḍin and the ninth century saw a landmark in Vāmana's *Kāvyālaṁkārasūtravṛtti*. He is considered as the chief protagonist of the *Rīti* school and he defines poetry as the integration of sound and sense, beautified by *guṇa*s (literary excellences) and *alaṁkāra* (poetic figures). Vāmana lays stress on *rīti* (*Viśiṣṭa pada-racanā-rītiḥ*,

KASV, I.2.7) or poetic diction which he defines as the special arrangement of words and establishes its three kinds — Vaidarbhī, Gauḍīya and Pāñcālī.

Vāmana was followed by Śrīśaṅkuka and Rudraṭa. An interval of a few decades saw another landmark in the form of Ānandavardhana's *Dhvanyāloka* which expounds the *dhvani siddhānta* (Verbal Symbolism in Literature).

The tenth century saw Rājaśekhara, Mukula, Bhaṭṭanāyaka, Bhaṭṭatouṭa, Kuntaka and Dhanañjaya. The eleventh century has some major Sanskrit critics — Abhinavagupta with contemporaries like Bhoja, Mahimabhaṭṭa and Kṣemendra. The twelfth century began with Mammaṭa's, *Kāvyaprakāśa* and also brought forward other critics like Ruyyaka and Hemacandra. The thirteenth century produced Jayaratha and Samudrabandha and after a gap, in the sixteenth century we have the critics Madhusūdana Sarasvatī and Prabhākara. The seventeenth century gave us two profound scholars: Jagannātha and Appayadīkṣita. Thus there is a continuous and cumulative development of thought within the tradition with each major thinker taking the cue from his predecessors.

In this continuous development Rājaśekhara holds an important place and in his *Kāvyamīmāṁsā*, we find many elements and issues pertinent to modern critical theory.

The two major issues of Sanskrit criticism are the art of poetic-composition and poetic-experience. The former concerns the poet and the latter the critic or ideal-reader (*sahṛdaya*). Rājaśekhara's major concern is with the poet and poetic composition though he does not leave out the *bhāvaka* (appreciator or ideal reader) who is able to appreciate the poetic genius of the poet. In Rājaśekhara as in Eliot, the emphasis is on the creative faculty of the poet rather than his emotional personality.

Rājaśekhara's *Kāvyamīmāṁsā* is not available in a complete English translation. There is a Hindī translation by Kedārnāth Śarmā Sārasvat published by the Bihar Rastrabhasa Parisad, Patna, 1965. This does not mention the MSS on which its text and translation are based. There is an edition with English notes, edited by Dalal and Śāstry (Gaekwad Oriental Series, 1934) and is based on two MSS from the Pattar Jain Bhandars, designated A and B.

The present translation would not have been possible but for the continuous support, encouragement, advice, suggestions and guidance rendered by my guru Prof. Kapil Kapoor.

I am also indebted to a number of people, first and foremost to Vivek Parashar without whose initiation, constant support and persistent efforts I would never have been able to get to the end of this work. The blessings of all my elders has equipped me with a spiritual resilience required for this effort.

A very special token of thanks for Subaha, Jaya, Anu and Rakesh.

I am also grateful to all the teachers past and present at the Centre for Linguistics and English, School of Language, Literature and Culture Studies, JNU, New Delhi.

Sadhana Parashar

The Śāstra Group at Jawaharlal Nehru University
— An Introduction —

At the Centre of Linguistics and English, Jawaharlal Nehru university, beginning in 1978, a conscious decision was taken to introduce courses in the Indian intellectual traditions in grammar, literary theory and philosophy so that the young post-graduates and research students who come to J.N.U., who are among the brightest minds in the country, are in a position to interact meaningfully with the western thought and on level ground. This intellectual tradition, we know, had three main contending schools of thought — the Brahmin (also called the Grammarians), the Buddhist and the Jaina. The Brahmin School, the Grammarians, were divided into *āstika* (theistic) and *nāstika* (atheistic) schools. These three traditions are enshrined mainly in Sanskrit and also in Pāli (Buddhist) and Prākṛt (Jaina). All the streams composed their major texts in Sanskrit which for more than 3000 years has continued to be the language of learning and scholarship in India. These three traditions, contrary to the popular perception, continue to be living traditions though through exigencies of history they have become relatively restricted to some traditional centres and institutes of learning. But the tradition is alive — this tradition of knowledge may be compared to a river, the *Gaṅgā pravāha*, which sometimes and/or at some places becomes narrow and elsewhere and at another time is a broad free flowing stream.

The task is to make this learning a part of the main-stream education, to establish a bridge between the wealth of scholarship in this tradition and the new centres of learning, the Indian universities. How is this to be achieved?

It can be achieved by making the seminal texts of the Indian intellectual traditions widely and inexpensively available. For this, we have —

1. to prepare editions of seminal intellectual texts *in different scripts*,
2. to translate/re-translate the seminal texts into English and into major Indian languages (and into major European languages), and prepare careful modern translations in contemporary idiom,
3. to expound the important theoretical frameworks in a modern idiom to bring out their contemporary relevance.

In this perspective, and with this end in view, the Centre of Linguistics and English, Jawaharlal Nehru University, New Delhi, had introduced courses first in the Indian intellectual traditions in grammar, literary theory and philosophy and then courses in the seminal texts — the grammar of Pāṇini, *Aṣṭādhyāyī*, Bharata's *Nāṭyaśāstra*, Bhartr̥hari's *Vākyapadīya* and Patañjali's *Yogasūtra*. *Aṣṭādhyāyī* is studied as a primary modeling device of knowledge; *Nāṭyaśāstra* is studied as a text of communication; *Vākyapadīya* is unrivaled as a text of philosophy of language; and, *Yogasūtra* is a text of cognition and cognitive processes. This, over the years, then led in due time to considerable expositional and comparative research by a growing body of brilliant young boys and girls who, with their minds engaged by the powerful texts, became deeply involved in and committed to the Indian traditions of thought and became convinced that the theoretical frameworks of this tradition can be meaningfully related to both the contemporary Indian realities and the modern western thought.

These young scholars have decided to form a group devoted to the task of opening out the Indian thought by (i) translating the seminal texts, (ii) writing expository commentaries on those texts, and (iii) applying the Indian theoretical frameworks to modern Indian and Western texts to show the power, validity and in-built development potential of these frameworks. This group, called **The Śāstra Group**, coordinated by me, has these founding members:

1. Ananya Vajpeyi
2. Anuradha Ghosh

3. Atanu Bhattacarya
4. Debashish Chatterji
5. Gaurhari Behera
6. Mayurika Chakravarti
7. Nabanita Banerji
8. Nitoo Das
9. Sadhana Parashar
10. Saugatha Bhaduri
11. Sunita Murmu
12. Sushant Kumar Mishra
13. Shankaranarayanan
14. Shruti Pant
15. Swati Mustafi
16. Rajnish Kumar Mishra

Objectives of Śāstra Group

1. to prepare inexpensive script variants of principal intellectual texts in the major Indian scripts,
2. to prepare modern translations of these texts in major Indian languages and produce both inexpensive student editions of each and multilingual CD texts,
3. to apply the Indian theoretical frameworks contemporary Indian texts and texts of other cultures,
4. to explore the possibility of producing reference bibliography of Sanskrit studies around the globe,
5. to prepare multi-lingual glossaries of intellectual terms in grammar, literary theory and philosophy, and
6. to start a *Journal of Indic Studies*.

The following texts have been identified in the first instance:

I. Grammar and Phonetics

1. Aṣṭādhyāyī
2. Vājasaneyi Prātiśākhya
3. Pāṇinīya Śikṣā
4. 1st Āhnika of Mahābhāṣya

II. Literary Theory

5. Bharata's Nāṭyaśāstra
6. Bhāmaha's Kāvyālaṁkāra
7. Daṇḍin's Kāvyādarśa
8. Mahimabhaṭṭa's Vyaktiviveka
9. Rājaśekhara's Kāvyamīmāṁsā
10. Anandavardhana's Dhvanyāloka
11. Abhinavagupta's Abhinavabhāratī
12. Visvanātha's Sāhityadarpaṇa

13. Pt. Jagannātha's Rasagaṅgādhara

III. Philosophy

14. Mīmāṁsāsūtra
15. Nyāyasūtra
16. Sāṁkhyasūtra
17. Vaiśeṣikasūtra
18. Yogasūtra
19. Vedāntasūtra
20. Mādhavācārya's Sarvadarśanasaṁgraha
21. Tattvārthasūtra
22. Dharmakīrti's Pramāṇavārttika
23. Jagadīśa's Śabdaśakti-prakāśikā

Some texts have already been translated — those at serial nos. 5, 6, 9, 14, 15, 16, 17, 18, 19. Those at no. 9 and 18 are under publication. Other are awaiting finalisation for publication. Besides, several research studies have been completed that expound the Indian theoretical frameworks and apply them to modern texts in a significant reversal of the existing data-theory relationship.

Rajnish Kumar Mishra's exposition of *Buddhist Theory of Meaning* was the first **Śāstra Group** research belonging to the 3rd part of the Objectives to be published in the ŚĀSTRA GROUP SERIES. Now Sadhna Parashar's translation of Rājaśekhara's *Kāvyamīmāṁsā* is being published as the second Śāstra Group Publication. *Kāvyamīmāṁsā* is a seminal 9th century text of literary theory; and it is different from the preceding texts in that for the first time, various issues and dimensions of literary creativity and composition are taken up for close analysis. The discussion is of great contemporary interest and is pertinent to issues of contemporary literary theory as well. The present is the only complete translation of this important text and has for years been used by succeeding batches of students in the Centre of Linguistics and English. I am very happy that this book is now being published. This will lead to a renewal of Rājaśekhara studies and a revival of interest in related issues. I feel extremely happy, and have a sense of fulfilment, at the publication of this work.

Prof. Kapil Kapoor
Professor of English
Dean, School of Language, Literature and Culture Studies
Jawaharlal Nehru University
New Delhi - 110 067

Contents

Scheme of Transliteration

VOWELS :

a	ā	i	ī	u	ū	e	ai	o	au
अ	आ	इ	ई	उ	ऊ	ए	ऐ	ओ	औ

r̥	l̥
ऋ	ऌ

anusvara : ṁ अं **visarga** ḥ (:) अः

CONSONANTS

gutturals :	k	kh	g	gh	ṅ
	क्	ख्	ग्	घ्	ङ्
palatals :	c	ch	j	jh	ñ
	च्	छ्	ज्	झ्	ञ्
cerebrals :	ṭ	ṭh	ḍ	ḍh	ṇ
	ट्	ठ्	ड्	ढ्	ण्
dentals :	t	th	d	dh	n
	त्	थ्	द्	ध्	न्
bilabials :	p	ph	b	bh	m
	प्	फ्	ब्	भ्	म्

SEMIVOWELS :

y	r	l	v
य्	र्	ल्	व्

SIBILANTS :

ś श्	ṣ ष्	s स्
(palatal)	**(cerebral)**	**(dental)**

ASPIRATE : h ह्

kṣ क्ष् tr त्र् jñ ज्ञ्

Introduction

THE objective of this study has been to attempt a translation of Rājaśekhara's work, *Kāvyamīmāṁsā*, an extensive treatise of poetics which deals with a large variety of issues in Sanskrit poetics which are also pertinent to literary theory.

Rājaśekhara, poet, dramatist and critic, belongs to the last quarter of ninth century AD and the first quarter of tenth century AD. He is believed to be the teacher and court poet of the kings' Mahendrapāla and Mahipāla.

The *Kāvyamīmāṁsā* is written in the *sūtra* style and is a kind of practical handbook for budding poets. But its interest lies much deeper than its just being a work on the education of the poet or a practical manual on the writing of poetry. The attempt in this study has been to remain faithful to the text and not fall into the trap of transcreation. The foot-notes at the end of each chapter are included as suggestions, incorporations, explanations or references relating to the text. A conscious effort has however been made to keep the length of the notes in check.

Language is central to literature. The description of language of literature is central to criticism.

Literary criticism in the context of Indian theories is an "extension of the scientific study of language into the field of the special use of language as a medium of art".[1]

The "linguistic analysis of literature is an attempt to make explicit prat of the process of reading by the use of terms and concepts appropriate to the reader's individually internalised yet culturally shared grammar

---

1. A.K. Warder, *The Science of Criticism in India*, Madras, Adyar Library and Research Centre, 1978, p. 29.

of the language".[2]

A work of literature can be seen as intricately interwoven with the total system of the natural language in which the work was written, which is in its turn linked with a system of ideological assumptions and cultural values prevalent in a given synchronic slice.

Translation as Practice

The complexity of the relation of language to literature and structures external to it is felt precisely when one attempts to translate from one language to another. To be able to retain the subtleties of enunciation in a particular language while expressing them in the translation is a challenging task.

> Translation continues to be an invisible practice. Efforts are on to make translation visible by developing a theoretical discourse to study the conditions of the translator's work, the discursive strategies and institutional structures which determine the production, circulation and reception of translated texts.[3]

Translation can be conceived of as a transference of a message from the source language text (in this case Sanskrit) to a target language (here English), based on the criterion of equivalence. Though we translate words literally aiming at their nearest equivalents yet we do not translate isolated words, rather we translate words bound by their syntactic, collocational, situational and cultural contexts.

To accept the possibility of translation is also to keep in view the recurring problems that arise during the practice of translation because each language divides the "continuum of the outside world into discrete units and there is rarely" if ever a one-to-one relationship of an item in language A with an item in language B.[4]

---

2. Roger Fowler, *The Languages of Literature : Some Linguistic Contributions to Criticism*, Routledge and Kegan Paul, London 1971, p. 68.

3. *See* Venuti Lawrence, *Rethinking Translation: Discourse, Subjectivity, Ideology*, Routledge, London, 1992, p. 6.

4. T.A. Sebeok (ed.), *Encyclopaedic Dictionary of Semiotics Tome 2*, Berlin, New York, mouton de gruyter, 1986, p. 1107.

It, therefore, becomes imperative for the translator to construct a viable typology across several factors while translating. In addition to lexical problems there is also the more serious case of grammatical difficulties specially in the case of interlinguistic translation involving Sanskrit and English.

When the signifier in a particular language is used to express certain social, aesthetic and associative-connotative functions, it may not be always possible to replace it by a denotative equivalent without the corresponding associations or connotations.

In Sanskrit which is a heavily accented language, changed accents in compound words may be used to obtain different connotations from the same words according to the rules of grammar and it may not be always easy to get dynamic equivalents in English. To take an example, in chapter thirteen we come across compounds like *aṁśujala* and *yāminīvanitayā*. Sanskrit lends itself to very effective and evocative compounding but when translating it into English we would have to paraphrase it into '*X* like *Y*' construction. However this construction seems to disperse the effect so a '*Y* like *X*' construction has been employed to capture the unity of the Sanskrit compound.

Some terms used in Sanskrit are also multidiscipline terms in the sense that certain words can have more than one meaning each belonging to different disciplines of study as for instance, *adhikaraṇa* can mean 'a discussion constituted of five parts', 'a court of justice' or 'the instrumental case in grammar'. There are numerous other terms like *saṁskāra*, *vṛtti*, *karma*, *vacana*, *araṇyarodana*, etc.

There are practical difficulties which crop up while translating from a classical language into any of the European languages because of a disjunction in their basic structure. As John Garner points out in *Aristotelian Literary Criticism* that the language employed by Aristotle poses problems in the translation

> since many Greek nouns lack distinct single equivalents in modern languages and since Aristotle, the great synthesiser is apt to subsume several ideas under a single term.[5]

5. *See* S.H. Butcher, *Aristotle's Theory of Poetry and Fine Arts*, Kalyani Publishers, Delhi, 1987.

Every language is bound by its cultural and ideological fields. It is more pertinent in this translation when the cultural context of medieval India which in being quite removed from the present-day Western civilisation also adds to the formidable tasks of the translator as she has to interpret the Sanskrit text in the totally alien culture of the English language though of course no critical concepts can be completely culture bound. If the translation had been into one of the modern Indian languages, the task would have been much simpler because the modes of discourse in the Sanskrit text could have been correspondingly adapted in the modern Indian languages. The primary objective has been to make available the text in English which has not been done so far. The purpose of translating the Sanskrit text into English is two-fold, one is to address it to a much wider audience comprising of not only teachers and students of English literature but also all others who wish to acquaint themselves with Rājaśekhara's text and have a working knowledge of the English language. The second reason is that the issues in critical theory raised by the Sanskrit theorists are no different from those of Western critical theories.

One of the problems which was felt often was in choosing the most appropriate equivalents in English to express the rich, penetrating and precise effects of words felt in the Sanskrit language. There is also a rhythmic pattern in Sanskrit in spite of its closely bound formal structures. It is not possible to reproduce the same rhythm in English but at places it has been maintained by adapting it to a suitable rhythm in English. As for instance in chapter three, note 2, the English translation is an idealised version of the text as it had indecent connotations.

> Niśād! Your fame will not be eternal,
> You who killed one heron,
> of the two in union blissful

The rhythm and essence, of the original however, has been maintained in this English translation. As attempt has been made to reconcile two requirements — one, the style of English should not be archaic and should make sense to the Modern reader — and second, the style at the same time should be formal to suit the technical language of a *śāstra* (text of a discipline).

The antiquated inversions of sentence structure have not been totally adhered to, but in certain cases they have been used to capture the elevated diction required for the same. The important technical terms have been paraphrased and the English equivalents have been put in parentheses in the translated text itself. There are however some Sanskrit terms which are conceptually difficult to translate and so have been retained in the original language. The effort has been to explain all such terms with the help of notes. The system of Transliteration followed is given at the beginning.

There are two Appendices provided at the end. Appendix I deals with the names of important persons which occur in the Sanskrit text and has been adapted from the Pt. Kedārnāth Śarmā Sārasvat edn. Appendix II deals with names of geographical equivalents and has been adapted from the C.D. Dalal edn. The continuous Sanskrit text has been taken from C.D. Dalal based on two MSS from the Pattar Jain Bhandar designated as A & B and is given at the end of the translation. Each chapter is divided into a number of lines to facilitate translation. The division of the lines and their break up has been at the discretion of the translator.

There are two maps placed after the Appendices depicting (i) India during Rājaśekhara's time and (ii) Linguistic analysis during the time of Rājaśekhara which have been taken from Dr. Śyām Vermā's *Ācārya Rājaśekhara* (in Hindī) (Bhopal: Madhya Pradesh Hindi Grantha Akadami, 1971).

Literary Criticism within the Tradition and Rājaśekhara's Place in it

Literary criticism does not necessarily have to choose between *textual* or *verbal* and *contextual* study. The distinction between the two types of linguistic meaning is also seen at two levels, formal and contextual. Formal meaning in poetry is the level at which stylistic patterns occur but these are not restricted to mere form. Formal patterns are found at three levels, *grammar*, *phonology* and *lexis*. Contextual meaning is the "relation of linguistic symbols to features of the world outside language".[6]

6. Roger Fowler, *op. cit.*, p. 223.

In case of Sanskrit poetics and for its poeticians, poetry is language and it is

> language caught in raher small compass: the individual verse forms of the *Varṇāvṛtta* metric; the stanza is its unit of composition, the whole in which its perfection is to be sought.[7]

Criticism not being linguistics, critical statements are not statements about grammar but they cannot but be improved by knowledge of what grammar is. As Roger Fowler[8] has argued for a 'unified criticism' based on a theory of language and a theory of the mutual interpenetration of language, conceptualisation and cultural organisation.

Pāṇini (fifth century BC) discusses in a few *sūtras* scattered over his works, the influence of the concept of language in various spheres of suffixes, primary and secondary derivatives and compounds.

Poetics is also indebted to grammar for the terms *jāti* (genus), *kriyā* (action), *guṇa* (quality) and *dravya* (individual/substance) which it uses in connection with certain poetic figures or while dealing with the expressive function of words.

The poet cannot avoid the ordinary grammatical connection between language and thought. Bhartṛhari makes the word essence, the Absolute Reality or the highest subtle principle which transcends all the limits of human experience.

> Even as their counterparts in the west do (e.g., Saussure), the Indian theorists conceived of meaning as a referential relation between the audible word form (*śabda*) or the signifier and the inaudible, mentally perceived sense or object content (*artha*) the signified.[9]

In addition to the grammarians, Indian poetics is also indebted to other

7. Edwin Gerow, *Indian Poetics* in *A History of Indian Literature*, Otto Harrassowitz Wiesbaden, 1977, p. 228.
8. Roger Fowler, *op. cit.*, p. 90.
9. *See* V.K. Chari, *Sanskrit Criticism*, Motilal Banarsidass, Delhi 1993, p. 5.

disciplines as for instance the philosophical schools. Daṇḍin[10] (AD 750-800) borrows the three-fold dividison of *karman* and four-fold classification of non-existence (*abhāva*) from the philosophical schools as also in the case of his treatment of the fault, *nyāyavirodhin*.

Literary criticism, in the Sanskrit tradition has been understood to be a *śāstra* by which is meant any systematic, well formulated body of knowledge.

A śāstraic exposition is supposed to involve three different kinds of inquiry:

(i) inquiry into the nature of substances or the categories of knowledge (*padārtha-mīmāṁsā*);

(ii) inquiry into the nature of language (*śabda-mīmāṁsā*) since language is the invariable medium in which knowledge is formulated; and

(iii) inquiry into the validity of critical statements (*prāmāṇya-mīmāṁsā*).[11]

Thus, a basic understanding of the grammatical and philosophical issues is a prerequisite for the understanding of critical questions.

In Sanskrit *Alaṁkāraśāstra*, the word *kāvya* is used in the wider sense which denotes all varieties of literature which fall within the purview of art and are not contributions to *śāstra*.

Bhāmaha (AD 700-750) defines *kāvya* as an integrated effect of words as well as their meanings (*śabdārthau sāhityau kāvyam*).[12] He goes on to explicitly differentiate between *śabdālaṁkāra*s which are connected to the disposition of the word, its form and structure and the *arthālaṁkāra*s which are associated with the meanings of words.

---

10. *See Daṇḍin's Kavyādarśa*, Sanskrit Text and English Translation. S.K. Belvalkar, Oriential Book Supplying Agency, Poona, 1924.
11. V.K. Chari, *op. cit.*, pp. 3-4.
12. *See Bhāmaha's Kāvyālaṁkāra*, tr. and ed. by P.V. Naganatha Sastry, Tanjore, The Lawley Press, 1928, I.16.

Daṇḍin in his definition of *kāvya* introduces the concept of body and 'soul', i.e., the spirit or essence which determines it. He defines *kāvya* as a series of words characterised by the desired sense (*iṣṭārtha*).[13]

Daṇḍin gives far more space to *śabdālaṁkāras* (regularities of phonetic features) thereby subscribing to the view of the poet as craftsman.

Vāmana[14] (AD 800-900) defines poetry primarily as such word and subject-matter as are beautified by diction and figures of speech and secondarily as mere word and subject-matter. His definition however cannot be complete without reference to Rīti which he considers as the animating principle or essence of *kāvya* (*Rītirātmā kāvyasaya*, *KASV*, I.2.6) and defines it as a special arrangement of words (*viśiṣṭa padaracanā rītiḥ*, *KASV*, I.2.7).

Rājaśekhara (AD 900-950) has given us in his *Kāvyamīmāṁsā* not one, but two definitions of *kāvya*. The first one is a fanciful definition in chapter three where he conceptualises *kāvya* as the legendary *kāvya-puruṣa* and in a symbolic mode goes on to enumerate its features. By elevating *kāvya* to a higher status, Rājaśekhara seems to hold it in very high esteem and a serious discipline to be followed in earnest.

Rājaśekhara also gives a functional definition of *kāvya* in chapter six where he defines it as sentences qualified with *guṇas* (technical excellences) and *alaṁkāras* (figures of speech). Thus for Rājaśekhara both the correctness and expressiveness of *kāvya* are important.

In ancient India literature was not studied as an end in itself. It was more often than not considered as a means to serve higher ends.

Bhāmaha holds a very noble conception of poetry, its ends being the realisation of the goals of human life (*dharma*, *artha*, *kāma* and *mokṣa*) with pleasure and fame as additives. Pleasure is directed to the ideal reader and fame to the poet. He does not conform to the view that poetry can be analysed by either concentrating on the mere manifestation of form or by devoting oneself to the evocation of content. Rather he argues

---

13. *See Kāvyādarśa*, I.10.

14. *See* Vāmana, *Kāvyālaṁkārasūtravṛtti*, tr. by Ganganath Jha, Oriental Book Agency, Poona, 1928, I.1.1.

explicitly for both by stating that he accepts both *śabdālaṁkāras* and *arthālaṁkāras* as also the distinction between them. Therefore, for him, the poet is not just a creator or a craftsman but a little of both (*KA*, I.15).

Daṇḍin conceives of poetry as an art form and says its immediate purpose is to give aesthetic pleasure both to the poet and the reader. Daṇḍin mentions delight (*ramaṇa*) and pleasure (*prīti*) for the reader and fame for the poet as the main ends of poetry.

Vāmana (*KASV*, I.1.5) also states that excellent poetry brings about pleasure and fame. Compositions of good poetry can lead to heaven and contrarily the composition of bad poetry leads poets to disrepute. His conception of a poet is that of a craftsman possessed of discriminating intelligence.

Rājaśekhara holds forth a very high position for poetry as well as poets. In fact, out of his ambitious project of composing eighteen *adhikaraṇas*, only the first remains, called the *kavirahasya*. The *Kāvyamīmāṁsā* is a treatise on instruction for poets. Rājaśekhara has classified poets into three classes which are further divisible into sub-classes. (chapter five).

According to him a poet could rise in proficiency and status through practice (*abhyāsa*). That the profession of a poet was taken very seriously is evident from the kind of instruction and information being made available to him through the *Kāvyamīmāṁsā*. In fact, he has devoted one entire chapter to *Kavicaryā* or the daily routine and duties of a poet.

As regards the prerequisites for creation of poetry Bhāmaha stresses primarily *pratibhā* and secondarily *vyutpatti* and *abhyāsa*.

According to Daṇḍin the requisites of a poet are *pratibhā*, vast-learning and assiduous application.

Rājaśekhara regards *pratibhā* as

> a power that illumines in the poet's heart the store of words, the assemblage of meanings, the paths of utterance, the mechanism of the figures of speech and other necessary materials.[15]

15. *See* R.S. Tiwary, *A Critical Approach to Classical Indian Poetics* Chaukhambha Orientalia, Delhi, p. 314.

The poetic imagination also called *kavitva* is said to be natural or inborn emanating from an antenatal capacity. Rājaśekhara has called it *śakti* or poetic-power (*KM*, Ch. IV). It has been defined as a poet's intelligence (*prajñā*) with a capacity of greater invention, or enhanced mental vision capable of creating expressive poetry using appropriate words. For Rājaśekhara there are four prerequisites essential for becoming a poet. They are: *śakti*, *pratibhā*, *vyutpatti* and *abhyāsa*.

Rājaśekhara while describing poetic perception shows the difference between scientific reality and poetic reality. The inherent value in a poetic description depends on the poet's experience just as poetic-truth depends on it and it is this experience of the poet that is expressed through his compositions. The perfection of this expression is through a perfect fusion of words and senses, which Rājaśekhara calls *sāhitya*.

Rājaśekhara — Life and Works

It is learnt from the evidence supplied by his works that Rājaśekhara was the *upādhyāya* of Mahendrapāla, the king of Kannauj and was also patronised by his son and successor Mahipāla. The approximate time in which Rājaśekhara lived and wrote is approximately AD 880-920.

It is not certain as to how many works Rājaśekhara actually wrote but we know of six works by him. The four plays are *Karpūramañjarī*, *Viddhaśālabhañjikā*, *Bālarāmāyaṇa* and *Bālabhārata*. Hemacandra, a poet critic has mentioned in his *Kāvyānuśāsana*, a poem (*kāvya*) of Rājaśekhara named *Haravilāsa*. And we have the *magnum opus*, *Kāvyamīmāṁsā*.

From his *Bālarāmāyaṇa* (I.6.13), we learn that he belonged to the *Yāyāvarakula* and some of his ancestors were inhabitants of Mahārāṣṭra. The *Yāyāvara* family had a great reputation for producing men of letters which has several times been mentioned in his work.

Rājaśekhara seems to have been proficient in many languages especially Sanskrit and Prākṛta which he uses in his works. His literary accomplishment earned him the title of a *kavirāja* which according to him is even higher than a *mahākavi*. From his *Kāvyamīmāṁsā*, it becomes amply clear that he was well informed in not only his own subject but also in different branches of knowledge associated with it.

The Kāvyamīmāṁsā

Kāvyamīmāṁsā appears to be the last work of the poet, critic and dramatist Rājaśekhara. It started off as an ambitious project to be completed in eighteen *adhikaraṇa*s but only the first *adhikaraṇa* which is divided into eighteen chapters is available.

The next is more in the form of a practical treatise for poets and it is for the first time in Sanskrit poetics that the new discipline of *kaviśikṣā* is dealt with so extensively. It is written in the form of *sūtra*s or aphoristic statements following the tradition set by *Kāmasūtra* and *Arthaśāstra*.

Rājaśekhara, not unlike a modern critic would do, adopts a systematic expository method by introducing at first the ideas and views of his predecessors and finally stating his own views at times substantiating it with illustrations drawn both from ancient poets as well as his contemporaries.

The first chapter, *Śāstrasaṁgrahaḥ* (Science of Poetics) gives a detailed account of the contents of the text and the subjects to be dealt with.

The second chapter, *Śāstranirdeśaḥ* (Nature and Division of Poetics) contains a discussion on the position and place of the science of poetics among other *śāstra*s.

The third chapter is *Kāvyapuruṣotpatti* (Origin of *Kāvya*) which follows the legendary-symbolic method of exposition. It relates the origin of *kāvya-vidyā* which is expounded by *kāvya-puruṣa*, the son of Sarasvatī, the goddess of wisdom and learning. In this chapter Rājaśekhara lays down physical action as *vṛtti* (*ceṣṭā-vinyāsa-krama*), dress and decoration as *pravṛtti* (*veśa-vinyāsa-krama*) and speech as *rīti* (*vacana-vinyāsa-krama*) which he delineates through the wanderings of *kāvya-puruṣa*.

Chapter four, *Pada-vākya-viveka* (Language, Word and Sentence) gives an account of the prerequisites for becoming a good poet. According to Rājaśekhara, *kāvya-śakti* (literary power) is the chief cause of poetical composition and posits *pratibhā* (innate-faculty) and *vyutpatti* as the objects or effects achieved by *kāvya-śakti*. He goes on to distinguish between two kinds of *pratibhā-kārayitrī* (poetical imagination) which is beneficial to the poet and *bhāvayitrī pratibhā* (critical imagination) which is of importance to the critic. There are further sub-divisions of both classes and he classifies poets on the basis of this into three types — *sārasvata*, *ābhyāsika* and *aupdeśika*.

Chapter five, *Vyutpatti and kāvya-pāka* (Vyutpatti and Maturity in Poetic Expression) begins with a definition of *vyutpatti*. Rājaśekhara states that the ability to 'discriminate between desirable and undesirable' is *vyutpatti*. In this chapter he reinforces the importance of *pratibhā* and *vyutpatti* for poets and classifies them into three as *śāstrakavi*, *kāvyakavi* and *ubhaya-kavi* with *kāvya-kavi* further sub-divided into eight classes of poets. He then goes on to give the ten stages of a poet and recalls his earlier distinction (in chapter four) of poets into *buddhimāna* (discriminating) and *āhārya buddhi* (of meagre intellect).

He also defines *vākya-pāka* (Maturity of expression in sentences) as the stringing together of words and meanings suffused with *guṇa*s (qualities) *alaṁkāra*s (rhetorical figures), *rīti* (verbal style) and *ukti* (proverbial quotes). He further gives nine kinds of *pāka* for poets.

Chapter six, *Pada-vākya-viveka* (Definition and Kinds of Sentences) defines word, *vṛtti* (compound word giving an aggregate sense different from the exact literal sense of the constituent words), sentences and *kāvya*. While giving a division of sentences, Rājaśekhara adopts two parameters — one which shows the marking of grammatical relations within a sentence and the second is the number of explicitly present verbs in a sentence.

Chapter seven, *Vākya-bheda* (Modes of Sentences and Intonation) details the appropriate language to be used by various ethnic and sub-ethnic groups which should be suitably employed in poetic-compositions. Then he goes on to define *kāku* (intonation) as the quality of recitation (*pāṭhadharmāḥ*) and gives the various divisions of *kāku* with illustrations drawn from various sources. He also mentions the languages used effectively or otherwise in different geographical regions.

In chapter eight, *Kavyārthyonyā* (Sources of Meaning in Poetry)

Rājaśekhara identifies the sources of meaning in poetry. He gives twelve sources and then adds four of his own to make sixteen sources of meaning. The four added by him are *uccitasaṁyoga* (juxtaposition for comparison) *yoktṛsaṁyoga* (extended simile), *utpādyasaṁyoga* (double simile) and *saṁyogavikāra* (modification produced by juxtapositioning). Each source is followed by an illustration.

Chapter nine, *Arthavyāptiḥ* (Description of Sources of Meaning) deals with the subject of description in meanings which may be *divya*, *divyamānuṣa*, *mānuṣa*, *pātālīya*, *mṛtya-pātālīya*, *divya-pātālīya* and *divya-mṛtya-pātālīya*. Rājaśekhara also gives us the difference between poetic reality (perception) and scientific reality and says that whatever the location may be the subject must be *rasavat*. The subject of description may be a *muktaka* (isolated verse) or a *prabandha* (literary-composition), each of which is of five kinds.

Chapter ten, *Kavicaryā and Rājacaryā* (Daily Routine and Duties of a Poet and a King) gives the *vidyā*s (important branches of knowledge for poets) and *upavidyā*s (the sixty-four accessory branches of knowledge) as essential knowledge for poets. The poet should be pure in body, speech and thought. The house of a poet, materials needed for writing, division of the day into eight parts and divisions of poets based on the time of poetic-composition are other points of consideration. Rājaśekhara, also invokes his learned wife, poetess, critic, Avantisundarī and comes out strongly in favour of women poets by saying 'women can be as good poets as men' and there need be 'no discrimination between men and women'. Considering the period when he was writing, this is a remarkable statement and again points to the modernity of Rājaśekhara. There are also instructions to kings on the assembly halls to be constructed, the evaluative discourses and assemblies to be held and eminent poets to be honoured.

Chapter eleven, *Śabdaharaṇa* (Appropriation of Words) delineates the use of words and ideas from the work of another. The different kinds of appropriation have been substantiated with examples.

Chapter twelve, *Arthaharaṇam* (Appropriation of Meanings) continues with the same subject but now considers the ideas or meanings used by ancient poets and the ways in which they can be adapted and adopted by the moderns. There are again a number of divisions and sub-divisions, each one illustrated with examples.

Chapter thirteen, *Arthaharaṇeṣvālekhyāprakhyādibhedāḥ* (Different Kinds of Appropriation) also continues with the same subject and deals with the eight sub-divisions of *Ālekhyaprakhyā*, the eight sub-divisions of *Tulyādehītulya* and the sub-divisions of *Parapūrapraveśasadṛśa*. Thus, in all thirty-two means of appropriation have been described.

Chapter fourteen, *Kavisamaya* (Conventions of a Poet) deals with poetic-conventions which according to Rājaśekhara are beneficial for a poet and should be followed meticulously. The divisions of poetic-conventions and their sub-divisions are given with special reference to *bhauma* (terrestrial) *kavi-samaya*.

Chapter fifteen, *Guṇa-Samaya-Sthāpanā* (Poetic-Conventions) continues with the conventions to be followed by poets relating to qualities as for instance *white laughter* and *black sin*. The manifestation of incorporeal qualities is depicted by white, blue and yellow colours in *Kavi-Samaya*.

Chater sixteen is *Svargya-Pātālīya-Kavi-Rahasya-Sthāpanā* (Poetic-Conventions Relating to Celestial and Nether Worlds). Just as poetic conventions relating to the terrestrial world were described in chapter fourteen, this chapter follows a description of conventions relating to celestial and nether-worldly time. Each kind is illustrated with examples. The terms which are used for certain ethnic groups are *dānavas*, *daityas* and *asuras*. These imply groups of people who shared a racial affinity with Indian Āryans but did not ṣubscribe to the same culture.

For a poet they can all be treated as one just as the twelve suns mentioned in the Purāṇas can be treated as one.

Chapter seventeen, *Deśa-Vibhāga* (Geographical Regions and its divisions) refers to the division of geographical regions followed by the divisions of space and time in chapter eighteen, *Kāla-Vibhāga* (Divisions based on Time).

Kāvyamīmāṁsā
of Rājaśekhara

Original Text in Sanskrit and Translation

1

शास्त्रसङ्ग्रहः

Śāstrasaṁgrahaḥ
(The Discipline of Poetics)

अथातः काव्यं मीमांसिष्यामहे यथोपदिदेश श्रीकण्ठः परमेष्ठिवैकुण्ठादिभ्यश्चतुःषष्टये शिष्येभ्यः। सोऽपि भगवान्स्वयम्भूरिच्छाजन्मभ्यः स्वान्तेवासिभ्यः। तेषु सारस्वतेयो वृन्दीयसामपि वन्द्यः काव्यपुरुष आसीत्। तं च सर्वसमयविदं दिव्येन चक्षुषा भविष्यदर्थदर्शिनं भूर्भुवस्वस्त्रितयवर्त्तिनीषु प्रजासु हितकाम्यया प्रजापतिः काव्यविद्याप्रवर्त्तनाय प्रायुङ्क्त। सोऽष्टादशाधिकरणीं दिव्येभ्यः काव्यविद्यास्नातकेभ्यः सप्रपञ्चं प्रोवाच।

Now[1] begins an analysis of poetics. Even as Śiva-Śrīkaṇṭha[2] expounded *Kāvya-vidyā* (poetics) to Parameṣṭhi,[3] Vaikuṇṭha and 64[4] pupils so also did Svayambhū[5] train his own pupils in this discipline.

---

1. Traditionally a treatise begins with the particle *atha* (now) as a sign of auspiciousness. The legendary origins are also a convention to signify the long history of the discipline. Legend is a favoured mode of discourse. Recourse to legends is also observed in other chapters as for example in chapter three.

2. Śiva is an important God of the Hindu pantheon, one of the trinity — Brahmā, Viṣṇu and Śiva. Śrīkaṇṭha is one of the thousand names of Śiva. For more details see John Dowson, *A Classical Dictionary of Hindu Mythology and Religion, Geography History and Literature*, Munshiram Manoharlal Publishers Pvt. Ltd., New Delhi, 1973, p. 296.

3. Parameṣṭhī and Vaikuṇṭha are names of Lord Viṣṇu, one of the gods of the Hindu Trinity. Cf. John Dowson, *Ibid.*, p. 331.

4. The number 64 recurs in the tradition, as for example, in *Ṛgveda*, *Kāmasūtra*, *Nāṭyaśāstra*, etc. There are 64 *kalās*, i.e., arts and crafts.

5. Svayambhū 'The Self-Existent', a name of Brahmā, the creator. See John Dowson, *op. cit.*, p. 314.

Kāvya-puruṣa,[6] the son of Sarasvatī,[7] revered by gods is also a pupil. He, on account of his insight is ordained to deliver the knowledge of the discipline of poetics to all the world. Poetics is divided into 18 *adhikaraṇas*.[8]

तत्र कविरहस्यं सहस्राक्षः समाम्नासीत्, औक्तिकमुक्तिगर्भः, रीतिनिर्णयं सुवर्णनाभः, आनुप्रासिकं प्रचेताः, यमो यमकानि, चित्रं चित्राङ्गदः, शब्दश्लेषं शेषः, वास्तवं पुलस्त्यः, औपम्यमौपकायनः, अतिशयं पाराशरः, अर्थश्लेषमुतथ्यः, उभयालङ्कारिकं कुबेरः, वैनोदिकं कामदेवः, रूपकनिरूपणीयं भरतः, रसाधिकारिकं नन्दिकेश्वरः, दोषाधिकरणं धिषणः, गुणौपादानिकमुपमन्युः, औपनिषदिकं कुचुमारः — इति। ततस्ते पृथक् पृथक् स्वशास्त्राणि विरचयाञ्चक्रुः।

इत्थङ्कारश्च प्रकीर्णत्वात् सा किञ्चिदुच्चिच्छिदे। इतीयं प्रयोजकाङ्गवती सङ्क्षिप्य सर्वमर्थमल्पग्रन्थेन अष्टादशाधिकरणी प्रणीता।

Sahasrākṣa[9] composed a treatise on *kavi-rahasya* (mystical doctrines of poets), Uktigarbha on *ukti* (poetic-expression), *Suvarṇanābha* on *rīti* (style), Pracetā on *anuprāsa* (alliteration), Citrāṅgada on *yamaka* (rhyme) and *citra-kāvya*, Śeṣa on *śabda- śleṣa* (paronomasia or pun), Pulastya on *vāstava* or *svābhāvokti* (description of nature), Aupkāyana on *upamālaṁkāra* (simile), Pārāśara on *atiśayokti* (hyperbole), Utathya on *artha-śleṣa* (pun playing upon the meanings), Kubera on *ubhaya-alaṁkāra* or *śabda* and *artha* (words and meanings), Kāmadeva on subjects related to *vinodas* (pleasure or gratification), Bharata on *Nāṭya-śāstra* (dramaturgy), Nandikeśvara on *rasa* (aesthetic appreciation), Dhīṣaṇa or Bṛhaspati on *doṣa* (faults), Upamanyu on *guṇa* (excellences) and Kucumāra on *aupniṣadika*.

In this way the discipline of poetics which comprises different genres

6. The narrative of Kāvya-puruṣa seems to have been borrowed from *Harṣa-carita*. Cf. Bāṇa — *Harṣa-carita*, tr. by E.B. Cowell and F.W. Thomas, Motilal Banarsidass, Delhi, 1968, chapter 1, pp. 4-34.

7. Sarasvatī, the goddess of speech and learning and patroness of the arts and sciences. Cf. John Dowson, *op. cit.*, pp. 284-85.

8. Rājaśekhara follows the division of a treatise into *adhikaraṇas*. An *adhikaraṇa* refers to a topic, a complete argument treating one subject. *See* Vamana Shivaram Apte, *The Practical Sanskrit-English Dictionary*, Motilal Banarsidass, Delhi, rpt. 1985, p. 43.

9. 17 thinkers are acknowledged here to have made contributions in different areas or concepts of literary theory. This is again a convention of scholarship acknowledging debt to the *pūrvācāryas* and enumerating them.

has been summarised into eighteen *adhikaraṇas* which together form this treatise *Kāvya-mīmāṁsā*.

तस्या अयं प्रकरणाधिकरणसमुद्देशः। शास्त्रसङ्ग्रहः, शास्त्रनिर्देशः, काव्यपुरुषोत्पत्तिः, पदवाक्यविवेकः, पाठप्रतिष्ठा, अर्थानुशासनं, वाक्यदिघयः, कविविशेषः, कविचर्या, राजचर्या, काकुप्रकाराः, शब्दार्थहरणोपायाः, कविसमयः, देशकालविभागः, भुवनकोश इति कविरहस्यं प्रथममधिकरणमित्यादि। इति सूत्राण्यथैतेषां व्याख्यामाध्यं भविष्यति।

The first *adhikaraṇa*, *Kavi-rahasya* comprises *Śāstra-saṁgraha* (The Discipline of Poetics), *Śāstra-nirdeśa* (Description of Poetics), *Kāvya-puruṣotpatti* (Origin of *Kāvya*), *Pada-Vākya-Viveka* (Language, Word and Sentence), *Pāṭha-pratiṣṭhā* (Modes of Poetry), *Arthānuśāsana* (Meaningful instruction), *Vākya-vidheya* (Definition and Kinds of Sentences),*Kavicaryā* (Daily Routine of a Poet),*Kavi-viśeṣas* (Description of Subjects), *Rājacaryā* (Routine of a Court-Poet), *Kākuprakāra* (Intonation), *Śabdārthaharaṇopāya* (Appropriation of words and meanings), *Kavisamaya* (Conventions of a Poet), *Deśakālavibhāga* (Divisions based on Time and Parts of a Country) and *Bhuvanakośa* (Geographical Divisions).[10]

समासव्यासविन्यासः सर्गे शिष्यहिताय नः।
चित्रोदाहरणैर्गुर्वी ग्रन्थेन तु लघीयसी ।

इयं नः काव्यमीमांसा काव्यव्युत्पत्तिकारणम् ।
इयं सा काव्यमीमांसा मीमांस्यो यत्र वाग्लवः ।।
वाग्लवं न स जानाति न विजानाति यस्त्विमाम् ।

यायावरीयः सङ्क्षिप्य मुनीनां मतविस्तरम्।
व्याकरोत्काव्यमीमांसा कविभ्यो राजशेखरः।।

For pupils' benefit the content of the treatise is kept concise but suitably elaborated. The text though brief abounds in examples. The *Kāvyamīmāṁsā* is a profound statement on the discipline of poetics. It is an analysis of poetics, of *śabda*, language and its constituent parts (words and meanings). Those who do not understand the power of words cannot follow its analysis. *Yāyāvarīya* (Rājaśekhara) has condensed the ideas of ancient thinkers in *Kāvyamīmāṁsā*.

10. Fifteen subjects are stated here as comprising the eighteen chapters of the first *adhikaraṇa*, *kavirahasya*. These fifteen subjects are treated in the eighteen chapters of *Kāvyamīmāṁsā*.

2

शास्त्रनिर्देशः

Śāstra-Nirdeśaḥ

(Nature and Division of Poetics)

इह हि वाङ्मयमुभयथा शास्त्रं काव्यं च। शास्त्रपूर्वकत्वात् काव्यानां पूर्वं शास्त्रेष्वभिनिविशेत। नह्यप्रवर्त्तितप्रदीपास्ते तत्त्वार्थसार्थमध्यक्षयन्ति।

तच्च द्विधा — अपौरुषेयं पौरुषेयं च। अपौरुषेयं श्रुतिः। सा च मन्त्र-ब्राह्मणे। विवृतक्रियातन्त्रा मन्त्राः। मन्त्राणां स्तुतिनिन्दा. . . विनियोगग्रन्थो ब्राह्मणम्।

ऋग्यजुःसामवेदास्त्रयी। अथर्वणश्च तुरीयः। तत्रार्थव्यवस्थितपादा ऋचः। ताः सगीतयः सामानि। अच्छन्दांस्यगीतानि यजूंषि। ऋचो यजूंषि सामानि चाथर्वणं त इमे चत्वारो वेदाः।

इतिहासवेदधनुर्वेदौ गान्धर्वायुर्वेदावपि चोपवेदाः। 'वेदोपवेदात्मा सार्ववर्णिकः पञ्चमो गेयवेदः' इति द्रौहिणिः।

VERBAL discourse may be divided into *kāvya* and *śāstra*. The prior knowledge of *śāstra* is essential for an appreciation of *kāvya*. Just as nothing is visible in the dark without the aid of light so also no poet can create without a knowledge of *śāstras*.

Śāstras are divisible into *apauruṣeya*[1] (revealed) and *pauruṣeya* (human).[2] The former is also known as *śruti*[3] which is divisible into

1-2. A *śāstra* is considered *apauruṣeya* when it cannot be attributed to a particular author and *pauruṣeya* when it can be traditionally attributed to a specific author: Cf. *Kāvyamīmāṁsā of Rājaśekhara*, ed. by C.D. Dalal & Pandit R.A. Sastry, 3rd edn., Oriental Institute, Baroda, 1934, p. 131.

3. *Śruti* has no beginning, exists in an unbroken tradition and it has not been written by any human author, while *smṛti* is created or composed by the

mantric and *Brāhmaṇa*[4]. The functional incantations are the *mantras*. Description of *mantras* comprise *Brāhmaṇa*.

Ṛgveda[5] (Study of Scriptures), *Yajurveda*[6] (Study of Various *yajña*-Practices) and *Sāmaveda*[7] (Devotional Cults based on Music) comprise the *trayī*[8] (threefold), *Atharvaveda* (Source book of Worldly Knowledge) is the fourth. In these the verses are called *Ṛk*. The song or choral portion is called *Sāma*. The one without rhyme or song is called *Yajus*.

Itihāsaveda (Historical Narratives), *Dhanurveda* (Science of Archery), *Gandharva* (Science of Fine Arts) and *Āyurveda* (Science of Life) are the four Upavedas. Ācārya Drauhiṇi posits *Gānaveda* which is available to all equally and is the soul of all Vedas as the fifth Veda.

"शिक्षा, कल्पो, व्याकरणं, निरुक्तं, छन्दोविचितिः,ज्यं, षडङ्गानि" इत्याचार्याः।
"उपकारकत्वादलङ्कारः सप्तमङ्गम् इति यायावरीयः। ऋते च तत्स्वरूपपरिज्ञानाद्वेदार्थानवगतेः।

---

disciplined and trained scholars. For more details see John Dowson, *op. cit.*, p. 305.

4. *Brāhmaṇa* literally means 'belonging to *Brāhmaṇa* or Veda'. A particular explanatory attempt with regard to a particular Veda is called as its *Brāhmaṇa*. The *Brāhmaṇa* portion of the Vedas shows the connection of the *mantras* to the rites or ceremonies. For details, see Benjamin Walker, *Hindu World: An Encyclopaedic Survey of Hinduism* (in two volumes), George Allen & Unwin Ltd., London, 1968, Vol. I, pp. 166-74.
5. *Ṛgveda* is the most ancient sacred book of the Hindus. It is a collection of hymns or verses. For details see Benjamin Walker, Vol. II, *op. cit.*, pp. 294-7.
6. *Yajurveda* is the second of the three principal Vedas. It is a collection of sacred texts in prose relating to sacrifices. For details see Benjamin Walker, *op. cit.*, Vol. II, pp. 613-14.
7. *Sāmaveda* (*Sāman*, melody), is the third Veda. Its *saṁhitā* or principal part is wholly metrical. For further reference, See Benjamin Walker, *op. cit.*, Vol. II, p. 343.
8. *Trayī* is comprised of three or three-fold. *Ṛk*, *Yajña* and *Sāman* are the three categories of Vedic *mantras*. All the *mantras* containing any kind of knowledge and used for their meaning and knowledge only are known as *Ṛk* literally meaning 'the *mantras* of Appraisal'. The *mantras*, containing the overtone of *yajña* and employed from that point of view and purpose only, are known as *Yajus*. The *mantras*, employed for the purpose of devotional singing at the time of *yajña* or at other occasions are known as *Sāman*. See under Veda for further reference in Benjamin Walker, *op. cit.*, Vol. II, pp. 556-9.

यथा —

"द्वा सुपर्णा सयुजा सखाया समानं वृक्षं परिषस्वजाते।
तयोरन्यः पिप्पलं स्वाद्वत्ति अनश्नन्नन्यो अभिचाकशीति।।"

"*Śikṣā* (The Science of Proper Articulation and Pronunciation or Phonetics), *Kalpa* (Rituals), *Vyākaraṇa* (Garmmar), *Chandas* (The Science of Prosody or Metrics), *Jyotiṣa* (Astronomy) and *Nirukta* (Etymology or Explanation of Difficult Vedic Words) are the six auxiliaries (Vedāṅgas)[9] to the study of Vedas" as posited by ancient *ācāryas*. Yāyāvarīya Rājaśekhara posits "*Alaṁkāra Śāstra* as the seventh Vedāṅga (discipline auxiliary to the Vedas)". Comprehension of the Vedas remains incomplete without an auxiliary knowledge of rhetorical figures as in (the *dvāsuparṇa mantra*) —

> Two birds, united always and known by the same name, closely cling to the same tree. One of them eats the sweet fruits, the other looks on without eating.[10]

---

9. Vedāṅgas (Ancillaries of the Vedas). The root *wid* in Sanskrit means *to know*. The books composed of the knowledge of Āryans were called the Vedas. At first the instruction was given in the Vedas. For a further exposition of these studies the *Brāhmaṇas* and Āraṇyakas were resorted to and in course of time these *Brāhmaṇas* and Āraṇyakas which contained discussions and expositions of the Vedas became independent branches of study or the six Vedāṅgas. For further reference see Vettam Mani, *Purāṇic Encyclopaedia: A Comprehensive Dictionary with Special Reference to the Epic and Purāṇic Literature*, Motilal Banarsidass, Delhi, 1979 rpt., pp. 841-3.

10. See Swami Nikhilananda, *The Upaniṣads. A Second Selection. Śvetāśvatara, Praśna* and *Māṇḍūkya* with *Gauḍapāda*'s *Kārikā*, Phoenix House Ltd., London, 1954, rpt., 1957.

    The embodied self and the Pure Self are described with a view to helping the aspirant attain the knowledge of ultimate reality.

    The *two birds* are the individual self and the supreme self. The former is Pure Consciousness conditioned by the body and mind on account of its association with ignorance (*avidyā*). The latter is Pure Consciousness unconditioned by any limiting factors — the Lord himself, who is eternally pure, free and illuminated and is the master or controller of *avidyā*. They are *united always* because the individual self is the reflection of the supreme self in the *buddhi*. The two are inseparable companions like an object and its reflection.

    They bear the *same name*, that is to say *ātman*. The tree is the body. *One of them*, that is the *individual self* or *jīva eats*, that is to say experiences. On account of

सेयं शास्त्रोक्तिः। प्रत्यधिकरणं ऋचं यजुः सामाथर्वणं ब्राह्मणं चोदाहृत्य भाषामुदाहरिष्यामः। तत्र वर्णानां स्थानकरणप्रयत्नादिभिः निष्पत्तिनिर्णयिनी शिक्षा आपिशलीयादिका। नानाशाखातीतानां मन्त्राणां विनियोजकं सूत्रं कल्पः। सा च यजुर्विद्या। शब्दानामन्वाख्यानं व्याकरणम्। निर्वचनं निरुक्तम्। छन्दसां प्रतिपादयित्री छन्दोविचितिः। ग्रहगणितं ज्योतिषम्। अलङ्कारव्याख्यानं तु पुरस्तात्।

This is *śāstrokti*. The following chapters include examples from all the Vedas.

Śikṣā (phonetics)[11] is a discipline auxiliary to the Vedas. It is the science of proper articulation and pronunciation of phonetic units or letters.

Different branches of study use separate *mantra*s (mystic formulae) and *sūtra*s (aphorisms) in rituals. This comes under *Yajurvidyā.*

A systematic analysis of the formation of words in a language is *Vyākaraṇa* or grammar.

The exposition of meaning of words is *Nirukta* (or etymology). The separation of words or lines of verse according to metre comes under *metrical poetics* (or *Chanda*). The study of planets and their positions is *Jyotiṣa-śāstra* (or astronomical science). Description of *Alaṁkāra-śāstra* (rhetorics) will follow.

पौरुषेयं तु पुराणम्, आन्वीक्षिकी, मीमांसा, स्मृतितन्त्रमिति शास्त्राणि। तत्र वेदाख्यानोपनिबन्धनप्रायं पुराणमष्टाद। यदाहुः —

> "सर्गः प्रतिसंहारः कल्पो मन्वन्तराणि वंशविधिः।
> जगतो यत्र निबद्धं तद्विज्ञेयं पुराणमिति।।"

"पुराणप्रविभेद एवेतिहासः" इत्येके। स च द्विधा परि(र)क्रियापुराकल्पाभ्याम्। यदाहुः —

---

lack of discrimination the *jiva* identifies itself with the body and experiences the pleasant or unpleasant truths of action. The *other* is the Lord, who is the witness or Pure consciousness. He is the controller of both the individual self and the body and is the detatched witness of their activities.

11. Phonetics is the branch of *bhāṣikā* or language study concerned with pronunciation (*śikṣā*) 'instruction'. It is regarded as one of the principal components of Sanskrit philological enquiry. See Benjamin Walker, *op. cit.*, p. 208.

"परि(र)क्रिया पुराकल्प इतिहासगतिर्द्विधा।
स्यादेकनायका पूर्वा द्वितीया बहुनायका।।"

तत्र रामायणं भारतं चोदाहरणे।

Pauruṣeya śāstras are four (1) *Purāṇas* (historical texts), (2) *Ānvīkṣikī* (Philosophy), (3) *Mīmāṁsā* (Epistemology) and (4) *Dharma-śāstra.*

Purāṇas consist of tales and legends of the Vedas retold in figurative language. They are eighteen. The subject division in Purāṇas are five.

> They are — creation of the Universe, inclusive creation or cosmogony, the period of different Manus, the historical description of mankind and destruction of the world.
>
> *Itihāsa* (historical narrative) is also a type of Purāṇa.[12]

It is of two types *parkriyā* and *purākalpa*.

> The progress of historical narrative is of two types *parkriyā* and *purākalpa*. The former has only one protagonist or central character while the latter has two or more. The examples of the two are *Rāmāyaṇa*[13] and *Mahābhārata.*[14]

आन्वीक्षिकीं तु विद्यावसरे वक्ष्यामः।

निगमवाक्यानां न्यायैः सहस्रेण विवेक्त्री मीमांसा। सा च द्विविधा विधिविवेचनी ब्रह्मनिदर्शनी च ।

---

12. *Purāṇa*: A class of Sanskrit writings giving a legandary account of earlier times. They are part of the *smṛti* (non-Vedic scriptures) and follow the *itihāsa* (epics) in point of time and importance. The Purāṇa according to its definition should contain *sarga* (creation of the universe), *pratisarga* (recreation of cosmogony), *vaṁśa* (the history of sages and patriarchs), *manvantara* (the period of different Manus) and *vaṁśānucarita* (genealogy of kings). For further reference see Benjamin Walker, *op. cit.*, Vol. II, pp. 253-7 and Vettam Mani, *op.cit.*, pp. 617-9.

13. *Rāmāyaṇa* is one of the two great epics of India — the other being *Mahābhārata.* It is said to have been composed by the sage Vālmīki. For more details see Benjamin Walker, *op. cit.*, pp. 287-9.

14. *Mahābhārata* is probably the longest of all the epics in the world and is a vast miscellany of pre-Āryan and Āryan material and tells the story of the descendants of Bharata, the eponymous founder of the great Indian families of yore, reaching its climax in the war of succession between the Kauravas and Pāṇḍavas. For details see Benjamin Walker, *op. cit.*, pp. 8-11.

अष्टादशैव श्रुत्यर्थस्मरणात्स्मृतयः। "तानीमानि चतुर्दश विद्यास्थानानि, यदुत वेदाश्चत्वारः, षडङ्गानि, चत्वारि शास्त्राणि" इत्याचार्याः। तान्येतानि कृत्स्नामपि भूर्भुवःस्वस्त्रयीं व्यासज्य वर्त्तन्ते। तदाहुः —

"विद्यास्थानानां गन्तुमन्तं न शक्तो
जीवेद्वर्षाणां योऽपि साग्रं सहस्रम्।

तस्मात्सङ्क्षेपादर्थसन्दोह उक्तो
व्यासः सन्त्यक्तो ग्रन्थभीरुप्रियार्थम्।।"

The description of *Ānvīkṣikī* is given in detail later.

Vedic sentences and their logical exposition is the subject of *Mīmāṁsa*. It is of two types — *Karma-Mīmāṁsā* or *Pūrva-Mīmāṁsā* and *Brahma-Mīmāṁsā* or *Vedānta Śāstra*.

Smṛtis[15] are the recollection of the meanings of Śruti or Vedas. They are eighteen. The ancient thinkers posit fourteen *Vidyāsthānas*. They are four Vedas, six Vedāṅgas and four *śāstras*. The knowledge acquired through these fourteen sources pertains to all things existing in the three worlds — the earth, the sky and the heaven.

Thus —

Man cannot reach the depths of this knowledge even after several years. Therefore their import is stated here in brief for the benefit of those who fear detailed description.

"सकलविद्यास्थानैकायतनं पञ्चदशं काव्यं विद्यास्थानम्" — इति यायावरीयः। गद्यपद्यमयत्वात् कविधर्मत्वात् हितोपदेशकत्वाच्च। तद्धि शास्त्राण्यनुधावन्ति।

"वार्त्ता कामसूत्रं शिल्पिशास्त्रं दण्डनीतिरिति। पूर्वैः सहाष्टादश विद्यास्थानानि" इत्यपरे।

आन्वीक्षिकी त्रयी वार्त्ता दण्डनीतिश्चेति विद्याः। "दण्डनीतिरेवैका विद्या" इत्यौशनसाः। दण्डभयाद्धि कृत्स्नो लोकः स्वेषु स्वेषु कर्मस्ववतिष्ठते। "वार्त्ता दण्डनीतिर्द्वे

15. *Smṛti* 'what was remembered'. Inspiration as distinguished from *śruti* or direct revelation. In its widest application the term includes the *vedāṅgas*, the *sūtras*, the *Rāmāyaṇa* the *Mahābhārata*, the *Purāṇas*, the *Dharma-Śāstras*, especially the works of Manu, Yājñavalkya and other law-givers and the *rīti-śāstras* or ethics. See Dowson, *op. cit.*, p. 301.

विद्ये" इति बार्हस्पत्याः। वृत्तिर्विनय ग्रहणं च स्थितिहेतुर्लोकयात्रायाः। "त्रयीवार्त्तादण्डनीतयस्तिस्रो विद्याः" इति मानवाः। त्रयी हि वार्त्तादण्डनीत्योरुपदेष्ट्री। "आन्वीक्षिकी त्रयी वार्त्तादण्डनीतयश्चतस्रो विद्या" इति कौटिल्यः। आन्वीक्षिक्या हि विवेचिता त्रयी वार्त्तादण्डनीत्योः प्रभवति।

Yāyāvarīya (Rājaśekhara) calls "*Kāvya* the fifteenth branch of knowledge". It is the basis of all the disciplines. *Kāvya* includes prose and verse, the works of poets and is useful. It is followed by all the *śāstras*.

In addition to the above fourteen, *Vārtā* (common speech), *Kāmasūtra* (erotics), *Śilpaśāstra* (archaeology) and *Daṇḍanīti* or *Arthaśāstra* (law) are additional disciplines. In all, these are eighteen genres.

Ānvīkṣikī, *Trayī*, *Vārtā* and *Daṇḍanīti* are the four disciplines. Uśnā posits *Daṇḍanīti* as the sole discipline. Fear of punishment induces people to work. Bṛhaspati posits two disciplines — '*Daṇḍanīti* (Law) and *Vārtā* (common speech)', because livelihood and discipline are essential to society. The followers of Manu posit, '*Trayī*, *Vārtā* and *Daṇḍanīti*', as the three most important disciplines since *Trayī*, instructs *Vārtā* and *Daṇḍanīti*. According to Kauṭilya, *Trayī*, *Ānvīkṣikī*, *Vārtā* and *Daṇḍanīti* are the four major disciplines.

"पञ्चमी साहित्यविद्या" इति यायावरीयः। सा हि चतसृणामपि विद्यानां निष्यन्दः। आभिर्धर्मार्थौ यद्विद्यात्तद्विद्यानां विद्यात्वम्।

तत्र त्रयी व्याख्याता। द्विधा चान्वीक्षिकी पूर्वोत्तरपक्षाभ्याम्। अर्हद्भदन्तदर्शने लोकायतं च पूर्वः पक्षः। सांख्यं न्यायवैशेषिकौ चोत्तरः। त इमे षट् तर्काः। तत्र च तिस्रः कथा भवन्ति वादो, जल्पो, वितण्डा च।

मध्यस्थयोस्तत्त्वावबोधाय वस्तुतत्त्वपरामर्शो वादः। विजिगीषोः स्वपक्षसिद्धये छलजातिनिग्रहादिपरिग्रहो जल्पः। स्वपक्षस्यापरिग्रहित्री परपक्षस्य दूषयित्री वितण्डा।

कृषिपाशुपाल्ये वणिज्या च वार्त्ता। आन्वीक्षिकीत्रयीवार्त्तानां योगक्षेमसाधनो दण्डस्तस्य नीतिर्दण्डनीतिः। तस्यामायत्ता लोकयात्रेति शास्त्राणि। सामान्यलक्षणं चैषाम् —

"सरितामिव प्रवाहास्तुच्छाः प्रथमं यथोत्तरं विपुलाः।
ये शास्त्रसमारम्भा भवन्ति लोकस्य ते वन्द्याः।।"

Yāyāvarīya (Rājaśekhara) names '*Sāhitya-Vidyā* as the fifth discipline'.

It is the soul of all other disciplines. Its knowledge leads to *dharma* and *artha* (prosperity and success).

Trayī has been analysed. *Ānvīkṣikī* is of two types — *Pūrvapakṣa* and *Uttarapakṣa*. The former comprises three philosophical schools (*darśana*)[16] — Cārvāka, Buddhist and Jaina. *Uttarapakṣa* also comprises three philosophical schools — Sāṁkhya (based on numeral discriminative tendencies), Nyāya (Logic) and Vaiśeṣika (Atomic School). These six schools of philosophy are collectively known as *tarka*. The arguments (or *kathā*) on which *tarka* is based has three varieties *vāda*, *jalpa* and *vitaṇḍa*. *Vāda* is an exposition. *Vitaṇḍa* is a fallacious controversy used for finding fault with the opponents defence. *Jalpa* is debate or disputation adopted to gain victory over the opponent.[17]

Agriculture, animal-care and trade, all together form *vārtā-śāstra* (popular usage). *Ānvīkṣkī*, *trayī* and *vārtā* together can be understood only on the basis of *Daṇḍanīti*.

Thus —

Just as rivers are thin and narrow in the beginning and gradually widen so also *śāstras* are small and gradually increase in dimension. These *śāstras* are revered by one and all.

सूत्रादिभिश्चैषां प्रणयनम्। तत्र सूत्रणात सूत्रम्। यदाहुः —

"अल्पाक्षरमसन्दिग्धं सारवद्विश्वतो मुखम्।
अस्तोभमनवद्यञ्च सूत्रं सूत्रकृतो विदुः।।"

16. *Darśana* 'Demonstration'. The six schools of Hindu philosophy are *Nyāya* (founded by Gotama, the logical School), *Vaiśeṣika* (founded by Kaṇāda, the Atomic School), *Sāṁkhya* (founded by the sage Kapila, takes its name from numeral or discriminative tendencies and is atheistical), Yoga (founded by Patañjali, is theistical and exerts the existence of one all-pervading spirit) Pūrva-Mīmāṁsā and Uttara-Mīmāṁsā which are included under a general term Vedānta. The former is founded by Jaimini and the latter by Vyāsa. For further reference See John Dowson, *op. cit.*, pp. 81-3. Also See Benjamin Walker, *op. cit.*, Vol. II, pp. 201-7, p. 541 for Vaiśeṣika, pp. 616-18 for Yoga, pp. 142-3 for Nyāya, pp. 344-5 for Sāṁkhya.

17. These are terms used in Logic. Cf. Lakshman Ramchandra Vaidya — *The Standard Sanskrit-English Dictionary*, Radhabai Amaram Sagoon Book-sellers and Publishers, Kalkadevi Road, Bombay, 1889, See pp. 652, 662 and 287.

सूत्राणां सकलसारविवरणं वृत्तिः। सूत्रवृत्तिविवेचनं पद्धतिः। आक्षिप्य भाषणाद्भाष्यम्। अन्तर्भाष्यं समीक्षा। अवान्तरार्थविच्छेदश्च सा। यथासम्भवमर्थस्य टीकनं टीका। विषमपदभञ्जिका पञ्जिका। अर्थप्रदर्शनकारिका कारिका। उक्तानुक्तदुरुक्तचिन्ता वार्त्तिकमिति शास्त्रभेदाः।

These *śāstras* are composed of *sūtras*,[18] etc. These are pithy aphorisms strung together.

> *Sūtras* can be defined as statements containing very few words, free from ambiguity, concise, devoid of superfluity, meaningful and far-reaching in its implications.

A commentary outlining the substance of a *sūtra* is called a *vṛtti*. A discussion of the *vṛtti* of the *sūtra* is called *padyati*. A learned commentary on an original work is called *bhāṣya*.[19] The close investigation of the deeper meaning of a *bhāṣya* is called a *samīkṣā*. The simplified gloss or commentary is called a *ṭīkā*. A running commentary which explains and analyses the difficult words is a *pañjikā*. The simplified meaning of a *sūtra* can be summarised in a verse called the *kārikā*. An exposition of the *ukta* (said), *anukta* (unsaid, extraordinary) and *durukta* (offensive, censorious or difficult words) of a *sūtra* is called a *vārttika*. These are the types of *śāstras*.

"भवति प्रथयन्नर्थं लीनं समभिप्लुतं स्फुटीकुर्वन्।
अल्पमनल्पं रचयन्ननल्पमल्पं च शास्त्रकविः।।"

शास्त्रैकदेशस्य प्रक्रिया प्रकरणम्। अध्यायादयस्त्ववान्तरविच्छेदाः। कृतिभिः स्वतन्त्रतया प्रणीता इत्यपरिसङ्ख्येया अनाख्येयाश्च।

> A *śāstra-kavi* is one who expounds the profound meaning of words. He clarifies the difficult prose, details the brevity of matter and concentrates the detailed exposition.

---

18. *Sūtra* is 'a thread or string'. A rule or aphorism. Cf. John Dowson *op. cit.*, pp. 312-14.

19. An exhaustive analysis of th e*sūtras*, raising of doubts and problems from outside (that is not explicitly stated in the text, but expected to be encountered by the reader in the interpretation of the *sūtras*) and then resolving them in the course of the analysis is called *bhāṣya*.

A part or section of the *śāstra* is called a *prakaraṇa* or a subject. However, the sections of extraneous subjects are denoted by means of words as for example *adhyāya*, *sarga*, *pariccheda*, etc. These have been composed independently by *ācāryas*. They are numerous and indescribable.

शब्दार्थयोर्यथावत्सहभावेन विद्या साहित्यविद्या। उपविद्यास्तु चतुःषष्टिः। ताश्च कला इति विदग्धवादः। स आजीवः काव्यस्य। तमौपनिषदिके वक्ष्यामः।

इत्यनन्तोऽभियुक्तानामत्र संरम्भविस्तरः।
त्यक्तो निपुणधीगम्यो ग्रन्थगौरवकारणात्।।

The discipline that studies the co-extension of words and meanings is called *sāhitya-vidyā*. This has sixty-four *upavidyās* or *kalās*. *Kalās* are the soul of *kāvya*. The detailed description of these will follow in the *aupniṣadika prakaraṇa*.

The creations of the learned in this world are endless and only the learned can follow them. For fear of increasing the size (of this text) we have left them out.

।। इति राजशेखरकृतौ काव्यमीमांसायां कविरहस्ये प्रथमेऽधिकरणे
द्वितीयोऽध्यायः शास्त्रनिर्देशः ।।

3

काव्यपुरुषोत्पत्तिः

Kāvyapuruṣotpattiḥ
(Origin of Kāvya)

एवं गुरुभ्यो गिरः पुण्याः पुराणीः शृणुमः स्म, यत्किल धिषणं शिष्याः कथाप्रसङ्गे पप्रच्छुः, कीदृशः पुनरसौ सारस्वतेयः काव्यपुरुषो वो गुरुः? — इति। स तान् बृहताम्पतिरूचे।

THE ancient thinkers proclaim that once Bṛhaspati's[1] pupils in the course of a narration asked him, "O Lord! Who is this Kāvya-puruṣa, son of Sarasvatī who is also the lord of your *kāvya-vidyā*?" Bṛhaspati then described the origin and features of Kāvya-puruṣa.

पुरा पुत्रीयन्ती सरस्वती तुषारगिरौ तपस्यामास। प्रीतेन मनसा तां विरिञ्चः प्रोवाच — 'पुत्रं ते सृजामि'।

अथैषा काव्यपुरुषं सुषुवे। सोऽभ्युत्थाय सपादोपग्रहं छन्दस्वतीं वाचमुदचीचरत्।

Sarasvatī,[2] desirous of a son performed penance in the Himālayas. Pleased with her devotion Brahmā[3] granted that a son be born to her. Thereafter, Sarasvatī begot a son, Kāvya-puruṣa. No sooner was he born,

1. Bṛhaspati. In mythology he appears as the prototype of priests, the teacher of *devatās* (gods) and later as a *ṛṣi*. See John Dowson, *op. cit.*, p. 64.
2. Sarasvatī, the goddess of speech and learning, inventress of the Sanskrit language and Devanāgarī letter and patroness of the arts and sciences, is also wife of Brahmā. Dowson, *ibid.*, p. 284.
3. Brahmā, the Supreme Being, the Creator, the first deity of the sacred Hindu Trinity, to whom is entrusted the work of creating the universe. Dowson, *ibid.*, p. 60.

he got up, touched his mother's feet and proclaimed in metrical verse.[4]

"यदेतद्वाङ्मयं विश्वमर्थमूर्त्या विवर्त्तते।
सोऽस्मि काव्यपुमानम्ब! पादौ वन्देय तावकौ।।"

Mother of verbal discourse round me revolves. The same Kāvya-puruṣa, I salute you in reverence.

तामाम्नायदृष्टचरीमुपलभ्य भाषाविषये छन्दोमुद्रां देवी ससम्मदमङ्कपर्यङ्केनादाय तमुदलापयत्। "वत्स सच्छन्दस्काया गिरःप्रणेतर्वाङ्मयमातरमपि मातरं मां विजयसे। प्रशस्यतमं चेदमुदाहरन्ति यदुत 'पुत्रात्पराजयो द्वितीयं पुत्रजन्म' इति। त्वत्तः पूर्वे हि विद्वांसो गद्यं ददृशुर्न पद्यम्। त्वदुपज्ञमथातः छन्दस्वद्वचः प्रवर्त्स्यति। अहो श्लाघनीयोऽसि।

"शब्दार्थौ ते शरीरं, संस्कृतं मुखं, प्राकृतं बाहु जघनमपभ्रंशः, पैशाचं पादौ, उरो मिश्रम्। समः प्रसन्नो मधुर उदार ओजस्वी चासि। उक्तिचणं च ते वचो, रस आत्मा, रोमाणि छन्दांसि, प्रश्नोत्तरप्रवह्लिकादिकं च वाक्केलिः, अनुप्रासोपमादयश्च त्वामलङ्कुर्वन्ति। भविष्यतोऽर्थस्याभिधात्री श्रुतिरपि भवन्तमभिस्तौति।।

Hearing metrical composition in familiar language, Sarasvatī was overjoyed and fondly said to the newborn infant, "Son, though I am the mother of all discourse, you, with your metrical composition have won me over. This is a matter of great joy. It is said, 'Losing out to a son is akin to the second birth of a son'. Prior to you, scholars have created prose, not poetry. You are the first creator of verse. Therefore, you are to be appreciated. "Words and meanings form your body, Sanskrit your mouth, Prākṛta dialects your limbs (arms), Apabhraṁśa your legs, Piśācī[5] your feet and Miśra languages your bosom. You are complete, happy, sweet and large-hearted. Your speech is elevated. *Rasa* is the soul[6], metrical composition the pores, questions and quizzes the forms of discourse and *anuprāsa* (alliteration), *upamā* (simile), etc., are the figures of speech

4. The legend makes 'literature', the Kāvya-puruṣa, 'son' of Sarasvatī, the goddess of knowledge. Literary discourse is a discourse of knowledge.

5. Piśācī is one of the Prākṛta dialects.

6. The aesthetic theory of *rasa* as the soul of *kāvya* was first conceived and developed by Bharata in his *Nāṭya-Śāstra* for the purpose of dramatic composition. See Bharatamuni's *The Nāṭya-Śāstra* tr. by A Board of Scholars, Sri Satguru Publications, Delhi, nd Ch. 6 and 7.

employed to ornament your language. *Śruti* (Vedas) also sing to your praise."[7]

"चत्वारि शृङ्गा स्त्र योऽस्य पादा द्वे शीर्षे सप्तहस्तासोऽस्य।
त्रिधा बद्धो वृषभो रोरवीति महो देवो मर्त्य (र्त्यां) माविवेश।।"

The one with four horns, three feet, two heads and seven hands tied in three ways and uttering words has been born on this earth.[8]

तथापि संवृणु प्रगल्भस्य पुंसः कर्म बालोचितं चेष्टस्व"।

इति निगद्य निवेश्य चैनमनोकहाश्रयिणि गण्डशैलतलतल्पे स्नातुमभ्रगङ्गां जगाम।

तावच्च कुशान् समिधश्च समाहर्त्तुं निःसृतो महामुनिरुशनाः परिवृत्ते पूषण्यूष्मोप्लुप्तं तमद्राक्षीत्। कस्यायमनाथो बाल इति चिन्तयन्स्वमाश्रमपदमनैषीत्।

क्षणादाश्वस्तश्च स सारस्वतेयस्तस्मै छन्दस्वतीं वाचं समचारयत्। अकस्माद्विस्मापयन्स चाभ्युवाच।

The infant is asked by Sarasvatī to mask his mature behaviour. Sarasvatī thus blessed her son, put him on a rock platform under a tree and proceeded to take a bath in the *ākāśa-gaṅgā*.[9] The great

7. Rājeśekhara in this chapter gives a legendary account of the origin of Kāvya-puruṣa and Kāvya-vidyā to represent in the allegorical mode the origin and spread of literary-compositions.

8. For different interpretations of this *Ṛk* (*Ṛgveda*, III.8.10.3) see Sāyaṇa's *Bhāṣya*, Yāska's *Nirukta* (XIII.18). Patañjali's *Mahābhāṣya* and Bharata's *Nāṭya-Śāstra* (Ch. 17). This hymn originally from the *Ṛgveda* has been employed by different disciplines in the tradition to define the scope of the discipline for example this has been employed by Patañjali in the first *āhnika* of *Mahābhāṣya* to denote the nature of language. Sāyaṇa has directed it to *yajña* and Bharata's *Nāṭya-śāstra* has employed it from the point of view of *nāṭya* and *kāvya*. The *vṛṣabha* which has four horns, three feet, two heads and seven hands and which is bound in three places cries that the Great God entered the mortals. The four horns — the four parts of speech-noun, verb, *upasarga* (preposition) and *nipāta*. Its three feet — the three tenses, past, future and present. Two heads — the two kinds of *śabda*, *nitya* (eternal) and *kārya* (non-eternal). Its seven hands — the seven cases. It is bound threefold. See *Lectures on Patañjali's Mahābhāṣya*, Vol. I (*Āhnika*s 1-3), P.S. Subrahmanya Sastri, Annamalainagar, 1944, *Āhnika* 1, p. 280.

9. Ākāśagaṅgā is the celestial Gaṅgā (Ganges). In astronomy, the Milky Way. See Dr. Ganga Ram Garg (ed.), *Encyclopaedia of the Hindu World*, Vol. 2, Concept Publishing Company, New Delhi, 1992, p. 293.

sage, Uśanas,[10] on his routine walk to collect grass and wood for fuel witnessed the sad plight of the baby due to the heat of the rising sun. Not seeing anyone around him, he picked up the infant and carried him to the *āśrama*. Sometime later the infant inspired Uśanas who all of a sudden proclaimed thus —

> "या दुग्धाऽपि न दुग्धेव कविदोग्धृभिरन्वहम्।
> हृदि नः सन्निधत्तां सा सूक्तिधेनुः सरस्वती।।" — इति

> The One who is forever being milked by poets,
> Yet who appears forever fresh,
> The one like Kāmadhenu[11] Sarasvatī,
> May forever abide in my heart.

तत्पूर्वकमध्येतॄणां च सुमेधस्त्वमादिदेश। ततः प्रभृति तमुशनसं सन्तः कविरित्याचक्षते। तदुपचाराच्च कवयः कवय इति लोकयात्रा। कविशब्दश्च 'कवृ वर्णे' इत्यस्य धातोः काव्यकर्मणो रूपम्। काव्यैकरूपत्वाच्च सारस्वतेयेऽपि काव्यपुरुष इति भक्त्या प्रयुञ्जते।

ततश्च विनिवृत्ता वाग्देवी तत्र पुत्रमपश्यन्ती मध्येहृदयं चक्रन्द। प्रसङ्गागतश्च वाल्मीकिर्मुनिवृषा सप्रश्रयं तमुदन्तमुदाहृत्य भगवत्यै भृगुसूतेराश्रमपदमदर्शयत्।

सापि प्रस्नुतपयोधरा पुत्रायाङ्कपालीं ददाना शिरसि च चुम्बन्ती स्वस्तिमता चेतसा प्राचेतसायाऽपि महर्षये निभृतं सच्छन्दांसि वचांसि प्रायच्छत्।

अनुप्रेषितश्च स तया निषादनिहतसहचरीकं क्रौञ्चयुवानं करुणक्रेङ्कारया गिरा क्रन्दन्तमुदीक्ष्य शोकवान् श्लोकमुज्जगाद।

After this metrical composition Uśanas came to be renowned as a poet in this world. Thereafter all composers were called poets. The word *kavi*[12] comes from the root *kavi-varṇe*.[13] Being steeped in poetics, this son of

---

10. Uśanas is son of Bhṛgu and preceptor of the *asuras*. See Śivarāma Vāmana Āpte, *The Student's Sanskrit-English Dictionary*, Motilal Banarsidass, Delhi, 1988.
11. Kāmadhenu the legendary miraculous cow of plenty who could get for her owner, the sage Vasiṣṭha whatever he desired. She was produced at the original churning of the ocean and is said to possess supernatural powers of creation. Here it stands for wishful fulfilment. See Benjamin Walker, *op. cit.*, pp. 515-16.
12. *Kavi* is best translated as 'composer' in the Indian literary tradition but for convenience of communication, we will use the word poet hereafter.
13. C.D. Dalal feels that Rājaśekhara's derivation of the word *kavi* is not possible according to the *uṇādi* rule. He follows the derivation of Ujjavaladatta in →

Sarasvatī also came to be known as Kāvya-puruṣa. Sarasvatī not finding her son on returning from her bath was disconsolate. Just then, the sage Vālmīki happened to pass that way. Sympathising with Sarasvatī, he took her to Uśanasa's *āśrama* closeby. Seeing the young boy in the *āśrama* the mother goddess Sarasvatī, with the milk overflowing in her breasts, picked him up and kissed him on the forehead. Thereafter Sarasvatī in gratitude blessed Vālmīki with the power to create verses. While returning to his own *āśrama*, Vālmīki witnessed the pathetic cries of a male heron at his mate's death from a *niṣād*'s arrow. Vālmīki's grief-stricken heart broke out in verse thus —

"मा निषाद प्रतिष्ठां त्वमगमः शाश्वतीः समाः।
यत्क्रौञ्चमिथुनादेकमवधीः काममोहितम्।।"

Niṣād! Your fame will not be eternal,
You who killed one heron,
Of the two in union blissful.[14]

ततो दिव्यदृष्टिर्देवी तस्मा अपि श्लोकाय वरमदात्, यदुतान्यदनधीयानो यः प्रथममेनमध्येष्यते स सारस्वतः कविः सम्पत्स्यत इति।

स तु महामुनिः प्रवृत्तवचनो रामायणमितिहासं समदृभत्; द्वैपायनस्तु श्लोक प्रथमाध्यायी तत्प्रभावेन शतसाहस्त्रीं संहितां भारतम्।

एकदा तु ब्रह्मार्षिवृन्दारकयोः श्रुतिविवादे दाक्षिण्यवान्देवः स्वयम्भूस्तामिमां निर्णेत्रीमुद्दिदेश। उपश्रुतवृत्तान्तश्च मातरं व्रजन्तीं सोऽनुवव्राज। वत्स, परमेष्ठिनाऽननुमतस्य ते न ब्रह्मलोकयात्रा निःश्रेयसायेत्यभिदधाना हठान्न्यवर्त्तयदेनमात्मना तु प्रववृते।

ततः स काव्यपुरुषो रुषा निश्चक्राम। प्रियं मित्रमस्य च कुमारः साक्रन्दं रुदन्नभ्यधीयत गौर्या — तात, तूष्णीमास्स्व, साऽहमेषा निषेधामीति निगदन्ती समचिन्तयत्। प्रायः प्राणभृतां प्रेमाणमन्तरेण नान्यद् बन्धनमस्ति, तदेतस्य वशीकरणं कामपि स्त्रियं सृजामीति विचिन्तयन्ती साहित्यविद्यावधूमुदपादयदादिशच्चैनामेष ते रुषा धर्मपतिः पुरः प्रतिष्ठते, तदनुवर्त्तस्वैनं निवर्त्तय च। भवन्तोऽपि हन्त मुनयः काव्यविद्यास्नातकाश्चरितमतयोः स्तुध्वमेतद्धि

→ accordance with the *uṇādi* rule (4-138) of his *Uṇādisūtravṛtti*. See C.D. Dalal and Pandit R.A. Sastry, ed., *Kāvya-mīmāṁsā* of *Rājeśekhara*, Baroda Oriental Institute, 1934, p. 143.

14. This is an idealised version of the text. The literal rendering would be *artha-duṣta* indecent, Cf. Bhāmaha, I.53.

वः काव्यसर्वस्वं भविष्यतीत्यभिधाय भगवती भवानी जोषमासिष्ट। तेऽपि तथा कर्त्तुमवतस्थिरे।

Sarasvatī, on learning this through divine vision, blessed Vālmīki's *śloka* and said, 'Whoever, even if he be unlettered, studies this *śloka*, will become a Sārasvata poet.

Thereafter, Vālmīki used ordinary language to compose the *Rāmāyaṇa*. Later, the sage Vyāsa after his study of this *śloka* composed the *Mahābhārata*, a collection of one lakh *ślokas*. Once in *Brahma-loka*, the *Brahmarṣis* and Gods engaged themselves in a Vedic debate. Brahmā directed Sarasvatī to be the judge. Sarasvatī proceeded to leave the earth for *Brahma-loka* and was followed by Kāvya-puruṣa when she told him, "Son, without Brahmā's desire you should not go to *Brahma-loka*. Thereafter turn back." Kāvya-puruṣa in annoyance ventured forth. Seeing him go, his friend Kārttikeya, son of Gaurī.[16] started to cry. Mother Gaurī said, "Son, do not cry, I will talk to him." So saying, she thought — 'For men there is no other bond stronger than love.' So to stop the runaway Kāvya-puruṣa. I will create a woman. Thus, Sāhitya-Vidyā-Vadhū[17] was created and ordered to run after Kāvya-puruṣa and plead with him to return. Then Gaurī told the sage disciples of Kāvya-vidyā to go behind the two and pray to them as they are the very essence of *kāvya*. Having said thus, Bhavānī[18] proceeded to sit quietly.[19]

---

15. Rājeśekhara gives a classification of poets in chapter four and Sārasvata poets are one of those.

16. Gaurī is one of the names of the consort of Śiva. See Dowson, *op. cit.*, p. 111.

17. Rājaśekhara extends the legend of Kāvya-puruṣa by creating Sāhitya-Vidyā-Vadhū who follows him from region to region to capture the attention of her truant lover. Here Rājaśekhara points to the existence of different styles of literary compositions. It alludes to the modes of dramaturgy by distinguishing speech, apparel and manners prevalent in different geographical regions.

18. Bhavānī is one of epithets of Parvatī, wife of Śiva.

19. As already mentioned the Indian codification of knowledge is in the legendary-symbolic mode. Here Kāvya-puruṣa, the son of Sarasvatī (goddess of wisdom and learning) stands for the domain of literary discourse. *Brahma-loka* symbolises the discourse of metaphysical concerns and the insistence on Kāvya-puruṣa to stay on earth is a pointer to the *laukika* (of this world) nature of literary discourse in the Indian tradition. Literary discourse is worldly and should not transcend its limits unlike philosophical discourse.

अथ सर्वे प्रथमं प्राचीं दिशं शिश्रियुर्यत्राङ्गवङ्गसुह्मब्रह्मपुण्ड्राद्या जनपदाः। तत्राभियुञ्जाना तमौमेयी यं वेषं यथेष्टमसेविष्ट। स तत्रत्याभिः स्त्रीभिरन्वक्रियत। सा प्रवृत्तिरौड्रमागधी। तां ते मुनयोऽभितुष्टुवुः —

Sāhitya-Vidya-Vadhū, disciples and sages followed Kāvya-puruṣa to the West. On reaching there the people of Aṅga, Vaṅga, Suha, Brahma and Puṇḍṛ[20] followed Kāvya-vidyā's dress and manners. This *pravṛtti*[21] is called Auḍhra-Māgadhī. The Kāvya-vidyā disciples paid obeisance to this *pravṛtti* thus —

"आर्द्रार्द्रचन्दनकुचार्पितसूत्रहारः
सीमन्तचुम्बिसिचयः स्फुटबाहुमूलः।
दूर्वाप्रकाण्डरुचिरास्वगुरूपभोगाद्
गौडाङ्गनासु चिरमेष चकास्तु वेषः।।"

Maidens are seen with sandalpaste covered breasts and garlands, the head cloth kissing the parting of hair, and with arms like the bent grass (*dūrvā*). May these maidens of Gauḍīya always enjoy these bright and shiny garments.

यदृच्छयाऽपि यादृङ्नेपथ्यः स सारस्वतेय आसीत् तद्वेषाश्च पुरुषा बभूबुः। साऽपि सैव प्रवृत्तिः। यदपरं नृत्तवाद्यादिकमेषा चक्रे सा भारती वृत्तिः। तां ते मुनय इति समानं पूर्वेण।

तथाविधाकल्पयापि तया यदऽवशंऽवदीकृतः समासवदनुप्रासवद्योगवृत्तिपरम्परागर्भं जगाद सा गौडीया रीतिः। तां ते मुनया इति समानं पूर्वेण।

वृत्तिरीतिस्वरूपं यथावसरं वक्ष्यामः।

The men of these regions also simulated the dress of Kāvya-puruṣa. This *pravṛtti* is known as Auḍhra-Māgadhī. The dance and song presented by Sāhitya-Vadhū, imitated by the women, praised by the sages, came to be

20. Some of these areas fall within the eastern side of the land as recorded in Bharata's *Nāṭyaśāstra*. *op. cit.*, p. 301. Also see Appendix II.

21. *Pravṛtti* according to Bharata's *Nāṭyaśāstra* gives the detailed information regarding dress types, languages, manners and customs followed and professions engaged in the different regions of the land. *Pravṛtti* has been classified into four by producers of plays — they are (a) Avantī, (b) Dākṣiṇāṭya, (c) Pāñcāli, and (d) Oḍhra-Māgadhī. Corresponding to these *pravṛttis* there are four different styles (*vṛttis*) such as Bhāratī, Sāttvatī, Kaiśikī and Ārabhaṭṭī. For further details see Bharata's *Nāṭyāśāstra, op. cit.*, ch. 14, pp. 200-1.

known as Bhāratī Vṛtti.[22] In the West Sāhitya-Vadhū tried to attract Kāvya-puruṣa with her dress and her speech which was composed of *samāsa* (long-compounds), *anuprāsa* (alliteration) and *yoga-vṛtti*. This came to be known as Gauḍīya *rīti*[23] and was appreciated by the sages. *Vṛtti*s and *rīti*s will be dealt with in detail later.

ततश्च स पाञ्चालान्प्रत्युच्चचाल यत्र पाञ्चालशूरसेनहस्तिनापुर-काश्मीरवाहीकबाह्लीकबाह्लवेयादयो जनपदाः। तत्राऽभियुञ्जाना तामौमेयीति समानं पूर्वेण। सा पाञ्चालमध्यमा प्रवृत्तिः। तां ते मुनयोऽभितुष्टुवुः —

Thereafter Kāvya-puruṣa proceeded to Pāñcāla, Śūrasena, Hastināpura, Kaśmīra, Vālhīka and Bālhīka.[24] Here, the women adopted the dress and manners of Sāhitya-Vidyā-Vadhū and the *pravṛtti* which was appreciated by the sages came to be known as Pāñcāla-*madhyama-pravṛtti*.

> "ताडङ्कवल्गनतरङ्गितगण्डलेख-
> मानाभिलम्बिदरदोलिततारहारम्।
> आश्रोणिगुल्फपरिमण्डलितान्तरीयं
> वेषं नमस्यत महोदयसुन्दरीणाम्।।"

> The apparel of the belles of Kanauja is worth appreciating. It has earrings, the movement of which makes the cheeks tremulous. There are long garlands reaching down to the navel and a *ghāgharā* (heavy-skirt) reaching down from the waist."

किञ्चिदार्द्रितमना यत्नेपथ्यः स सारस्वतेय आसीदिति समानं पूर्वेण। सापि

22. Bhāratī-*vṛtti* is the verbal style according to Bharata's *Nāṭyaśāstra, op. cit.*, ch. 22, pp. 302-3.

23. For the *rīti* theorists, it is the type or mode of language, specifically lexis, chosen and employed which constitutes the essence of literariness. See Kapil Kapoor, *Alaṁkāra and the Theory of Metaphor*, in M.S. Kushwaha (ed.), *Indian Poetics and Western Thought*, Argo Publications, Delhi, 1988.

    The history of the concept of *rīti* has three stages, the first is when it was a living geographical mode of literary criticism (as in Rājaśekhara) the second was when it lost its geographical associations and came to be standardised with reference to the subject; and third is its reinterpretation by Kuntaka. See D.K. Gupta, *A Critical Study of Daṇḍiṅ and his Works*, Meharchand Lachmandas, Delhi, 1970, pp. 131-81.

24. For the geographical provinces see Bharata's *Nāṭyaśāstra*, p. 201. Also see Appendix II.

यदीषन्नृत्तगीतवाद्यविलासादिकं दर्शयाम्बभूव सा सात्त्वती वृत्तिः। आविद्धगतिमत्त्वात्सा चारभटी। तां ते मुनय इति समानं पूर्वेण। तथाविधाकल्पयापि तया यदऽद्धशंवदीकृतः ईषदसमासं ईषदनुप्रासमुपचारगर्भञ्च जगाद सा पाञ्चाली रीतिः। तां ते मुनय इति समानं पूर्वेण।

It was in this province that Kāvya-puruṣa was enamoured of Kāvya-vidyā. The dance, song and music demonstrated by Sāhitya-vadhū and appreciated by the sages can be placed under Sāttvatī or Ārabhaṭṭī *pravṛtti*. Kāvya-puruṣa thus moved by Sāhitya-vadhū used *samāsa* (compounds) and *anuprāsa* (alliteration) in his sentences which was then called Pāñcālī *rīti*.

ततः सोऽवन्तीन्प्रत्युच्चचाल यत्रावन्तीवैदिशसुराष्ट्रमालवार्बुदभृगुकच्छादयो जनपदाः। तत्राऽभियुञ्जाना तमौमेयीति समानं पूर्वेण। सा प्रवृत्तिरावन्ती। पाञ्चालमध्यमा दाक्षिणात्ययोरन्तरचारिणी हि सा। अत एव सात्त्वतीकैशिक्यौ तत्र वृत्ती। तां ते मुनयोऽभितुष्टुवुः —

After that Kāvya-puruṣa moved towards Avantī, Vidiśā, Saurāṣṭra, Mālavā, Arbudeyaka, Bhṛgu and Kutch.[25] The natives adopted Sāhitya-Vidyā-Vadhū's attire and the *pravṛtti* was named Avantī *pravṛtti* which is midway between Pāñcāla and Dakṣiṇa *pravṛttis*. Avantī has two *vṛttis* namely Sāttavatī *vṛtti* (grand style) and Kauśikī *vṛtti* (graceful style). The sages have praised this *pravṛtti* thus —

"पाञ्चालनेपथ्यविधिर्नराणां स्त्रीणां पुनर्नन्दतु दाक्षिणात्यः।
यज्जल्पितं यच्चरितादिकं तदन्योन्यसम्भिन्नमवन्तिदेशे।।"

The apparel, speech and manners of the men of Pāñcāla and women of the south is very pleasing and a blend of the two can be found in Avantī.

ततश्च स दक्षिणां दिशमाससाद यत्र मलयमेकलकुन्तलकेरलपालमञ्जर-महाराष्ट्रवङ्गकलिङ्गादयो जनपदाः। तत्राऽभियुञ्जाना तमौमेयीति समानं पूर्वेण। सा दाक्षिणात्या प्रवृत्तिः। तां ते मुनयोऽभितुष्टुवुः —

After this Kāvya-puruṣa proceeded to the south with regions like Malaya, Mekala, Kuntala, Kerala, Pāla, Manjar, Mahārāṣṭra, Gaṅga and Kaliṅga.

25. See Bharata's *Nāṭyaśāstra*, p. 201. Also see Appendix II.

The natives followed Sāhitya-Vidyā-Vadhū and this came to be known as Dākṣiṇātyā *pravṛtti*.

> "आमूलतो वलितकुन्तलचारुचूड-
> श्चूर्णालकप्रचयलाञ्छितभालभागः।
> कक्षानिवेशनिबिडीकृतनीविरेष
> वेषश्चिरं जयति केरलकामिनीनाम्।।"

Hair tied neatly, curled wavelets falling over the face and *sārī*s tied tightly below the arms makes these pretty Kerala women appear unusually graceful.

तामनुरक्तमनाः स यत्रोपथ्यः सारस्वतेय आसीदिति समानं पूर्वेण। सापि यद्विचित्रनृत्तगीतवाद्यविलासादिकमाविर्भावयामास सा कैशिकीवृत्तिस्तां ते मुनय इति समानं पूर्वेण। यदत्यर्थं च स तया वशंवदीकृतः स्थानानुप्रासवदसमासं योगवृत्तिगर्भञ्च जगाद सा वैदर्भी रीतिः। तां ते मुनय इति समानं पूर्वेण। तत्र वेषविन्यासक्रमः प्रवृत्तिः, विलासविन्यासक्रमो वृत्तिः, वचनविन्यासक्रमो रीतिः। चतुष्टयी गतिर्वृत्तीनां प्रवृत्तीनां च, देशानां पुनरानन्त्यं तत्कथमिव कार्त्स्न्येन परिग्रहः" इत्याचार्याः। अनन्तानपि हि देशांश्चतुर्धैवाकल्प्य कल्पयन्ति 'चक्रवर्तिक्षेत्रं सामान्येन, तदवान्तरविशेषैः पुनरनन्ता एव' इति यायावरीयः।

दक्षिणात्समुद्रादुदीचीं दिशं प्रति योजनसहस्रं चक्रवर्तिक्षेत्रं, तत्रैष नेपथ्यविधिः। ततः परं दिव्याद्या अपि यं देशमधिवसेयुस्तद्देश्यं वेषमाश्रयन्तो निबन्धनीयाः। स्वभूमौ तु कामचारः। द्वीपान्तरभवानां तदनुसारेण वृत्तिप्रवृत्ती।

रीतयस्तु तिस्रस्तास्तु पुरस्तात्।

तत्रास्ति मनोजन्मनो देवस्य क्रीडावासो विदर्भेषु वत्सगुल्मं नाम नगरम्। तत्र सारस्वतेयस्तामौमेयीं गन्धर्ववत्परिणिनाय। ततस्तद्वधूवरं विनिवृत्त्य तेषु प्रदेशेषु विहरमाणं तुषारगिरिमेवाजगाम, यत्र गौरी सरस्वती च मिथः सम्बन्धिन्यौ तस्थतुः। तौ च कृतवन्दनौ दम्पती दत्त्वाशिषं प्रभावमयेन वपुषा कविमानसनिवासिनौ चक्रतुः।

तयोश्च कविलोकस्वर्गसर्गं तमकल्पतां, यत्र काव्यमयेन शरीरेण मर्त्यमधिवसन्तो दिव्येन देहेन कवय आकल्पं मोदन्ते।

> इत्येष काव्यपुरुषः पुरा सृष्टः स्वयम्भुवा।
> एवं विभज्य जानानः प्रेत्य चेह च नन्दति।।

Kāvya-puruṣa was now captivated by Sāhitya-Vidyā-Vadhū. She sported various dresses and performed dances to songs and music. This came to be known as Kauśikī *vṛtti*. Kāvya-puruṣa's compositions were now devoid of *samāsa* (compounds) but characterised by *anuprāsa* and *yoga-vṛtti*. This came to be known as Vaidarbhī.[26]

Ācāryas posit that *vṛttis* and *pravṛttis* are only four whereas there are numerous geographical regions. Rājaśekhara says that this entire geographical greater region is called *cakravarttī kṣetra* and is further divisible into four major regions with a number of provinces in each.

Cakravarttī kṣetra is from the Southern Sea to the Himālayas in the north covering an area of one thousand *yojana* (miles). The poets can describe the apparel, manners, customs and speech of these geographical areas.

Rītis are of three kinds. They will be described later. In Vaidarbha there is an abode of Kāmadeva called Vatsagulma Kāvya-puruṣa was married to Sāhitya-Vidyā-Vadhū in the Gāndharva manner.

Then the pair reached Himālayā where Gaurī and Sarasvatī were sitting together. Kāvya-puruṣa and Sahitya-Vidyā-Vadhū bent to touch their feet in reverence and received their blessings which granted for them a permanent place in the hearts of poets.

Thus, a new heavenly poetic-world was created for them, enabling the poets to stay in their mortal frames in this world and in the divine form in the celestial world.

Thus Svayambhu, Brahmā created Kāvya-puruṣa. The poet who is able to comprehend the real depth of this legend gains happiness in this world and the world beyond.

।। इति राजशेखरकृतौ काव्यमीमांसायां कविरहस्ये प्रथमेऽधिकरणे तृतीयोऽध्यायः काव्यपुरुषोत्पत्तिः ।। ५ ।।

---

26. Rājaśekhara gives four geographical/cultural divisions:

Western Regions	*Pāñcāla*	*Avantī*	*Southern states*
Bhāratī *vṛtti*	Sāttvati *vṛtti* or Ārabhaṭṭī *vṛtti*	Kauśikī or Sāttvatī *vṛtti*	Kauśikī *vṛtti*
Auḍhra-Māgadhī *pravṛtti*	Pāñcāla *madhyamā pravṛtti*	Avantī *pravṛtti*	Dākṣiṇātyā *pravṛtti*
Gauḍīyā *rīti*	Pāñcālī *rīti*		Vaidarbhī *rīti*

4

पदवाक्यविवेकः

Pada-Vākya-Vivekaḥ
(Language, Word and Sentence)

द्विविधं शिष्यमाचक्षते यदुत बुद्धिमानाहार्यबुद्धिश्च। यस्य निसर्गतः शास्त्रमनुधावति बुद्धिः स बुद्धिमान्। यस्य च शास्त्राभ्यासः संस्कुरुते बुद्धिमसावाहार्यबुद्धिः।

DISCIPLES are two types: *buddhimān* (discriminatory) and *āhārya-buddhi* (of meagre intellect). Those who are naturally inclined to the *śāstra*s are *buddhimān*. Others who under the guidance of a teacher practise the *śāstra*s possess *āhārya-buddhi*.

त्रिधा च सा — स्मृतिर्मतिः प्रज्ञेति। अतिक्रान्तस्यार्थस्य स्मर्त्री स्मृतिः। वर्त्तमानस्य मन्त्री मतिः। अनागतस्य प्रज्ञात्री प्रज्ञेति। सा त्रिप्रकाराऽपि कवीनामुपकर्त्री।

The *buddhi* (intellect) is of three types — *smṛti*, *mati* and *prajñā*. The intellect which recollects things of the past is *smṛti*. *Mati* is the intellect capable of recalling matters related to the present and *prajñā* is intellect capable of looking into the future. All three are essential to a poet.

तयोर्बुद्धिमान् शुश्रूषते शृणोति गृह्णीते धारयति विजानात्यूहतेऽपोहति तत्त्वं चाभिनिविशते। आहार्यबुद्धेरप्येत एव गुणाः किन्तु प्रशास्तारमपेक्षन्ते। अहरहः सुगुरूपासना तयोः प्रकृष्टो गुणः। सा हि बुद्धिविकाशकामधेनुः। तदाहुः —

Of the two types of disciples, one with discrimination desires to hear, comprehends, raises doubts and provides solutions. In the process he learns new facts. The *āhārya-buddhi* pupil also has these qualities but needs an able teacher to guide him. To revere an able teacher is a quality desirous in both pupils, because reverence of a teacher is akin to a *kāma-*

dhenu[1] for the intellect. Thus —

> "प्रथयति पुरः प्रज्ञाज्योतिर्यथार्थपरिग्रहे
> तदनु जनयत्यूहापोहक्रियाविशदं मनः।
> अभिनिविशते तस्मात्तत्त्वं तदेकमुखोदयं
> सह परिचयो विद्यावृद्धैः क्रमादमृतायते।।"

Acquaintance with learned teachers is found to be like nectar. At first it helps the wise and discerning to receive knowledge required to light up the truth of substances. Thereafter, the mind is made capable of imagining solutions to various problems and in the end the mind becomes capable of resorting to that one ultimate truth.

ताभ्यामन्यथाबुद्धिर्दुर्बुद्धिः। तत्र बुद्धिमतः प्रतिपत्तिः। स खलु सकृदभिधानप्रतिपन्नार्थः कविमार्गंमृगयितुं गुरुकुलमुपासीत। आहार्यबुद्धेस्तु द्वयमप्रतिपत्तिः सन्देहश्च। स खल्वप्रतिपन्नमर्थं प्रतिपत्तुं सन्देहं च निराकर्त्तुमाचार्यनुपतिष्ठेत।

Contrary to the preceding two, the third category of disciples is of *durbuddhi* (ignorant). The *buddhimān* (discriminatory) observes correctly, comprehends in the first instance and should certainly enter a *gurukula* (to stay near his teacher) for advanced study in poetics. The *āhārya-buddhi* (of meagre intellect) is filled with doubt on two counts — he fails to comprehend in the first instance and even after that remains doubtful. Therefore to remove these two doubts he should stay near a teacher and learn the art of poetic-composition.

दुर्बुद्धेस्तु सर्वत्र मतिविपर्यास एव। स हि नीलीमेचकितसिचयकल्पोऽनाधेय-गुणान्तरत्वात्तं यदि सारस्वतोऽनुभावः प्रसादयति तमौपनिषदिके वक्ष्यामः।

The *durbuddhi* (ignorant) disciple cannot acquire knowledge from anywhere. His intellect is like a blue-coloured cloth on which no other colour can show.

"काव्यकर्मणि कवेः समाधिः परं व्याप्रियते" इति श्यामदेवः। मनस एकाग्रता समाधिः। समाहितं चित्तमर्थान्पश्यति। उक्तञ्च —

Śyāmadeva posits '*samādhi* (meditation) as the most essential factor in poetical composition'. Concentration of the mind (on a particular subject)

1. Kāma-dhenu, see ch. 3, Note 11.

is *samādhi*. A concentrated mind can meditate on profound subjects. Thus —

> "सारस्वतं किमपि तत्सुमहारहस्यं
> यद्गोचरे च विदुषां निपुणैकसेव्यं।
> तत्सिद्धये परमयं परमोऽभ्युपायो
> यच्चेतसो विदितवेद्यविधेः समाधिः।।"

The secret of eloquent speech (or poetical composition) relating to Sarasvatī[2] is profound and indescribable. It is within the power of the wise (and the skilful) only. There is only one supreme path to strive after it and that is concentration of an informed mind or *samādhi*.

'अभ्यासः' इति मङ्गलः। अविच्छेदेन शीलनमभ्यासः। स हि सर्वगामी सर्वत्र निरतिशयं कौशलमाधत्ते। समाधिरान्तरः प्रयत्नो बाह्यस्त्वभ्यासः। तावुभावपि शक्तिमुद्भासयतः। 'सा केवलं काव्ये हेतुः' इति यायावरीयः।

Maṅgala posits '*abhyāsa* (practice)', as most essential for poetical composition. *Abhyāsa* is continued and uninterrupted practice. It is essential for all subjects and helps to form reputed scholars. *Samādhi* is an inward endeavour while *abhyāsa* is outward. Both *samādhi* and *abhyāsa* strengthen *kāvya-śakti* (literary-power). Yāyāvarīya (Rājaśekhara) posits '*kāvya-śakti* as the chief cause of poetical composition'.

विप्रसृतिश्च सा प्रतिभाव्युत्पत्तिभ्याम्। शक्तिकर्त्तृके हि प्रतिभाव्युत्पत्तिकर्मणी। शक्तस्य प्रतिभाति शक्तश्च व्युत्पद्यते। या शब्दग्राममर्थसार्थमलङ्कारतन्त्रमुक्तिमार्गमन्यदपि तथाविधमधिहृदयं प्रतिभासयति सा प्रतिभा। अप्रतिभस्य पदार्थसार्थः परोक्ष इव, प्रतिभावतः पुनरपश्यतोऽपि प्रत्यक्ष इव। यतो मेधाविरुद्रकुमारदासादयो जात्यन्धाः कवयः श्रूयन्ते।

Kāvya-śakti is different from *pratibhā* (innate faculty) and *vyutpatti*. Actually *kāvya-śakti* is *kartṛ-rūpa*[3] while *vyutpatti* and *pratibhā* are

---

2. Sarasvatī, refer to ch. 1, Note 7. From here onwards, Rājaśekhara discusses the sources of literary creativity.

3. *Kartṛ-rūpa*: The agent of an action or subject. Instrument of an action which produces the fruit or result of an action. See Kashinath Vasudev Abhyankar and J.M. Shukla, *A Dictionary of Sanskrit Grammar*, Oriental Institute, Baroda, 1961, 3rd edn. 1986, p. 109.

karma-rūpa.[4] *Kāvya-śakti* can help in achieving *pratibhā* and *vyutpatti*. *Pratibhā* helps to perceive words, meanings, figures of speech, expressions and other poetic imagery in the mind. For one who is without *pratibhā* even perceptible objects appear non-present while for one who possesses it, non-present objects are as if directly perceived. It has been heard that Medhāvirudra and Kumāradāsa were born blind but their descriptions suffused with their *pratibhā* appear realistic.

किञ्च महाकवयोऽपि देशद्वीपान्तरकथापुरुषादिदर्शनेन तत्रस्थां व्यवहृतिं निबध्नन्ति स्म। तत्र देशान्तरव्यवहारः —

Poets (endowed with *pratibhā*) visualise and describe the customs and manners of people belonging to different geographical regions and islands without the personal knowledge of the same. Description of places and manners is seen thus —

"प्राणानामनिलेन वृत्तिरुचिता सत्कल्पवृक्षे वने
तोये काञ्चनपद्मरेणुकपिशे पुण्याभिषेकक्रिया।
ध्यानं रत्नशिलागृहेषु विबुधस्त्रीसन्निधौ संयमो
यत्काङ्क्षन्ति तपोभिरन्यमुनयस्तस्मिंस्तपस्यन्त्यमी।।"

Here in this forest of *kalpa*-trees, they draw from air life's necessary sustenance, in waters yellow with the golden dust of the lotus, they perform ablutions for religious vows; on jewelled slabs they meditate; and restrain their passions in the midst of celestial nymphs; they practice penance in a place where other sages by their austerities seek to win.[5]

द्वीपान्तरव्यवहारः —

"अनेन सार्द्धं विहराम्बुराशे-

---

4. *Karma-rūpa*: The object defined as 'something which the agent or doer of an action wants primarily to achieve' Abhyankar, *op. cit.*, p. 110. In other words Rājaśekhara posits *pratibhā* and *vyutpatti* as the effects or objects achieved by *kāvya-śakti*. The former only strengthens the literary power or *kāvya-śakti* which alone can create poetry. For the theory of creative process, Cf. Ananda Coomaraswamy, *The Dance of Śiva,* Indian edn. rev., Sagar Publications, New Delhi, 1982, Ch. 2-3, pp. 39-60.

5. See C.R. Devadhar (ed. & tr.), *Abhijñānaśākuntalam* from *Works of Kālidāsa*, Vol. 1, Motilal Banarsidass, Delhi, rpt. 1986, VII. 12 p. 219.

स्तीरेषु तालीवनमर्मरेषु।
द्वीपान्तरानीतलवङ्गपुष्पै-
रपाकृतस्वेदलवा मरुद्भिः।।"

Description of islands

O Princess, sport with him on the shores of the sea full of rumbling whispers of the palm groves. The beads of perspiration from your body will be swabbed by the cool breezes waving close flowers from other islands.[6]

कथापुरुषव्यवहारः —

"हरोऽपि तावत्परिवृत्तधैर्य-
श्चन्द्रोदयारम्भ इवाम्बुराशिः।
उमामुखे बिम्बफलाधरौष्ठे
व्यापारयामास विलोचनानि।।"

Description of characters in a story —

Like the Moon's influence on the sea at rest,
Came passion stealing over the Hermit's breast,
While on the maiden's lip that mocked the dye,
Of ripe red fruit, he bent his melting eye.[7]

"तथागतायां परिहासपूर्वं
सख्यां सखी वेत्रभृदाबभाषे।
बाले व्रजामोऽन्यत इत्यथैनां
वधूरसूयाकुटिलं ददर्श।।"

When Sunanda ceased to speak, the Princess shed her shyness and reserve and by her ardent glance proclaimed her love for the Prince. Yet modesty prevented her casting around his neck the wreath that sealed her choice until Sunanda noting her maidenly confusion, recalled her to herself by pretending to lead her away, saying: 'Come, gracious lady, let us pass on to the others!' The

---

6. See Kālidāsa's *Raghuvaṁśa*, A Study by Padma Ranganathan, The Gondals Press, New Delhi, 1964, p. 42.
7. See Kālidāsa's *Kumārsaṁbhavam* (3-67), S.R. Sehgal, Munshiram Manoharlal, Delhi, 1959, p. 36.

maiden gave her an indignant glance and at once threw the wreath around the blushing Prince's neck.[8]

सा च द्विधा कारयित्री भावयित्री च। कवेरुपकुर्वाणा कारयित्री। साऽपि त्रिविधा सहजाऽऽहार्यौपदेशिकी च। जन्मान्तरसंस्कारापेक्षिणी सहजा। जन्मसंस्कारयोनिराहार्या। मन्त्रतन्त्राद्युपदेशप्रभवा औपदेशिकी। ऐहिकेन कियतापि संस्कारेण प्रथमां तां सहजेति व्यपदिशन्ति। महता पुनराहार्या। औपदेशिक्याः पुनरैहिक एव उपदेशकालः, ऐहिक एव संस्कारकालः।

Pratibhā[9] is of two types — *kārayitrī* (poetical imagination) and *bhāvayitrī* (critical imagination). *Kārayitrī pratibhā* is beneficial to the poet. It is of three types — *sahaja*, *āhāryā* and *aupdeśiki*. That which is inborn and inherited from pior birth is *sahaja pratibhā*, that acquired by the practice of *śāstras* and *kāvyas* is *āhāryā-pratibhā* and that obtained by the blessings of others and a deep study of *mantras-tantras*[10] is *aupdeśiki*. *Sahaja kāryitrī-pratibhā* being temporal and innate is manifested as the natural disposition seen after birth. On the other hand, *āhārya kāryitrī-pratibhā* requires extensive practice. *Aupdeśikī kāryitrī-pratibhā* is acquired by charms and secret divinations in this world itself. It is not congenital.

त इमे त्रयोऽपि कवयः सारस्वतः, आभ्यासिकः, औपदेशिकश्च।

---

8. See Kālidāsa's *Raghuvaṁśa*, *op. cit.* (4-72).

9. 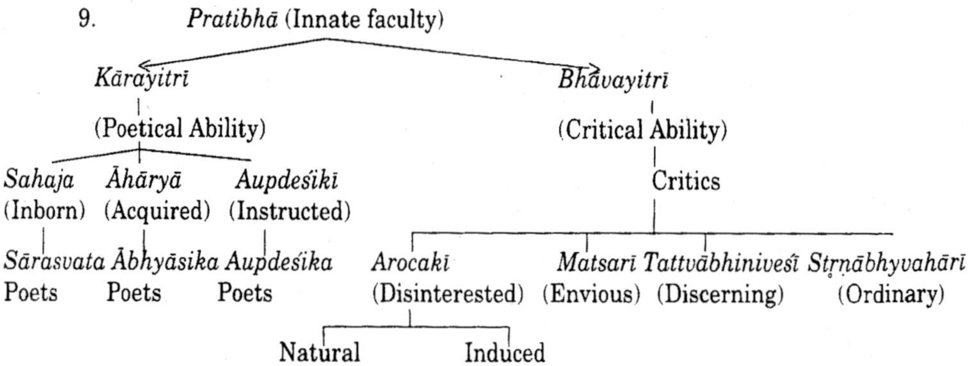

10. The ability which develops in a person as a result of the deep study of *Mantra* literature (portions of the Vedas), and systems of thought or philosophical systems (*tantra*).

जन्मान्तरसंस्कारप्रवृत्तसरस्वतीको बुद्धिमान्सारस्वतः। इह जन्माभ्यासोद्भासितभारतीक आहार्यबुद्धिराभ्यासिकः। उपदेशितदर्शितवाग्विभवो दुर्बुद्धिरौपदेशिकः। तस्मान्नेतरौ तन्त्रशेषमनुतिष्ठताम्। 'नहि प्रकृतिमधुरा द्राक्षा फाणितसंस्कारमपेक्षते' इत्याचार्याः। 'न' इति यायावरीयः एकार्थं हि क्रियाद्वयं द्वैगुण्याय सम्पद्यते। 'तेषां पूर्वः पूर्वः श्रेयान्' इति श्यामदेवः। यतः—

Based on the three types of *kāryitrī-pratibhā*, poets are also of three types, *sārasvata*, *ābhyāsika* and *aupdeśika*. *Sārasvata* poets are those *buddhimān* (discriminating) poets who manifest an innate, natural wisdom or learning (Sarasvatī). Those in whom the wisdom (Sarasvatī) is gained in this life through exercise and practice are the *āhāryā buddhi ābhyāsika* poets. Though of meagre intellect, the *aupdeśika* poets can express with instruction, practice and exercise. *Ācārya*s posit that — "Both *sārasvata* and *ābhyāsika* poets, do not require *mantra-tantra*, just as grape-juice, the natural disposition of which is sweet does not become sweeter on being cooked with sugary syrup." Yāyāvarīya (Rājaśekhara) holds a different opinion. If for the same cause, two means are adopted, the effect is also doubled. In the opinion of Śyāmadeva the third poet is better than the second while the first mentioned poet is the best because —

"सारस्वतः स्वतन्त्रः स्याद्भवेदाभ्यासिको मितः।
औपदेशिककविस्त्वत्र वल्गु फल्गु च जल्पति।।"

A *sārasvata* poet composes independently, an *ābhyāsika* poet composes in a measured way whereas an *aupdeśika* poet composes attractive but unsubstantial compositions.

'उत्कर्षः श्रेयान्' इति यायावरीयः। स चानेकगुणसन्निपाते भवति। किञ्च —

Rājaśekhara states "Eminence should be attained." Eminence can be achieved only by accumulation of several excellences. Thus —

"बुद्धिमत्त्वं च काव्याङ्गविद्यास्वभ्यासकर्म च।
कवेश्चोपनिषच्छक्तिस्त्रयमेकत्र दुर्लभम्।।

Sagacity, *kāvya* and its subsidiaries, *abhyāsa* and poetic power are very rarely found together.

काव्यकाव्याङ्गविद्यासु कृताभ्यासस्य धीमतः।
मन्त्रानुष्ठाननिष्ठस्य नेदिष्ठा कविराजता।।"

A poet comes nearer to being a *kavirāja* if he becomes proficient in *kāvya* and its subsidiaries, discriminating and a faithful follower of *mantra*.

कवीनां तारतम्यतश्चैष प्रायो वादः।

"एकस्य तिष्ठति कवेर्गृह एव काव्य-
मन्यस्य गच्छति सुहृद्भवनानि यावत्।
न्यस्याविदग्धवदनेषु पदानि शश्वत्
कस्याऽपि सञ्चरति विश्वकुतूहलीव।।"

Amongst the poets there is relative importance of —

The compositions of some poets remain confined within the four walls of their own house, for some others they travel to their friends' homes and in case of a few, they travel and trample upon the face of well read and unlettered people with their footsteps (words) like one eager to see the world.

सेयं कारयित्री।

भावकस्योपकुर्वाणा भावयित्री। सा हि कवेः श्रममभिप्रायं च भावयति। तया खलु फलितः कवेर्व्यापारतरुरन्यथा सोऽवकेशी स्यात्। 'कः पुनरनयोर्भेदो यत्कविर्भावयति भावकश्च कतिः' इत्याचार्याः। तदाहुः —

In this way *kārayitrī-pratibhā* was analysed. *Bhāvayitrī-pratibhā* favours the *bhāvaka* or critic. It completes the poet's meaning. It certainly brings forth the poetic imagination and without it a poetic composition appears fruitless. *Ācāryas* state that, 'there is no difference between a poet and a critic'. Thus —

"प्रतिभातारतम्येन प्रतिष्ठा भुवि भूरिधा।
भावकस्तु कविः प्रायो न भजत्यधमां दशाम्।।"

Distinctive *pratibhā* imparts abundant prestige in this world. A poet who is himself a critic, usually will not be in an unfavourable state.

'न' इति कालिदासः। पृथगेव हि कवित्वाद्भावकत्वं, भावकत्वाच्च कवित्वं। स्वरूपभेदाद्विषयभेदाच्च। यदाहुः —

Kālidāsa does not hold this view. He holds the opinion that the critical and poetical faculties are quite distinct and are rarely found together in one and the same person. The subject of one is word formation while that if the other is aesthetic appreciation. As it has been said —

> "कश्चिद्वाचं रचयितुमलं श्रोतुमेवाऽपरस्तां
> कल्याणी ते मतिरुभयथा विस्मयं नस्तनोति।
> नह्येकस्मिन्नतिशयवतां सन्निपातो गुणाना-
> मेकः सूते कनकमुपलस्तत्परीक्षाक्षमोऽन्यः।।"

> Someone is skilled in (sound) poetic composition while the other in hearing it. Blessed though amazing is the co-existence of the two kinds of intellect. For many excellences to be found in harmony together in the same person is a difficult task. One stone brings forth gold while the other is used to test it.

'ते च द्विधाऽरोचकिनः, सतृणाभ्यवहारिणश्च' इति मङ्गलः। 'कवयोऽपि भवन्ति' इति वामनीयाः। 'चतुर्द्धा' इति यायावरीयः मत्सरिणस्तत्त्वाभिनिवेशिनश्च। 'तत्र विवेकिनः पूर्वं तद्विपरीतास्तु ततोऽनन्तराः' इति वामनीयाः।

Maṅgala posits that, critics are of four kinds — *arocakī* (discontented) and *sṛṇābhyvahārī* (feeding on grass, i.e., vulgar), *matsarī* (envious) and *tatvābhiniveśī*. The followers of Vāmana feel that of these four, '*arocakī* and *tatvābhiniveśī* are discriminating whereas *sṛṇābhyvahārī* and *matsarī* are indiscriminate.'

अरोचकिता हि तेषां नैसर्गिकी ज्ञानयोनिर्वा। नैसर्गिकीं हि संस्कारशतेनाऽपि रङ्गमिव कालिकां ते न जहति। ज्ञानयोनौ तु तस्यां विशिष्टज्ञेयवतिव चसि रोचकितावृत्तिरेव" इति यायावरीयः।

Arocakī (discontented) are those who possess innate disinterestedness. They are of two kinds (1) naturally disinterested and (2) induced. The former will never become interested but in the latter interest may be generated by an excellent poetic composition. This is Rājaśekhara's view.

किञ्च सतृणाभ्यवहारिता सर्वसाधारणी। तथाहि व्युत्पित्सोः कौतुकिनः सर्वस्य सर्वत्र प्रथमं सा। प्रतिभाविवेकविकलता हि न गुणागुणयोर्विभागसूत्रं पातयति। ततो बहु त्यजति

बहु च गृह्णाति। विवेकानुसारेण हि बुद्धयो मधु निष्यन्दन्ते। परिणामे तु यथार्थदर्शी स्यात्। विभ्रमभ्रंशश्च निःश्रेयसं सन्निधत्ते।

Stṛṇābhyvahārī critics are ordinary. They, out of enthusiasm are always ready with words for every composition. Indiscriminate imagination cannot distinguish between excellences and blemishes. These critics take away from and also leave a lot in a poetic composition. The intellect can function only on the basis of its discriminatory power. The result should be seen in real terms. Indiscrimination should be disillusioned.

मत्सरिणस्तु प्रतिभातमपि न प्रतिभातं, परगुणेषु वाचंयमत्वात्। स पुनरमत्सरी ज्ञाता च विरलः। तदुक्तम् —

Matsarī critics close their eyes to the truth, as they do not wish to express the excellences of others. The existence of an excellent critic who is not jealous or envious is a rarity. As it has been said —

"कस्त्वं भोः कविरस्मि काप्यभिनवा सूक्तिः सग्वे पठ्यतां
त्यक्ता काव्यकथैव सम्प्रति मया कस्मादिदं श्रूयताम्।
यः सम्यग्विविनक्ति दोषगुणयोः सारं स्वयं सत्कविः
सोऽस्मिन्भावक एव नास्त्यथ भवेद्दैवान्न निर्मत्सरः।।

Question — Brother, who are you?

Answer — I am a poet.

Question — Then friend, Let's hear a verse.

Answer — Brother, I have left off even talking of poetry.

Question — Why?

Answer — Listen, that able poet who is able to understand the excellences and faults of a composition himself is not a critic. If he is, then he is not without envy.

तत्त्वाभिनिवेशी तु मध्येसहस्रं यद्येकस्तदुक्तम् —

"शब्दानां विविनक्ति गुम्फनविधीनामोदते सूक्तिभिः
सान्द्रं लेढि रसामृतं विचिनुते तात्पर्यमुद्रां च यः।
पुण्यैः सङ्घटते विवेक्तृविरहादन्तर्मुखं ताम्यतां

केषामेव कदाचिदेव सुधियां काव्यश्रमज्ञो जनः।।

Tattvābhiniveśī critic in one in a thousand. Thus —

> 'A poet whose heart is grief-stricken due to the lack of a true critic, finds a wise critic who analyses the word construction, exults at the poetic fancies, enjoys the aesthetic charm of the composition and finally succeeds in locating the profound meaning of a work.

स्वामी मित्रं च मन्त्री च शिष्यश्चाचार्य एव च।
कवेर्भवति ही चित्रं किं हि तद्यन्न भावकः।।

A critic or *bhāvaka* is a master, friend, a counsellor, pupil and a teacher together to the poet.

काव्येन किं कवेस्तस्य तन्मनोमात्रवृत्तिना।
नीयन्ते भावकैर्यस्य न निबन्धा दिशो दश।।

There is no use of the poetic compositions which remain within the poet's heart and are not spread all over by critics.

सन्ति पुस्तकविन्यस्ताः काव्यबन्धा गृहे गृहे।
द्वित्रास्तु भावकमनःशिलापट्टनिकुट्टिताः।।

Books with papers filled with poetic compositions are lying in every house but critical compositions found engraved in the hearts of critics are only two to three in numbers.

सत्काव्ये विक्रियाः काश्चिद्भावकस्योल्लसन्ति ताः।
सर्वाभिनयनिर्णीतौ दृष्टा नाट्यसृजा न याः।।

On reading an excellent poetic composition, the varied states of mind which are produced within the heart of a critic have not been seen even by Brahmā — the creator of *Nāṭyaśāstra*.

वाग्भावको भवेत्कश्चित्कश्चिद्धृदयभावकः।
सात्त्विकैराङ्गिकैः कश्चिदनुभावैश्च भावकः।।

Some critics express their appreciation through words, others through the essence of poetry and some by means of mental and physical effort.

गुणादानपरः कश्चिद्दोषादानपरोऽपरः।
गुणदोषाहृतित्यागपरः कश्चन भावकः।।

Some critics discover the qualities to be praised in a composition, some the blemishes to be condemned. There are very few who appreciate the aesthetic essence.

अभियोगे समानेऽपि विचित्रो यदयं क्रमः।
तेन विद्मः प्रसादोऽत्र नृणां हेतुरमानुषः।।

Critics are of many types and are interested in different aspects of appreciation of compositions. This is because of the difference in the interest and temperament of different people.

न निसर्गकविः शास्त्रे न क्षुण्णः कवते च यः।
विडम्बयति सात्मानमाग्रहग्रहिलः किल।।

A poet who is neither naturally endowed with poetic power nor increases his intellect by means of *abhyāsa* and yet stubbornly tries to compose poetry certainly invites derision on himself.

कवित्वं न स्थितं यस्य काव्ये च कृतकौतुकः।
तस्य सिद्धिः सरस्वत्यास्तन्त्रमन्त्रप्रयोगतः।।

पदान्तरं वेत्ति सुधीः स्ववाक्यपरवाक्ययोः।
तदा स सिद्धो मन्तव्यः कुकविः कविरेव वा।।

The one who does not possess natural poetic power but is enthusiastic about composing poetry should try to attain perfection through blessings. (Sarasvatī-*mantra*). The discriminating critic who understands the difference between his own and others' verse, even if he is not a good poet should be considered superior.

कारयित्रीभावयित्र्याविती मे प्रतिभाभिदे।
अथातः कथयिष्यामो व्युत्पत्तिं काव्यमातरम्।।

In this way the difference between *kārayitrī*-and *bhāvayitrī-pratibhā* or between a poet and a critic has been brought out. *Vyutpatti* will be analysed in the next chapter.

।। इति राजशेखरकृतौ काव्यमीमांसायां कविरहस्ये प्रथमेऽधिकरणे चतुर्थोऽध्यायः पदवाक्यविवेकः। काव्यविशेषेषु कारयित्री भावयित्री नाम समीक्षा।।

5

व्युत्पत्तिः काव्यपाकश्च

Vyutpatti and Kāvya-Pāka
(Vyutpatti and Maturity in Poetic Expression)

'बहुज्ञता व्युत्पत्तिः' इत्याचार्यः। सर्वतोदिक्का हि कविवाचः। तदुक्तम् —

प्रसरति किमपि कथञ्चन नाभ्यस्ते गोचरे वचः कस्य।
इदमेव तत्कवित्वं यद्वाचः सर्वतोदिक्काः।।

VYUTPATTI is '*knowledge of various subjects*' say the ancient *ācāryas*. The poets' words reach out on all sides. Thus — Speech cannot be expressive in describing subjects (without *vyutpatti*). Poetic expression is a description of known and unknown subjects by means of words.

'उचितानुचितविवेको व्युत्पत्तिः' इति यायावरीयः। 'प्रतिभाव्युत्पत्त्योः प्रतिभा श्रेयसी' इत्यानन्दः। सा हि कवेरव्युत्पत्तिकृतं दोषमशेषमाच्छादयति। तदाह —

Rājaśekhara posits that the 'discrimination between desirable and undesirable is *vyutpatti*'. Ānandavardhana says that, 'out of *pratibhā* and *vyutpatti*, *pratibhā* is superior', because it helps to hide the lack of *vyutpatti*.

अव्युत्पत्तिकृतो दोषः शक्त्या संव्रियते कवेः।
यस्त्वशक्तिकृतस्तस्य झगित्येवावभासते।।

A poet with his poetic power is able to hide his ignorance or lack of *vyutpatti* but the faults in a poet due to his incapacity cannot be hidden. The *bhāvakas* (critics) can gather them at once.

शक्तिशब्दश्चायमुपचरितः प्रतिभाने वर्त्तते।

एतत्किं शिरसि स्थितं मम पितुः खण्डं सुधाजन्मनो
लालाटं किमिदं विलोचनमिदं हस्तेऽस्य किं पन्नगाः।
इत्थं क्रौञ्चरिपोः क्रमादुपगते दिग्वाससः शूलिनः
प्रश्ने वामकरोपरोधसुभगं देव्याः स्मितं पातु वः।।

The suggestive power of words is *pratibhā*. For example, 'Seeing Śiva standing, the young Kārttikeya innocently asked his mother Pārvatī, "What is the shiny curve on father's head?" The mother replied that it was a piece of the moon. He then asked, "What is this on the forehead?" Pārvatī replied that it was an eye. Kumāra then asked, "What is there in the hand?" Pārvatī said it was a snake. Observing the series of questions Pārvatī raised her left hand to hide a half smile. May this benign smile bless and protect you."

'व्युत्पत्तिः श्रेयसी' इति मङ्गलः। सा हि कवेरशक्तिकृतं दोषमशेषमाच्छादयति। तथाहि —

Ācārya Maṅgala posits '*Vyutpatti* as superior to *Pratibhā*', because with *vyutpatti* a poet can hide faults due to his inability. Thus —

कवेः संव्रियतेऽशक्तिर्व्युत्पत्त्या काव्यवर्त्मनि।
वैदग्धीचित्तचित्तानां हेया शब्दार्थगुम्फना।।

In creating poetry by means of *vyutpatti* the poet can hide his inability. Critics are attracted by the essence of the poem and do not pay attention to the words and the means of stringing those words together.

व्युत्पत्तिर्यथा —

कृतः कण्ठे निष्को नहि किमुत तन्वी मणिलता
कृशं लीलापत्रं श्रवसि निहितं कुण्डलमुचि।
न कौशेयं चित्रं वसनमवदातं तु वसितं
समासन्नीभूते निधुवनविलासे वनितया।।

An example of *vyutpatti* —

At night as the time for union with the husband came nearer, the wife removed a *hasalī* (a thick neck band) and wore a thin necklace of beads, long hanging earrings were exchanged with flowers and leaves in the ear-lobes and a heavy intricately woven silk *sārī* was exchanged for an ordinary clean *sārī*.

'प्रतिभाव्युत्पत्ती मिथः समवेते श्रेयस्यौ' इति यायावरीयः। न खलु लावण्यलाभादृते रूपसम्पदृते रूपसम्पदो वा लावण्यलब्धिर्महते सौन्दर्याय।

Yāyāvarīya (Rājaśekhara) says, 'the presence of both *pratibhā* and *vyutpatti* together is beneficial for creating poetry'. Just as without *lāvaṇya*[1] the beauty of form and shape remains incomplete and unattractive.

उभययोगो यथा —

> जङ्घाकाण्डोरुनालो नखकिरणलसत्केसरालीकरालः
> प्रत्यग्रालक्तकाभाप्रसरकिसलयो मञ्जुमञ्जीरभृङ्गः।
>
> भर्त्तुर्नृत्यानुकारे जयति निजतनुस्वच्छलावण्यवापी-
> सम्भूताम्भोजशोभां विदधदभिनयाद्दण्डपादो भवान्याः।।

Example of *ubhayayoga* —

> Glorious is Bhavānī's foot lifted in dance (*daṇḍapāda*) in imitating her husband's, bearing the lustre of a lotus grown in the pure beauty of her own body, with thighs as its long stalk, full with the rays of the sun with nails as its pollen, having the splendour of fresh red dye as its petals and the pretty (resonant) anklets as its bees.[2]

प्रतिभाव्युत्पत्तिमांश्च कविः कविरित्युच्यते।

स च त्रिधा। शास्त्रकविः काव्यकविरुभयकविश्च।

'तेषामुत्तरोत्तरीयो गरीयान्' इति श्यामदेवः।

---

1. *Lāvaṇya*, usually translated as beauty or charm is inexact and semantically uninteresting. The *Śabdakalpadruma* (a traditional Sanskrit dictionary) defines it as follows: "*Lāvaṇyam* is a glow of the body that resembles the tremulous glitter of pearls." It may be translated as a 'glowing loveliness!' See Kālidāsa's *Kumāra-saṁbhava, The Origin of the Young God*, tr. with annotation and an Introduction by Hank Heifetz, University of California Press, Berkeley, 1985, Notes 1.35, p. 139.
2. See *The Poetic Light* or *Kāvyaprakāśa* of Mammaṭa, Vol. II (Ullāsas VII-X) tr. by Dr. R.C. Dwivedi, Motilal Banarasidass, Delhi, 1970, pp. 204-5.

'न' इति यायावरीयः। यथा स्वविषये सर्वो गरीयान्। नहि राजहंसश्चन्द्रिकापानाय प्रभवति, नापि चकोरोऽद्भ्यः क्षीरोद्धरणाय। यच्छास्त्रकविः काव्ये रससम्पदं विच्छिनत्ति। यत्काव्यकविः शास्त्रे तर्ककर्कशमप्यर्थमुक्तिवैचित्र्येण श्लथयति। उभयकविस्तूभयोरपि वरीयान्यद्युभयत्र परं प्रवीणः स्यात्। तस्मात्तुल्यप्रभावावेव शास्त्रकाव्यकवी।

उपकार्योपकारकभावं तु मिथः शास्त्रकाव्यकव्योरनुमन्यामहे। यच्छास्त्रसंस्कारः काव्यमनुगृह्णाति शास्त्रैकप्रवणता तु निगृह्णाति। काव्यसंस्कारोऽपि शास्त्रवाक्यपाकमनुरुणद्धि काव्यैकप्रवणता तु विरुणद्धि।

तत्र त्रिधा शास्त्रकविः। यः शास्त्रं विधत्ते, यश्च शास्त्रे काव्यं संविधत्ते, योऽपि काव्ये शास्त्रार्थं निधत्ते।

काव्यकविः पुनरष्टधा। तद्यथा रचनाकविः, शब्दकविः, अर्थकविः, अलङ्कारकविः, उक्तिकविः, रसकविः, मार्गकविः, शास्त्रार्थकविरिति।

A poet needs both *pratibhā* and *vyutpatti* equally. A true poet is formed by a union of the two. Poets are of three kinds — *śāstra-kavi*,[3] *kāvya-kavi*, and *ubhaya-kavi* or a poet proficient in both *śāstra* and *kāvya*. Śyāmadeva posits that, '*ubhaya-kavi* is the most superior followed by *kāvya-kavi* and then by *śāstra-kavi*'. Yāyāvarīya (Rājaśekhara) refutes this by saying that each kind of poet is distinct in his own way. A flamingo (*rājahaṁsa*) cannot partake of moonshine and a partridge (*cakora*) is not discriminating. In this way a *śāstra-kavi* with his seriousness composes poetry suffused with *rasa* and *dhvani* (poetry of suggestion) and a *kāvya-kavi* throws an aesthetic charm over harsh, logical and technical subjects also. *Ubhaya-kavi*,[4] being adept at both kinds of expression should be

3. For definitions of *śāstrakavi*, *śāstra* and its divisions, See chapter 2.

4. *Division of poets*

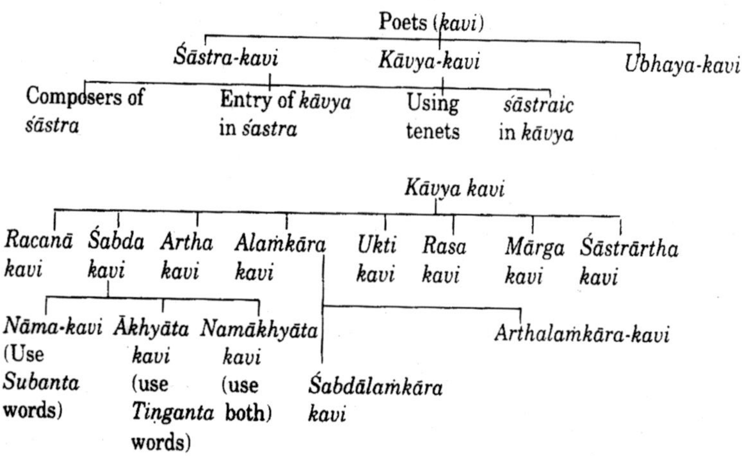

considered superior. Thus, *śāstra-kavi* and *kāvya-kavi* may be considered to be at a similar level. *Śāstra* and *kāvya* are mutually associative and beneficial to each other. If a poet is proficient in *śastra*s, his compositions become marked with seriousness and excellence. With only knowledge of *śāstra*s, one cannot become a poet. A profound study of *kāvya* also helps to attain a perfect understanding of technical literature. With only knowledge of *kāvya*, a poet lacks in seriousness. *Śāstra-kavi*s are of three kinds — (1) composers of *śāstra*, (2) using *kāvya* in *śāstra* and (3) using *śāstric* tenets in *kāvya*. *Kāvya-kavi*s are of eight kinds — (1) *racanā-kavi* (one whose composition reflect craftsmanship of poets), (2) *śabda-kavi* (one whose compositions are distinguished by the use of language), (3) *artha-kavi* (one whose compositions are distinguished by ideas or meanings), (4) *alaṁkāra-kavi* (rhetorical poets), (5) *ukti-kavi* (quotable poets), (6) *rasa-kavi* (aesthetic poets), (7) *mārga-kavi* (poets of verbal style), and (8) *śāstrārtha-kavi* (poets of rational discourses).

तत्र रचनाकविः —

> "लोलल्लाङ्गूलवल्लीवलयितबकुलानोकहस्कन्धगोलै-
> र्गोलाङ्गूलैर्नदद्भिः प्रतिरसितजरत्कन्दरामन्दिरेषु।
> खण्डेषूद्दण्डपिण्डीतगरतरलकाः प्रापिरे येन वेला-
> मालङ्घ्योत्तालतल्लस्फुटितपुटकिनीबन्धवो गन्धवाहाः।।"

Illustration of *racanā-kavi* (craftsmanship in the choice of sounds and words)

> The King after crossing the sea reached the mountains with tall date palms on it and took a breath of the sweet-scented breeze wafted from the lotuses in the ponds. The natural caves in the mountains echoed with the screeches of monkeys who were chattering with their long tails clinging around thick trees.[5]

त्रिधा च शब्दकविर्नामाख्यातार्थभेदेन। तत्र नामकविः —

> "विद्येव पुंसो महिमेव राज्ञः
> प्रज्ञेव वैद्यस्य दयेव साधोः।

---

5. This verse is quoted in Bhojadeva's, *Sarasvatīkaṇṭhābharaṇa* (2-69). The verse in Sanskrit is appealing with its alliteration which is lost when rendered in English.

लज्जेव शूरस्य मृजेव यूनो
विभूषणं तस्य नृपस्य सैव।।"

Sabda-kavis are of three types (1) *nāma-kavi* (preponderance of names, nouns or *subanta*[6] words), (2) *ākhyāta-kavi* (in whose discourse verbs or *tiṅganta*[7] words abound), and (3) *nāmākhyāta-kavi* (in whose language there is preponderance of both kinds of words).

Example of *nāma-kavi*

> Just as knowledge is to a man, glory to a king, intellect to a physician, perception to a foreteller of the future, piety to a good man, modesty to the brave and humility to a young man, so are the ornamental qualities of that king.

आख्यातकविर्यथा —

"उच्चैस्तरां जहसुराजहृषुर्जगर्जु-
राजघ्निरे भुजतटीनिकरैः स्फुरद्भिः।
सन्तुष्टुवुर्मुमुदिरे बहु मेनिरे च
वाचं गुरोरमृतसम्भवलाभगर्भाम्।।"

Example of *ākhyāta-kavi*

> On hearing of the acquisition of nectar during the churning of the ocean the gods laughed, enjoyed, thundered, playfully attacked each other, prayed and were overjoyed.

नामाख्यातकविः —

"हतत्विषोऽन्धाः शिथिलांसबाहवः श्रियो विषादेन विचेतना इव।
न चुक्रुशुर्नो रुरुदुर्न सस्वनुर्न चेलुरासुर्लिखिता इव क्षणम्।।"

Example of *namākhyāta-kavi*

> Languid, blind, dejected, with tired shoulders and hands, grieved and disconsolate due to the lack of riches the demons did not scream, shout, cry, speak or move. They appeared to be in an unconscious state.

6. *Subanta* is a name given to a word formed with the addition of a case-affix. The ancient grammarians gave four kinds of words, viz., *nāma*, *ākhyāta*, *upsarga* and *nipāta*. See Abhyankar, *op. cit.*, p. 431.

7. *Tiṅganta* words ending in verbs. See Abhyankar, *ibid.*, p. 187.

अर्थकविः —

> "देवी पुत्रमसूत नृत्यत गणाः किं तिष्ठतेत्युद्भुजे
> हर्षाद्भृङ्गिरिटावुदाहृतगिरा चामुण्डयाऽऽलिङ्गिते।
> पायाद्वो जितदेवदुन्दुभिघनध्वानप्रवृत्तिस्तयो-
> रन्योन्याङ्कनिपातजर्जरजरत्स्थूलास्थिजन्मा रवः।।"

Example of *artha-kavi*

On the birth of Kārttikeya Bhṛngrīṭi[8] was seen coming from one side happily exclaiming to the people, 'Why are you sitting?' 'Pārvatī has given birth to a son. Sing and dance.' Cāmuṇḍā[9] was coming from the other end. They both met and started dancing together. The garlands of dry bones around their necks made terrible sounds which drowned the deafening sound of the drums of gods.

द्विधाऽलङ्कारकविः शब्दार्थभेदेन। तयोः शब्दालङ्कारः —

> "न प्राप्तं विषम-रणं प्राप्तं पापेन कर्मणा विष-मरणं च।
> न मृतो भागीरथ्यां मृतोऽहमुपगुह्य मन्दभागी रथ्याम्।।"

Alaṁkāra-kavi are of two kinds — *śabdālaṁkāra-kavi* and *arthālaṁkāra-kavi*.

Example of *śabdālaṁkāra-kavi*

It is unfortunate that due to my bad deeds I could not attain the inaccessible battlefield but instead received poisonous death. Instead of dying in the Bhāgīrathī (Gaṅgā) I died in an ordinary lane.

अर्थाऽलङ्कारः —

> "भ्रान्तजिह्वापताकस्य फणच्छत्रस्य वासुकेः।
> दंष्ट्राशलाकादारिद्यूं कर्तुं योग्योऽस्ति मे भुजः।।"

Example of *arthālaṁkāra-kavi*

With a flag flying like a tongue and bearing a hood like covering sat the king of snakes, Vāsuki. It only needs one arm for me to

---

8. Bhṛngiriṭi is the name of an attendant of Śiva. See Apte, *op. cit.*
9. Cāmuṇḍā is the terrific form of Durgā who drowned the deafening sounds of drums of the gods.

crush his teeth like bones.

उक्तिकविः —

"उदरमिदमनिन्द्यं मानिनीश्वासलाव्यं
स्तनतटपरिणाहो दोर्लतालेह्यसीमा।
स्फुरति च वदनेन्दुर्दृक्प्रणालीनिपेय-
स्तदिह सुदृशि कल्याः केलयो यौवनस्य।।"

Example of *ukti-kavi*

Youth is playing charmingly upon this lovely young woman. Her thin and beautiful waist is an object of fancy, the expanse of her breasts embraces her like a creeper and her moon-face is attractive to the eyes.

यथा वा —

"प्रतीच्छत्याशोकीं किसलयपरावृत्तिमधरः
कपोलः पाण्डुत्वादवतरति ताडीपरिणतिम्।
परिम्लानप्रायामनुवदति दृष्टिः कमलिनी-
मितीयं माधुर्यं स्पृशति च तनुत्वं च भजते।।"

Another example

This young maiden's lips may be exchanged with the tender red leaves of a young *aśoka* plant. Her cheeks are pale white like the fruits of a palmyra and her eyes resemble the closing petals of a lotus. There is an increase in the sweetness of this young and slender beauty.

रसकविः —

"एतां विलोकय तनूदरि ताम्रपर्णी—
मम्भोनिधौ विवृतशुक्तिपुटोद्धृतानि।
यस्याः पयांसि परिणाहिषु हारमूर्त्या
वामभ्रुवां परिणमन्ति पयोधरेषु।।"

Example of *rasa-kavi*

Behold the Tāmraparṇī[10] river which falls into the ocean. The

10. Tāmraparṇī is the name of a river rising in Malaya, celebrated for its pearls. Vidhyadhar Vaman Bhide, *A Concise Sanskrit-English Dictionary*, Gian Publishing House, Delhi, 1986, p. 508.

drops of water emerging from the oyster shells are like a necklace of pearls around the expansive breasts of beautiful maidens.

मार्गकविः —

"मूलं वालकवीरुधां सुरभयो जातीतरूणां त्वचः
सारश्चन्दनशाखिनां किसलयान्यार्द्राण्यशोकस्य च।
शैरीषी कुसुमोद्गतिः परिणमन्मोचं च सोऽयं गणः
ग्रीष्मेणोष्महरः पुरा किल ददे दग्धाय पञ्चेषवे।।"

Example of *mārga-kavi*

In days gone by, when the heat from Śiva's eyes burnt Kāmadeva's skin, his friend Grīṣma provided him with medicines to allay the inflammation. These included fragrant leaves, sweet-smelling flowers, sandalpaste, tender young shoots of the *aśoka* tree, flowers of the *śiriṣa* tree and ripe fruits of banana.

शास्त्रार्थकविः —

"आत्मारामा विहितरतयो निर्विकल्पे समाधौ
ज्ञानोद्रेकाद्विघटिततमोग्रन्थयः सत्त्वनिष्ठाः।
यं वीक्षन्ते कमपि तमसां ज्योतिषां वा परस्ता-
त्तं मोहान्धः कथमयममुं वेत्ति देवं पुराणम्।।"

An example of *śāstrārtha-kavi*

How can Duryodhana who is under the delusion of evil, recognise the great human God-Kṛṣṇa who possesses a spiritual soul and a mind awakened to true knowledge — the one who can concentrate exclusively on the sole divine entity.

एषां द्वित्रैर्गुणैः कनीयान्, पञ्चकैर्मध्यमः, सर्वगुणयोगी महाकविः।

दश च कवेरवस्था भवन्ति। तत्र च बुद्धिमदाहार्यबुद्ध्योः सप्त, तिस्रश्च औपदेशिकस्य। तद्यथा काव्यविद्यास्नातको, हृदयकविः, अन्यापदेशी, सेविता, घटमानो, महाकविः, कविराज, आवेशिकः, अविच्छेदी, सङ्क्रामयिता च।

यः कवित्वकामः काव्यविद्योपविद्याग्रहणाय गुरुकुलान्युपास्ते स विद्यास्नातकः।

यो हृदय एव कवते निह्नुते च स हृदयकविः।

यः स्वमपि काव्यं दोषभयादन्यस्येत्यपदिश्य पठति सोऽन्यापदेशी।

यः प्रवृत्तवचनः पौरस्त्यानामन्यतमच्छायामभ्यस्यति स सेविता।

योऽनवद्यं कवते न तु प्रबध्नाति स घटमानः।

योऽन्यतरप्रबन्धे प्रवीणः स महाकविः।

यस्तु तत्र तत्र भाषाविशेषे तेषु प्रबन्धेषु तस्मिंस्तस्मिंश्च रसे स्वतन्त्रः स कविराजः। ते यदि जगत्यपि कतिपये।

यो मन्त्राद्युपदेशवशाल्लब्धसिद्धिरावेशसमकालं कवते स आवेशिकः।

यो यदैवेच्छति तदैवाविच्छिन्नवचनः सोऽविच्छेदी।

यः कन्याकुमारादिषु सिद्धमन्त्रः सरस्वतीं सङ्क्रामयतिस सङ्क्रामयिता।

काव्यपाकः

सततमभ्यासवशतः सुकवेः वाक्यं पाकमायाति। 'कः पुनरयं पाकः?' इत्याचार्याः। 'परिणामः' इति मङ्गलः। 'कः पुनरयं परिणामः?' इत्याचार्याः। 'सुपां तिङां च श्रवः (प्रि?) या व्युत्पत्तिः' इति मङ्गलः। सौशब्द्यमेतत्। 'पदनिवेशनिष्कम्पता पाकः' इत्याचार्याः। तदाहुः —

Out of the qualities enumerated above, a poet who possesses two to three qualities is called *kaniṣṭha* (inferior), one possessing five qualities is called *madhyamā* (medium) and the one with all the qualities is called a *mahākavi* (eminent poet).

There are ten stages of a poet. *Buddhimān* and *āhārya-buddhi* poets have seven and *aupdeśikī* poets have three stages. The names of the stages are (1) *kāvya-vidya-snātaka*s (classical disciples), (2) *hṛdaya-kavi* (diffident), (3) *anyapdeśī* (using the names of other poets), (4) *sevitā* (follows a specific poet or period), (5) *ghaṭamāna* (diffused poet), (6) *mahākavi* (poet of eminence), (7) *kavirāja* (poet-*par-excellence*), (8) *āveśika* (instructive poet), (9) *avicchedī* (spontaneous composer), and (10) *saṁkrāmiyatā* (composer using spells and powers).

The one who enters a *gurukula* to attain poetic perfection and learn about poetics, metres, figures of speech, etc., is a *kāvya-vidyā-snātaka*.

The one who composes poetry secretly and does not disclose it out of hesitation or fear of fault finding is a *hṛdaya-kavi*.

The one who reads out his own composition proclaiming it as another poet's out of fear of fault finding is an *anyāpdeśī* poet.

The one who follows a particular specific classical poet as a model and composes accordingly is a *sevitā*.

The one whose compositions are diffused and scattered rather than on a single subject is called a *ghaṭamāna* poet.

The one who composes an important and entire essay or poetic is called a *mahākavi*.

The one who has the capability to compose (freely) epics and other forms of narrative in different languages using various states of emotions (*rasa*) is called a *kavirāja*. They are very few in number.

The one who perfects his poetic faculty by means of instruction and advice is called an *āveśika* poet.

The one who can quickly compose impromptu on any subject whatsoever is called an *avicchedī* poet.

The one who uses the spells and powers associated with Sarasvatī on young unmarried girls and boys and makes them compose is called a *saṁkrāmiyatā* poet.

The poet's words and sentences attain maturity with continuous practice. "What is this *pāka* (maturity)?" *Ācārya* Maṅgala says that, 'this is the result of continuous practice'. Again the question is — "What is this result?" Maṅgala answers that, 'the correct use, *vyutpatti* of *subanta* and *tiṅganta* words is the result'. Other thinkers posit that, 'the result is the meaning assigned to a word or the unambiguous use of a word'. Thus —

"आवापोद्धरणे तावद्यावद्दोलायते मनः।
पदानां स्थापिते स्थैर्ये हन्त सिद्धा सरस्वती।।"

In poetry if the intellect remains indecisive in removing or adding words then it is an imperfect state. When stability is reached in the arrangement of words, perfection is said to be accomplished.

'आग्रहपरिग्रहादपि पदस्थैर्यपर्यवसायस्तस्मात्पदानां परिवृत्तिवैमुख्यं पाकः' इति वामनीयाः।

Vāmana feels that, 'sometimes doubt persists in placing a word. Thus, a word once written must never be changed and this is what is *pāka* (maturity of expression).

तदाहुः —

"यत्पदानि त्यजन्त्येव परिवृत्तिसहिष्णुतां।
तं शब्दन्यायनिष्णाताः शब्दपाकं प्रचक्षते।।"

Thus —

The learned scholars define *śabdapāka* as the unchangeable status of a word.

'इयमशक्तिर्न पुनः पाकः' इत्यवन्तिसुन्दरी। यदेकस्मिन्वस्तुनि महाकवीनामनेकोऽपि पाठः परिपाकवान्भवति। तस्माद्रसोचितशब्दार्थसूक्तिनिबन्धनः पाकः। यदाह —

Avantisundarī says, 'this is poetic power not *pāka*'. In the poetry of *mahākavi* (eminent poets) there are several readings for one and each one is mature in expression. Thus, to use words for aesthetic essence and for their quotable and epigrammatic density, while composing is *pāka* (maturity of expression). Thus —

"गुणालङ्काररीत्युक्तिशब्दार्थग्रथनक्रमः।
स्वदते सुधियां येन वाक्यपाकः स मां प्रति।।"

तदुक्तम्— "सति वक्तरि सत्यर्थे शब्दे सति रसे सति।
अस्ति तन्न बिना येन परिस्रवति वाङ्मधु।।"

The stringing together of words and meaning suffused with *guṇas* (qualities), *alaṁkāras* (rhetorical figures), *rīti* (verbal style) and *ukti* (proverbial quotes) is attractive to *sahṛdayas* (ideal readers) and *bhāvakas* (critics). This is also called *vākyapāka* (maturity of expression in sentences). The aesthetic charm inherent in literature does not arise out of the presence of words and meanings, it requires *pāka* (maturity of expression). The maturity (*pāka*) adds perfection to a composition.

'कार्यानुमेयतया यत्तच्छब्दनिवेद्यः परं पाकोऽभिधाविषयस्तत्सहृदयप्रसिद्धसिद्ध एव व्यवहाराङ्गमसौ' इति यायावरीयः।

स च कविग्रामस्य काव्यमभ्यस्यतो नवधा भवति।

तत्राद्यन्तयोरस्वादु पिचुमन्दपाकम्,

आदावस्वादु परिणामे मध्यमं बदरपाकम्,

आदावस्वादु परिणामे स्वादु मृद्वीकापाकम्,

आदौ मध्यममन्ते चास्वादु वार्ताकपाकम्,

आद्यन्तयोर्मध्यमं तिन्तिडीकपाकम्,

आदौ मध्यममन्ते स्वादु सहकारपाकम्,

आदावुत्तममन्ते चास्वादु क्रमुकपाकम्,

आदावुत्तममन्ते मध्यमं त्रपुसपाकम्,

आद्यन्तयोः स्वादु नालिकेरपाकमिति।

तेषां त्रिष्वपि त्रिकेषु पाकाः प्रथमे त्याज्याः। वरमकविर्न पुनः कुकविः स्यात्। कुकविता हि सोच्छ्वासं मरणम्। मध्यमाः संस्कार्याः। संस्कारो हि सर्वस्य गुणमुत्कर्षति। द्वादशवर्णमपि सुवर्णं पावकपाकेन हेमीभवति। शेषा ग्राह्याः।

स्वभावशुद्धं हि न संस्कारमपेक्षते। न मुक्तामणेः शाणस्तारतायै प्रभवति।

Yāyāvarīya (Rājaśekhara) presents his own point of view. 'Unchangeable status of words in a *kāvya* is *śabdapāka* (maturity in words). Where there is an intermingling of *rasa* (aesthetic charm), *guṇa* (quality) and *alaṁkāra* (rhetorical figures), the *vākyapāka* is visible (maturity of expression in sentences). This can be analysed by *sahṛdaya*s (ideal readers) and *bhāvaka*s (critics).

Pāka is of nine kinds for poets.

Poetic compositions which are insipid both in the beginning and the end come under *Pichumanda*[11] *pāka*.

Poetic compositions which are insipid and dry in the beginning but gradually become a little interesting till the end come under *badarpākam*.[12]

Poetic compositions which are uninteresting in the beginning but

---

11. *Pichumanda*, the *nimba* tree, *Azadirachta indica*. See Bhide, *op. cit.*, p. 692.
12. *Badar*, the jujube tree. See Bhide, *op. cit.*, p. 790.

rapidly gain interest in the end fall under *mṛdvīkāpākam.*[13]

Poetic compositions which are moderately pleasing in the beginning but absolutely disinteresting in the end are *vārttāka pākam.*[14]

Compositions which are moderately sweet and pleasing both in the beginning and the end are *titindītpākam.*[15]

Compositions which are moderately pleasing in the beginning but very interesting in the end fall under *sahakārapākam.*[16]

Compositions which are interesting in the beginning but insipid in the end fall under *kramukapākam.*[17]

Compositions which are interesting in the beginning but moderately pleasant in the end are called *trapuspākam.*[18]

Compositions which are pleasing from the beginning till the end fall under *nārikelapākam.*[19]

Out of these *pichumandapāka*, *vārttapāka* and *kramukapāka* ought to be forsaken. It is better not to be a poet than a bad poet. This is because to write bad poetry is a matter of unhappiness and like death.

Badar, *titindika* and *trapusa* poets should improve their compositions to make them pleasing. Refining leads to an increase in the qualities. Gold which is a mixture of many metals becomes pure after undergoing refinement under fire. The rest of the three *pākas* — *mṛdīka*, *sāhkāra* and *nārīkela* are to be grasped.

Those with a pure natural disposition do not need improvement. A bead does not become more lustrous on refinement.

अनवस्थितपाकं पुनः कपित्थपाकमामनन्ति। तत्र पलालधूननेन अन्नकणलाभ-वत्सुभाषितलाभः।

13. *Mṛdvīkā* (grapes), a vine or bunch of grapes. See Bhide, *op. cit.*, p. 889.
14. *Vārttāka*, the egg-plant, See Bhide, *op. cit.*, p. 969.
15. *Titinḍī*, the tamarind tree. See Bhide *op. cit.*, p. 511.
16. *Sahakāra*, a mango tree. See Bhide, *op. cit.*, p. 1118.
17. *Kramuka*, the betel nut tree. See Bhide, *op. cit.*, p. 394.
18. *Trapus*, a cucumber plant.
19. *Nārikela*, the coconut tree. See Bhide, *op. cit.*, p. 597.

सम्यगभ्यस्यतः काव्यं नवधा परिपच्यते।
हानोपादानसूत्रेण विभजेत्तद्धि बुद्धिमान्।।
अयमत्रैव शिष्याणां दर्शितस्त्रिविधो विधिः।
किन्तु विविधमप्येतत्त्रिसतगत्यस्य वर्त्तते।।

The poetical compositions which have an irregular distribution, i.e., they are interesting at places while at others are moderately so and prosaic in still other parts, fall under *kapitha-pāka.*[20] Just as on beating the husk, one gets only a grain or two, similarly in a *kapitha-pāka* composition, one can find a *sūkti* here or there.

In this way for a practising poet the *pāka* of poetical compositions is of nine kinds. An intelligent poet should first distinguish between the kinds of *pāka* to be grasped and the one's to be forsaken.

In this way, for pupils of poetics, three divisions have been given though a number of divisions can be made.

।। इति राजशेखरकृतौ काव्यमीमांसायां कविरहस्ये प्रथमेऽधिकरणे शिष्यविशेषेषु काव्यपाककल्पः पञ्चमोऽध्यायः ।।

20. *Kapittha*, the wood apple tree. See Bhide, *op. cit.*, p. 332.

6

पदवाक्यविवेकः

Pada-Vākya Vivekaḥ
(Definition and Kinds of Sentences)

व्याकरणस्मृतिनिर्णीतः शब्दो निरुक्तनिघण्ट्वादिभिर्निर्दिष्टस्तदभिधेयोऽर्थस्तौ पदम्।

तस्य पञ्च वृत्तयः — सुब्वृत्तिः, समासवृत्तिः, तद्धितवृत्तिः कृद्वृत्तिः, तिङ्वृत्तिश्च। गौरश्वः पुरुषो हस्तीति जातिवाचिनः शब्दाः। हरो हरिर्हिरण्यगर्भः काल आकाशं दिगिति द्रव्यवाचिनः। श्वेतः कृष्णो रक्तः पीत इति च गुणवाचिनः। प्रादयश्चादयश्चासत्त्ववचनाः। नगरमुपप्रस्थितः पन्थाः, वृक्षमनुद्योतते विद्युदिति कर्मप्रवचनीयाः।

'सेयं सुब्वृत्तिः पञ्चतय्यपि वाङ्मयस्य माता' इति विद्वांसः। सुब्वृत्तिरेव समासवृत्तिः। व्याससमासावेवानयोर्भेदहेतू। सा च षोढा द्वन्द्वादिभेदेन। तत्र षट्समासीसमाससूक्तम् —

A ŚABDA (word)[1] is a grammatically viable construct (substantiated by *vyākaraṇa smṛti*[2]). The meaning signified by a word on the basis of the *Nirukta*,[3] *Nighaṇṭu*,[4] *Kośa*, etc., is its *artha*. *Śabda* and *artha* together

1. *Śabda* has been roughly translated as word. Hereafter we will use the word *śabda* instead of word.

   'The entire store of words' is divided into two large grammatical classes, The BASES and the AFFIXES, and all utterances are seen as built up by successive AFFIXATION. See Kapil Kapoor, *Text and Interpretation: The Indian Tradition*, Motilal Banarsidass, Delhi, forthcoming, p. 8.

2. *Vyākaraṇa* or grammar is also considered one of the *smṛtis* because the grammarians distinguish the correct words from their incorrect forms with the help of memory. Cf. Dalal, *op.cit.*, p. 162.

3. *Nirukta* — 'Etymology, glossary' one of the Vedāṅgas, the only one known to us is by Yāska. Cf. John Dowson, *op. cit.*, p. 223 and Abhyankar, *op. cit.*, p. 223.

4. *Nighaṇṭu* — a name given to a collection of words which are mainly Vedic, cf. Abhyankar, *op. cit.*, p. 218.

form a *pada*.[5]

The *padas* have *vṛttis*[6] — *subvṛtti*,[7] *samāsavṛtti*,[8] *taddhitavṛtti*,[9] *kṛdvṛtti*[10] and *tiṅgvṛtti*.[11] Cows, horses, elephants and men etc. are *jāti-vācaka* words (class-denoting). Sky, time, etc., are *dravya-vācaka* (denoting substance). White, yellow, red, black, etc., are *guṇa-vācaka* (denoting qualities). *Pra*, *sam*, *ch*, *h*, etc., are *avyaya-vācaka* (indeclinables). 'The traveller went near the town', 'the lightning struck behind the tree'. Here 'near' and 'behind' are indeclinables.

The wise scholars feel that, 'the five kinds of *subvṛtti* is the mother of the universe of verbal discourse (*vāṅmaya*). *Subvṛtti* is also *samāsavṛtti*. The difference is only in compound or extension. Compounds are of six kinds. As in a *sūtra* —

> "द्वन्द्वोऽस्मि द्विगुरस्मि च गृहे च मे सततमव्ययीभावः
> तत्पुरुष कर्मधारय येनाऽहं स्यां बहुव्रीहिः।।"

The householder says that though his family consists only of two members (*dvandva*) and a couple of cows (*dvigu*), there is no

5. *Pāda* — a unit forming a part of a sentence. The definition '*artha-padam*' is attributed to the ancient grammarian 'Indira' who is believed to have been the first grammarian of India. Cf. Abhyankar, *op. cit.*, p. 233.

6. *Vṛttis* — This is a technical term with a number of different connotations. Here it refers to 'a compound word giving an aggregate sense different from the exact literal sense of the constituent words'. For other meanings consult Abhyankar, *op. cit.*, pp. 366-7.

7. *Subvṛtti* or *subanta* — Those words that take nominal endings with the addition of a case-affix. These include nouns, pronouns and adjectives. Also see, Abhyankar, *op. cit.*, p. 431.

8. *Samāsavṛtti* or *samasānta* — Compound words which are formed by the addition of secondary suffixes. They are of various kinds — *dvandva* (copulative), *dvigu* (numeral appositional), *karmadhāraya* (appositional), *bahuvrīhi* (attributive), *avyayībhāva* (adverbial) and *tatpuruṣa* (determinative). Also see, Abhyankar, *op. cit.*, pp. 416-17.

9. *Taddhitavṛtti* or *taddhitānta* — Secondary derived nominals. For more details see Abhyankar, *op. cit.*, pp. 181-2.

10. *Kṛdvṛtti* or *kṛdanta* are the primary derived nominals. Also see Abhyankar, *op. cit.*, p. 127.

11. *Tiṅgvṛtti* or *tiṅganta* are those that take the verbal endings. It includes verbs and verb phrases. See Abhyankar, *op. cit.*, p. 187.

reduction in household expenditure (*avyaya*); he asks his servant, therefore, to work more (*karamdhāraye*), in order that his labour may enrich him with a good quantity of paddy (*bahuvrīhi*).[12]

तद्धितवृत्तिः पुनरनन्ता। तद्धि शास्त्रप्रायो वादो यदुत तद्धितमूढाः पाणिनीयाः। माञ्जिष्ठं रौचनिकं सौरं सैन्धवं वैयासीयमिति तद्धितान्ताः। प्रातिपदिकविषया चेयम्। कृद्वृत्तिश्च धातुविषया। कर्त्ता हर्त्ता कुम्भकारो नगरकार इति कृदन्ताः।

तिङ्वृत्तिर्दशधा दशलकारीभेदेन। द्विधा च सा धातुसुब्धातुविषयत्वेन। अपाक्षीत् पचतिप क्ष्यतीति धातवीयान्याख्यातानि। अपल्लवयत् पल्लवयति पल्लवयिष्यतीति सौब्धातवीयानि।

Taddhita vr̥tti is endless. It is often quoted from the *śāstras* that the Pāṇinian grammarians are ignorant of *taddhita*. The words *mañjiṣṭha*, *raucanika*, *saur*, *saindhava*, *vaiyāsīya*, etc., are formed from *taddhita* suffixes.[13] *Taddhita* words are derived from a substantive (*pratipādika*) by the application of suffixes and thus become *subanta* (conventional nouns or pronouns). *Kr̥t* terminations (*pratyaya*)[14] are derived from roots (*dhātu*)[15] for example, *karta* from the root *kr̥*, *harta* from the root *hyā*, *kumbhakāra* from the word *kumbha* and root *kr̥* and *nāgarakāra*. All these words are *kr̥danta* (primary derived nominals).

Tiṅganta words (verbs) are of ten kinds corresponding to the ten divisions of *lakāra* (personal endings affixed to roots). The *tiṅganta* words are also of two kinds depending on the roots (*dhātu*) and *sup-dhātu* (derived verb). The words *pacati*, *apākṣīta*, *pakṣyati*, etc., are formed from roots and *pallavayati*, *appllavayat* and *pallavayiṣyati* are formed from the *sup-dhātu*.

तदिदमित्थङ्कारं पञ्चप्रकारमपि पदजातं मिथः समन्वीयमानमानन्त्याय कल्पते।

---

12. The translated version has been taken from C.D. Dalal, *op. cit.*, p. 163.

13. Pāṇini has used the word *taddhita* not for words, but for suffixes which are added to form such words at all places (e.g., in I.1.38, IV.I.17, 76, VI.I.61, etc). See Abhyankar, *op. cit.*, p. 181.

14. *Pratyayas* — affix, suffix, a termination, as contrasted with *prākr̥ti* the base. Cf. Abhyankar, *op. cit.*, p. 264.

15. *Dhātu*, a root; the basic word of a verbal form, a word denoting a verbal activity. Cf. Abhyankar, *op. cit.*, pp. 207-8.

तज्जन्मा चैष विदुषां वादो यत्किल दिव्यं समासहस्रं बृहस्पतिर्वक्ता शतक्रतुरध्येता तथापि नान्तः शब्दराशेरासीत्।

तत्र दयितसुब्वृत्तयो विदर्भाः। वलभसमासवृत्तयो गौडाः। प्रियतद्धिता दाक्षिणात्याः। कृत्प्रयोगरुचय उदीच्याः। अभीष्टतिब्वृत्तयः सर्वेऽपि सन्तः। तेषां च विशेषलक्षणानुसन्धानेनावर्द्धताख्यातगणः। उक्तश्च—

In this way these five kinds of *padas* combine together in innumerable ways resulting in endless forms. According to ancient scholars it is widely reported that the *guru* Bṛhaspati[16] could not teach, even after a period of one thousand celestial years, the entire ocean of words (grammar) to his pupil Indra.[17]

Out of these five *vṛttis*, the people of *vidarbhā*[18] prefer and use *subanta* words (nouns and pronouns). The people of Gauḍa[19] are fond of *samāsānta pada* (compounds). The people of South prefer *taddhita* (secondary derived nominals). The northerners prefer *kṛdanta* words (primary derived nominals) and *tiṅganta padas* (verbs) are favoured by all. These five kinds of words, when used in constructions according to special rules for their application, enrich the sentence.[20]

"विशेषलक्षणविदां प्रयोगाः प्रतिभान्ति ये।
आख्यातराशिस्तैरेष प्रत्यहं ह्युपचीयते।।"

New applications are observed by persons who are aware of special constructions which can be applied to words. This helps to increase the number of *tiṅganta* verbs and sentences (*ākhyāta*).

---

16. Bṛhaspati in the *Ṛgveda* appears as the prototype of the priests and priestly order. In later times he is a *ṛṣi* and also regent of the planet Jupiter and the name is commonly used for the planet itself. Known for his eloquence, called, Gīsh-pati, 'lord of speech'. Cf. Dowson., *op. cit.*, pp. 63-4.

17. Indra — One of the celestial gods. There are a number of myths associated with him. Cf. Dowson, *op. cit.*, pp. 123-6.

18. *Vidarbhā* is a geographical region. See Appendix II.

19. For the region Gauḍa, refer to Appendix II.

20. See C.D. Dalal, *op. cit.*, p. 163. Where he points out that the word *ākhyāta* used in this verse and the next denotes a sentence and is not used in its usual signification of a verb.

पदानामभिधित्सितार्थग्रन्थनाकरः सन्दर्भो वाक्यम्। 'तस्य च त्रिधाऽभिधाव्यापारः' इत्योद्भटाः। वैभक्तः शाक्तः शक्तिविभक्तिमयश्च।

प्रतिपदं श्रूयमाणसूपपदविभक्तिषु कारकविभक्तिषु वा वैभक्तः।

लुप्तास्वपि विभक्तिषु समाससामर्थ्यात्तदर्थावगतौ शाक्तः। उभयात्मा च शक्तिविभक्तिमयः। तत्र वैभक्तः —

'An organised unity of all properly structured *pada*s needed to express the desired/intended meaning is *vākya.*'[21] According to the followers of *ācārya* Udbhaṭa there are three kinds of sentences based on the *abhidhā-vyāpāra* (overt marking of the grammatical relation between different parts of a sentence). These are *vaibhakta*, *śākta* and *śakti-vibhaktimaya.*[22]

A sentence in which (grammatical relations) like case-terminations (*upapāda-vibhakti*)[23] and case-endings *kāraka-vibhakti*[24] are explicitly marked in each *pada* is called a *vaibhakta* sentence.

Sentences in which the power, inherent in the words without case-endings as in a compound, expresses the sense of the omitted case-terminations are called *śākta.*[25]

Sentences which have both kinds of *pada*s (explicit and implicit) are called *ubhayātmaka*.

"नमस्तस्मै वराहाय लीलयोद्धरते महीम्।
खुरयोर्मध्यगो यस्य मेरुः खणखणायते।।"

An example of *vaibhakta* —

Obeisance is paid to Varāha (Viṣṇu in his third incarnation as

21. Cf. Kapil Kapoor: *Sylvia Plath's 'Daddy' in the other Tradition. An Example Analysis in Rajasekhara's Model* unpublished paper, p. 22.
22. For this triadic division of sentences also, see Kapil Kapoor, *ibid.*, pp. 21-2.
23. *Upapāda-vibhakti* is a case-ending which is due to the presence of another noun; such as the *caturthī*, due to the combination of nouns *namāh*, *hasti*, etc. See C.D. Dalal, *op. cit.*, p. 163.
24. *Kāraka-vibhakti* is a case-ending which has direct connection only with the verb. Dalal, *op. cit.*, p. 163.
25. These are sentences 'in which all grammatical relations are implicit (not overtly marked).' See Kapil Kapoor's paper on *Sylvia Plath*, *op. cit.*, p. 22.

boar) who has lifted the earth easily and the Sumerū mountain caught in its hooves makes a resounding sound.[26]

शाक्तः —

"वित्रस्तशत्रुः स्पृहयालुलोकः
प्रपन्नसामन्त उदग्रसत्त्वः।
अधिष्ठितौदार्यगुणोऽसिपत्र-
जितावनिर्नास्ति नृपस्त्वदन्यः।।

यथा वा —

"कण्ठदोलायितोद्दामनीलेन्दीवरदामकाः।
हरिभीत्याश्रिताशेषकालियाहिकुला इव।।"

An example of *śākta* —

(O King!) There is no other king like you, who has the ability to destroy the arrogance of your enemy, a favourite of the people, a saviour of the neighbouring kings, heroic, magnanimous and capable of conquering the world with his sword.[27]

Another example —

Looking at the garland of blossoming blue-lotuses it appeared as if the entire family of black serpents had coiled itself around his neck to save themselves from Kṛṣṇa.[28]

शक्तिविभक्तिमयः —

"अथागादेकदा स्पष्टचतुराशामुखद्युतिः।
तं ब्रह्मेव शरत्कालः प्रोत्फुल्लकमलासनः।।"

An example of *śakti-vibhakti-ubhaya* —

Spreading out its light in the face of four directions and filled with

---

26. Every *pada* in this sentence is formed of different case-endings or terminations without any use of compounds.

27. In this verse there are six words (describing the excellences of the king) in the *bahuvrīhi* compound and they retain the power of expressing the meanings of one or the other of the six case-endings from *dvitīya* to *saptamī*.

28. This sentence has only four *padas*, two of the compounds are *tatpuruṣa* and two are *bahuvrīhi*. Though the *case-terminations* are not explicitly marked, their meaning is apparent.

the blossoms of lotus and *asana* (a kind of tree) came the *śarad* season like Brahmā[29].

तत्र वाक्यं दशधा। एकाख्यातम्, अनेकाख्यातम्, आवृत्ताख्यातम्, एकाभिधेयाख्यातम्, परिणताख्यातम्, अनुवृत्ताख्यातम्, समुचिताख्यातम्, अध्याहृताख्यातम्, कृदभिहिताख्यातम्, अनपेक्षिताख्यातमिति।

Sentences are of ten kinds *ekākhyāta*, *anekākhyāta*, *āvṛttākhyāta*, *ekābhidheyākhyāta*, *pariṇatākhyāta*, *anuvṛttākhyāta*, *samuchhitākhyāta*, *adhyāhṛthākhyāta*, *kṛdabhihitākhyāta* and *anapekṣitākhyāta*.

तत्रैकाख्यातम् —

"जयत्येकपदाक्रान्तसमस्तभुवनत्रयः।
द्वितीयपदविन्यासव्याकुलाभिनयः शिवः।।"

An example of *ekākhyāta* (with one verb) sentence —

Glory to Śiva who is in the midst of the *tāṇḍava* (furious dance performed by Śiva) with one foot pervading the entire world and in his attempt to put the other foot down (due to lack of space) he enacts out his frustration.[31]

अनेकाख्यातम्। तच्च द्विधा सान्तरं निरन्तरम्। तयोः प्रथमम् —

"देवासुरास्तमथ मन्थगिरां विरामे
पद्मासनं जय जयेति बभाषिरे च।
द्रागभेजिरे च परितो बहु मेनिरे च
स्वाग्रेसरं विदधिरे च ववन्दिरे च ।।"

Anekākhyāta (more than one verb) sentences are of two types: *sāntara* {which has *subanta padas* (nouns) in between the verbs} and *nirantara* (which has only verbs).

---

29. In this verse *śleṣālaṁkāra* has been used to describe the *śarad* season. *Śākta abidhā-vyāpāra* has been used in description of the season. Brahmā — whose radiance spreads in all directions and who is seated on a lotus is described by *vaibhakta-abhidhā-vyāpāra*.

30. Here Rājaśekhara adopts the second parameter for division of sentences and that is the number of explicitly present verbs (*ākhyāta*) in a sentence.

31. There is only one verb *jayati* in this sentence.

An example of *sāntara* —

After the churning of the ocean, once the sound had subsided, all the gods and demons greeted Brahmā with shouts of joyous welcome, started surrounding him on all sides, paying respects to him, making a leader out of him and greeting him.[32]

द्वितीयम् —

"त्वं पासि हंसि तनुषे मनुषे बिभर्षि
विभ्राजसे सृजसि संहरसे विरौषि।
आस्से निरस्यसि सरस्यसि रासि लासि
सङ्क्रीडसे ब्रुडसि मेघसि मोदसे च ।।"

The second (an example of *nirantara anekākhyāta*) —

(O god!) You protect, destroy, expand, agree, follow, ornament, create, destruct, make speech, create silence, throw, make agreeable, take, give, play, drown and remain happy.[33]

'आख्यातपरतन्त्रा वाक्यवृत्तिरतो यावदाख्यातमिह वाक्यानि' इत्याचार्याः। 'एकाकारतया कारकग्रामस्यैकार्थतया च वचोवृत्तेरेकमेवेदं वाक्यम्' इति यायावरीयः।

The *ācāryas* state that each sentence ends with one *ākhyāta pada* (verb). Thus, in the above example there are as many sentences as the number of verbs. Yāyāvarīya (Rājaśekhara) however feels that 'it is one sentence'. The reason is that there is one agent and the import of the sentence is also one.

आवृत्ताख्यातम् —

"जयत्यमलकौस्तुभस्तबकितांशपीठो हरि-
र्जयन्ति च मृगेक्षणाञ्चलदपाङ्गदृष्टिक्रमाः।
ततो जयति मल्लिका तदनु सर्वसंवेदना-
विनाशकरणक्षमो जयति पञ्चमस्य ध्वनिः।।"

Avṛttākhyāta (an example of a sentence with one verb attatched to different agent-nominatives) —

32. In this verse in addition to verbs there are also a number of nouns, therefore it is an example of *sāntara*.

33. The word *tvam* for 'you' and *ca* for 'and' are the two *subanta* words while the remaining are verbs. Thus, it is a *nirantara anekākhyāta* sentence.

Praise to the Lord's chest adorned with pure and transparent gems, to the vivacious sidelong glances of beautiful maidens, praise to the jasmine flowers and then praise to the *pañcam* notes of the nightingale capable of destroying all life.[34]

एकाभिधेयाख्यातम् —

"हृष्यति चूतेषु चिरं तुष्यति बकुलेषु मोदते मरुति।
इह हि मधौ कलकूजिषु पिकेषु च प्रीयते रागी।"

Ekābhidheyākhyāta (an example of a sentence in which the same agent is connected to many verbs) —

During the spring season the traveller is pleased with mangoes, satisfied with the *bakula* (a kind of tree), delighted with the *malaya* breeze, and happy at the sweet sound of the nightingale.

परिणताख्यातम् —

"सोऽस्मिन्जयति जीवातुः पञ्चेषोः पञ्चमध्वनिः।
ते च चैत्रे विचित्रैलाकक्कोलीकेलयोऽनिलाः।।"

Pariṇatākhyāta (an example of a sentence in which the same verb attached to one agent is also used for another one). Thus —

Praise to the *pañcam dhvani* of the nightingale which is the life source of Kāmadeva (Cupid, God of Love) in this month of *Caitra* and (praise also to the) *malaya* breeze sporting with the cardamom and *kaṅkola* trees.[35]

अनुवृत्ताख्यातम् —

"चरन्ति चतुरम्भोधिवेलोद्यानेषु दन्तिनः।
चक्रवालाद्रिकुञ्जेषु कुन्दभासो गुणाश्च ते।।"

Anuvṛttākhyāta (an example where the same verb is carried over to the following sentence) —

(O King !) Your elephants travel all over the bordering forests of

34. In this verse the verb *jayati* has been repeated with a number of agents.

35. Here the verb *jayati* used for the *pañcam dhvani* is also applicable to the *malaya* breeze.

the four oceans and your excellences like blossoms of *kunda* (jasmines) travel all over the mountains of the world.[36]

समुचिताख्यातम् —

"परिग्रहभराक्रान्तं दौर्गत्यगतिचोदितं।
मनो गन्त्रीव कुपथे चीत्करोति च याति च।।"

Samucittākhyāta (the same verb proper to an analogy is extended to another agent-nominative) —

The mind weighed down by the wife, family and misfortune is like a train which goes on the wrong track and also screams. The train which is weighed down and at high speed also goes off track and makes a screeching sound.

यथा च —

"स देवः सा दंष्ट्रा कृतकिटिविलासस्मितसिता
द्वयं दिश्यात्तुभ्यं मुदमिदमुदारं जयति च।
उदञ्चद्भिर्भूयस्तरलितनिवेशा वसुमती
यदग्रे यच्छ्वासैर्गिरिगुडकलीलामुदवहत्।।"

And also —

May Lord Varāha (Viṣṇu in his third incarnation as the boar) and the pure tusk supporting the earth, both be a source of happiness for you, the long breaths (of the lord) causes the earth which adorns the tusk like a ball, to move.[37]

अध्याहृताख्यातम् —

"दोर्दण्डताण्डवभ्रष्टमुडुखण्डं बिभर्ति यः।
व्यस्तपुष्पाञ्जलिपदे चन्द्रचूडः श्रिये स वः।।"

Adhyāhṛtākhyāta (where the verb is not apparent but elided) —

The scattered parts of lunar *asterisms* due to *tāṇḍava* of the arms

---

36. The verb *caranti* is used both for the elephants and for qualities.

37. Of the examples quoted above in the first one the mind which 'appears to go off track' and 'screams' is appropriate. In the second verse the verb *udvahat* seems appropriate because the earth is not a ball but bears a resemblance and the tusk bears the earth.

are taken in by the hands of Śiva instead of diffused flowers. May, this Candracūḍa (an epithet of Śiva) Śiva be always there to adorn you.[38]

कृदभिहिताख्यातम् —

"अभिमुखे मयि संहृतमीक्षितं
हसितमन्यनिमित्तकथोदयं।
विनयबाधितवृत्तिरतस्तया
न विवृतो मदनो न च संवृतः।।"

Kṛdabhihitākhyāta (where the *kṛdanta* words are used as verbs instead of *tiṅganta*) —

On coming before me the maiden (Śakuntalā) lowered her eyes and broke into laughter with reference to some other context. In this way she neither exhibited nor hid her desire which might have been in opposition to her sense of decorum (or modesty).[39]

अनपेक्षिताख्यातम् —

"कियन्मात्रं जलं विप्र? जानुदघ्नं नराधिप।
तथापीयमवस्था ते न सर्वत्र भवादृशाः।।"

Anapekṣitākhyāta (a verbless sentence) —

Thus —

King — Brāhmaṇa ! How much water (is there)?

Brāhmaṇa — King ! Knee-deep !

King — Why this state (of yours)?

Brāhmaṇa — Everybody is not like you[40] !

---

38. The verbs *astu* or *bhavatu* are elided but the sentence does not make complete sense without them.

39. Here the words — *īkṣita, hansita, vivṛta, saṁvṛta,* etc., which have *kṛt* suffixes have been used to function as *ākhyāta* (or verbs).

40. Verbless sentences are static images. They usually codify a memory or reminiscence.

गुणवदलङ्कृतञ्च वाक्यमेव काव्यम्। 'असत्यार्थाभिधायित्वान्नोपदेष्टव्यं काव्यम्' इत्येके। यथा —

Some people say that '*kāvya* consists of false figurative descriptions. Thus it is not worth consideration.' Thus —

"स्तेमः स्तोकोऽपि नाङ्गे श्वसितमविकलं चक्षुषां सैव वृत्तिः
मध्येक्षीराब्धि मग्नाः स्फुटमथ च वयं कोऽयमीदृक्प्रकारः।
इत्थं दिग्भित्तिरोघःक्षतविसरतया मांसलैस्त्वद्यशोभिः
स्तोकावस्थानदुस्थैस्त्रिजगति धवले विस्मयन्ते मृगाक्ष्यः।।"

(O King !) Your fame first spread to the four directions of this earth. When it rebounded from the walls like directions, it collected in abundance and entered the ocean but its body did not get wet, its breath did not stop and nor did its eyes close. After whitening the ocean and because of lack of space it started brightening the sky. In this way, your fame has brightened all the three worlds and this is a matter of amazement for (doe-eyed) maidens.

यथा च —

"भ्रश्यद्भूभुग्रभोगीश्वरफणपवनाध्मातपातालतालुः
त्रुट्यन्नानगिरीन्द्रावलिशिखरखरास्फाललोलाम्बुराशिः।
उद्यन्नीरन्ध्रधूलीविधुरसुरवधूमुच्यमानोपशल्यः
कल्योद्योगस्य यस्य त्रिभुवनदमनः सैन्यसम्मर्द आसीत्।।"

And also

The valour of the king's army has caused an upheaval in all the three worlds. The weight of the colossal army has pressed the earth down which has resulted in the bursting open of the hoods of the Śeṣanāga. When the Śeṣanāga gave out a hot and angry hiss, it heated up the upper crust of *pātāla* (nether world). On the earth, a number of high mountains broke off and fell into the ocean due to the fierce action of the army. This inundated the oceans. When the heavy dust raised by the army reached the heaven the celestial damsels left the borders of Heaven and in fright took refuge in mansions. Thus the king's army has resulted in the destruction of the three worlds.[41]

आहुश्च —

> "दृष्टं किञ्चिददृष्टमन्यदपरं वाचालवार्त्तार्पितं
> भूयस्तुण्डपुराणतः परिणतं किञ्चिच्च शास्त्रश्रुतम्।
> सूक्तया वस्तु यदत्र चित्ररचनं तत्काव्यमव्याहतं
> रत्नस्येव न तस्य जन्म जलधेर्नो रोहणाद्वा गिरेः ।।"

It is said —

Some of the things in *kāvya* are perceptible while others are imperceptible. Some things are engendered by the imagination of garrulous poets while others appear to be old wives tales from the Purāṇas. Some things are *śāstrīya* (technical) while others are due to the skill of poets. Unlike other gems this gem of *kāvya* does not appear to be born either out of the sea or the Rohana mountain (a mountain in Ceylon).

'न' इति यायावरीयः।

> "नासत्यं नाम किञ्चन काव्ये यस्तु स्तुत्येष्वर्थवादः।
> स न परं कविकर्मणि श्रुतौ च शास्त्रे च लोके च ।।"

Rājaśekhara does not agree to this. He says that

It is not a fact that *kāvya* can remain free of *atiśayokti* (hyperbole) or of improbable descriptions. The descriptions pertaining to people or to things in *kāvya* which employ *atiśayokti* need not be untrue or improbable. Similar meanings have been identified in the Vedas, *śāstra*s and *loka* (world).

तत्र श्रौतः —

> "पुष्पिण्यौ चरतो जङ्घे भूष्णुरात्मा फलेग्रहिः।
> शेरेऽस्य सर्वे पाप्मानः श्रमेण प्रपथे हताः ।।"

Thus —

(O mendicant !) With walking a person develops flower like

41. The two examples given above are instances of *atiśayokti-alaṁkāra* (hyperbole). Extreme exaggeration is evident here and so the realistic is transformed into make-believe.

strong legs, his soul strengthens and he gets the fruit of good health. All his sins are washed away (because as he travels he comes across a number of places of pilgrimage).[42]

शास्त्रीयः —

"आपः पवित्रं प्रथमं पृथिव्या-
मपां पवित्रं परमं च मन्त्राः।
तेषां च सामर्ग्यजुषां पवित्रं
महर्षयो व्याकरणं निराहुः।।"

An example from the *śāstras* —

The purest thing on this earth is water, purer than even that is *mantra*. Out of these *mantras*, the *Ṛk*, *Yajuṣa* and *Sāma mantras* are the purest but sages declare *vyākaraṇa-śāstra* (grammar) to be even purer than the *mantras* of the *trayī* (threefold Vedas).[43]

किञ्च —

"यस्तु प्रयुङ्क्ते कुशलो विशेषे शब्दान्यथावद्व्यवहारकाले।
सोऽनन्तमाप्नोति जयं परत्र वाग्योगविद् दुष्यति चापशब्दैः।।

The wise man who possesses the knowledge of *vyākaraṇa* (grammar) and uses the correct word at the correct place, has a command over language, achieves glory in the next world and the one who knows the language but uses incorrect forms of words corrupts himself and falls into hell.

"कः? वाग्योगविदेव। कुत एतत्? यो हि शब्दाञ्जानात्यपशब्दानप्यसौ जानाति। यथैव हि शब्दज्ञाने धर्मः, एवमशब्दज्ञानेऽप्यधर्मः। अथवा भूयानधर्मः प्राप्नोति। भूयांसो ह्यपशब्दा अल्पीयांसः शब्दाः। एकैकस्य हि शब्दस्य बहवोऽपभ्रंशाः। तद्यथा। गौरित्यस्य शब्दस्य गावी गोणी गोता गोपोतलिकेत्येवमादयोऽपभ्रंशाः। अथ योऽवाग्योगवित् अज्ञानं तस्य शरणम्। नात्यन्तायाज्ञानं शरणं भवितुमर्हति। यो ह्यजानन्वै ब्राह्मणं हन्यात्सुरां वा पिबेत्सोऽपि मन्ये पतितः स्यात्। एवं तर्हि सोऽनन्तमाप्नोति जयं परत्र वाग्योगविद्दुष्यति

42. The above verse is from the *Aitareya Brāhmaṇa* where it is connected to a tale about Hariścandra and his son Rohita. Indra, not wanting Rohita to go home gave the above advice to him.

43. This is not true but one can witness exaggeration being employed in *śāstras* like in *kāvyas*.

चापशब्दैः। कः? अवाग्योगविदेव। अथ यो वाग्योगवित् विज्ञानं तस्य शरणम्। क्व पुनरिदं पठितम्? भ्राजा नाम श्लोकाः।

किञ्च भोः श्लोका अपि प्रमाणम्? किञ्चातः? यदि प्रमाणमयमपि श्लोकः प्रमाणं भवितुमर्हति —

Here the *question* arises —

"Who corrupts himself ?" The one who knows the language or the ignorant (fool).

The *answer* : Not the fool. It is the one who knows the language who corrupts himself.

Then the *question*: "Why so?"

The *answer* : The one who knows the pure (correct) form of words also knows the incorrect forms. Just as the knowledge of correct words leads to *dharma* (righteousness, one of the four ends of human life) so also the usage of incorrect forms leads to *adharma* (in greater quantity). The reason is that the number of incorrect words is much larger than the pure words for example *gau* is the correct form of the word and it has many corrupt forms (*apabhraṁśa*) like *gāvī*, *gaunī*, *gotā*, *gopotalikā*, etc.

Thus it is only the knowledgeable who is lead to *adharma*. The one who does not know *vyākaraṇa-śāstra* (grammar) is bound to use incorrect forms due to his ignorance. It cannot be called *adharma*. But ignorance cannot be used as an excuse because in spite of ignorance a man who indulges in taking alcoholic spirits, kills a cow or kills a brāhmaṇa, is considered fallen and cannot be absolved of his sin. Leaving this issue, we can conclude that the one who knows and uses the pure forms of words achieves glory in the next world and the one who does not know, falls into hell. Thus, an attempt should be made to know the pure forms of words with the study of *vyākaraṇa-śāstra* (grammar).

The question is where has this *śloka* been written?

Answer — This is the *bhraja śloka* (of Kātyāyana).

Question — Can a *śloka* be used as evidence in matters relating to *dharma* and *adharma*?

If yes, then this *śloka* should also be treated as evidence.

Thus —

"यद्युदुम्बरवर्णानां घटीनां मण्डलं महत्।
पीतं न गमयेत्स्वर्गं किं तत्क्रतुगतं नयेत्।।" इति।

If these bottles filled with spirit, red in colour like ripe molasses, are unable to obtain heaven then how can an insignificant amount of spirit taken from the *sautramaṇi* (eastern) *yajña* help in attaining Heaven?

'प्रमत्तगीत एष तत्रभवतो यस्त्वप्रमत्तगीतस्तत्प्रमाणमेव' इति गोनर्दीयः।

लौकिकः —

"गुणानुरागमिश्रेण यशसा तव सर्पता।
दिग्वधूनां मुखे जातमकस्मादर्द्धकुङ्कमम्।।"

On this *ācārya* Gonārdīya (an epithet of Patañjali, author of *Mahābhāṣya*) answers that, 'this *śloka* is the nonsensical prattle of an insane person'. 'If the *śloka* is by a worthy person it can be taken as evidence for the matter of *dharma*.'

An example from *laukika* (of this world) —

(O, King!) Your fame constituted of your excellences and affection appears to have placed a half *kum-kum* (a red mark on the forehead of young brides signifying matrimony) on the foreheads of young bride like four directions.[44]

'असदुपदेशकत्वात्तर्हि नोपदेष्टव्यं काव्यम्' इत्यपरे। यथा एवम् —

"वयं बाल्ये डिम्भांस्तरुणिमनि यूनः परिणता-
वपीच्छामो वृद्धान्परिणयविधेस्तु स्थितिरियं।
त्वयारब्धं जन्म क्षपयितुममार्गेण किमिदं
न नो गोत्रे पुत्रि क्वचिदपि सतीलाञ्छनमभूत्।।"

Some people are of the opinion that, '*kāvyas* propagate false beliefs and thus should be abandoned'.

44. The colour of qualities is white and that of love is red, according to poetic convention a mixture of the two has produced a half *kum-kum*.

Thus —

(When the daughter pledges to live her life with one man, *veśyā* (following the profession of prostitution) mother advises—

> Daughter, the marriage ties in our community of *veśyās* state that one should love young boys in adolescence, young men in youth and old men in one's old-age — this is the *veśyā-dharma.* You are thinking of choosing the wrong path. Our community has never faced such an appellation before.[45]

'अस्त्ययमुपदेशः किन्तु निषेध्यत्वेन न विधेयत्वेन' इति यायावरीयः। या एवंविधा विधयः परस्त्रीषु पुंसां सम्भवन्ति तानवबुध्येतेति कवीनां भावः। किञ्च कविवचनायत्ता लोकयात्रा। 'सा च निःश्रेयसमूलम्' इति महर्षयः। यदाहुः —

Yāyāvarīya (Rājaśekhara) says — 'this is advice but in the form of prohibition (or negation) and not as a sacred precept'. The men visiting the *veśyās* should be aware of their contemptible natures and should not expect loyalty from them. Secondly, women should be protected from such characters. This is the import of the poet's words. The worldly actions propagated by the poet are always beneficial for the human race.

> "काव्यमय्यो गिरो यावच्चरन्ति विशदा भुवि।
> तावत्सारस्वतं स्थानं कविरासाद्य मोदते।।"

Thus —

> Till pure poetic speech spreads (remains) on this earth, the poet will always have a place in *sārasvata loka* (abode of Sarasvatī, goddess of wisdom) and remain happy.

किञ्च —

> "श्रीमन्ति राज्ञां चरितानि यानि
> प्रभुत्वलीलाश्च सुधाशिनां याः।
> ये च प्रभावास्तपसामृषीणां
> ताः सत्कविभ्यः श्रुतयः प्रसूताः ।।"

The powerful characters of old kings, ascendancy of gods, and the

45. In this verse the profession being glorified is against accepted societal norms and the sanctity of marriage vows is being questioned, thus these kinds of meanings should be abandoned.

other-worldly (*alaukika*) effect of sages and saints — all this has been realised and become well-known with the poets' speech and words.

उक्तश्च —

"ख्याता नराधिपतयः कविसंश्रयेण
राजाश्रयेण च गताः कवयः प्रसिद्धि।
राज्ञा समोऽस्ति न कवेः परमोपकारी
राज्ञो न चास्ति कविना सदृशः सहायः ।।

वल्मीकजन्मा स कविः पुराणः
कवीश्वरः सत्यवतीसुतश्च।
यस्य प्रणेता तदिहानवद्यं
सारस्वतं वर्त्म न कस्य वन्द्यम्।।"

It has been said —

The kings became famous because of the poets and the poets' gained acclaim under the patronage of the king. Thus there is none other to help the poets cause except the king and there is no one to help the king except the poets.

The *sārasvata mārga* (path of poetic creation) which has amongst its first founder the sage Vālmīki and the great poet composer Vyāsa opens out a path which can have no fault. Who will not worship such a pathway? (i.e., everyone will revere it).

'असभ्यार्थाभिधायित्वान्नोपदेष्टव्यं काव्यम्' इति च केचित्।

यथा —

"प्रसर्पन्प्रग्रीवैर्भृतभुवनकुक्षिर्झणझणा-
करालः प्रागल्भ्यं वदति तरुणीनां प्रणयिषु।
विलासव्यत्यासाज्जघनफलकास्फालनघन-
स्फुटच्छेदोत्सिक्तः कलकनककाञ्चीकलकलः।।"

Some people feel that, '*kāvyas* contain indecent meanings which bring out uncivilised undertones'. Thus it should be avoided.

As in —

In the act of love making there is witnessed a reversal of roles. The women intoxicated with passion are pinning down the husbands when the sound produced by the golden girdle (furnished with small tinkling bells or other ornaments) due to the movement of their limbs spreads out and covers the entire sky. This boldness of wives seems to be an indicator of their shamelessness.

अपि च—

"नित्यं त्वयि प्रचुरचित्रकपत्रभङ्गी-
ताडङ्कताडनविपाण्डुरगण्डलेखाः।
स्निह्यन्तु रत्नरशनारणनाभिराम-
कामार्त्तिनर्त्तितनितम्बतटास्तरुण्यः।।"

Another example —

When the wives reverse their roles during love making the long ear ornaments dangling from their ears rub against their cheeks thus reddening them and the gems studded girdle at the wrist dances and makes a lot of pleasant sound.[46]

'प्रक्रमापन्नो निबन्धनीय एवायमर्थः' इति यायावरीयः। तदिदं श्रुतौ शास्त्रे चोपलभ्यते। तत्र याजुषः—

Yāyāvarīya (Rājaśekhara) says that one has to make these descriptions depending on the context. Similar kinds of meanings can be traced to the Vedas and *śāstras* also.

"योनिरुदूलूखलं शिश्नं मुशलं मिथुनेमे तत् प्रजननं क्रियते।।"

आर्चः —

"उपोप मे परामृश मा मे दभ्राणि मन्यथाः।
सर्वाऽहमस्मि रोमशा गन्धारीणामिवाविका।।"

Thus, in the *Yajurveda* —

A boiling vessel like the uterus and the pestle like male organ of regeneration are together called *mithun* (copulation). This union is the cause of regeneration.

46. In both the examples given above one can witness indecent connotations and such *kāvya* should be avoided on this count.

Another example (from the *Ṛgveda*) —

> (Romśā, Bṛhaspati's daughter invites her husband for union).
>
> (O, Svāmī !) Come and embrace me. Don't underestimate the size of pores on my body. I have pores all over my body. I am Romśā (shaggy) just like the sheep of Gāndhāra-deśa.

शास्त्रीयः —

> "यस्याः प्रसन्नधवलं चक्षुः पर्यन्तपक्ष्मलं।
> नवनीतोपमं तस्या भवति स्मरमन्दिरम्।।"
>
> पदवाक्यविवेकोऽयमिति किञ्चित्प्रपञ्चितः।
> अथ वाक्यप्रकारांश्च कांश्चिदन्यान्निबोधत।।

An example from the *śāstras* —

> The woman who has clear, white eyes with long eyelashes also possesses a soft female organ like fresh butter.[47]

In this way, some description of *pada* and *vākya* has been attempted in this chapter. The next chapter will deal with various other kinds of sentences.

।। इति राजशेखरकृतौ काव्यमीमांसायां कविरहस्ये प्रथमेऽधिकरणे षष्ठोऽध्यायः पदवाक्यविवेकः।।

---

47. By giving these examples Rājaśekhara points out that when the context demands, such verses have also been included in Vedas and *śāstras*.

7

वाक्यभेदाः

Vākya-Bhedaḥ

(Modes of Sentences and Intonation)

वाक्यं वचनमिति व्यवहरन्ति। तच्च त्रिधा प्रणेतृभेदेन ब्राह्मं, शैवं, वैष्णवमिति। तदिदं वायुप्रोक्तपुराणादिभ्य उपलब्धं यदुत ब्राह्मं वचः पञ्चधा स्वायम्भुवमैश्वरमार्षमार्षीकमार्षिपुत्रकं च।

स्वयम्भूर्ब्रह्मा तस्य स्वायम्भुवम्। तन्मनोजन्मानो भृगुप्रभृतयः पुत्रास्ते ईश्वरास्तेषामैश्वरम्। ईश्वराणां सुता ऋषयस्तेषामार्षम्। ऋषीणामपत्यानि ऋषीकास्तेषामार्षीकम्। ऋषीकाणां सूनव ऋषिपुत्रकास्तेषामार्षिपुत्रकम्।

स्वयम्भुवः प्रथमं वचाः श्रुतिः, श्रुतेरन्यच्च स्वायम्भुवम्। तदाहुः —

THE other name for *vākya* is *vacana* (statement). *Vacana* is of three kinds — *brāhma* (of Vedic literature) *śaiva* (of *vidyās* or disciplines) and *vaiṣṇava* (of literary discourse and daily concourse). It is learnt from the *Vāyu Purāṇa* that *brāhma vacana* is of five kinds — *svāyambhuva*, *aiśvara*, *ārṣa*, *ārṣīka*, and *ārṣiputraka*.

Svayambhū[2] is Brahmā and his *vacana* (statement) is *svāyambhuva*

1. "Four factors interact to form these categories — (*i*) the type of discourse, (*ii*) the person speaking, (*iii*) the nature of meaning, and (*iv*) the mode of expression. This threefold division thus divides discourse on the basis of status of meaning and nature of devices used in the language." See Kapil Kapoor, *Sylvia Plath's 'Daddy' op. cit.*, p. 26.

2. Svayambhū is 'the self-existent'. A name of Brahmā the creator. See Dowson, *op. cit.*, p. 314.

(of the creator). The sons of Brahmā consist of gods like Bhr̥gu[3] and their *vacana* is *aiśvara* (of divine beings). The sons of gods are *r̥ṣi*s and their *vacana* is called *ārṣa* (of great thinkers). The progeny of *r̥ṣi*s are called *r̥ṣīka* and their *vacana* are known as *ārṣīka*. The sons of *r̥ṣīka*s are *r̥ṣi-putraka* and their *vacana* are known *ārṣiputraka*.

The *vacana* of Svayambhū (Brahmā) are the Vedas. There are also other statements in addition to the Vedas. Thus —

"सर्वभूतात्मकं भूतं परिवादं च यद्भवेत्।
कुचिन्निरुक्तमोक्षार्थं वाक्यं स्वायम्भुवं हि तत्।।"

The *vacana* which is an epitomy of truth beneficial to all living things and in some instances even leads to salvation, is *svāyambhuva*.

तदेव स्तोकरूपान्तरपरिणतमैश्वरं वचः। उक्तश्च —

"व्यक्तक्रममसंक्षिप्तं दीप्तगम्भीरमर्थवत्।
प्रत्यक्षं च परोक्षं च लक्ष्यतामैश्वरं वचः।।"

आर्षम्—

"यत्किञ्चिन्मन्त्रसंयुक्तं युक्तं नामविभक्तिभिः।
प्रत्यक्षाभिहितार्थं च तदृषीणां वचः स्मृतम्।।"

आर्षीकम् — "नैगमैर्विविधैः शब्दैर्निपातबहुलं च यत्।
न चापि सुमहद्वाक्यमृषीकाणां वचस्तु तत् ।।"

आर्षिपुत्रकम् —

"अविस्पष्टपदप्रायं यच्च स्याद्बहुसंशयम्।
ऋषिपुत्रवचस्तत्स्यात्ससर्वपरिदेवनम्।।"

तदुदाहरणानि पुराणेभ्य उपलभेत।

An insignificant portion of the above is *aiśvara vacana*, Thus —

The exposition of connected, detailed, clear, profound, meaningful, explicit and implicit meanings comes under *aiśvara vacana*.

Ārṣa vacana —

---

3. Bhr̥gus — "A class of mythical beings who belonged to the middle or aerial class of gods." See John Dowson, *op. cit.*, p. 55.

Arṣa vacana comprises of some *mantras* in correspondence with nouns and case affixes and involves an exposition of explicit meanings.

Ārṣīkam vacana

The *ārṣīkam vacana* largely abound in Vedic words, use indeclinables extensively and are composed of small and concise sentences.

Ārṣiputrakam

The *vacanas* of *ṛṣi-putrakas* are filled with unclear words, doubtful meanings which confuse people (make them cry). Their examples can be found in Purāṇas.

सारस्वताः कवयो नः पूर्वे इत्थङ्कारं कथयन्ति। ब्रह्मविष्णुरुद्रगुहबृहस्पतिभार्गवादिशिष्येषु चतुःषष्टावुपदिष्टं वचः पारमेश्वरम्। क्रमेण च सञ्चरद्देवैर्देवयोनिभिश्च यथामत्युपजीव्यमानं दिव्यमिति व्यपदिश्यते। देवयोनयस्तु —

"विद्याधराप्सरोयक्षरक्षोगन्धर्वकिन्नराः।
सिद्धगुह्यकभूताश्च पिशाचा देवयोनयः।।"

Sarasvatī's son (our ancestral poet) states that the statements of advice given by Brahmā, Viṣṇu, Rudra, Kārttikeya, Bṛhaspati, Bhārgava and 64 disciples fall under the category of *parameśvara*. These sentences are used repeatedly by gods, other sub-ethnic groups[4] (*devajāti*s) and spread out according to one's wisdom are called *divya* sentences. The different sub-ethnic groups of *deva*s are as under —

vidyādhara, *apsarasa*, *yakṣa*, *rākṣasa*, *gandharva*, *kinnara*, *siddha*, *guhyaka*, *bhūta* and *piśāca* are the sub-ethnic groups (of *deva*s).

तत्र पिशाचादयः शिवानुचराः स्वभूमौ संस्कृतवादिनः, मर्त्ये तु भूतभाषया व्यवहरन्तो निबन्धनीयाः। अप्सरसस्तु प्राकृतभाषया। तद्दिव्यं वचश्चतुर्धा। वैबुधं वैद्याधरं गान्धर्वं योगिनीगतं च। शेषाणामेतेष्वेवोपलक्षणं प्रकृतिसादृश्येन। तत्र वैबुधम् —

"समासव्याससंदृब्धं शृङ्गाराद्भुतसम्भृतं।

4. These are sub-ethnic groups with each group having its own distinctive attributes.

सानुप्रासमुदारं च वचः स्यादमृताशिनाम्।।"

यथा —

"यच्चन्द्रकोटिकरकोरकभारभाजि
बभ्राम बभ्रुणि जटाकुहरे हरस्य।
तद्वः पुनातु हिमशैलशिलानिकुञ्ज-
झात्कारडम्बरविरावि सुरापगाम्भः।।"

Out of these, *piśāca* and other followers of Śiva in their own abode — *Śivaloka* use the Sanskrit language. If they are made to speak in this world (*mṛtyaloka*) they should use *bhūta-bhāṣā* and the *apsara's* (celestial maidens) should use *prākṛta bhāṣā*. *Divya vacana* (celestial statements) are of four kinds — (1) *baibudha*, (2) *vaidyādhara*, (3) *gāndharva*, and (4) *yoginīgata*. The remaining sub-ethnic groups can use one of these statements.

Baibudha statements (used by celestial beings) —

> The statements of *devatā*s are dignified, ornamental having pleasant effect (*rasayukta*), alliterative, detailed in some places and concentrated in others.

Thus —

> May the water of the holy river Gaṅgā which rotates in the hollow of the brown matted locks of Śiva which are weighed down by the digits of the moon and its rays and which produces a pleasant sound in the caves of the Himālayas (mountains) purify you all.[5]

वैद्याधरम् —

"स्तोकानुप्राससच्छायं चतुरोक्तिप्रसादि च।
द्राघीयसा समासेन विद्धि वैद्याधरं वचः।।"

यथा —

"प्रणतसुरकिरीटप्रांशुरत्नांशुवंश-
च्छुरितनखशिखाग्रोद्भासमानारुणाङ्घ्रे।

---

5. In this verse *candrakoṭi* and *himśaila* are the long compounds, some other words are moderate in length, alliterative like *rakāra*, *kakāra*, *sakāra* and *hakāra* and the expressive description of the Gaṅgā in Śiva's locks is an example of elevated expression.

उदिततरणिवृन्दोद्दामधामोर्ध्वनेत्र-
ज्वलननिकरदग्धानङ्गमूर्त्ते नमस्ते।।"

Vaidyādharam

The statements of *vidyādharas* are alliterative, clear, expressive and with long compounds.

Thus —

The rows of nails which mirror the bright flame reflected from the attractive gems in the crowns of heads of kings who have bowed down in the shining feet of Śiva and like the heat of the rising orb of the sun, the third eye sends out rays of heat to incinerate Kāmadeva (Cupid, God of Love). Greetings to the same Lord Śiva.[6]

यथा वा —

"भ्रमति भ्रमरकरम्बितनन्दनवनचम्पकस्तवकगौरः।
वात्याहत इव वियति स्फुटलक्ष्मा रोहिणीरमणः।।"

गान्धर्वम् —

"ह्रस्वैः समासैर्भूयोभिर्विभूषितपदोच्चया।
तत्त्वार्थग्रथनग्राह्या गन्धर्वाणां सरस्वती।।"

यथा —

"नमः शिवाय सोमाय सगणाय ससूनवे।
सवृषव्यालशूलाय शकपालाय सेन्दवे।।"

योगिनीगतम् —

"समासरूपकप्रायं गम्भीरार्थपदक्रमम्।
सिद्धान्तसमयस्थायि योगिनीनामिदं वचः।।"

यथा —

"दुःखेन्धनैकदहनामृतवर्षमेघ
संसारकूपपतनैककरावलम्ब।
योगीन्द्रदर्पण जगद्गतकृत्स्नतेजः
प्रत्यक्षचौरवर वीरपते नमस्ते।।"

6. This verse contains long compounds and also exhibits alliteration.

And also —

> Pure like the clusters of jasmine flowers surrounded by bees in the forests (Nandana-Vana) and clear the marked moon rotates in the sky as if it has been thrown up by a whirlwind.

Gāndharvam (*statements of gandharvā*s).

> The sentences of *gandharvā*s are composed of small compounds, with many phrases, strung together to bring out the main import, all of which adds to their charm.

Thus —

> Obeisance is paid to Śaṅkara Śiva who is with Umā (Pārvatī, his wife), with *gaṇa*s,[7] with his sons, with Nandī (attendant of Śiva), with serpents and trident (*triśūla*) and with a bowl.

Statement of *yoginī*s

> The statements of *yoginī*s are composed of compounds and metaphors, a string of serious meanings and follow the principles of poetic-conventions.

Thus —

> O fire, which can burn unhappiness like coal! O clouds, which can provide nectar like rain! The only shelter for one who is ready to fall in this world like well! A mirror of the senses. Filler of the entire world with a bright light!, A visible thief and lord of courageous men. Greetings to you!

महाप्रभावत्वाद्भौजङ्गममपि दिव्यमित्युपचर्यते।

> "प्रसन्नमधुरोदात्तसमासव्यासभागवत्।
> अनोजस्विपदप्रायं वचो भवति भोगिनाम्।।"

यथा —

> "सुसर्जितां श्रोत्रसुखां सुरूपा-
> मनेकरत्नोज्जवलचित्रिताङ्गीम्।

7. *Gaṇa* — A troop of demigods considered as Śiva's attendants and under the special superintendence of Gaṇeśa, a demigod of this troop.

विद्याधरेन्द्रः प्रतिगृह्य वीणां
पिनाकिने गायति मङ्गलानि।।"

The statements regarding serpents and snakes because of their powerful nature are also considered as *divya* (celestial).

The statements of snakes are infused with many excellences like *prasāda*, *mādhurya*, *udātta*,[8] use compounds and are composed of pleasant words and phrases.

Thus —

The king of *vidyādharas* is singing verses in praise of Lord Śiva with a *vīṇā* (a musical instrument) which is beautiful, sweet-sounding and studded with beautiful gems.

'किमर्थं पुनरनुपदेश्ययोर्ब्राह्मपारमेश्वरयोर्वाक्यमार्गयोरुपन्यासः?' इत्याचार्याः। 'सोऽपि कवीनामुपदेशपरः' इति यायावरीयः। यतो नाटकादावीश्वरादीनां देवानां च प्रवेशे तच्छायावन्ति वाक्यानि विधेयानीति। दिव्यम्।

इह हि प्रायो वादो यदुत मर्त्यावतारव्यवहाररुचेर्भगवतो वासुदेवस्य वचो वैष्णवं तन्मानुषमिति व्यपदिशन्ति। तच्च त्रिधा रीतित्रयभेदेन। तदाहुः —

"वैदर्भी गौडीया पाञ्चाली चेति रीतयस्तिस्रः।
आशु च साक्षान्निवसति सरस्वती तेन लक्ष्यन्ते।।"
रीतिरूपं वाक्यत्रितयं। काकुः पुनरनेकयति।

The *ācāryas* put a question that the *brāhma* and *parmeśvara* statements are never used practically. Then why are they being described here? Yāyāvarīya (Rājaśekhara) says that, '*brāhma* and *pārmeśvara* statements are also essential for poets because in a dramatic composition, if the characters are celestial their speech should correspond to their elevated status'.

It is traditionally observed that in *mṛtya-loka* (of this world) the statements of the god in human form Vāsudeva (a name of Kṛṣṇa) are

8. *Prasāda, mādhurya* and *udātta* are three *guṇas* or qualities. *Prasāda* refers to perspicuity or clearness of style. Cf. Apte, *op. cit.*, p. 672. *Mādhurya* stands for sweetness in poetic-compositions Cf. Apte, *op. cit.*, p. 756. *Udātta* refers to a figure of speech which employs the use of praiseworthy epithets. Cf. S.K. De, *op. cit.*, p. 238.

known as *vaiṣṇava* or *mānuṣa vacana* (mortal statements). These statements correspond to three *rītis*[9] and are of three kinds.

> Vaidarbhī, Gauḍīya and Pāñcālī are the three *rītis*. Sarasvatī (goddess of learning and wisdom) manifests herself in these *rītis*. The sentences pertaining to these three *rītis* are of various kinds due to *kāku* (intonation).

वाकु - निरूपण

'काकुर्वक्रोक्तिर्नाम शब्दाऽलङ्कारोयम्' इति रुद्रटः। 'अभिप्रायवान्पाठधर्मः काकुः, सा कथमलङ्कारी स्यात्?' इति यायावरीयः।

सा च द्विधा साकाङ्क्षा निराकाङ्क्षा च। वाक्यान्तराकाङ्क्षिणी साकाङ्क्षा, वाक्योत्तरभाविनी निराकाङ्क्षा। तदेव वाक्यं काकुविशेषेण साकाङ्क्षम्। तदेव काक्वन्तरेण निराकाङ्क्षम्। आक्षेपगर्भा, प्रश्नगर्भा, वितर्कगर्भाचेतिसाकाङ्क्षा। विधिरूपा, उत्तररूपा, निर्णयरूपेति निराकाङ्क्षा।

Ācārya Rudraṭa[10] states that, '*kāku* is an *alaṁkāra* called *vakrokti*.' Yāyāvarīya (Rājaśekhara) says that, '*kāku* is the quality of recitation on reading (*pāṭhadharmāḥ*).' How can it be designated as an *alaṁkāra*?[11]

तत्राक्षेपगर्भा —

> "यदि मे वल्लभा दूती तदाऽहमपि वल्लभा।
> यदि तस्याः प्रिया वाचः तन्ममाऽपि प्रियप्रियाः।।"

एवमेय निर्देष्टुर्विधिरूपा।

प्रश्नगर्भा —

> "गतः स कालो यत्रासीन्मुक्तानां जन्म वल्लिषु।

---

9. *Rīti* is indicative of the styles of poetic writing, Vāmana (eighth century AD), author of *Kāvyālaṁkāra Sūtra* VII (1-2-17) is considered the founder of the *rīti* school. For a comprehensive exposition, see R.S. Tiwary, *A Critical Approach to Classical Indian Poetics* (Chaukhambha Orientalia, Delhi, 1984), chapter 3, pp. 208-15.

10. See Rūdraṭa's *Kāvyālaṁkāra*, ed. with commentary of Namīsādhu by Durgaprasad and V.L. Sastri, Nirnayasagar Press, 1928, p. 16.

11. Rājaśekhara here criticises Rūdraṭa for laying down *kāku-vakrokti* as a figure of sound. He points out that it is the modulation of the voice which attempts to evocate the meaning intended by the poet. Thus it cannot be designated as an *alaṁkāra*.

वर्त्तन्ते साम्प्रतं तासां हेतवः शुक्तिसम्पुटाः।।"

Kāku is of two kinds — *sākāṁkṣā* and *nirākāṁkṣā*. That which raises an expectancy about another sentence is *sākāṁkṣā* and that which ends once the answer is provided is *nirākāṁkṣā*. A sentence can become *sākāṁkṣā* with a particular *kāku* whereas with a different *kāku* it can become *nirākāṁkṣā*, also *sākāṁkṣā kāku* is threefold, being based upon *ākṣepa-garbhā*, *praśna-garbhā* and *vitarka-garbhā*. *Nirākāṁkṣā kāku* is also threefold, being based upon *vidhīrūpa*, *uttararūpa* and *nirṇayarūpa.*[12]

An example of *ākṣepagarbhā*

> (The heroine says to her friends) — If he (the hero) finds the lady messenger sent by me attractive then he will find me also attractive and if he finds my lady messenger's speech pleasant then he will find my words also pleasant.[13]

If this sentence is stated simply the meaning would be that he finds both my lady-messengers and my speech pleasant.

An example of *praśnagarbhā*

The time when pearls use to hang on tender plants has gone forever, now they (the pearls) originate in oyster shells.

इयमेवोपदेष्टुरुत्तररूपा।

वितर्कगभा —

> "नवजलधरः सन्नद्धोऽयं न दृप्तनिशाचरः
> सुरधनुरिदं दूराकृष्टं न नाम शरासनम्।
> अयमपि पटुर्धारासारो न बाणपरम्परा

---

12. *Kāku* (Intonation)
    - *Sākāṁkṣā*
        - *ākṣepa garbhā*
        - *praśna garbhā*
        - *vitarka garbhā*
    - *Nirākāṁkṣā*
        - *vidhirūpa*
        - *uttararūpa*
        - *nirṇayarūpa*

13. The example of *ākṣepa-garbhā* (censure) suggests that if this sentence is read or recited with a particular intonation it will suggest a meaning which is negative in character. If on the other hand this very sentence is recited with a different intonation the meaning turns affirmative in character.

कनकनिकषस्निग्धा विद्युत्प्रिया न ममोर्वशी।।"

Here the question (Has the time gone by?) is an indication of *praśnagarbhā sākāṁkṣā.*[14]

An example of *vitarkagarbhā*

(A statement of Purūravā from the play *Vikramorvaśīya*) —

> Is this dark-coloured body a new cloud? Is it not a *rākṣasa*? Is it a rainbow which stretches far and wide? Is it not a bowstring to send out arrows of love? Is this a vigorous shower of rain? Is it not a shower of arrows? Is its presence like the testing criteria of the golden threshold (a streak of lightning)? Is it not my lovely Urvaśī?

इयमेवोपदेष्टुर्निर्णयरूपा। ता इमास्तिस्रोऽपि नियतनिबन्धाः। तद्विपरीताः पुनरनन्ताः।

तत्राभ्युपगमानुनयकाकु—

"युष्मच्छासनलङ्घनाम्भसि मया मग्नेन नाम स्थितं
प्राप्ता नाम विगर्हणा स्थितिमतां मध्येऽनुजानामपि।
क्रोधोल्लासितशोणितारुणगदस्योच्छिन्दतः कौरवा-
नद्यैकं दिवसं ममाऽसि न गुरुर्नाऽहं विधेयस्तव।।"

This sentence (on the basis of its debatable questions) is an example of *vitarkagarbhā*. If we change its intonation, then the suggested meaning (by *dhvani*) would make it an instance of *nirṇayarūpa nirākākāṁkṣā.*[15] These three varieties of *kāku* (intonation) follow restrictions. The kinds of intonation without these restrictions are numerous.

An example of *abhyupagamānunaya kāku* (a statement of the angry Bhīmasena to Yuddhiṣṭhira

---

14. If this very sentence was treated like an imperative statement then the suggestion would be in the form of the answer — 'Yes, the time has gone' which would thus be an instance of *uttararūpa nirākāṁkṣā*.

15. If the debatable questions are changed to decisive answers then the meanings changes entirely. 'This is a cloud and not a *rākṣasa*, a rainbow and not a bow-string , a shower of rain and not of arrows and it is a streak of lightning, not my Urvaśī.' Since this rendering gives us a decisive answer, we would place it under *nirṇayarūpa nirākāṁkṣā*.

(O, Yuddhiṣṭhira) Till today, I was inactive as I was submerged in non-violation of your wishes like water and was ready to suffer insults of even younger brothers but now as a result of intense anger and with this enemies' blood soaked club I am ready for destruction of the Kauravas. Today, for a day, I am neither your obedient younger brother and nor are you my ruler and elder brother.[16]

अभ्यनुज्ञोपहासकाकू —

**"मथ्नामि कौरवशतं समरे न कोपाद्
दुःशासनस्य रुधिरं न पिबाम्युरस्तः।
सञ्चूर्णयामि गदया न सुयोधनोरू
सन्धिं करोतु भवतां नृपतिः पणेन।।"**

An example of *abhyanugyopahāsa kāku*

(Bhīmasena's statement to the younger brothers on hearing of the peace-treaty between Yuddhiṣṭhira and Duryodhana)

I should not kill a hundred Kauravas in the battlefield, I should not take the blood from Duḥśāsana's chest and drink it, I should not crush Duryodhana's thigh with my club and your king Yuddhiṣṭhira is ready to sign a peace-treaty with the Kauravas.[17]

एवं त्रिचतुरकाकुयोगोऽपि।

तत्र त्रियोगः —

**"सेयं पश्यति नो कुरङ्गकवधूस्त्रस्तैवमुद्वीक्षते
तस्याः पाणिरयं न मारुतवलत्पत्राङ्गुलिः पल्लवः।
तारं रोदिति सैव नैष मरुता वेणुः समापूर्यते**

16. Here 'I was inactive' and 'suffered insults of even younger brothers' is an instance of *abhyupagama kāku*. And 'for today you are not my elder brother' and 'I am not your obedient younger brother' are examples of *anunaya kāku*. The suggestion (*dhvani*) here is that after today I will again be your obedient servant and you my lord.

17. Here the statements concerning Bhīmasena's pledge are examples of *abhyanugya kāku* and 'your king' is an instance of *upahāsa kāku*.

सेयं मामभिभाषते प्रियतमा नो कोकिलः कूजति।।"

Similarly a sentence may be formed with the union of three to four varieties of *kāku* (intonation).

An example of the union of three kinds of *kāku* — (A statement of *Purūrava*) —

> This is my beloved looking at me with agitated eyes and not a deer. It is her hand and not a new and tender leaf shaking in the wind. It is she who is crying with a loud voice and not the sound of bamboos in the wind. And it is the same beloved who is talking to me and not the sound of the nightingale.[18]

चतुर्योगः —

"उच्यतां स वचनीयमशेषं
नेश्वरे परुषता सखि साध्वी।
आनयैनमनुनीय कथं वा
विप्रियाणि जनयन्ननुनेयः।।"

(An example of the union of four varieties of intonation).

(Statement of the heroine to her lady companion)

> (O, friend !) you may say whatever you want, to him (the hero) but it is not suitable to show harshness towards the lord, try to get him here for a conciliation but how can you be reconciled to one who opposes my wishes.[19]

"सख्या वा नायिकाया वा सखीनायिकयोरथ।
सखीनां भूयसीनां वा वाक्ये काकुरिह स्थिता।।

पदवाक्यविदां मार्गो योऽन्यथैव व्यवस्थितः।
स त्वङ्गाभिनयो द्योत्या (नयद्योत्यः?) तं काकुः कुरुतेऽन्यथा।।

अयं काकुकृतो लोके व्यवहारो न केवलम्।

---

18. Here the first is *praśnarūpa vitarkagarbhā kāku*. It may also be taken as *nirṇayagarbhā* if treated decisively.

19. Here 'to say or not to do so' and 'how to reconcile to one who opposes' there are two varieties of *kāku* in *nirdeśa-rūpa* and two in *upadeśa-rūpa*, thus altogether there are four kinds of *kāku*.

शास्त्रेष्वप्यस्य साम्राज्यं काव्यस्याप्येष जीवितम्।।

कामं विवृणुते काकुरर्थान्तरमतन्द्रिता।
स्फुटीकरोति तु सतां भावाभिनयचातुरीम्।।

इत्थं कविर्निबध्नीयादित्थं च मतिमान्पठेत्।
यथा निबन्धनिगदश्छायां काञ्चिन्निषिञ्चति।।

Intonation is generally found in the speeches of the lady-companions or the heroine and her lady-companions.

The speech composed of words and sentences as adopted by people (like grammarians and Mīmāṁsakas) is straightforward (and direct). They use the parts of the body for intonation. But speech as used by poets (and dramatists) is quite different (owing to the importance they give to voice modulations).

The use of *kāku* is not prevalent in this *loka* (ordinary speech of this world) only. It also has a prominent place in the Vedas but of poetry it is the very soul.[20]

Kāku when appropriately used reveals unmistakably a meaning different from the expressed one without any cause for doubt or confusion. It also represents one's skill in the representation of various moods to the *sahṛdayas* (ideal readers).

In a poetic-composition the poet should use *kāku* in such a way and the reader should recite in a manner which clearly shows off the brilliance of the composition.

पाठ–प्रतिष्ठा

करोति काव्यं प्रायेण संस्कृतात्मा यथा तथा।
पठितुं वेत्ति स परं यस्य सिद्धा सरस्वती।।

यथा जन्मान्तराभ्यासात्कण्ठे कस्यापि रक्तता।
तथैव पाठसौन्दर्यं नैकजन्मविनिर्मितम्।।

ससंस्कृतमपभ्रंशं लालित्यालिङ्गितं पठेत्।
प्राकृतं भूतभाषां च सौष्ठवोत्तरमुद्गिरेत्।।

20. By calling *kāku* (intonation) as the very life soul of poetry, Rājaśekhara has shown the importance of modulation of voice in poetry and its effect on meaning.

प्रसन्ने मन्द्रयेद्वाचं तारयेत्तद्विरोधिनि।
मन्द्रतारौ च रचयेन्निर्वाहिणि यथोत्तरम्।।

Poets who are good composers may create poetic compositions but a good reciter is the one who has attained Sarasvatī (or one who has acquired skill and proficiency not less than the goddess of learning).

Just as one who is endowed with a sweet voice from birth is due to traces (*saṁskāra*) from previous generations so also a good reciter of poetry is made after generations of practice.

Poetry of Sanskrit and Apabhraṁśa[21] should be ready with charm and grace and that of Prākṛta[22] and Bhūt-bhāṣā[23] should be read with ever-increasing beauty.

The poetry with *prasāda*[24] (a *guṇa* or a quality) should be read seriously and with depth while the one possessing *ojas*[25] should be read at a high pitch. *Ubhaya-guṇa* in poetry should be read appropriately (at times a low pitch or depth and at others a high pitch should be adopted).

ललितं काकुसमन्वितमुज्ज्वलमर्थवशकृतपरिच्छेदम्।
श्रुतिसुखविविक्तवर्णं कवयः पाठं प्रशंसन्ति।।

अतितूर्णमतिविलम्बितमुल्बणनादं च नादहीनं च।
अपदच्छिन्नमनावृतमतिमृदुपरुषं च निन्दन्ति।।

गम्भीरत्वमनैश्वर्यं निर्व्यूढिस्तारमन्द्रयोः।
संयुक्तवर्णलावण्यमिति पाठगुणाः स्मृताः।।

यथा व्याघ्री हरेत्पुत्रान्दंष्ट्राभिश्च च पीडयेत्।
भीता पतनभेदाभ्यां तद्वद्वर्णान्प्रयोजयेत्।।

---

21. Apabhraṁśa is one of the forms of Prākṛta dialect used by common people. Apte, *op. cit.*, p. 98.
22. Prākṛta is a vernacular or provincial dialect derived from and akin to Sanskrit. See Apte, *op. cit.*, p. 677.
23. Bhūta-bhāṣā is the language usually ascribed to certain sub-ethnic groups.
24. *Prasāda* is an excellence, lucidity arising from carefully selected words which leads to the intended sense at once. See. S.K. De, *History of Sanskrit Poetics*, *op. cit.*, p. 238.

25 *Ojas* is a *guṇa* which refers to strength due to the presence of compounds. See S.K. De., *HSP*, *op. cit.*, p. 238.

विभक्तयः स्फुटा यत्र समासश्चाकदर्थितः।
अम्लानः पदसन्धिश्च तत्र पाठः प्रतिष्ठितः।।

To read with a sweet sound, proper intonation, clear, stressed according to the meaning, pleasant to the ears and uttering each letter distinctly is to be appreciated (are some of the essential ingredients required of good reading).

To read quickly or haltingly, very loudly or too softly, without stressing at the correct places, and either too sweetly or too harshly is to be censured (are some of the features to be avoided while reading).

The letters should be uttered in such a fashion just as a tigress holds cubs tenderly in her teeth but without allowing them to get hurt or fall down.

The reading in which the cases are clearly marked, compounds appear distinctly and *sandhis* are apparent is deemed to be an excellent one.

न व्यस्तपदयोरैक्यं न भिदां तु समस्तयोः।
न चाख्यातपदम्लानिं विदधीत सुधीः पठन्।।

आगोपालकमायोषिदास्तामेतस्य लेह्यता।
इत्थं कविः पठन्काव्यं वाग्देव्या अतिवल्लभः।।

येऽपि शब्दविदो नैव नैव चार्थविचक्षणाः।
तेषामपि सतां पाठः सुष्ठु कर्णरसायनम्।।

पठन्ति संस्कृतं सुष्ठु कुण्ठाः प्राकृतवाचि ते।
वाराणसीतः पूर्वेण ये केचिन्मगधादयः।।

आह स्म —

"ब्रह्मन्विज्ञापयामि त्वां स्वाधिकारजिहासया।
गौडस्त्यजतु वा गाथामन्या वाऽस्तु सरस्वती।।

The wise scholars should not read words which are meant to be separate together, one should not read compounds separately (by breaking them up) and should utter the verbs clearly.

A poet who renders a recitation which is attractive to even cowherds and women is like a beloved of Sarasvatī (goddess of wisdom and learning).

The wise poets render a recitation which is pleasing even for those who have no knowledge of words or their meanings.[26]

The poets belonging to regions west of Vārāṇasī render Sanskrit poetry beautifully but are dull when it comes to Prākṛta poetry

It is said that —

> Sarasvatī wanting to relingquish her position said to Brahmā that either the people of Gauḍa should give up reading poetry in Prākṛta or else he, (Brahmā), should appoint another Sarasvatī in place of her. (Suggestion is that Gauḍīya are incapable of reciting poetry in Prākṛta).

नातिस्पष्टो न चाश्लिष्टो न रूक्षो नातिकोमलः।
न मन्द्रो नातितारश्च पाठी गौडेषु वाडवः।।

रसः कोऽप्यस्तु काप्यस्तु रीतिः कोऽप्यस्तु वा गुणः।
सगर्वं सर्वकर्णाटाष्टङ्कारोत्तरपाठिनः।।

The recitation rendered by scholars of Gauḍa[27] is mediocre. It is neither clear nor unclear, neither harsh nor soft and neither read in a loud tone nor a deep one.

The poets of Karṇāṭa[28] region are very clear in their recitation. Whatever be the *rīti*, *rasa* or excellence they recite proudly and distinctly.

गद्ये पद्येऽथवा मिश्रे काव्ये काव्यमना अपि।
गेयगर्भे स्थितः पाठे सर्वोऽपि द्रविडः कविः।।

पठन्ति लटभं लाटाः प्राकृतं संस्कृतद्विषः।
जिह्वया ललितोल्लापलब्धसौन्दर्यमुद्रया।।

सुराष्ट्रत्रवणाद्या ये पठन्त्यर्पितसौष्ठवम्।
अपभ्रंशावदंशानि ते संस्कृतवचांस्यपि।।

---

26. Rājaśekhara here is referring to the purely auditory pleasure which can be derived through a good recitation.

27. For geographical regions, See Appendix II.

28. For geographical regions, See Appendix II.

The poets of Dravida[29] region although with a deep insight into poetry, sing each composition, be it poetic, prose or mixed.

The poets belonging to Lāṭa[30] region are enemies of Sanskrit but render the Prākṛta pieces very beautifully. The movement of their tongues appears very graceful while in the act of reading.

The poets of Saurāṣṭra, Gurjara, Travaṇa[31], etc., read and render clearly and beautifully, poetry in both, Sanskrit and Apabhraṁśa.

शारदायाः प्रसादेन काश्मीरः सुकविर्जनः।
कर्णे गुडूचीगण्डूषस्तेषां पाठक्रमः किमु।।

ततः पुरस्तात्कवयो ये भवन्त्युत्तरापथे।
ते महत्यपि संस्कारे सानुनासिकपाठिनः।।

मार्गानुगेन निनदेन निधिर्गुणानां
सम्पूर्णवर्णरचनो यतिभिर्विभक्तः।

पाञ्चालमण्डलभुवां सुभगः कवीनां ।
श्रोत्रे मधु क्षरति किञ्चन काव्यपाठः।।

ललल्लकारया जिह्वं जर्जरस्फाररेफया।
गिरा भुजङ्गाः पूज्यन्ते काव्यभव्यधियो न तु।।

पञ्चस्थानसमुद्भववर्णेषु यथास्वरूपनिष्पत्तिः।
अर्थवशेन च विरतिः सर्वस्वमिदं हि पाठस्य।।

सकाकुकलना पाठप्रतिष्ठेयं प्रतिष्ठिता।
अर्थानुशासनस्याथ प्रकारः परिकीर्त्यते।।

With the blessings of Śāradā the poets of Kāśmīra[32] are good but when they recite, it is as if one is washing the mouth with a dose of medicine, to the ears (that is, it sounds very harsh to the ears).

Further than this, the poets belonging to the north, however learned they may be in the science of grammar, their recitation is always nasal.

The recitation of poets of Pāñcāla[33] region is very sweet. They follow the correct use of stress, employ the right tone and utter each letter

29. For geographical regions, See Appendix II.

30. For geographical regions, See Appendix II.

distinctly. When they recite, it is as if honey is poured into the ears.

The wise scholars who utter the *lakāra* with a force and the entire *rakāra* with the force of only the letter '*r*', in spite of their brilliance as Naiyāyikās and Vaiyākaraṇas will gain no respect with poets because for poets respect is due only with a soft, pleasing and correct utterance rendered in recitation.

The syllables (*varṇas*) have five positions — *svar*, *kāla*, *sthāna*, *prayatna* and *anupradāna*. The syllables uttered with distinct clarity and with proper stresses and pauses keeping the meaning in mind is the secret of a good recitation.

In this way this chapter dealt with intonation and recitation or modulation and the analytic description thereof.

The next chapter will deal with sources of meaning.

।। इति राजशेखरकृतौ काव्यमीमांसायां कविरहस्ये प्रथमेऽधिकरणे सप्तमोऽध्यायः समाप्तः।।

8

काव्यार्थयोनयः

Kāvyārthyonyaḥ

(Sources of Meaning in Poetry)

'श्रुतिः, स्मृतिः इतिहासः, पुराणं, प्रमाणविद्या, समयविद्या, राजसिद्धान्तत्रयी, लोको, विरचना, प्रकीर्णकं च काव्यार्थानां द्वादश योनयः' इति आचार्याः। 'उचितसंयोगेन, योक्तृसंयोगेन, उत्पाद्यसंयोगेन, संयोगविकारेण च सह षोडश' इति यायावरीयः। तत्र श्रौतः।

'उर्वशीहाप्सराः पुरूरवसमैडं चकमे'। अत्रार्थे —

"चन्द्राद्बुधः समभवद्भगवान्नरेन्द्र-
माद्यं पुरूरवसमैडमसावसूत।
तं चाप्सराः स्मरवती चकमे किमन्य-
दत्रोर्वशी स्मितवशीकृतशक्रचेताः।।"

ĀCĀRYAS have identified twelve sources of meaning in poetry. These are *śruti* (cultural patronymic texts, the Vedas), *smṛti* (*śāstras*), *itihāsa* (historical narratives), *purāṇas* (mythology), *pramāṇa-vidyā* (epistemology), *rāja-siddhānta trayī* (*arthaśāstra* or polity, *nāṭyaśāstra* or dramaturgy and *kāmaśāstra* or science of erotics), *loka* (experience of the poet), *viracanā* (works of other poets) and *prakīrṇaka* (64 Arts and Sciences[1], five sub-Vedas — *Itihāsa*, *Dhanurveda*, *Gandharvaveda*, *Āyurveda*, *Gānaveda*. Seven auxiliary sciences: *śikṣā*, *kalpa*, *vyākaraṇa*, *nirukta*, *chanda*, *jyotiṣa*, *kāvya*. Six *vidyās* — *vārtā*, *kāmasūtra*, *śilpa-śāstra*, *artha-śāstra*, *sāhitya-vidyā*, *ānvīkṣikī* and others like *vṛkṣaśāstra*, *aśvagajaśāstra*, etc.).

1. See chapter 10, note 1.

Yāyāvarīya (Rājaśekhara) has added four more sources to these twelve to make a total of sixteen sources. These are *uccitsaṁyoga* (juxtaposition for comparison), *yoktṛsaṁyoga* (extended simile), *utpādyasaṁyoga* (double simile) and *saṁyogavikāra* (modification produced by juxtapositioning).

An example of *śruti* (or Veda) —

'(According to a Veda) Urvaśī the celestial nymph desired the son of Ilā or the king Purūrava.' Thus —

> The moon bore a son called Buddha, Buddha and his wife Ilā had a son called Purūrava who was the first king of Candravaṁśa (lunar race). In relation to his beauty it is enough to state that the celestial beauty Urvaśī who is known for the charming smile and is said to have attracted Indra, has also fallen prey to attraction of Purūrava.[2]

यथा वा —

"यदेतन्मण्डलं तपति तन्महदुक्थं ता ऋचः स ऋचां लोकोऽथ यदेतदर्चिर्दीप्यते तन्महाव्रतं तानि सामानि स साम्नां लोकोऽथ य एष तस्मिन्मण्डले पुरुषः सोऽग्निस्तानि यजूंषि स यजुषां लोकः सैषा त्रय्येव विद्या तपति।"

Thus also —

> That blazing orb (*uktham*)[3] is the abode (substratum) of distinguished gods who are objects of *Ṛk*. The blazing rays of the orb are *sāma* (hymns of praise). They are the great worship, form of His lustre, abode of the distinguished gods of *Sāmaveda* and the *puruṣa* (the life principle) in that orb is *Agni*, the *Yajuṣ*. The distinguished gods of *Yajuṣ* dwell in them. In this way the orb, the rays and *puruṣa* — all three get heated and are like the *trayī vidyā*.[4]

---

2. Purūravās was a prominent king of Candravaṁśā (lunar race). Descending in order from Brahmā came Attri-Candra-Buddha-Purūravās. The dynasty which came from Candra was Candravaṁśā. For further reference see Vettam Mani, *op. cit.*, pp. 620-1.
3. *Uktham* a particular portion of the *Sāmaveda*. See Vettam Mani *op. cit.*, p. 805.
4. *Trayī* see chapter 2, note 8 and Vettam Mani, *op. cit.*, p. 791.

अत्रार्थे —

"एतद्यन्मण्डलं खे तपति दिनकृतस्ता ऋचोऽर्चींषि यानि
द्योतन्ते तानि सामान्ययमपि पुरुषो मण्डलेऽणुर्यजूंषि।
एव यं वेद वेदत्रितयमयमयं वेदवेदीसमग्रो
वर्गः स्वर्गापवर्गप्रकृतिरविकृतिः सोऽस्तु सूर्यः श्रिये वः।।"

तच्चेदं वेदहरणं। यदित्थं कथयन्ति —

"नमोऽस्तु तस्यै श्रुतये यां दुहन्ति पदे पदे।
ऋषयः शास्त्रकाराश्च कवयश्च यथामति।।"

Another example —

The orb of the sun which heats up in the sky is like the verses (of *Ṛgveda*), the rays are the *Sāma* (*Veda*) and the minute particle or *puruṣa* is *Yajurveda*. In this way the sun is the epitome of the three Vedas. The sun is an aggregation of the thoughts of *dharma*, *artha*, *kāma* and *mokṣa*[5] expressed in the Vedas. It is the principle behind heaven and final emancipation. May this unimpaired source (the sun) add to your esteem.

In this way the ancient *ācārya*s while referring to appropriation of meanings from the Vedas say —

Homage is due to the *śruti*s (the meaning of which) is like a cow who is milked at every step by sages, learned men and poets.

स्मार्तः —

"बह्वर्थेष्वभियुक्तेन सर्वत्र व्यपलापिना।
विभावितैकदेशेन देयं यदभियुज्यते।।"

अत्रार्थे —

"हंस प्रयच्छ मे कान्तां गतिस्तस्यास्त्वया हृता।
सम्भावितैकदेशेन देयं यदभियुज्यते।।"

An example of meaning related to *smṛti* —

5. The four *puruṣārthas* (four human ends) of life are: *dharma* (righteousness or discharge of duty), *artha* (acquisition of wealth), *kāma* (gratification), and *mokṣa* (final emancipation, deliverance of the soul from recurring births or transmigration). See Apte, *op. cit.*, p. 774.

If a person who is accused of stealing many things refuses to admit his crime but later on admits to a part of the crime or some part of the stolen goods are recovered from him, then he is liable to return the entire stolen property.

Another example

O swan! You must give your gait back to my beloved wife. You have stolen her walk. This is in accordance with the precept laid down by the *dharamaśāstra* that even if a part of the looted goods is found in one's possession then he is held responsible for the entire stealth.

ऐतिहासिकः —

"न स स सङ्कुचितः पन्थाः येन वाली इतो गतः।
समये तिष्ठ सुग्रीव मा वालिपथमन्वगाः।।"

अत्र —

"मदं नवैश्वर्यलवेन लम्भितं
विसृज्य पूर्वः समयो विमृश्यताम्।
जगज्जिघत्सातुरकण्ठपद्धति-
र्न वालिनैवाहततृप्तिरन्तकः।।"

An example from a historical narrative[6]

(O, Sugrīva!)[7] The path which led to the destruction of your brother Vālī[8] is not yet closed. You should remember your pledge and abide by it. You should not follow Vālī.

Thus —

(O, Sugrīva!) Remember your old pledge and do not loose yourself in your newly-acquired prosperity. Death which is the cause of the destruction of the entire world is not satisfied with just Vālī (in other words you may be the next victim).

---

6. The *śloka* is taken from *Kiṣkindhākāṇḍa*, Vālmīki's *Rāmāyaṇa*, chapter 24, *śloka* 18.
7. Sugrīva — Bālī's brother, sons of Arunā. For more details see Vettam Mani, *op. cit.*, p. 756.
8. Bālī — A mighty monkey king. For further reference, see Vettam Mani, *op. cit.*, pp. 105-6.

पौराणिकः —

"हिरण्यकशिपुर्दैत्यो यां यां स्मित्वाऽप्युदैक्षत।
भयभ्रान्तैः सुरैश्चक्रे तस्यै तस्यै दिशे नमः।।"

अत्र —

"स सञ्चरिष्णुर्भुवनत्रयेऽपि यां
यदृच्छयाशिश्रियदाश्रयः श्रियः।
अकारि तस्य मुकुटोपलस्खलत्-
करैस्त्रिसन्ध्यं त्रिदशैर्दिशे नमः।।"

An example of meaning from Paurāṇic sources —

When the king of demons, Hiraṇyakaśipu[9] smiled in different directions, the petrified gods in terror paid homage to those directions.

And also —

The lord of the wealth of three worlds, Hiraṇyakaśipu happened to travel through the worlds whichever direction he took, the gods removed their crowns and bowed to him in all directions.

अत्राहुः —

"श्रुतीनां साङ्गशाखानामितिहासपुराणयोः।
अर्थग्रन्थः कथाभ्यासः कवित्वस्यैकमौषधम्।।

इतिहासपुराणाभ्यां चक्षुर्भ्यामिव सत्कविः।
विवेकाञ्जनशुद्धाभ्यां सूक्ष्ममप्यर्थमीक्षते।।

वेदार्थस्य निबन्धेन श्लाघ्यन्ते कवयो यथा।
स्मृतीनामितिहासस्य पुराणस्य तथा तथा।।"

Thus also —

Stringing together and composing the meanings from various sources such as Vedas, Vedāṅgas, *itihāsa* and Purāṇas, etc., and relating legends depicted in them is the sole criterion and like a medicinal drug for the poetic faculty.

Good poets use the discriminative collyrium to purify their

9. A *dānava*, son of Diti, cf. Vettam Mani, *op. cit.*, p. 314.

itihāsa-purāṇa like eyes to see the subtle and minute facts present in them.

Just as poets who follows the meanings available in Vedic sources for composing poetry are to be appreciated, similarly poets who use *dharma-śāstra*, *itihāsa* and *purāṇa* for composing poetry are to be appreciated.

द्विविधः प्रामाणिको मैमांसिकस्तार्किकश्च। तत्र प्रथमः। शब्दस्य सामान्यमभिधेयं विशेषश्चार्थः। अत्र —

"सामान्यवाचि पदमप्यभिधीयमानं
मां प्राप्य जातमभिधेयविशेषनिष्ठम्।
स्त्री काचिदित्यभिहिते सततं मनो मे
तामेव वामनयनां विषयीकरोति।।"

Pramāṇika meanings are of two kinds — *mīmāṁsaka* and *tārkika*. The principle behind *Mimāṁsā Śāstra*[10] is that though a word usually expresses only its ordinary meaning but it can acquire a specific meaning depending on the context in which it is used.

Thus —

A commonly used word 'woman' has a special meaning for me. When 'some woman' is being talked of my mind goes to my beloved, Sulocanā.

Tārkika artha (logic) is again of two kinds — Sāṁkhya[11]-*śāstrīya* and

---

10. *Mīmāṁsā* is the name of the six chief *darśanas* or systems of Indian philosophy. It was originally divided into two systems — the Pūrva-Mīmāṁsā or Karma-Mīmāṁsā founded by Jaiminī and the Uttara-Mīmāṁsā or Brahma-Mīmāṁsā ascribed to Bādarāyaṇa; but the two systems have very little in common between them, the first concerning itself chiefly with the correct interpretation of the ritual of the Veda and the settlement of dubious points in regard to Vedic texts and the latter dealing chiefly with the nature of *Brahman* of the Supreme Spirit. See Vaman Shivram Apte, *op. cit.*, p. 762.

11. Sāṁkhya is the name of one of the six systems of Hindu philosophy attributed to the sage Kapila. This philosophy is so-called because it 'enumerates' 25 *tattvas* or true principles and its chief object is to effect the final emancipation of the 25th *tattva*, i.e., the *puruṣa* or soul from the bonds of the worldly existence →

Nyāya[12] -Vaiśesika[13] -*śāstra*.

तर्केषु साङ्ख्यीयः —

"नासतो विद्यते भावो नाभावो विद्यते सतः।
उभयोरपि दृष्टोऽन्तस्त्वनयोस्तत्त्वदृष्टिभिः।।"

अत्र —

"य एते यज्वानः प्रथितमहसो येऽप्यवनिपा
मृगाक्ष्यो याश्चैताः कृतमपरसंसारकथया।
अमी ये दृश्यन्ते फलकुसुमनम्राश्च तरवो
जगत्येवंरूपा विलसति मृदेषा भगवती।।"

An example of *Sāṁkhya-śāstrīya* meaning —

The unreal has no existence; the real never ceases to be. The truth about both has been realised by the seers.[14]

Set aside the movable world. These performers of sacrificial rituals, famous kings, these women with their beautiful eyes and in the immovable world the trees are laden with fruits and flowers. In all these one can see the sportive earth in various forms (i.e., this world is ultimately reduced to dust).

न्यायवैशेषिकीयः — स किंसामग्रीक ईश्वरः कर्त्ता? इति पूर्वपक्षः। निरतिशयैश्वर्यस्य तस्य कर्तृत्वमिति सिद्धान्तः।

→ — the fetters of phenomenal creation — by conveying a correct knowledge of 24 other *tattva*s and by properly discriminating the soul from them. See Apte, *op. cit.*, p. 978.

12. Nyāya is founded by the sage Gotama. The word *nyāya* means prosperity or fitness, the proper method of arriving at a conclusion by analysis. This school has been called the Logical School. Cf. John Dowson, *op. cit.*, p. 81.

13. Vaiśeṣika is founded by a sage named Kaṇāda, who lived about the same time as Gotama. It is supplementary to the Nyāya and these two schools are classed together. It is called the Atomic School, because it teaches the existence of a transient world composed of aggregations of eternal atoms. Both the Nyāya and the Vaiśeṣika recognise a Supreme Being. Cf. Dowson, *op. cit.*, p. 81.

14. *Tattva-darśana* is seeing into the reality of things. The seers of truth behold the body and the pleasure and pain associated with it as unreal. Cf. *The Bhagvad Gītā*, tr. by Swami Chidbhava Nanda, Sri Ramakrishna Tapuvanan, Madras, 1970, chapter 2, *śloka* 16, pp. 134-6.

अत्र —

"किमीहः किंकायः स खलु किमुपायस्त्रिभुवनं
किमाधारो धाता सृजति किमुपादान इति च।
अतर्क्यैश्वर्ये त्वय्यनवसरदुःस्थो हतधियः
कुतर्कोऽयं कांश्चिन्मुखरयति मोहाय जगतः।।"

बौद्धीयः —

विवक्षापूर्वा हि शब्दास्तामेव विवक्षां सूचयेयुः।

In *Nyāyaśāstra* in answer to the question, 'what are the different materials used by God for creation?, a principle is formulated which states that God is gifted with unimaginable powers. He does not need any material to create, he himself is the Creator'.

Thus —

(O God!), Certain thoughtless, materialistic and ignorant people come up with this logic concerning you to confuse the world. What is the desire which motivates? What is form? What is the process? What is the basis and reason adopted by the Creator in the process of Creation!

According to Buddhist principles[15]

The word is an indicator of the speaker's intention (or desire).

अत्र —

"भवतु विदितं शब्दा वक्तुर्विवक्षितसूचकाः
स्मरवति यतः कान्ते कान्तां बलात्परिचुम्बति।
न न न म म मा मा मां स्प्राक्षीर्निषेधपरं वचो
भवति शिथिले मानग्रन्थौ तदेव विधायकम्।।"

---

15. Buddhism is based on the teachings of Gautama Buddha and is one of the great world faiths. His doctrine concerning the *atta*, the soul or ego was that the soul does not exist. What is called the soul is in reality a physical and mental aggregate of five evanescent or impermanent conditions called *khaṇḍa* namely *rūpa* form of the physical body, *vedanā* (feelings), *saṁjñā* (idea or understanding), *saṁkhāra* (will) and *vijñāna* (or pure consciousness). See Benjamin Walker, *op. cit.*, pp. 183-7.

Thus —

> It is true that words are an indication of the speaker's desire because after the quietening of the lover's quarrel between the hero and the heroine, when the love-sick hero forcibly desired the maiden she at once uttered words of denial — No! No! Don't touch me! These words of denial (on the loosening of pride) are presented (function) as the principle (which voices the heroine's desire).

लौकायतिकः —

> भूतेभ्यश्चैतन्यं मदशक्तिवत्। अत्र —
>
> "बहुविधमिह साक्षिचिन्तकाः
> प्रवदन्त्यन्यमितः कलेवरात्।
> अपि च सुदति ते सचिन्तकाः
> प्रलयं यान्ति सहैव चिन्तया।।"

आर्हतः —

> शरीरपरिमाण आत्मा, अन्यथा शरीराफल्यमात्माफल्यं वा।

Loka as a source of meaning —

In Cārvāka's opinion the living being is not separate from the body.

> According to him just as intoxicants (seeds) on being mixed with other stimulants produce intoxication so also five elements go to form a living thing.

(An example in poetry)

> (O maiden!) with beautiful teeth, eminent philosophers call this soul separate from the body but these people who appear to be anxious about you will be destroyed by anxiety.

Thus —

The Jaina[16] philosophers say that the size or dimension of each living

---

16. Jainism is Hindu sect of extreme antiquity whose last reformer 'Mahāvīra' is regarded as its historical founder. They accept the dualistic principles of *jīva* (eternal soul) and *ajīva* (eternal element). The *jīva* acts and is affected by acts; it is a knowing self; the *ajīva* is atomic and unconscious. *Ajīvas* exist in various →

being's soul is in proportion to the size of its body.

अत्र —

"शरीरमात्रमात्मानं ये वदन्ति जयन्ति ते।
तद्युम्बनेऽपि यज्जातः सर्वाङ्गपुलकोऽस्य मे।।"

सर्वपार्षदत्वात्काव्यविद्यायाः तानिमानन्यांश्चार्थान्व्युत्पत्तये प्रत्यवेक्षेत।

आहुश्च —

"यांस्तर्ककर्कशानर्थान्सूक्तिष्वाद्रियते कविः।
सूर्यांशव इवेन्दौ ते काञ्चिदर्चन्ति कान्तताम्।।"

Thus —

The philosophers who say that the size of the body is in proportion to the size of the soul are the most superior because the touch of his body has sent thrills through my body and enraptured me.

समयविद्यासु शैवसिद्धान्तीयः —

"घोरघोरतरातीतब्रह्मविद्याकलातिगः।
परापरपदव्यापी पायाद्वः परमेश्वरः।।"

पाञ्चरात्रः —

"नाद्यन्तवन्तः कवयः पुराणाः सूक्ष्मा बृहन्तोऽप्यनुशासितारः।
सर्वज्वरान् घ्नन्तु ममानिरुद्धप्रद्युम्नसङ्कर्षणवासुदेवाः।।"

Kāvya-vidyā is supported by all the *śāstras*. A poet in addition to being aware of the above philosophical principles should also take care of other philosophical systems which is the cause of *vyutpatti*.

A poet who expounds the meanings difficult to comprehend with the help of his sayings transforms the complex matter into charming sense just as the inflamed and heated rays of the sun get transformed into the cool shady and soft moonlight of the moon.

→ relationships, five categories or *tattva* of *ajīva* being distinguished, namely (i) *ākāśa*, ether or space in its universal aspect and not the space in which we live, the world only exists in one specialised segment of the space condition, (ii) *dharma* (not to be confused with the term as used in Hinduism) a condition of movement, (iii) *adharma*, a tertiary space which permits of rest, (iv) *kāla* or time, and (v) *pudgala* matter; what is received by the senses. See Benjamin Walker, *op. cit.*, pp. 492-7.

An example of Śaiva Siddhānta[17] being used in poetry —

> May the knowledge which is beyond time and relates to Śiva who is found everywhere bless and protect you.

Pañcarātra (Vaiṣṇava)[18] principle and its example —

> Ancient and eminent poets, endless, rulers of the narrow and wide domains of the world. May Aniruddha,[19] Pradyumna,[20] Sankarṣaṇa[21] and Vāsudeva[22] rid us of the heat (both mental and physical) of our bodies.

बौद्धसिद्धान्तीयः —

> "कलिकलुषकृतानि यानि लोके मयि निपतन्तु विमुच्यतां स लोकः।।
> मम हि सुचरितेन सर्वसत्त्वाः परमसुखेन सुखावनीं प्रयान्तु।।"

An example of Buddhist siddhānta —

> All the unhappiness and suffering in the world due to the evil of the people in it should be mine. May every living being be free of all suffering. May my good deeds bring about happiness in the life of human beings and may they live peacefully.

एवं सिद्धान्तान्तरेष्वपि।

राजसिद्धान्तत्रय्यामर्थशास्त्रीयः —

> "शमव्यायामाभ्यां प्रतिविहिततन्त्रस्य नृपतेः
> परं प्रत्यावापः। फलति कृतसेकस्तरूरिव।

---

17. Śaivism is the religion devoted to the worship of Śiva and his symbols. For further details and its distinguishing features, see Benjamin Walker, *op. cit.*, pp. 328-30.

18. Vaiṣṇavism is the religion devoted to the worship of Viṣṇu and two of his chief incarnations Rāma and Kṛṣṇa with their consorts. Pañcarātra is an early Vaiṣṇavaite sect whose origins are lost in obscurity. For further reference, see Benjamin Walker, *op. cit.*, pp. 176-7.

19. Aniruddha, son of Pradyumna and grandson of Kṛṣṇa. See Dowson. *op. cit.*, p. 17.

20. Pradyumna son of Kṛṣṇa by Rukmiṇī. See Dowson. *op. cit.*, pp. 237-8.

21. Saṅkarṣaṇa — a name of Balarāma, Dowson, *op. cit.*, p. 279.

22. Vāsudeva — a name of Kṛṣṇa, Dowson, *op. cit.*, p. 343.

बहुव्याजं राज्यं न सुकरमराजप्रणिधिभि-
दुराराधा लक्ष्मीरनवहितचित्तं छलयति।।"

Similarly the meanings should be appropriated from other principles.

Out of the three *Rājasiddhāntas*, an example from *Arthaśāstra* (in poetry)

When a tree (*pālit*) is nourished with water it yields fruits. Similarly a kingdom which is organised on the principles of peace and hard work yields power to the king. Kingdoms can be brimming with malpractices. They cannot function without secret agents. It is very difficult to capture wealth and keep it within control. It always slips through the fingers of an inattentive and unorganised person. Thus after one is satisfied with one's kingdom one should direct one's attention to the other kingdom.

नाट्यशास्त्रीयः —

"एवं धारय देवि बाहुलतिकामेवं कुरुष्वाङ्गकं
मात्युच्चैर्नम कुञ्चयाग्रचरणं मां पश्य तावत्स्थितं।
देवीं नर्त्तयतः स्ववक्त्रमुरजेनाम्भोधरध्वानिना
शम्भोर्वः परिपान्तु लम्बितलयच्छेदाहतस्तालिकाः।।"

An example from the subject of *Nāṭyaśāstra* (Dramaturgy)

Goddess, keep your hand thus, move your gentle body in this fashion, don't bend too much, bring the toes of your feet together. Look at me. Thus a cloud like face and *mṛdaṅga* (a kind of drum) like sound was used by Śiva while giving instructions to Pārvatī. May the beat set on the long notes used by Śiva protect you.

कामसूत्रीयः —

"नाश्चर्यं त्वयि यल्लक्ष्मीः क्षिप्त्वाऽधोक्षजमागता।
असौ मन्दरतस्त्वं तु प्राप्तः समरतस्तया।।"

लौकिकस्तु द्विधा प्राकृतो व्युत्पन्नश्च। तयोः प्रथमः —

"स्फुटितपिठरीबन्धश्लाघ्यो विपक्षगृहेप्यभूत्
प्रियतम ययोः स्नेहग्रन्थिस्तथा प्रथमं स नौ।
जनवदधुना सन्नन्यावां वसाव इहैव तौ

धिगपरिचितं प्रेम स्त्रीणां चिराय च जीवितम्।।"

यथा वा —

"इक्षुदण्डस्य मण्डस्य दध्नः पिष्टकृतस्य च।
वाराहस्य च मांसस्य सैष गच्छति फाल्गुनः।।"

An example from the subject of *Kāmasūtra* (love)

(O King!) It is not surprising that Lakṣmī has left Viṣṇu to go along with you because Viṣṇu had attained her by Mandarācala (churning of the ocean) whereas you have obtained her through war.[23]

Laukika artha (of this world) is of two kinds *prākṛta* and *vyutpanna*.

An example of *prākṛta* (natural meaning)

The heroine remembering the time before her marriage tells her husband that previously (before the marriage) though they lived in different houses their knot of love was beautiful like the two halves of a broken pot which has been pasted together. Now in spite of living in the same house they are like ordinary people. This is a blemish on the unparalleled love and long life of women.

And also —

The month of *Phālguna* which is suitable for feeding on sugarcane, curd, paste of lentils and the flesh of a wild pig is slowly passing away.

द्वितीयो द्विधा समस्तजनजन्यः कतिपयजनजन्यश्च। तयोः प्रथमो ऽनेकधा देशानां बहुत्वात्।

तत्र दाक्षिणात्यः —

"पिबन्त्यास्वाद्य मरिचं ताम्बूलविशदैर्मुखैः।
प्रियाधरावदंशानि मधूनि द्रमिलाङ्गनाः।।"

यथा वा —

"विरम मदन कस्त्वं चैत्र का शक्तिरिन्दो-

23. There is a pun on the word *mandarata* and *samarata* where the former also stands for a person with a lack of passion and the latter who is passionate. It is poetically appropriate to use pun while referring to such a subject.

रिह हि कुसुमबाणाः कुण्ठिताग्राः स्खलन्ति।
हृदयभुव इमास्ताः कुन्तलप्रेयसीनां
प्रहतिकिणकठोरग्रन्थयो वज्रसाराः।।"

Vyutpanna artha is again of two kinds. One is *samastajana-jānya* (of all common people) and the second is *katipayajanjānya* (certain specific people). The former is of various kinds depending on the variety of countries.

An example of the south —

> The women of the Draviḍa[24] region eat excessive betel leaf (due to which they loose the sense of taste) and they take a pinch of pepper before partaking of wine from their beloved's lips.

Another example —

> The beautiful maidens of Kuntala[25] region have developed knots in their hearts and they have got hardened due to continuously being attacked by cupid's arrows. Thus O, Kāmadeva (Cupid, God of Love) stop your arrows. The month of *Caitra* has also lost its force (the moonlight docs not move them). The arrows aimed at them also become crooked, loose their force and fall apart.

उदीच्यः —

"नेपाल्यो वल्लभैः सार्द्धमार्द्रैणमदमण्डनाः।
ग्रन्थिपर्णकपालीषु नयन्ति ग्रीष्मयामिनीः।।"

द्वितीयः —

"मिथ्यामीलदरालपक्ष्मणि वलत्यन्तः कुरङ्गीदृशो
दीर्घापाङ्गसरित्तरङ्गतरले तल्पोन्मुखं चक्षुषि।
पत्युः केलिमतः कथां विरमयन्नन्योन्यकण्डूयनात्
कोऽयं व्याहरतीत्युदीर्य निरगात्सव्याजमालीजनः।।"

An example from the north (region)

The maidens of Nepāla[26] paste their bodies with camphor and spend

---

24. Name of a geographical place. See Appendix II.
25. Kuntala — Name of a place. See Appedix II.
26. Nepāla — Name of a place. See Appendix II.

their nights under the bushes (of *granthiparṇa*) with their lovers.

An example of *katipayajana-jānya* —

> Some friends were talking amongst themselves in the bedroom of a beautiful maiden. They saw the beautiful eyes of the maiden with long brows and vivacious like the waves of the river, with thick eyelashes bent and under the pretence of feigned sleep which were often diverted to the bed. The friends who were talking amongst themselves about their husbands' stopped their chatter and pinched the maiden and with a gesture suggestively told her that she was being called by someone.

कविमनीषानिर्मितं कथातन्त्रमर्थमात्रं वा विरचना। तत्राद्या —

> "अस्ति चित्रशिखो नामखड्गविद्याधराधिपः।
> दक्षिणे मलयोत्सङ्गे रत्नवत्याः पुराः पतिः।।
> तस्य रत्नाकरसुता श्रियो देव्याः सहोदरी।
> स्वयंवरविधावासीत्कलत्रं चित्रसुन्दरी।।"

When a poet uses his own imagination and comes up with a story or uses free description, it is called *viracanā*.

Thus —

> In the southern region, there stands the Malaya mountain in the valley of which exists the city of Ratnāvatī, the king of which is called Citraśikhā. His wife was called Citrāsundarī who was the daughter of Lakṣmī's co-sister and the ocean Ratnākara. Citraśikhā married her in a *svayaṁvara*.[27]

द्वितीया —

> "ज्योत्स्नां लिम्पति चन्दनेन स पुमान्सिञ्चत्यसौ मालती-
> मालां गन्धजलैर्मधूनि कुरुते स्वादून्यसौ फाणितैः।
> यस्तस्य प्रथितान्गुणान्प्रथयति श्रीवीरचूडामणेः
> तारत्वं स च शाणया मृगयते मुक्ताफलानामपि।।"

---

27. *Svayaṁvara* is a kṣatriya custom of princesses selecting their husbands themselves. There are three kinds of *svayaṁvara*, see Vettam Mani, *op. cit.*, p. 779.

अत्राहुः —

"नीचैर्नार्थकथासर्गे यस्य न प्रतिभाक्षयः।
स कविग्रामणीरत्र शेषास्तस्य कुटुम्बिनः।।"

The next example —

> The person who strives to spread the fame of the already famous qualities of the King Vīrcūḍāmaṇi appears to be applying sandalpaste on moonlight, watering a garland of *mālatī* flowers with perfumed water, sweetening the *mahuā* flowers with jaggery and bringing the pearls to a shine.

Thus also —

The wise old scholars have stated that the chief among poets are those whose poetic genius does not dwindle even after composing verses with original and new meanings. The other poets are his followers.

अभिहितेभ्यो यदन्यत्तत्प्रकीर्णकम्। तत्र हस्तिशिक्षीयः —

"मेघानां क्षणहासतामुपगतो हारः प्रकीर्णो दिशा-
माकाशोल्लसितामितामरवधूपीनस्तनास्फालकः।
क्षुण्णश्चन्द्र इवोल्वणो मदवशादैरावणप्रेरितः
पायाद्वः परिपाकपाण्डुलवलीश्रीतस्करः शीकरः।।"

For poets in addition to the above sources of meaning, there are other sources of meaning also. These are called *prakīraṇaka* (miscellaneous).

An example of meaning related to reading the hand —

> Those little drops of water which are a source of momentous amusement for the clouds, appear to be like garlands of *muktā* flowers in different directions, particles of moonlight shining on the breasts of celestial goddesses moving in the skies and like the beauty of the ripe *lovely* flowers which is reflected in the scattered droplets of water from the trunks of intoxicated Airāvata[28] elephants. May these water drops be a source of pleasure for you.

रत्नपरीक्षीयः —

"द्वौ वज्रवर्णौ जगतीपतीनां

28. Airāvata is the name of the elephant of Lord Indra. Cf. Apte, *op. cit.* p. 318.

सद्भिः प्रदिष्टौ न तु सार्वजन्यौ।
सः स्याज्जपाविद्रुमभङ्गशोणो
यो वा हरिद्रारससंनिकाशः।।"

An example of *ratna-parīkṣā* (inspection of gems)

Experts in the art of *ratna-parīkṣā* have stated that for kings there are two colours of diamonds which are not commonly found. One is *red* like the fully blossomed *china rose* and the other is *yellow* like the juice of *haldī* (turmeric).

धनुर्वेदीयः —

"स दक्षिणापाङ्गनिविष्टमुष्टिं
नतांसमाकुञ्चितसव्यपादं।
ददर्श चक्रीकृतचारुचापं
प्रहर्त्तुमभ्युद्यतमात्मयोनिम्।।"

An example from *dhanurvidyā* (archery)

Then he saw the mind-born one (Cupid), his clenched fist resting at the corner of his right eye, his shoulders bent (forward) and his left foot drawn in, ready to strike with his beautiful bow bent to (the figures of) a circle.[29]

योगशास्त्रीयः —

"यः सर्वेषां हृदयकमले प्राणिनामेकहंस-
स्त्वं जागर्षि स्वपिषि च मुहुर्बुध्यसे नापि बुद्धः।
तं त्वाराध्य प्रविततधियो बन्धभेदं विधाय
ध्वस्तातङ्का विमलमहसस्ते भवन्तो भवन्ति।।"

An example from *Yogaśāstra* (the Yoga philosophy)

(O, God!) You are like the swan which resides in the hearts of all living things. You are there in sleep and wakefulness (you are Omnipresent), yet no one really knows you. The wise amongst

---

29. See Kālidāsa's *Kumārasambhava* (Cantos I-VIII), ed. with the commentary of Mallinātha a Literal English Translation, Notes and Introduction by M.R. Kale, Motilal Banarsidass, Delhi, 1981, 7th edn. (Canto 3, *śloka* 70. p. 18) of Translation.

scholars search for you inwards and break the bonds born of ignorance thereby attaining real knowledge and realisation.

एवं प्रकीर्णकान्तरमपि।

उचितसंयोगः —

> **"पाण्ड्योऽयमंसार्पितलम्बहारः**
> **क्लृप्ताङ्गरागो हरिचन्दनेन।**
> **आभाति बालातपरक्तसानुः**
> **सनिर्झरोद्गार इवाद्रिराजः।।"**

Similarly the other subjects related to arts and sciences can also be used in poetic descriptions[30].

An example of *uccitasaṁyoga* (in appropriate context) —

> Here sits the king of the Pāṇḍus, who has applied scented paste of red sandal to his body from whose shoulders hang down the pearl-garlands and who looks like the king of the mountains whose summits are reddened with the rays of the morning sun and which has rivulets flowing downwards.[31]

योक्तृसंयोगः —

> **"कुर्वद्भिः सुरदन्तिनो मधुलिहामस्वादु दानोदकं**
> **तन्वानैर्नमुचिद्रुहो भगवतश्चक्षुः सहस्रव्यथां।**
> **मज्जन्स्वर्गतरङ्गिणीजलभरे पङ्कीकृते पांसुभि-**
> **र्यद्यात्राव्यसनं निनिन्द विमनाः स्वर्लोकनारीजनः।।"**

An example of *yokṛtsaṁyoga* (joining together of contexts) —

> The celestial nymphs are unhappy over the victory march of a certain king because during the victory celebrations, numerous soldiers, carriages, elephants and horses raise a lot of dust which settles in the corner of the eyes of celestial elephants. This makes the ichor flowing from them turn bitter for the celestial bees.

---

30. Rājaśekhara now adds four more sources of meaning to the twelve already stated.

31. See *The Raghuvaṁśa* of Kālidāsa by Gopal Raghunath Nandargikar, Motilal Banarsidass, Delhi, 1971, 4th edn., *sarga* 6, *śloka* 60, p. 180.

Then the dust flies into the thousand eyes of Lord Indra thereby troubling him and in the end this collected dust flows into the celestial Gaṅgā thus dirtying its water.

उत्पाद्यसंयोगः —

"उभौ यदि व्योम्नि पृथक्प्रवाहा-
वाकाशगङ्गापयसः पतेताम्।
तेनोपमीयेत तमालनील-
मामुक्तमुक्तालतमस्य वक्षः।।"

An example of *utpādyasaṁyoga* (where likeness can be shown)—

If the celestial Gaṅgā would fall down from the sky in two separate streams they could be compared to the two sides of a pearl necklace around the blue chest of Śrī Kṛṣṇa.

संयोगविकारः —

"गुणानुरागमिश्रेण यशसा तव सर्पता।
दिग्वधूनां मुखे जातमकस्मादर्द्धकुङ्कुमम्।।

यथा वा —

"उन्माद्यत्यम्बुराशिर्विदलति कुमुदं सङ्कुचन्त्यम्बुजानि
स्यन्दन्ते चन्द्रकान्ताः पतितसुमनसः सन्ति शेफालिकाश्च।
पीयन्ते चन्द्रिकाम्भः क्रमसरलगलं किञ्च किञ्चिच्चकोरा-
श्चन्द्रे कर्पूरगौरद्युतिभृति नभसो याति चूडामणित्वम्।।"

इदं कविभ्यः कथितमर्थोत्पत्तिपरायणम्।
इह प्रगल्भमानस्य न जात्वर्थकदर्थना।।

An example of *saṁyogavikāra* (change of form due to union)

The qualities and fame joined together and appeared in the form of a half saffron mark on the foreheads of the bride like directions.[32]

Another example

Pure (white) like camphor, the moon, when it shines like a jewel

---

32. Here the qualities or excellences are conventionally depicted as red and fame as white which together (on getting mixed) formed a half saffron mark on the foreheads of brides which have been compared to the four directions.

in the night sky, it induces a storm in the sea, the buds begin to blossom, lotuses begin to droop, the moonlight (rubies) seems to melt and the *śefālikā* flowers fall from the branches.[33]

The sources of meaning from poetic compositions have been described in this chapter. A poet who becomes eloquent in this matter does not remain short of subjects of meaning.

।। इति राजशेखरकृतौ काव्यमीमांसायां कविरहस्ये प्रथमेऽधिकरणे अर्थानुशासने षोडश काव्यार्थयोनयः अष्टमोऽध्यायः ।।

33. Here a number of changes are induced due to the rising of the moon.

9

अर्थव्याप्तिः

Arthavyāptiḥ
(Description of Sources of Meaning)

"स त्रिधा" इति द्रौहिणिः; दिव्यो, दिव्यमानुषो, मानुषश्च। "सप्तधा" इति यायावरीयः; पातालीयो, मर्त्यपातालीयो, दिव्यपातालीयो, दिव्यमर्त्यपातालीयश्च।

ĀCĀRYA Drauhiṇī states that, 'meanings are of three kinds' — *divya* (celestial), *divya-mānuṣa* (celestial and mortal) and *mānuṣa* (mortal). Yāyāvarīya (Rājaśekhara) adds another four to the above three and comes up with 'seven kinds of meanings'. The other four are — *pātālīya* (nether-worldly), *mṛtya-pātālīya* (of this world and nether-worldly) *divya-pātālīya* (celestial, and nether-worldly) and *divya-mṛtya-pātālīya* (celestial, of this world and nether-worldly).

तत्र दिव्यः —

"स्मृत्वा यन्निजवारवासगतया वीणासमं तुम्बुरो-
रुद्गीतं नलकूबरस्य विरहादुत्कश्चुलं रम्भया।
तेनैरावणकर्णचापलमुषा शक्रोऽशि निद्रां जहद्-
भूयः कारित एव हासिनि शचीवक्त्रे दृशां सम्भ्रमम्।।"

Divya meaning (celestial) is the one which has its basis in celestial characters and situations.

Thus —

Rambhā[1], languishing in her water reservoir due to separation

1. Rambhā is the name of an *apsarā* (celestial beauty), wife of Nalakūbara and considered as the most beautiful woman in the paradise of Indra. See Apte, *op. cit.*, p. 795.

from her beloved Nalakūbara (son of Kubera, god of riches) sang beautifully in her sweet voice like Gandharva's[2] musical *vīṇā*, that the Airāvata[3] elephant concentrated on the song and forgot to move its ears while Indra shed his sleep and looked upon Indrā's[4] face under the impression of watching Rambhā.

दिव्यमानुषस्तु चतुर्धा। दिव्यस्य मर्त्यागमने, मर्त्यस्य च स्वर्गगमन इत्येको भेदः। दिव्यस्य मर्त्यभावे, मर्त्यस्य च दिव्यभाव इति द्वितीयः। दिव्येतिवृत्तपरिकल्पनया तृतीयः। प्रभावाविर्भूतदिव्यरूपतया चतुर्थः।

The *divya-mānuṣa* (celestial and mortal) meaning is again of four kinds — (1) A celestial being coming in the world and a mortal being going to Heaven. (2) A celestial being transformed into a mortal being after being born on this earth and a mortal transformed into celestial after his death. (3) The divine imaginings of a mortal being (4) Though mortal yet with the ability to produce divine energy due to an innate power.

तत्र दिव्यस्य मर्त्यागमनम् —

"श्रियः पतिः श्रीमति शासितुं जगज्जगन्निवासो वसुदेवसद्मनि।
वसन्ददर्शावतरन्तमम्बराद्धिरण्यगर्भाङ्गभुवं मुनिं हरिः।।"

An example of a celestial being becoming a mortal —

Śrī Kṛṣṇa who took birth in the house of Vāsudeva, with the purpose of setting the world right witnessed the approach of the sage Nārada[6] born of one of the organs of Brahmā coming down

2. Gandharva is a celestial musician, a class of demi-gods regarded as the musicians of gods and said to grant a good and agreeable voice to girls. See Apte, *op. cit.*, p. 398.
3. Airāvata is the elephant of Indra. See Apte, *op. cit.*, p. 248.
4. Indrāṇī is the wife of Indra. Also the name of Durgā considered as one of the eight mothers on divine energies. See Apte, *op. cit.*, p. 248.
5. All the characters in this verse are drawn from the celestial world. Therefore it is an example of celestial meaning.
6. Nārada is the name of a celeberated *devarṣi* (deified sage or divine sage). He is one of the ten mind born sons of Brahmā, supposed to have sprung from his thigh. He is represented as a messenger from the gods to men and *vice-versa* and as being very fond of promoting discord among gods and men, hence his epithet Kālipriyā. See Apte, *op. cit.*, p. 542.

to earth by the celestial pathway.

मर्त्यस्य स्वर्गगमनम् —

"पाण्डोर्नन्दन नन्दनं वनमिदं सङ्कल्पजैः सीधुभिः
क्लृप्तापानककेलि कल्पतरुषु द्वन्द्वैः सुधालेहिनाम्।
अप्यत्रेन्दुशिलालवालवलयं सन्तानकानां तले
ज्योत्स्नास्रं गलदच्छनिर्झरजलैर्यत्नं विना पूर्यते।।"

An example of a mortal going to the Heavens —

O, Pāṇḍuputra (Arjuna)[7]. This is a celestial garden (Nandanvana).[8] The celestial beings take part in various playful activities after their wishes have been fulfilled by these *dvandva* (of both sexes) *kalpavṛkṣa*[9] trees, in this garden. The other kinds of *santānaka kalpavṛkṣa*s are always surrounded by water obtained by the association of moonstones.[10]

दिव्यस्य मर्त्यभावः —

"इति विकसति तस्मिन्नन्ववाये यदूनां
समजनि वसुदेवो देवकी यत्कलत्रम्।
किमपरमथ तस्मात्षोडशस्त्रीसहस्र-
प्रणिहितपरिरम्भः पद्मनाभो बभूव।।"

An example of earthiness of a celestial being —

In this way with an expansion of Yaduvaṁśa,[11] Vāsudeva was born in this clan and his wife was Devakī. From the union of Devakī and Vāsudeva was born Padmanābha[12] who is known to

---

7. Arjuna is one of five Pāṇḍavas, son of Pāṇḍu, a major character in the Epic *Mahābhārata*.
8. Nandanvana is the name of the garden of Indra, the Elysium. See Apte, *op. cit.*, p. 535.
9. *Kalpavṛkṣa* is a mythological tree or plant that is supposed to grant all desires. See Chaturvedi, *op. cit.*, p. 124.
10. Moonstones or *cañcamaṇi*, the moonstone is supposed to ooze away under the influence of the moon. See Apte, *op. cit.*, p. 427.
11. Yaduvaṁśa — Yaduḥ is the name of an ancient king, the eldest son of Yayāti and Devayāṇī and ancestor of the Yādavas. See Apte, *op. cit.*, p. 781.
12. Padmanābha is an epithet of Viṣṇu. See Apte, *op. cit.*, p. 585.

have been with 16 thousand women.

मर्त्यस्य दिव्यभावः —

"आकाशयानतटकोटिकृतैकपादा-
स्तद्धेमदण्डयुगलान्यवलम्ब्य हस्तैः।
कौतूहलात्तव तरङ्गविघट्टितानि
पश्यन्ति देवि मनुजाः स्वकलेवराणि।।"

An example of the celestial aspects of a mortal —

O, goddess (Gaṅgā)! People who have died on your banks while going up to heaven (in planes) and while climbing up the golden steps, look down in amazement at their own bodies going along the flowing waters.[13]

दिव्येतिवृत्तपरिकल्पना —

"ज्योत्स्नापूरप्रसरविशदे सैकतेऽस्मिन्सरय्वा
वादद्यूतं चिरतरमभूत्सिद्धयूनोः कयोश्चित्।
एको ब्रूते प्रथमनिहतं कैटभं कंसमन्यः
स त्वं तत्त्वं कथय भवता को हतस्तत्र पूर्वम्।।"

An example of an imaginary celestial narrative —

Lord! The moonlight was shining on the river Sarayū and on its sandy shore two learned youths were arguing for a long time on a certain subject. The former said that Viṣṇu first killed Kaiṭabha[14] while the latter said that he killed Kaṁsa.[15] Thus, please tell us the truth. Whom did you kill first?

प्रभावाविर्भूतदिव्यभावः —

"मा गाः पातालमुर्वि स्फुरसि किमपरं पाट्यमानः कुदैत्य

---

13. The suggestion here is that according to traditional Hindus if their dead are given the last bath in the Gaṅgā after their death, their sins are washed off and they acquire a place in Heaven.

14. Kaiṭabha is the name of a powerful demon killed by Viṣṇu. He and Madhu are said to have sprung from the ears of Viṣṇu while he was asleep; and when they were about to devour Brahmā, they were slain by Viṣṇu. See Apte, *op. cit.*, p. 797.

15. Kaṁsa is a tyrannical king of Mathurā, the son of Ugrasena and cousin of Devakī, the mother of Kṛṣṇa. Kaṁsa became the great persecutor of Kṛṣṇa but was eventually killed by him. See Dowson, *op. cit.*, p. 149.

त्रैलोक्यं पादपीतप्रथिम नहि बले पूरयस्यूनमङ्घ्रेः।
इत्युत्स्वप्नायमाने भुवनभृति शिशावङ्कसुप्ते यशोदा
पायाच्चक्राङ्कपादप्रणति पुलकितस्मेरगण्डस्थला वः।।"

Suggested manifestation of celestial aspects —

> Lord Kṛṣṇa who is asleep in Yaśodā's lap utters these words in his sleep. "Earth! Do not go down to hell (the lower world). O, evil *rākṣasa*! Your body has been slaughtered, yet you seem to be moving. O, Bālī, the measure of all the three worlds cannot be more than one footstep. Why don't you fill the empty space with your step." Yaśodā who lay with the young Kṛṣṇa in her lap, was delighted and paid obeisance to the marked feet of the Lord. May the smiling mother protect you.[16]

मर्त्यः —

"वधूः श्वश्रूस्थाने व्यवहरति पुत्रः पितृपदे
पदे रिक्ते रिक्ते विनिहितपदार्थान्तरमिति।
नदीस्रोतोन्यायादकलितविवेकक्रमघनं
न च प्रत्यावृत्तिः प्रवहति जगत्पूर्णमथ च।।"

An example of this world (*mṛtyaloka*) —

> This life in all its manifestations is like the flowing waters of the river. The water which flows by does not return to fill the same space. Similarly a girl who today is a daughter-in-law will in time be called a mother-in-law. The same man who is a son today will be called a father in course of time. The space created by one person is filled by another and thus the world goes on.

पातालीयः —

"कर्कोटः कोटिकृत्त्व प्रणमति पुरतस्तक्षके देहि चक्षुः
सज्जः सेवाञ्जलिस्ते कपिलकुलिकयोः स्तौति च स्वस्तिकस्त्वां।
पद्मः सद्मैष भक्तेरवलगति पुरः कम्बलोऽयं बलोऽयं
सोत्सर्पः सर्पराजो व्रजतु निजगृहं प्रेष्यतां शङ्खपालः।।"

---

16. Lord Kṛṣṇa here recollects the incarnation of Varāha and Vāmana, thereby depicting his celestial nature.

An example of the nether-world (*pātālīya*) —

> O Lord! Karkoṭaka[17] Nāga pays obeisance to you. Shower your blessings on Takṣaka,[18] Kapilā and Kūlikā[19] who are offering water ceremoniously and the Svāstika[20] Nāga is praying to you, Padma[21] *nāga* is ready to serve you, Balvāna[22] and Kambala[23] *nāgas* are tossing and turning before you. Bless and allow the king of serpents, Vāsuki[24] and another *nāga śaṅkhapāla* to depart.

मर्त्यपातालीयः —

> "आर्द्रावले व्रज न वेत्स्यपकर्ण कर्णं
> द्विः सन्दधाति न शरं हरशिष्यशिष्यः।
> तत्साम्प्रतं समिति पश्य कुतूहलेन
> मर्त्यैः शरैरपि किरीटिकिरीटमाथम्।।"

Of this world and nether-worldly (*mṛtyapātālīya*) —

> (Karṇa's words to snakes pulling the carriage). "O, moist ones, O, offenders! Don't you know me (Karṇa)? I am the disciple of Parśurāma,[25] a follower of Lord Śiva, therefore I do not string the bow twice. The arrow always finds its mark. You will see the

17. Karkoṭaka, a serpent born to Kaśyapa by his wife Kadrū. See Vettam Mani, *op. cit.*, pp. 390-1.
18. Takṣaka, a serpent son of Kadrū and chief of snakes. Cf. John Dowson, *op. cit.*, p. 316.
19. Kūlikā is one of the eight serpent kings, described as of a dusty brown colour and having a half moon on his head.
20. Svastika, a *nāga* (serpent) who lived in Girivrāja. It is mentioned in *Mahābhārata*, Sabhā Parva, chapter 9, verse 9, that this serpent lives in the palaces of Varuṇa. See Vettam Mani, *op. cit.*, p. 779.
21. Padma, a serpent born to sage Kaśyapa of his wife Kadrū (*śloka* 10, chapter 35. Ādi Parva). See Vettam Mani, *op. cit.*, p. 544.
22. Balvāna a kind of serpent.
23. Kambala is a prominent serpent of the family of Kaśyapa (chapter 35, Ādi Parva, *Mahābhārata*). See Vettam Mani, p. 381.
24. Vāsuki is the king of Nāgas. He was the eldest son of Kadrū and Prajāpatī Kaśyapa. See Vettam Mani, *op. cit.*, p. 838.
25. Paraśurāma was an incarnation of Mahāviṣṇu as man. For further details, see Vettam Mani, *op. cit.*, p. 568.

destruction of Arjuna or Kirīṭa (a synonym of Arjuna) with these arrows.[26]

इहापि पूर्ववत्समस्तमिश्रभेदानुगमः।

दिव्यपातालीयः —

"स पातु वो यस्य शिखाश्मकर्णिक
स्वदेहनालं फणपत्रसञ्चयम्।
विभाति जिह्वायुगलोलकेसरं
पिनाकिनः कर्णभुजङ्गपङ्कजम्।।"

One can also understand the different divisions of *mṛtya-pātālīya* similar to *divya-mānuṣa divyapātālīya.*

May lord Śaṅkara protect you who has serpents hanging from the ears as ornaments, the rubies shining on the foreheads of these serpents are like the interior of the lotuses, their long bodies are like the lotus stalks and their broad hoods are like the lotus leaves and their forked tongues are like the saffron (pollen) of the lotus.[27]

स्वर्गमर्त्यपातालीयः —

"आस्तीकोऽस्ति मुनिः स्म विस्मयकृतः पारीक्षितीयान्मखा-
त्त्राता तक्षकलक्ष्मणः फणभृतां वंशस्य शक्रस्य च।
उद्वेल्लन्मलयाद्रिचन्दनलतास्वान्दोलनप्रक्रमे
यस्याद्यापि सविभ्रमं फणिवधूवृन्दैर्यशो गीयते।।"

Divya mṛtya-pātālīya

The sage Āstīka[28] while performing the sacrificial ritual conducted

26. Since both Karṇa and a serpent have been described this is an instance of *mṛtya-pātālīya* meaning.
27. Here the description is of the celestial Śiva and the nether-worldly snake, thus depicting the *divya-pātālīya* meaning.
28. Āstīka is an ancient sage, son of Jaratkāru by a sister of the great serpent Vāsukī. He saved the life of the serpent Takṣaka when Janamejaya made his great sacrifice of serpents and induced that king to forego his persecution of the serpent race. See John Dowson, *op. cit.,* p. 27.

    Thus Indra is the celestial character, Āstīka is mortal and the wives of serpents are from the nether world. This is therefore an instance of *divya-mṛtya-pātālīya* meaning.

by Janmejaya, son of king Parīkṣita, prays for the protection of the serpent king Takṣaka and their protector Indra. Even today, the wives of serpents while swinging on the sandal creepers in the Malayācala mountains sing praises of the sage Āstīka.

"सोऽयमित्थङ्कारमुल्लिख्योपजीव्यमानो निःसीमार्थसार्थः सम्पद्यते। अस्तु नाम निःसीमार्थसार्थः। किन्तु द्विरूप एवासौ विचारितसुस्थोऽविचारितरमणीयश्च। तयोः पूर्वमाश्रितानि शास्त्राणि तदुत्तरं काव्यानि" इत्यौद्भटाः।

*Ācārya*s state that the sources of meaning for poetic exposition by poets with genius is unlimited. Other *ācārya*s feel that though the sources of meaning may be vast but they are divisible into two main groups only — *vicārit-sustha* and *avicārit-ramaṇīya*. The former is expressed in *śāstra*s while the latter is described in *kāvya*s.

This is stated by *ācārya* Udbhaṭa.

यथा —

"अपां लङ्घयितुं राशिं रुचा पिञ्जरयन्नभः।
खमुत्पपात हनुमान्नीलोत्पलदलद्युतिः।।"

Thus —

Hanumān (the monkey god, a character in the Epic *Rāmāyaṇa*), to cross the ocean flew in the sky casting his brilliance onto the sky thus changing it to a yellow colour and taking the blue from the sky to appear as a blue lotus.[29]

यथा वा —

"त आकाशमसिश्यामम्मुत्पत्य परमर्षयः।
आसेदुरोषधिप्रस्थं मनसा समरंहसः।।"

यथा च —

तदेव वारि सिन्धूनां महत्स्थेमार्चिषामिति इत्यादि।

29. Though a rhetorical figure is used here to denote the exchange of colours and this is a source of pleasure and charm but in reality the sky is colourless. It does not have its own colour or the capacity to take on colour. This meaning does not remain fixed on second thought but disintegrates. Thus, it is an instance of *avicārita ramaṇīya*.

"न स्वरूपनिबन्धनमिदं रूपमाकाशस्य सरित्सलिलादेर्वा किन्तु प्रतिभासनिबन्धनम्। न च प्रतिभासस्तादात्म्येन वस्तुन्यवतिष्ठते यदि तथा स्यात्सूर्याचन्द्रमसोर्मण्डले दृष्ट्या परिच्छिद्यमानद्वादशाङ्गुलप्रमाणे पुराणाद्यागमनिवेदितधरावलयमात्रे न स्तः" इति यायावरीयः। एवं नक्षत्रादीनां सरित्सलिलादीनामन्येषां च। यथाप्रतिभासं च वस्तुनः स्वरूपं शास्त्रकाव्य योर्निबन्धोपयोगि। शास्त्रे यथा —

> The great sages, too having jumped into the sky, which was dark like a sword, and equalling the mind in velocity, reached *oṣadiprastha*.[30]

And also —

Other examples may be cited like "The water of rivers is the source of heat."

Yāyāvarīya (Rājaśekhara) says,

It is correct that the things which have been described above like the colour of the sky and the river as a source of heat are not real (or natural) but are apparent.

The apparent and the real is not present naturally in a thing. If appearances were real, then the solar-systems of the sun and the moon which appear to be only equal to twelve fingers, could not be equal to or larger than the earth which has been described by the Purāṇas. Similarly one should understand about the other satellites, mountains, rivers.

It is not the natural disposition of a thing to be manifested apparently and in reality. One should describe a thing according to one's perception.

> "प्रशान्तजलभृत्पङ्के विमले वियदम्भसि।
> ताराकुमुदसम्बन्धे हंसायत इवोडुराट्।।"

काव्यानि पुनरेतन्मयान्येव।

---

30. See Kālidāsa, *Kumārsambhava*, tr. by Kale, *op. cit.*, canto 6. *śloka* 36, p. 34 (of English translation).

The swords are dark only in poetic description. In reality they are white. This is again an instance of *avicārita-ramaṇīya*.

'अस्तु नाम निःसीमार्थसार्थः। किन्तु रसवत एव निबन्धो युक्तो न नीरसस्य' इति आपराजितिः।

यदाह —

> "मज्जनपुष्पावचयनसन्ध्याचन्द्रोदयादिवाक्यमिह।
> सरसमपि नातिबहुलं प्रकृतरसानन्वितं रचयेत्।।"
>
> "यस्तु सरिदद्रिसागरपुरतुरगरथादिवर्णने यत्नः।
> कविशक्तिख्यातिफलो विततधियां नो मतः स इह।।"

Without clay like clouds, blessed with satellite like flowers, pure sky like water, the moon appeared to be like a swan.

Similarly in *kāvya*s and *śāstra*s, things can be described only on the basis of sudden perception.

Āparājita's son Bhaṭṭalollaṭa says,

Even though the source of meanings may be wide and comprehensive it also remains necessary to include aesthetic meanings rather than mere content.

Thus —

Water-sporting, gathering of flowers, dusk, rise of the moon when described should not be overdone and should not be in opposition to the context and the aesthetic state of mind (*rasa*) being evoked.

A poet often describes rivers, mountains, oceans, cities, houses, elephants, carriages, etc., and these indicate his creative capacity. Learned scholars do not approve of it.

'आम्' इति यायावरीयः। अस्ति चानुभूयमानो रसस्यानुगुणो विगुणश्चार्थः, काव्ये तु कविवचनानि रसयन्ति विरसयन्ति च नार्थाः। अन्वयव्यतिरेकाभ्यां चेदमुपलभ्यते।

तत्र सरिद्वर्णनरसवत्ता —

> "एतां विलोकय तलोदरि ताम्रपर्णी —
> मम्भोनिधौ विवृतशुक्तिपुटोद्धृतानि।
> यस्याः पयांसि परिणाहिषु हारमूर्त्या
> वामभ्रुवां परिणमन्ति पयोधरेषु।।"

Yāyāvarīya (Rājaśekhara) declares, 'It is true'. Yet it has also been observed that there are some meanings which are favourable to a particular *rasa* (aesthetic state of mind) and others which are unfavourable to it. It is an established fact that in poetic compositions it is the poets' sentences that add to or detract from the aesthetic effect of the entire creation. Yet it is not meanings which attract or detract because a poet with *pratibhā*, (innate faculty) can transform even mundane and commonplace things into aesthetic wonders and those who lack *pratibhā* may diminish the aesthetic meaning and reduce its worth.

Description of a river —

> (O, Kṛśodarī!) Look at this Tāmraparṇī river falling into the ocean, the water-drops (or pearls) obtained from the hollow of oysters, decorate the expansive bosoms of beautiful maidens in the form of garlands of pearl necklaces.

अद्रिवर्णनरसवत्ता —

> **"एतास्ता मलयोपकण्ठसरितामेणाक्षि रोधोभुव-**
> **श्चापाभ्यासनिकेतनं भगवतः प्रेयो मनोजन्मनः।**
> **यासु श्यामनिशासु पीततमसो मुक्तामयीश्चन्द्रिकाः**
> **पीयन्ते विवृतोर्ध्वचञ्चुविचलत्कण्ठं चकोराङ्गनाः।।"**

A description of mountains —

> (O, doe-eyed maidens!) These are the shores of the rivers flowing in the highlands of the Malayācala[31] mountain which are a favourite haunt of Kāmadeva (Cupid, God of Love) and his beloveds to practise with a bow-string. The female *cakora* (partridge) in the dark nights drink in the pearl like bright moonlight with their open beaks.

सागरवर्णनरसवत्ता —

> **"धत्ते यत्किलकिञ्चितैकगुरुतामेणीदृशां वारुणी**

---

31. Malayācala is the name of a mountain range in the south of India abounding in sandal trees; poets usually represent the breeze from the Malaya mountain as wafting the odour of sandal tree and other plants growing thereon, which peculiarly affect persons who are smitten with love. See Apte, *op. cit.*, p. 746.

वैधुर्यं विदधाति दम्पतिरुषां यच्चन्द्रिकार्द्रं नभः।
यच्च स्वर्गसदां वयः स्मरसुहृन्नित्यं सदा सम्पदां
यल्लक्ष्मीरधिदैवतं च जलधेस्तत्कान्तमाचेष्टितम्।।"

The description of the sea —

> The intoxicating wine which induces a playful and sportive state of mind in beautiful maidens eagerly awaiting the desired union with their lovers, the moonlight which is manifest in the sky and which is capable of putting to an end quarrels between the husband and wife, which helps even the gods to maintain their youth and wealth (Lakṣmī) which is considered supreme amongst riches on the earth — all these are the result of the beautiful effort put in by the sea.[32]

एवं पुरतुरगादिवर्णनरसवत्तापि।

विप्रलम्भेप्यतिरसवत्ता —

"विधर्माणो भावास्तदुपहितवृत्तेर्न धृतये
सरूपत्वादन्ये विहितविफलौत्सुक्यविरसाः।
ततः स्वेच्छं पूर्वेष्वसजदितरेभ्यः प्रतिहतं
क्व हीनं प्रेयस्या हृदयमिदमन्यत्र रमताम्।।"

कुकविर्विप्रलम्भेऽपि रसवत्तां निरस्यति।
अस्तु वस्तुषु मा वा भूत्कविवाचि रसः स्थितः।।

Similarly one can find many examples of even cities, houses, etc., which are an indication of the superiority or eminence of a poet.

An example of violation of *śṛṅgāra rasa* (in separation) —

> For the separated lover whose mind is suffused with thoughts of his beloved, dwelling upon her negative points makes him restless and on thinking about her qualities, he becomes anxious. In this state he himself feels a distate for the things which she has a dislike for and his suffering increases when he thinks of things

32. The significance of this verse is that wine, the moon, ambrosia and wealth — these four are the gifts of the sea. The poet has made use of *śṛṅgāra rasa* while depicting the importance of the sea.

dear to her. Where can a separated lover look for rest and peace? (That is, nowhere).

To describe separation in love, an aesthetic sense is needed but a bad poet makes it insipid. Thus even if a substance lacks aesthetic charm, the voice of the poet should carry the aesthetic sensiblity — this is an undebatable principle.

"यथा तथा वास्तु वस्तुनो रूपं, वक्तप्रकृतिविशेषायत्ता तु रसवत्ता। तथा च यमर्थं रक्तः स्तौति तं विरक्तो विनिन्दति मध्यस्थस्तु तत्रोदास्ते" इति पाल्यकीर्त्तिः।

"येषां वल्लभया समं क्षणमिव स्फारा क्षपा क्षीयते
तेषां शीततरः शशी विरहिणामुल्केव सन्तापकृत्।
अस्माकं न तु वल्लभा न विरहस्तेनोभयभ्रंशिना-
मिन्दू राजति दर्पणाकृतिरयां नोष्णो न वा शीतलः।।"

'विदग्धभणितिभङ्गिनिवेद्यं वस्तुनो रूपं न नियतस्वभावम्' इति अवन्तिसुन्दरी। तदाह —

Pālyakīrti (a Jain *ācārya*) says,

whatever be the appearance of a thing, the aesthetic sense of a poet lies in his natural disposition. A contented person may worship something, an indifferent person may criticise the same thing while a mediocre person may be contemplative about it.

(Thus a mediocre person may say) —

For those who spend the long nights with their beloveds', the entire night seems to last for a moment and for them the moon is a thing of intense coolness. For the separated lovers the same moon is hot like burning embers. I have no beloved and no pangs of separation. Thus free of the two, this moon is like a piece of glass for me. It is neither hot nor cold. It neither gives happiness nor unhappiness.

Avantīsundarī[33] (wife of Rājaśekhara) says —

33. Avantīsundarī, worthy wife of Rājaśekhara and generally supposed to be the sister of Dharmapāla. Rājaśekhara refers to her as his wife in the Prologue to his drama *Karpūramañjarī* and says that his drama was staged at her request. She was a very illustrious member of Cauhāna family and probably she, a kṣatriya by caste had a romantic marriage with the brāhmaṇa Rājaśekhara. →

The form of a substance is not restricted, rather it is indefinite' (that is, it does not possess faults or excellences. It is the poet who infuses these into them with his words).

"वस्तुस्वभावोऽत्र कवेरतन्त्रो
गुणागुणावुक्तिवशेन काव्ये।
स्तुवन्निबध्नात्यमृतांशुमिन्दुं
निन्दंस्तु दोषाकरमाह धूर्तः।।"

Thus —

In this poetic world the nature of a thing is not certain. It is because of the poets' words (*ukti*) that it develops certain excellences or faults. Those who wish to worship the moon call in *amṛtāṁśu* and the rogues who wish to find fault with it name it *doṣākāra* (with a mark).

"उभयमुपपन्नम्" इति यायावरीयः।

स पुनर्द्विधा। मुक्तकप्रबन्धविषयत्वेन। तावपि प्रत्येकं पञ्चधा। शुद्धः, चित्रः, कथोत्थः, संविधानकभूः, आख्यानकवांश्च। तत्र मुक्तेतिवृत्तः शुद्धः। स एव सप्रपञ्चश्चित्रः। वृत्तेतिवृत्तः कथोत्थः। सम्भावितेतिवृत्तः संविधानकभूः। परिकल्पितेतिवृत्तः आख्यानकवान्।

Yāyāvarīya (Rājaśekhara) says that both (Pālyakīrti and Avantīsundarī) are in the right.

The meanings are further divisible into two kinds. One is *muktaka kāvya* and the second is *prabandha kāvya*. *Muktaka* means dispersed, free and simple *kāvya* and *prabandha* is a long and continuous *kāvya* or *mahākāvya*.

Both *muktaka* and *prabandha* are of five kinds each — (1) *śuddha*, (2) *citra*, (3) *kaṭhottha*, (4) *samvidhānakabhū*, and (5) *ākhyānakauāna*.

The meanings devoid of history is *śuddha*. To describe it in detail is

→ Avantīsundarī was herself a learned woman of those days. She was a rhetorician of outstanding merit as she has been quoted thrice by Rājaśekhara in his celebrated work *Kāvyamīmāṁsā*. She has also been referred to thrice by Hemacandra in his *Deśīnāma-māla*. From these verses it is known that Avantīsundarī was a Prākṛta poetess of great poetic abilities. See Dr. Ganga Ram Garg, *Encyclopaedia of the Hindu World*, Vol. 3, *op. cit.*, pp. 612-8.

citra. The old tales or historically related meaning is *kaṭhottha*. Where the incidents are possible it is called *saṁvidhānkabhū* and where the history is imagined it is known as *ākhyānakauāna*.

तत्र मुक्तके शुद्धः —

> "सा पत्युः प्रथमापराधकरणे शिक्षोपदेशं विना
> नो जानाति सविभ्रमाङ्गवलनावक्रोक्तिचित्रां गतिम्।
> स्वच्छैरच्छकपोलभित्तिगलितैः पर्यस्तनेत्रोत्पला
> बाला केवलमेव रोदिति लुठल्लोलोदकैरश्रुभिः।।"

An example of *muktaka kāvya* in *śuddha artha* (a friend relating a newly wed bride's experience) —

> The new bride does not know the kind of behaviour to be exhibited on learning of her husband's indiscretion (of being unfaithful). She does not know how to arch the brows, to pass snide remarks and to appear offended and retire in mock anger. She is, after learning of her husband's first indiscretion, continuously dripping tears which wash her cheeks and has bent her head and eyes in shame and embarassment.[34]

चित्रः —

> "दूरादुत्सुकमागते विवलितं सम्भाषिणि स्फारितं
> संश्लिष्यत्यरुणं गृहीतवसने कोपाञ्चितभ्रूलतम्।
> मानिन्याश्चरणानतिव्यतिकरे बाष्पाम्बुपूर्णं क्षणा-
> च्चक्षुर्जातमहो प्रपञ्चचतुरं जातागसि प्रेयसि।।"

An example of *citra* —

> The indiscreet husband came near his wife eagerly, the wife watched him from afar with eager eyes, on his drawing near her eyes bent and were cast aside, dilated when he spoke, turned red on his embracing her, on his touching her clothes, her brows arched up in anger and on his falling at her feet, they filled up with tears. In this way the Mānini's[35] eyes manifested a number

34. Since there is a description of the natural and real state of the heroine without any historical description it is called *śuddha*.

35. Mānini is a woman offended with her husband through jealous pride.

of emotions after her husband's indiscretion.[36]

कथोत्थः —

"दत्त्वा रुद्धगतिः खसाधिपतये देवीं ध्रुवस्वामिनीं
यस्मात्खण्डितसाहसो निववृते श्रीशर्मगुप्तो नृपः।
तस्मिन्नेव हिमालये गुरुगुहाकोणक्वणत्किन्नरे
गीयन्ते तव कार्त्तिकेयनगरस्त्रीणां गणैः कीर्त्तयः।।"

An example of *kaṭhottha.*

(O King!) The king Śrīśarmagupta who after losing the battle, his courage and valour left his wife Dhruvsvāminī for Khasādhipatī[37] and retired to the Himālayas. From the corners of these caves comes the sounds of lutes and the women of Kārttikeya singing songs in your praise.

संविधानकभूः —

"दृष्ट्वैकासनसंस्थिते प्रियतमे पश्चादुपेत्यादरा-
देकस्या नयने निमील्य विहितक्रीडानुबन्धच्छलः।
ईषद्वक्रितकन्धरः सपुलकः प्रेमोल्लसन्मानसा-
मन्तर्हासिवलत्कपोलफलकां धूर्तोऽपरां चुम्बति।।"

Saṁvidhānakabhū —

When the rogue with two wives entered his house, he saw both his wives sitting together on the same seat with their backs towards him. With the intention of pleasing both of them, he softly crept up to them and closed the eyes of one and bending his neck tenderly and lovingly kissed the cheeks of the other one.[38]

यथा च —

"कुर्वत्या कुङ्कुमाम्भःकपिशितवपुषं यत्तदा राजहंसीं
क्रीडाहंसो मयासावजनि विरहितश्चक्रवाकीभ्रमेण।

---

36. Here the subject of the first verse has been dealt with in greater detail, therefore it is *citrakāvya.*
37. For reference to these names and the tale, see Appendix I.
38. In this verse imagination seems to have played a part in the delineation, thus it is an instance of *saṁvidhānakabhū.*

तस्य तत्पाप्मनो मे परिणमति फलं यत्पुरे प्रेमबन्धा-
देकत्रावां वसावो न च दयितदृशाऽप्यस्ति नौ सन्निकर्षः।।"

And also —

(O, Beloved!) Once due to an unfortunate chance, I happened to separate a swan and his mate, the brown she swan, which had undergone a colour change due to bathing in saffron coloured water mistaking its identity for a ruddy goose. It is because of the sin committed then that in spite of our staying in the same city, we cannot even see each other.[39]

आख्यानकवान् —

"अर्थिजनार्थधृतानां वनकरिणां प्रथमकल्पितैर्दशनैः।
चक्रे परोपकारी हैहयजन्मा गृहं शम्भोः।।"

Ākhyānakavāna —

Sahastrārjnua acquired the first pair of tusks to get a temple made for Lord Śiva from the elephants which had been kept for the purpose of donation.[40]

These were the five kinds under *muktaka*. Now we will go on to *prabandha*.

निबन्धे शुद्धः —

"स्तिमितविकसितानामुल्लसद्भ्रूलतानां
मसृणमुकुलितानां प्रान्तविस्तारभाजां।
प्रतिनयननिपाते किञ्चिदाकुञ्चितानां
सुचिरमहमभूवं पात्रमालोकितानाम्।।"

Śuddha artha (in *prabandha*)

(Describing the glances of Mālatī in the play *Mālatīmādhava*, Mādhava declares) —

---

39. Even here the condition of the swans is being described and imagination comes into play again, thus it is an instance of *saṁvidhānakabhū*.
40. Here a tale relating to Sahastrārjuna has been mentioned, thus it is an *ākhyānakabāna*.

I was the object of those steady and expansive looks, the eyes with raised brows, tender with bashful love as though extending to far off regions yet hesitating with the fall of each eyelash.[41]

चित्रः —

"अलसवलितमुग्धस्निग्धनिष्पन्दमन्दै-
रधिकविकसदन्तर्विस्मयस्मेरतारैः।
हृदयमशरणं मे पक्ष्मलाक्ष्याः कटाक्षै-
रपहृतमपविद्धं पीतमुन्मूलितं च।।"

An example of *citra*

Those thick lashes cover the slightly dazed, side long, innocent, affectionate, steady, soft eyes with pupils dilated in wonder. Her glances have caught and held my heart, partaken of it and extirpated it.

कथोत्थः —

"अभिलाषमुदीरितेन्द्रियः
स्वसुतायामकरोत्प्रजापतिः।
अथ तेन निगृह्य विक्रिया-
मभिशप्तः फलमेतदन्वभूत्।।"

Prajāpatī (the Lord of Creation) felt a lustful desire for his own daughter, his senses being excited by Kāma, he then having curbed the excitement, cursed Kama who has thus experienced the fruit (of his own act).[42]

संविधानकभूः —

"क्रोधं प्रभो संहर संहरेति
यावद्गिरः खे मरुतां चरन्ति।
तावत्स वह्निर्भवनेत्रजन्मा
भस्मावशेषं मदनं चकार।।"

Ere the cries of the gods — Restrain thy ire, restrain thy ire, O,

---

41. This is a natural description of various looks of the heroine.
42. See Kālidāsa, *Kumārasambhava*, tr. by M.R. Kale, *op. cit.*, canto IV, *śloka* 41, p. 22 (of translation).

Lord — could rise in the sky, the fire, born of the eye of Śiva, left only the ashes of Madana.[43]

आख्यानकवान् —

"त्पयुः शिरश्चन्द्रकलाममनेन
स्पृशेति सख्या परिहासपूर्वम्।
सा रञ्जयित्वा चरणौ कृताशी-
र्माल्येन तां निर्वचनं जघान।।"

When blessed by her friend after dyeing her feet (with lac-dye) joyously saying — "Touch (strike) the digit of the moon on thy husband's head with this" — She (Pārvatī) struck her (friend) with a wreath of flowers without uttering a word.[44]

किञ्च। संस्कृतवत्सर्वास्वपि भाषासु यथासामर्थ्यं यथारुचि यथाकौतुकं चावहितः स्यात्। शब्दार्थयोश्चाभिधानाभिधेयव्यापारप्रगुणतामवबुध्येत।

तदुक्तम् —

एकोऽर्थः संस्कृतोक्त्या ससुकविरचनः प्राकृतेनापरोऽस्मिन्-
अन्योऽपभ्रंशगीर्भिः किमपरमपरो भूतभाषाक्रमेण।
द्वित्राभिः कोऽपि वाग्भिर्भवति चतसृभिः किञ्च कश्चिद्विवेक्तुं
यस्येत्थं धीः प्रगल्भा स्नपयति सुकवेस्तस्य कीर्त्तिर्जगन्ति।।

इत्यङ्कारं घनैरर्थैर्व्युत्पन्नमनसः कवेः।
दुर्गमेऽपि भवेन्मार्गे कुण्ठिता न सरस्वती।।

A poet should compose not only in Sanskrit but also in Prākṛta[45] and other languages depending on his capacity and interest in accordance with his mental disposition. However the *vākya-vācaka* (denotative/ verbal) relation and its maturity should always be kept in mind.

The one and the same meaning may be the subject of an ideal Sanskrit poet or in Prākṛta of another good poet or for that matter in

---

43. See Kālidāsa's *Kumārasambhava*, tr. M.R. Kale *op. cit.*, canto 3, *śloka* 71, p. 18 (of translation).

44. Śee Kālidāsa's *Kumarāsambhava*, cantos I-VIII, ed. and tr. by M.R. Kale, Motilal Banarsidass, Delhi, 1980, 2nd edn., canto 7, *śloka*, 19, p. 91.

45. Prākṛta is a vernacular or provincial dialect derived from and akin to Sanskrit. See Apte, *op. cit.*, p. 677.

Apabhraṁśa,[46] or in Bhūt-bhāṣā.[47] Some poets use two-three languages while others are proficient in four to five languages. In this way with the wisdom of poets his fame spreads all over the world.

।। इति राजशेखरकृतौ काव्यमीमांसायां कविरहस्ये प्रथमेऽधिकरणे अर्थानुशासने अर्थव्याप्तिर्नवमोऽध्यायः।।

46. One of the forms of Prākṛta dialect used by common people. Apte, *op. cit.*, p. 98.
47. Bhūt-bhāṣā is the language usually ascribed to certain subethnic groups.

10

कविचर्या राजचर्या च

Kavicaryā and Rājacaryā
(Daily Routine and Duties of a Poet and a King)

गृहीतविद्योपविद्यः काव्यक्रियायै प्रयतेत। नामधातुपारायणे, अभिधानकोशः, छन्दोविचितिः, अलङ्कारतन्त्रं च काव्यविद्याः। कलास्तु चतुःषष्टिरुपविद्याः। सुजनोपजीव्यकविसन्निधिः, देशवार्त्ता, विदग्धवादो, लोकयात्रा, विद्वद्गोष्ठ्यश्च काव्यमातरः पुरातनकविनिबन्धाश्च। किञ्च —

> **स्वास्थ्यं प्रतिभाभ्यासो भक्तिर्विद्वत्कथा बहुश्रुतता।**
> **स्मृतिदार्ढ्यमनिर्वेदश्च मातरोऽष्टौ कवित्वस्य।।**

STUDENTS of the discipline of Poetics should study the *vidyās* (the important branches of knowledge for poets) and *upavidyās* (the sixty-four accessory branches of knowledge)[1] for learning the art of poetic composition.

---

1. The sixty-four arts are as under:

(1) *gīta* (music), (2) *vādya* (instrumental music), (3) *nr̥tya* (dancing), (4) *nāṭya* (histrionics), (5) *citra* (painting), (6) *acccunirmāṇa* (making of types), (7) *puṣpanirmāṇa* (flower-gardening), (8) *pūmetta-racanā* (artistic flower laying), (9) *dehālaṁkaraṇa* (dressing), (10) *gr̥hālaṁkaraṇa* (furnishing of houses), (11) *śayyānirmāṇa* (making of beds), (12) *jalataraṅga* (music with water), (13) *jalavādya* (music on water), (14) *vividha veṣadhāraṇa* (wearing different kinds of dresses), (15) *mālānirmāṇa* (making of flower garlands), (16) *keśālaṁkāra* (hair-dressing), (17) *vastradhāraṇa* (wearing of dresses), (18) *karṇābhūṣaṇa nirmāṇa* (making of ear-ornaments), (19) *sugandha puṣpasañcayana* (collection of sweet smelling flowers), (20) *alaṁkr̥tahāra* (decorating food articles), (21) *indrajāla* (magic), (22) *bhaṅgikaraṇa* (beautification), (23) *karaśucīkaraṇa* (cleaning of the hands), (24) *modakanirmāṇa* (making of sweet-meats), (25)

→

The important branches of knowledge (*vidyās*) are four: *nāmadhātu-pārāyaṇa* (grammar), *abhidhāna kośa* (lexicon), *chandoviciti* (prosody) and *alaṁkāra* (poetics). Sixty-four *kalās* are called *upavidyās* (accessory-studies). In addition to these there are other subjects which are a source of inspiration for poets. Acquaintance with poets who are patronised by good men (*deśa-vārttā*) knowledge of geographical regions (*vidagdha-vāda*) speeches and sayings of learned men and popular local beliefs (*loka-yātrā*) dramatic compositions or assemblies (*vidvād-goṣṭhī*) and ancient literary compositions (*purātana-kavi nibandha*).

Thus —

The eight mothers of poetic-composition are health, *pratibhā* (innate faculty), *abhyāsa* (practice), *bhakti* (devotion), *vidvād* (assemblies of learned scholars), commerce with the learned knowledge of various subjects, retentive memory and enthusiasm.

अपि च। नित्यं शुचिः स्यात्। त्रिधा च शौचं वाक्शौचं, मनःशौचं, कायशौचं च। प्रथमे शास्त्रजन्मनी। तार्तीयीकं तु सनखच्छेदौपादौ, सताम्बूलं मुखं, सविलेपनमात्रं वपुः,

---

→ *pānīya nirmāṇa* (making of drinks), (26) tailoring, (27) *jālanirmāṇa* (making of nets), (28) riddle, (29) *akṣaraśloka* (competition in reciting of poems according to certain rules), (30) *arthaviṣādīkaraṇa* (clarification of meaning), (31) *granthapārāyaṇa* (reading of books), (32) *nāṭakadarśana* (enacting of plays), (33) *samasyāpurāṇa* (part of a verse, generally the last line, proposed by one person to be completed by another as a trial of skill), (34) *nirmāṇa* (making of cots of cane), (35) carpentry, (36) logic, (37) *vāstuvidyā* (science of building homes), (38) *svarṇaratna pariśodhana* (connoisseurship of gold and diamonds), (39) *dhātusaṁskaraṇa* (purification of metals), (40) skill in distinguishing the colour of diamonds, (41) *khaniparīkṣaṇa* (finding out of mines), (42) *vṛkṣāyurvedayoga* (understanding trees and their values), (43) cockfight (44) understanding the language of words like *mainā*, (45) massaging, (46) *keśaprakṣālaṇa*, (47) *akṣara muṣṭika kathana*, (48) *videśabhāṣāpāṭhana* (learning of foreign language), (49) *deśabhāṣā-jñāna* (knowledge of language of one's own country), (50) *bhāvikalpapravacana* (fortune telling), (51) *yantranirmāṇa* (making of machines), (52) *smaraṇaśaktipoṣaṇa* (increasing memory power), (53) *śravaṇapāṭha* (studying by hearing), (54) *nimiṣakavana* (instant poetry-making), (55) *kriyāvikalpa*, (56) *kapaṭabhāva* (false poses), (57) *chandojñāna* (knowledge of the different metres), (58) *vastragopana*, (59) game of dice, (60) another gambling game, (61) *bālalīlā* (entertainment of children), (62) *vinayācārakrama* (etiquette), (63) *vaitālikavaidyājñāna* (panegyrics), and (64) *kārya grahaṇa* (comprehension of facts) (*śabdasāgara*).

Vettam Mani, *Purāṇic Encyclopaedia, op. cit.*, p. 367.

महार्हमनुल्बणं च वासः, सकुसुमं शिर इति। शुचि शीलनं हि सरस्वत्याः संवननमामनन्ति।

स यत्स्वभावः कविस्तदनुरूपं काव्यम्। यादृशाकारश्चित्रकरस्तादृशाकारमस्य चित्रमिति प्रायो वादः। स्मितपूर्वमभिभाषणं, सर्वत्रोक्तिगर्भमभिधानं सर्वतो रहस्यान्वेषणं परकाव्यदूषणवैमुख्यमनभिहितस्य, अभिहितस्य तु यथार्थमभिधानम्।

In addition a poet should remain pure. Purity is of three kinds — of speech, of the mind and of the body. Purity of the mind and speech is obtained by a study of *śāstras*. For purity of the body the nails of the hands and the feet should be clipped. There should be a betel-leaf in the mouth. The body should be pasted with perfumes, etc. To inculcate the various kinds of purity and to follow Sarasvatī (goddess of wisdom) is to respect learning.

A poet's composition reflects his own natural disposition. It is well-known that a painter paints according to his own mental disposition. A poet should be ever-smiling. His speech should be marked with archedness (*vakrata*). The mystical doctrine should be explored in all its forms. One should not find fault in others' work without asking and on being asked one should attempt a real and appropriate criticism.

तस्य भवनं सुसंमृष्टं ऋतुषट्कोचितविविधस्थानम्, अनेकतरुमूलकल्पितापाश्रयवृक्षवाटिकं, सक्रीडापर्वतकं, सदीर्घिकापुष्करिणीकं, ससरित्समुद्रावर्त्तकं, सकुल्याप्रवाहं, सबर्हिणहरिणहारीतं, ससारसचक्रवाकहंसं, सचकोरक्रौञ्चकुररशुकसारिकं, घर्मक्लान्तिचौरं, सभूमिधारागृहयन्त्रलतामण्डपकं, सदोलाप्रेङ्खं च स्यात्। काव्याभिनिवेशखिन्नस्य मनसस्तद्विनिर्वेदच्छेदायाज्ञामूकपरिजनं विजनं वा तस्य स्थानम्। अपभ्रंशभाषणप्रवणः परिचारकवर्गः, समागधभाषाभिनिवेशिन्यः परिचारिकाः। प्राकृतसंस्कृतभाषाविद आन्तःपुरिका, मित्राणि चास्य सर्वभाषाविन्दि भवेयुः।

सदःसंस्कारविशुद्ध्यर्थं सर्वभाषाकुशलः, शीघ्रवाक्, चार्वक्षरः, इङ्गिताकारवेदी, नानालिपिज्ञः, कविः, लाक्षणिकश्च लेखकः स्यात्। तदसन्निधावतिरात्रादिषु पूर्वोक्तानामन्यतमः।

A poets' abode should be clean and painted. There should be separate seating places for different seasons. There should be seating places under trees and climbers in the garden. There should be winding paths and artificial hills in the garden. There should also be present small ponds, water-reservoirs and artificial rivers and lakes — small streams and rivulets should also run through the garden. Peacocks, parrots, swans, geese, partridges, etc., are the birds which should be present.

There should be shady places to act as shelters against the sun and rain. Small caves (alcoves) decorated with fountains and creepers and also swings should be present.

When the poet after the intense activity of poetic composition wishes for relaxation, the inmates of his family and his followers should not speak without his desire. His servants should be proficient in Apabhraṁśa,[2] his lady attendants should be proficient in Māgadhī[3] and other languages, the wives or women of the family should have a knowledge of the above as well as other languages.

The writer who has to edit the poets' work should be adept in a large number of languages, receptive, well-versed, aesthetic, with a knolwedge of different dialects and a possessor of a good handwriting. If such a person is unable to keep long hours in the night with the poet, the same work could be done by an educated personal attendant of the poet.

स्वभवने हि भाषानियमं यथा प्रभुर्विदधाति तथा भवति। श्रूयते हि मगधेषु शिशुनागो नाम राजा;, तेन दुरुच्चारानष्टौ वर्णानपास्य स्वान्तःपुर एव प्रवर्त्तितो नियमः, टकरादयश्चत्वारो मूर्द्धन्यास्तृतीयवर्जमूष्माणस्त्रयः क्षकारश्चेति।

Kings could make their own rules for language usage for their own countries. As for instance, the king of Magadha namely Śiśunāga had made use of this particular usage in his homeland whereby the eight sounds which are difficult to pronounce should not be used in the spoken language. The use of these eight letters (*t*, *ṭh*, *ḍa*, *ḍh*, *ś*, *ṣ*, *h* and *kṣa*) was prohibited.

श्रूयते च सूरसेनेषु कुविन्दो नाम राजा, तेन परुषसंयोगाक्षरवर्जमन्तःपुर एवेति समानं पूर्वेण।

श्रूयते च कुन्तलेषु सातवाहनो नाम राजा, तेन प्राकृतभाषात्मकमन्तःपुर एवेति समानं पूर्वेण।

श्रूयते चोज्जयिन्यां साहसाङ्को नाम राजा, तेन च संस्कृतभाषात्मकमन्तःपुर एवेति समानं पूर्वेण।

---

2. Apabhraṁśa is the deformed utterance of standard correct forms or words; corrupt form e.g., *gāvī*, *goṇī*, etc. Cf. Abhyankar, *op. cit.*, p. 32. It is also one of the dialects used by common people in the early middle ages.

3. A dialect of the people of Magadha which seems to have acquired its name from the region. Magadha, the southern part of modern Bihar.

It has also been heard that the king Kuvinda of Mathurā had also prohibited the use of difficult sounds in his homeland.

Similarly the King Sātavāhana of Kuntala helped in the spread of Prākṛta[4] language in his homeland.

The King of Sāhasāṅka of Ujjayinī was a patron of the Sanskrit language and helped in the spread of the same in his homeland.

तस्य सम्पुटिका सफलकखटिका, समुद्गकः, सलेखनीकमषीभाजनानि ताडिपत्राणि भूर्जत्वचो वा, सलोहकण्टकानि तालदलानि, सुसम्मृष्टा भित्तयः, सततसन्निहिताः स्युः। 'तद्धि काव्यविद्यायाः परिकरः' इति आचार्याः। 'प्रतिभैव परिकरः' इति यायावरीयः।

The materials which should always be found near a poet are a box which can be closed, a slate, a box to hold his materials, pen, ink-pot and pen-holder, palm-leaves, brass-plates and well rubbed or clean walls. *Ācārya*s say that all these materials are needed for composition by a poet. Yāyāvarīya (Rājaśekhara) feels that the collection of materials mentioned above is not the real requisite for the composition of poetry but the poetical-genius (or *pratibhā*) alone is its chief necessity.

"कविः प्रथममात्मानमेव कल्पयेत्। कियान्मे संस्कारः, क्व भाषाविषये शक्तोऽस्मि, किंरुचिर्लोकः परिवृढो वा, कीदृशि गोष्ठ्यां विनीतः, क्वास्य वा चेतः संसजत इति बुद्ध्वा भाषाविशेषमाश्रयेत" इति आचार्याः। 'एकदेशकवेरियं नियमतन्त्रणा, स्वतन्त्रस्य पुनरेकभाषावत्सर्वा अपि भाषाः स्युः' इति यायावरीयः।

देशविशेषवशेन च भाषाश्रयणं दृश्यते।

*Ācārya*s say that a poet should evaluate himself. He should be able to size up the extent of his own knowledge, his competence in a particular language, the interest of the people and the King at that particular moment, the level of education and the areas of interest of his patron. Keeping the above issues in mind he should then take up an appropriate and favourable language for poetic-composition.

Yāyāvarīya (Rājaśekhara) says that all these injunctions are for a poet who belongs to a particular region (*ekadeśīya* or regional poet). For a non-regional poet, all languages are one as he has an

4. Prākṛta is a vernacular or provincial dialect derived from Sanskrit.

equal right on all languages.

Poets prefer to use regional dialects due to their specific abode in particular geographical regions.

तदुक्तम् —

> "गौडाद्याः संस्कृतस्थाः परिचितरुचयः प्राकृते लाटदेश्याः
> सापभ्रंशप्रयोगाः सकलमरुभुवष्टक्कभादानकाश्च।
> आवन्त्याः पारियात्राः सह दशपुरजैर्भूतभाषां भजन्ते
> यो मध्ये मध्यदेशं निवसति स कविः सर्वभाषानिषण्णः।।"
>
> जानीयाल्लोकसाम्मत्यं कविः कुत्र ममेति च।
> असम्मतं परिहरेन्मतेऽभिनिविशेत च।।
>
> जनापवादमात्रेण न जुगुप्सेत चात्मनि।
> जानीयात्स्वयमात्मानं यतो लोको निरङ्कुशः।।
>
> गीतसूक्तिरतिक्रान्ते स्तोता देशान्तरस्थिते।
> प्रत्यक्षे तु कवौ लोकः सावज्ञः सुमहत्यपि।।
>
> प्रत्यक्षकविकाव्यं च रूपं च कुलयोषितः।
> गृहवैद्यस्य विद्या न कस्मैचिद्यदि रोचते।।

Thus —

> Poets belonging to regions like Gauḍīya[5], etc., show a special interest in Sanskrit. The ones who are residents of Lāṭadeśa love the Prākṛta language. Those who are residents of Marubhūmi (Mārwāḍa — Rājpūtānā) and Punjāb are interested in Apabhraṁśa and show an increased use of *takāra*, *kakāra* and *jhakāra*. Poets of Avantikā, Pariyātrā and Daśapurā are proficient in Bhūtabhāṣā or Paiśācī[6] while the resident poets of Madhya-deśa show a similar inclination towards all languages.

It is of utmost importance for a poet to know the interest and expectations of the people. He should analyse and describe the subjects dear to his own heart as well as close to the interest of the people. He should abandon the

---

5. Gauḍīya, Lāṭadeśa, Marubhūmi, Punjāb, Avantikā and Madhyadeśa — for the modern equivalents of these places, See Appendix II.

6. Paiśācī is one of the lowest forms of Prākṛta dialects.

use of subjects which are of no interest to him or to the people.

Yet one should also not belie one's own conscience. A poet should attempt to analyse and understand his own true self. Common people have no constraints. Sometimes they find fault even with excellent compositions.

A poets' composition is praiseworthy if it does not belong to this world alone. It should live on even after the poets' death. It should be praised even by critics who come from far off places. However it is generally observed that during the poets' time, his compositions are not praised but severely criticised.

The poetic compositions of the present day are like the beauty of a woman of the family or the treatment prescribed by the family physician (*vaid*) which is not appreciated by everyone but only by some.

इदं महाहासकरं विचेष्टितं
परोक्तिपाटच्चरतारतोऽपि यत्।
सदुक्तिरत्नाकरतां गतान्कवीन्
कवित्वमात्रेण समेन निन्दति।।

It is a matter of amusement that a poet who is adept at appropriation of beautiful verses from other poets and thus acquires renown in his self-esteem finds fault with a new collection of verses of eminent poets (*mahākavis*).

वचः स्वादु सतां लेह्यं लेशस्वाद्वपि कौतुकात्।
बालस्त्रीहीनजातीनां काव्यं याति मुखान्मुखम्।।

कार्यावसरसञ्जानां परिव्राजां महीभुजाम्।
काव्यं सद्यः कवीनां च भ्रमत्यह्ना दिशो दश।।

पितुर्गुरोर्नरेन्द्रस्य सुतशिष्यपदातयः।
अविविच्यैव काव्यानि स्तुवन्ति च पठन्ति च।।"

Even if a poetic composition is devoid of extraordinary qualities but is simple and pleasing, it is heard by people and because of their innate curiosity is carried far and wide by children, women and people of lower divisions in society.

Sometimes compositions composed by Āśukavis, kings and saints spread all around without any delay.

The compositions of a poet father are carried over by the son, of a king by his flatterers and of a teacher (*guru*) by his pupils. These followers appreciate these compositions even without considering their worth and thus help to spread them all over.

'किञ्च नार्द्धकृतं पठेदसमाप्तिस्तस्य फलम्' इति कविरहस्यम्।

न नवीनमेकाकिनः पुरतः। स हि स्वीयं ब्रुवाणः कतरेण साक्षिणा जीयेत।

न च स्वकृतिं बहु मन्येत। पक्षपातो हि गुणदोषौ विपर्यासयति।

न च दृप्येत। दर्पलवोऽपि सर्वसंस्कारानुच्छिनत्ति।

परैश्च परीक्षयेत्। यदुदासीनः पश्यति न तदनुष्ठातेति प्रायो वादः।

कविमानिनं तु छन्दोनुवर्त्तनेन रञ्जयेत् कविम्मन्यस्य हि पुरतः सूक्तमरण्यरुदितं स्याद्विप्लवेत च। तदाह —

> A poet should never recite his incomplete composition to anybody because then there might arise a difficulty in its completion.

This is the essence of the mystical doctrine which should be followed.

A new composition should never be recited in front of a single poet. If the latter claims to be the creator of that particular composition, it becomes difficult to find evidence to the contrary. It is difficult to win such an argument.

One should not be extravagant in praising one's own composition. To do so shows prejudice. Prejudice can make an excellence appear a fault and *vice-versa* which could be the cause of infamy.

A poet should never be proud. Pride can result in the extirpation of all the excellences.

One's own poetic composition should be tested by others. It is a famous saying that 'others can judge their actions better than the doers themselves'.

The foolish poet who considers himself to be a good poet should not be disagreed with on any account because even if excellent compositions are rectified in front of such a poet, it would be as futile as crying in the wilderness (*araṇyarodana*).[7]

इदं हि वैदग्ध्यरहस्यमुत्तमं
पठेन्न सूक्तिं कविमानिनः पुरः।
न केवलं तां न विभावयत्यसौ
स्वकाव्यबन्धेन विनाशयत्यपि।।

It is a test of a poets' cleverness that he should never recite his composition even before a highly esteemed poet for he may not comprehend the worth of the composition and completely destroy its effect with his interference.

कविचर्या

अनियतकालाः प्रवृत्तयो विप्लवन्ते तस्माद्दिवसं निशां च यामक्रमेण चतुर्द्धा विभजेत्। स प्रातरुत्थाय कृतसन्ध्यावरिवस्यः सारस्वतं सूक्तमधीयीत। ततो विद्यावसथे यथासुखमासीनः काव्यस्य विद्या उपविद्याश्चानुशीलयेदाप्रहरात्। न ह्येवंविधमन्यत्प्रतिभाहेतुर्यथा प्रत्यग्रसंस्कारः।

द्वितीये काव्यक्रियाम्। उपमध्याह्नं स्नायादविरुद्धं भुञ्जीत च। भोजनान्ते काव्यगोष्ठीं प्रवर्त्तयेत्। कदाचिच्च प्रश्नोत्तराणि भिन्दीत। काव्यसमस्याधारणा, मातृकाभ्यासः, चित्रा योगा इत्यायामत्रयम्।

चतुर्थ एकाकिनः परिमितपरिषदो वा पूर्वाह्णभागविहितस्य काव्यस्य परीक्षा। रसावेशतः काव्यं विरचयतो न च विवेक्त्री दृष्टिस्तस्मादनुपरीक्षेत। अधिकस्य त्यागो, न्यूनस्य पूरणं, अन्यथास्थितस्य परिवर्त्तनं, प्रस्मृतस्यानुसन्धानं चेत्यहीनम्।

Work done without an appropriate division of time falls into confusion. Thus day and night may be divided into four major parts (*prahar*)[8]. A poet should get up early in the morning and after his prayers should recite the *Sarasvatīstotra*[9]. Thereafter he should retire to the study room and devote the next hour to an intensive study of *vidyā*s and *upavidyā*s related to poetics. The only means to sharpen the poetic-genius (*pratibhā*) is practice.

---

7. *Araṇyarodana* is a Nyāya both *laukika* (of common Indian life) and also of *śāstra*, i.e., disciplines. See for more details Col. G.A. Jacob, *Laukikānyāyāñjali: A Second Handful of Popular Maxims Current in Sanskrit Literature*, The Nirnaya Sagar Press, Bombay, 1925, p. 4.

8. *Prahar* are the eight parts of the whole day with each *prahar* lasting for roughly 3 hours.

9. A hymn or verse in praise of Sarasvatī is known as *Sarasvatī- stotra*.

The second part (*prahar*) of the day should be devoted to the practice of the art of poetic-composition. Just a little before noon, the poet should take a bath and have some suitable food. Thereafter he should take part in a stimulating talk (*kāvya-goṣṭhī*) relating to poetics in a gathering of poets. During this talk, analysis can be carried on by means of questions, answers and counter-questions on subjects pertaining to poetics. Poets should also attempt to create beautiful verses and *citra kāvya*.

सायं सन्ध्यामुपासीत सरस्वतीं च। ततो दिवा विहितपरीक्षित –स्याभिलेखनमाप्रदोषात्। यावदार्त्ति स्त्रियमभिमन्येत। द्वितीयतृतीयौ साधु शयीत। सम्यक्स्वापो वपुषः वरमारोग्याय। चतुर्थे सप्रयत्नं प्रतिबुध्येत। ब्राह्मे मुहूर्ते मनः प्रसीदत्तांस्तानर्थानध्यक्षयतित्याहोरात्रिकम्।

In the next *prahar*, the poet should collect two to four close friends and again analyse the compositions created in the morning.

The analysis should take into consideration both excellences and faults. During creation of a composition and in an emotional outpouring detailed analysis is not possible. Thus it becomes essential to analyse it after a lapse of time. During this analysis, the additional quarters can be removed, incomplete verses can be completed, the couplets scattered here and there can be collected and placed in an appropriate order and forgotten words or verses can be added. This is to be done in the fourth *prahar*.

कविप्रकार

चतुर्विधश्चासौ। असूर्यम्पश्यो, निषण्णो, दत्तावसरः, प्रायोजनिकश्च।

यो गुहागर्भभूमिगृहादिप्रवेशान्नैष्ठिकवृत्तिः कवते, असावसूर्यम्पश्यस्तस्य सर्वे कालाः।

यः काव्यक्रियायामभिनिविष्टः कवते न च नैष्ठिकवृत्तिः, स निषण्णः स्तस्यापि त एव कालाः।

यः सेवादिकमविरुन्धानः कवते, स दत्तावसरस्तस्य कतिपये कालाः। निशायास्तुरीयो यामार्द्धः। स हि सारस्वतो मुहूर्त्तः। भोजनान्तः सौहित्यं हि स्वास्थ्यमुपस्थापयति; व्यवायोपरमः यदार्त्तिविनिवृत्तिरेकमेकाग्रतायतनं। याप्ययानयात्रा। विषयान्तरविनिवृत्तं हि चित्तं यत्र यत्र प्रणिधीयते तत्र तत्र गुडूचीलागं लगति। यदा यदा चात्मनः क्षणिकतां मन्यते स स काव्यकरणकालः।

यस्तु प्रस्तुतं किञ्चन संविधानकमुद्दिश्य कवते, स प्रायोजनिकस्तस्य प्रयोजनवशात्कालव्यवस्था।

बुद्धिमदाहार्यबुद्ध्योरियं नियममुद्रा। औपदेशिकस्य पुनरिच्छैव सर्वे कालाः, सर्वाश्च नियममुद्राः।

Poets are of four kinds: *asūryampaśya*, *niṣaṇṇa*, *dattāvasara* and *prāyojanika*.[10]

The poets who enter deep caves and in a stable state of mind compose poetry are referred to as *asūryampaśya* poets. There is no fixed time for such a poet as he can compose poetry on all occasions.

A poet who creates poetry only due to a wish or desire expressed by people but does not remain collected in mind is referred to as a *niṣaṇṇa kavi*. For such a poet also time is not a restraining factor as he can compose poetry at all times.

The poet who uses his time for specific work and only occasionally, at an opportune moment, composes poetry is referred to as *dattāvasara* poet. There is a fixed time for him to create poetry for instance, the first half of the fourth *prahar* at night is called *sārasvata muhūrta* and is an opportune time. The time after meals is also favourable because satisfaction of the appetite induces concentration in the mind. The time during long journeys is also conducive to poetic-compositions because the mind remains concentrated and free of other worries. A mind undisturbed by objects of senses is effective for the composition of poetry in the same way as the effect of medicinal drugs on diseases. In addition to these, whenever a *dattāvasara* poet finds time, he uses it for poetic-composition.

A poet who takes up a subject in a given context and composes accordingly is referred to as a *prāyojanika*. The time of his poetic-composition depends on his own discretion.

The above restrictions are for *buddhimān* and *āhāryabuddhi* poets only. *Aupadeśika* (instructed) poets do not have these divisions for such poets there is no time or restriction. His desire to compose is everything for him.

---

10. These kinds of poets are defined subsequently.

पुरुषवत् योषितोऽपि कवीभवेयुः। संस्कारो ह्यात्मनि समवैति, न स्त्रैणं पौरुषं वा विभागमपेक्षते। श्रूयन्ते दृश्यन्ते च राजपुत्र्यो महामात्यदुहितरो गणिकाः कौतुकिभार्याश्च शास्त्रप्रहतबुद्धयः कवयश्च।

Women[11] can be as good poets as men. Poetic power is born of *saṁskāra*[12] (traces or impressions). These impressions are a part of the inner soul. Thus there need be no discrimination between men and women. There are any number of princesses, daughters of ministers and performing artistes who are endowed with ability born of knowledge of the *śāstra*s and with the ability to compose poetry.

सिद्धं च प्रबन्धमनेकादर्शगतं कुर्यात्। यदित्थं कथयन्ति —

"निक्षेपो विक्रयो दानं देशत्यागोऽल्पजीविता।
त्रुटिको वह्निरम्भश्च प्रबन्धोच्छेदहेतवः।।
दारिद्र्यं व्यसनासक्तिरवज्ञा मन्दभाग्यता।
दुष्टे द्विष्टे च विश्वासः पञ्च काव्यमहापदः।।"

A poet should recite his entire poetic *prabandha* only after it is complete in all respects in an assembly of poets. Learned people should be informed well in advance. A number of copies should be made of the poets' work and distributed by a variety of means. It is said that *prabandha*s if left in someone's custody, or sold, or given as alms, or sacrificed due to change of place, or due to a short life or if left incomplete are lost by fire or water.

There may be other reasons for destruction of these *prabandha*s such as poverty, bad company, misfortune, humiliation of the art of poetic-composition and faith in evil persons or enemies.

पुनः समापयिष्यामि, पुनः संस्करिष्यामि, सुहृद्भिः सह विवेचयिष्यामीति कर्तुराकुलता राष्ट्रोपप्लवश्च प्रबन्धविनाशकारणानि।

अहर्निशाविभागेन य इत्थं कवते कृती।
एकावलीव तत्काव्यं सतां कण्ठेषु लम्बते।।

---

11. Rājaśekhara's wife Avantīsundarī is an outstanding instance. See chapter 6 note.

12. Of the many meanings of the term *saṁskāra* here the reference is to impressions and the faculty of recollection.

When a poetic composition is being composed or when it is being edited (*saṁskāra*) or when it is being tested and evaluated, if one leaves it incomplete with the thought of finishing it at some other time, or correcting it at a later date or after consultation with friends, even then the poetic composition may be destroyed or left incomplete.

The poet, who follows the method given above and composes poetry based on the division of day and night (into four *prahar*s) creates verses which appear to be like a single string of pearls beautifying the necks of learned people.

यथा यथाभियोगश्च संस्कारश्च भवेत्कवेः।
तथा तथा निबन्धानां तारतम्येन रम्यता।।

मुक्तके कवयोऽनन्ताः सङ्घाते कवयः शतं।
महाप्रबन्धे तु कविरेको द्वौ दुर्लभास्त्रयः।।"

As the mind of a poet starts gaining insights into creation and attains maturity, his composition, language, expression, etc., also become correspondingly finer and thus the beauty of his poetic-compositions increases.

There are innumberable poets who compose on varied issues and subjects, there may be thousands who can compose on one subject but those who can compose a *mahākāvya* (epic) are extremely rare. There may be one or two but even to find a third is extremely difficult.

अत्राह स्म —

"बह्वपि स्वेच्छया कामं प्रकीर्णमभिधीयते।
अनुज्झितार्थसम्बन्धः प्रबन्धो दुरुदाहरः।।"

रीतिं विचिन्त्य विगणय्य गुणान्विगाह्य
शब्दार्थसार्थमनुमृत्य च सूक्तिमुद्राः।
कार्यो निबन्धविषये विदुषा प्रयत्नः
के पोतयन्त्ररहिता जलधौ प्लवन्ते।।

लीढाभिधोपनिषदां सविधे बुधाना-
मभ्यस्यतः प्रतिदिनं बहुदृश्वनोऽपि।
किञ्चित्कदाचन कथञ्चन सूक्तिपाका-

द्राक्तत्त्वमुन्मिषति कस्यचिदेव पुंसः।।

इत्यनन्यमनोवृत्तेर्निःशेषेऽस्य क्रियाक्रमे।
एकपत्नीव्रतं धत्ते कवेर्देवी सरस्वती।।

सिद्धिः सूक्तिषु सा तस्य जायते जगदुत्तरा।
मूल्यच्छायां न जानाति यस्याः सोऽपि गिरां गुरुः।।

Thus —

A lot can be said on diffused subjects but there are very few verses with reference to *śāstras*.

A learned poet should acquaint himself with the *rīti*s like *vaidarbhī*, etc., and qualities like *ojas*, etc. They should understand the words, meanings and their interrelations, follow the style adopted by ancient composers and then turn to his own poetic compositions. No one can cross the sea without a ship.

He who practises *(abhyāsa)* in close association with experts who have a deep knowledge of *vyākaraṇa* (grammar) and other technical sciences, his compositions will never lack in intrinsic charm.

Thus, for the poet who practises with single-minded devotion, Sarasvatī (goddess of learning and wisdom) takes up the vow of the only wife for him (or remains at his command) for ever.

A poet who follows this practice and these steps religiously attains great heights and the beauty of his compositions cannot be measured by even Bṛhaspati himself.

राजचर्या

राजा कविः कविसमाजं विदधीत। राजनि कवौ सर्वो लोकः कविः स्यात्। स काव्यपरीक्षायै सभां कारयेत्। सा षोडशभिः स्तम्भैचतुर्भिद्वारैरष्टभिर्मत्तवारणीभिरुपेता स्यात्। तदनुलग्नं राज्ञः केलिगृहम्। मध्येसभं चतुःस्तम्भान्तरा हस्तमात्रोत्सेधा समणिभूमिका वेदिका। तस्यां राजासनम्। तस्य चोत्तरतः संस्कृताः कवयो निविशेरन्। बहुभाषाकवित्वे यो यत्राधिकं प्रवीणः स तेन व्यपदिश्यते। यस्त्वनेकत्र प्रवीणः संक्रम्य तत्र तत्रोपविशेत्।

ततः परं वेदविद्याविदः प्रामाणिकाः पौराणिकाः स्मार्त्ता भिषजो मौहूर्त्तिका अन्येऽपि तथाविधाः।

पूर्वेण प्राकृताः; कवयः, ततः परं नटनर्त्तकगायनवादनवाग्जीवनकुशीलवतालावचरा अन्येऽपि तथाविधाः।

पश्चिमेनापभ्रंशिनः कवयः, ततः परं चित्रलेप्यकृतो माणिक्यबन्धका वैकटिकाः स्वर्णकारवर्द्धकिलोहकारा अन्येऽपि तथाविधाः।

दक्षिणतो भूतभाषाकवयः, ततः परं भुजङ्गगणिकाः प्लवकशौभिकजम्भकमल्लाः शस्त्रोपजीविनोऽन्येऽपि तथाविधाः।

If the king himself is a poet he can establish a poetic community. If a king is a poet his people also turn into poets. A king should get an assembly hall constructed for evaluating poetic-compositions. There should be sixteen pillars in the assembly hall. There should be four entrances inside. Next to this assembly hall should be the king's own play house. In the centre of the assembly hall and in between four pillars should stand a raised platform studded with precious stones. The king's throne should be placed on this. The Sanskrit poets should sit to the north of the king's throne. Sanskrit poets can be composers of other languages also. But if a large part of his work is in Sanskrit or he is more successful in this language then he may be known as a Sanskrit poet. The poet who has an equal right on a number of languages may sit wherever he so desires.

After the Sanskrit poets in the same row may be seated, scholars of Vedas and its auxiliary branches, philosophers, scholars of Purāṇas (or mythology), scholars of Dharmaśāstra (polity), physicians, astrologers and other such professionals.

The poets of Prākṛta languages should sit on the east of the king's throne. After him should sit the actors, dancers, singers, vocalists, theatre artists, bards, story-tellers, those who dance to the beat of hands and other such artisans.

The poets of the Apabhraṁśa languages should sit towards the west of the king's throne. They should be followed by painters, those who polish on walls, paint pictures on walls, jewellers, goldsmiths, blacksmiths and other such craftsmen.

The poets of Paiśācī or Bhūta-bhāṣā should sit to the right of the king's throne. These should be followed by swimmers, rope-dancers, magicians and wrestlers, etc.

तत्र यथासुखमासीनः काव्यगोष्ठीं प्रवर्त्तयेत् भावयेत्परीक्षेत च। वासुदेव सातवाहनशूद्रकसाहसाङ्कादीन्सकलान्सभापतीन्दानमानाभ्यामनुकुर्यात्।

तुष्टपुष्टाश्चास्य सभ्या भवेयुः, स्थाने च पारितोषिकं लभेरन्। लोकोत्तरस्य काव्यस्य च यथार्हा पूजा कवेर्वा। अन्तरान्तरा च काव्यगोष्ठीं शास्त्रवादाननुजानीयात्। मध्वपि नानवदंशं स्वदते।

काव्यशास्त्रविरतौ विज्ञानिष्वभिरमेत। देशान्तरागतानां च विदुषामन(न्य?)द्वारा सङ्गं कारयेदौचित्याद्यावत्स्थितिं पूजां च। वृत्तिकामांश्चोपजपेत् संगृह्णीयाच्च। पुरुषरत्नानामेक एव राजोदन्वान्भाजनम्। राजचरितं च राजोपजीविनोप्यनुकुर्युः। राज्ञ एव ह्यसावुपकारो यद्राजोपजीविनां संस्कारः।

In this fashion the king who sits happily in the assembly hall can begin the poet's assembly and initiate an evaluation and criticism of the work of poets. The king should also give his own critical estimate according to his own capability. Just as the kings of olden times who themselves were poets such as Vāsudeva, Sātavāhana, Śūdraka and Sāhāsanka used to honour the learned scholars with money and prestige so also the king should shower the poets with honour and wealth.

The king's assembly of poets should remain happy and prosperous. The poet should be rewarded from time to time. If amongst them there appears a poet or poetic-composition which is superior or extraordinary it should be suitably honoured. The king should invite scholars to discuss critical and (technical) śāstric aspects in between the poetic discussions. This is because even while taking our food we enhance its taste with the addition of sauces and spices.

After poetic discourse the king should also participate in the scientific discourse. There should be a meeting between the scientists from outside his region with his own scientists. They should be appropriately honoured and accorded a suitable welcome. The one who is qualified and desires a job should be suitably given one. The one's who are fit to be elevated should be elevated. For the jewels or brilliant men the only hope is the king. The men who take shelter under the king should follow him. The good nature, manners and behaviour of the king's assemblage is of great advantage to the ruler.

This also is of immense help to the king and a means of satisfaction for the people.

महानगरेषु च काव्यशास्त्रपरीक्षार्थं ब्रह्मसभाः कारयेत्। तत्र परीक्षोत्तीर्णानां ब्रह्मरथयामं पट्टबन्धश्च।

श्रूयते चोज्जयिन्यां काव्यकारपरीक्षा

The king should organise assemblies of brāhmaṇas and learned scholars of Vedas to examine works of *kāvya* and *śāstra* in famous cities of learning.

The learned scholars who qualify in this evaluation should be taken around in a royal carriage, they should be honoured with a suitable designation and a royal grant should be fixed for them.

It has been heard that in olden times there used to be an evaluation of poets in the city of Ujjayinī. Thus —

"इह कालिदासमेण्ठावत्रामररूपसूरभारवयः।
हरिचन्द्रचन्द्रगुप्तौ परीक्षिताविह विशालायाम्।।"

श्रूयते च पाटलिपुत्रे शास्त्रकारपरीक्षा —

"अत्रोपवर्षवर्षाविह पाणिनिपिङ्गलाविह व्याडिः।
वररुचिपतञ्जली इह परीक्षिताः ख्यातिमुपजग्मुः।।"

इत्थं सभापतिर्भूत्वा यः काव्यानि परीक्षते।
यशस्तस्य जगद्व्यापि स सुखी तत्र तत्र च।।

In this city of Ujjayinī, famous poets like Kālidāsa, Bhaṭṭramentha, Amara, Rāpā, Āryāsura, Bhāravi, Haricandra and Candragupta were examined.

It has also been heard that learned scholars of *śāstra*s were examined in Pāṭliputra.

Thus —

Upavarṣa, Varṣa, Pāṇini, Piṅgala, Vyāḍi, Vararūci and

Patañjali were examined here (in Pāṭaliputra) and became famous throughout the country.

Thus the king who arranges assemblies and discourses and presides over the evaluation of poetic compositions becomes famous throughout the world and attains happiness.

।। इति राजशेखरकृतौ काव्यमीमांसायां कविरहस्ये प्रथमेऽधिकरणे कविचर्या राजचर्या च दशमोऽध्यायः।।

11

शब्दहरणम्

Śabdaharaṇam
(Appropriation of Words)

परप्रयुक्तयोः शब्दार्थयोरुपनिबन्धो हरणम्। तद्द्विधा परित्याज्यमनुग्राह्यं च। तयोः शब्दहरणमेव तावत्पञ्चधा पदतः, पादतः, अर्द्धतः वृत्ततः, प्रबन्धतश्च।

'तत्रैकपदहरणं न दोषाय' इति आचार्याः। 'अन्यत्र द्व्यर्थपदात्' इति यायावरीयः।

तत्र श्लिष्टस्य श्लिष्टपदेन हरणम् —

THE using of words and ideas from the work of another (and passing them off as one's own) is called appropriation. It is two- fold (1) that which should be avoided and (2) that which should be adopted. Of the two kinds of appropriation (one of words and another of ideas) that of words alone is five-fold, arising from

> (a) *pada* (word), (b) a *pada* (quarter of a stanza), (c) *ardha* (a hemistich), (d) *vṛtta* (metre), and (e) *prabandha* (a long continuous composition).

*Ācārya*s say that 'borrowing one word cannot be called a fault', Yāyāvarīya (Rājaśekhara) says that 'borrowing a word which has two meanings is certainly not a fault'.

> **"दूराकृष्टशिलीमुखव्यतिकरान्नो किङ्किरातानिमा-**
> **नाराद्व्यावृतपीतलोहितमुखान्किं वा पलाशानपि।**
> **पान्थाः केसरिणं न पश्यत पुरोऽप्येनं वसन्तं वने**
> **मूढा रक्षत जीवितानि शरणं यात प्रियां देवताम्।।"**

यथा च —

> "मा गाः पान्थ प्रियां त्यक्त्वा दूराकृष्टशिलीमुखम्।
> स्थितं पन्थानमावृत्य किं किरातं न पश्यसि।।"

On appropriation of paranomastic words

> O travellers! Can you not see the swarms of *śilimukha* (arrows and bees) being attracted from afar to the *kirātas* (barbarians and flowers). Besides can you not see the *palāśa* (trees and *rākṣasas*) with their yellow and red colour respectively. Also can you not see the *kesarī* (serpents and lions) standing in the forest. You fools, to save yourself rush to the shelter of your favourite gods.[1]

And also

> O traveller! Do not leave your beloved and venture out. Can you not see these *kirātas* (barbarians and flowery trees) standing in the pathway and attracting towards themselves *śilimukha* (arrows and bees).

श्लिष्टपदैकदेशेन हरणम् —

> "नाश्चर्यं यदनार्याप्तावस्तप्रीतिरयं मयि।
> मांसोपयोगं कुर्वीत कथं क्षुद्रहितो जनः।।"

यथा च —

> "कोपान्मानिनि किं स्फुरत्यतितरां शेभाधरस्तेऽधरः
> किं वा चुम्बनकारणाद्दयित नो वायोर्विकारादयम्।
> तस्मात्सुभ्रु सुगन्धिमाहितरसं स्निग्धं भजस्वादरा-
> न्मुग्धे मांसरसं ब्रुवन्निति तया गाढं समालिङ्गितः।।"

Borrowing a part of the paranomastic word —

> It is not a matter of surprise that the one who has fallen into bad company should stop loving me just as one who is not hungry cannot make use of the meat.

And also —

1. The paranomastic words such as *kirāta*, *śilīmukha*, *palāśa* and *kesarī*, etc., occur in both the verses. The second verse borrows two of these words from the first one.

(The husband said to his wife) your soft lips are trembling due to anger or passion.

(The beloved replied) — They are trembling due to the strong wind.

(The husband then said) — If that be so then make use of either the sweet smelling meat curry or sweet and amorous lover like myself. Thus saying he embraced her tightly.[2]

श्लिष्टस्य यमकेन हरणम् —

"हलमपारपयोनिधिविस्तृतं
प्रहरता हलिना समराङ्गणे।
निजयशश्च शशाङ्ककलामलं
निरवधीरितमाकुलमासुरम्।।"

यथा च —

"दलयता विशिखैर्बलमुन्मदं
निरवधीरितमाकुलमासुरम्।
दशसु दिक्षु च तेन यशः सितं
निरवधीरितमाकुलमासुरम्।।"

Appropriation of an entire line by using Yamaka (a figure of speech) —

Balarāma (elder brother of Lord Kr̥ṣṇa) by using his massive ocean like plough attacked the despairing army of demons repelled and petrified them thus helping to spread his renown all over the earth and heaven.

And also

Lord Viṣṇu using his arrows on the army of demons repelled and petrified them and thus helped to spread his own renown in all the ten directions — the earth and heaven.[3]

2. The word *māusa* is borrowed by the poet in the second verse and combined with the *sarasam* to come up with two meanings (*māṁsarasa* or meat curry and *ma-saras*, i.e., a lover like myself).

3. Here the word *mīrvadhīrīlam* has two meanings: (a) repelled, and (b) unlimited spreading. These two meanings are expressed with reference to (i) the army of the *asuras*, and (ii) the fame of Baladeva. These are borrowed by the second verse which forms an example of *yamaka* and expresses the same sense.

श्लिष्टस्य प्रश्नोत्तरेण हरणम् —

"यस्यां भुजङ्गवर्गः कर्णायतेक्षणं कामिनीवदनं च।।"

यथा च —

"किं करोति कियत्कालं वेश्यावेश्मनि कामुकः।
कीदृशं वदनं वीक्ष्य तस्याः कर्णायतेक्षणम्।।"

Appropriation of paranomastic words in the form of a questionnaire

The land in which paramours behave like Karṇa (known for his large heartedness) and the faces of women have eyes reaching up to the ears.

And also

Question: What does the paramour do in the house of a prostitute, and for what time? What kind of a face does he look at?

Answer: He acts as *Karṇa* for a moment. After he looks at the woman with eyes long enough to reach her ears.

यमकस्य यमकेन हरणम् —

"वरदाय नमो हरये पतति जनोऽयं स्मरन्नपि न मोहरये।
बहुशश्चक्रन्द हता मनसि दितिर्येन दैत्यचक्रं दहता।।"

यथा च —

"चक्रं दहतारं चक्रन्द हतारं। खड्गेन तवाजौ राजन्नरिनारी"।।
एवमन्योन्यसमन्वयेऽन्येऽपि भेदाः।

नन्विदमुपदेशयमेव न भवति। यदित्थं कथयन्ति —

"पुंसः कलातिपातेन चौर्यमन्यद्विशीर्यति।
अपि पुत्रेषु पौत्रेपु वाक्चौर्यं च न शीर्यति।।"

Appropriation of Yamaka[4] by means of Yamaka *alaṁkāra* —

Obseisance to Lord Viṣṇu, the mere thought of whom helps mortals to keep their worldly attachments under control, and the

---

4. *Yamaka* is a rhetorical figure in which there is a repitition of words or syllables similar in sound, but different in meaning, a kind of rhyme. It can occur in the same stanza (or in any part of it) See Apte, *op. cit.*, p. 782.

> one who was responsible for destroying the entire race of demons thus inducing Dīti (Mother of *daityas*) to mourn the loss (of her sons).

And also —

> (O king!) When you vanquished your enemies in the battle, with your sword, their wives, mourned the loss'.

Similarly there can be many variations in the appropriation of words and lines in different combinations.

Here a doubt is raised that appropriation is not advisable. It has been said —

> While all other thefts committed by a person pass away with the lapse of time, literary theft endures even to sons and grandsons.

"अयमप्रसिद्धः प्रसिद्धिमानहम्, अयमप्रतिष्ठःप्रतिष्ठावानहम्, अप्रक्रान्तमिदमस्य संविधानकं प्रक्रान्तं मम, गुडूचीवचनोऽयं मृद्वीकावचनोऽहम्, अनादृतभाषाविशेषोऽयमहमादृतभाषाविशेषः, प्रशान्तज्ञातृकमिदं देशान्तरितकर्तृकमिदम्, उच्छिन्ननिबन्धनमूलमिदं म्लेच्छितकोपनिबन्धन-मूलमिदमित्येवमादिभिः कारणैः शब्दहरणेऽर्थहरणे चाभिरमेत" इति अवन्तिसुन्दरी।

Avantīsundarī (Rājaśekhara's wife, a learned scholar in her own right) says —

> This poet is unknown, I am a celebrated poet, this one is not established, I have established myself. His subject-matter (*saṁvidhānaka*) or plot is not of contemporary interest, mine is, 'his words are like medicine, mine are like grape-vine', this poet's language is not distinguished, mine is distinctive'. 'This work is obsolete; this is by a foreign author', 'This one has a worn out origin or theme'. 'This was composed with mere unrefined knowledge' — due to these and other similar considerations, borrowing of words and borrowing of meanings or subjects may be resorted to'.

'त्रिभ्यः पदेभ्यः प्रभृति त्वश्लिष्टेभ्यो हरणम्' इत्याचार्याः।

यथा —

"सा पातु वो यस्य जटाकलापे

स्थितः शशाङ्कः स्फुटहारगौरः।
नीलोत्पलानामिव नालपुञ्जे
निद्रायमाणः शरदीव हंसः।।"

यथा च —

"स पातु वो यस्य हतावशेषा-
स्तत्तुल्यवर्णाञ्जनरञ्जितेषु।
लावण्ययुक्तेष्वपि वित्रसन्ति
दैत्याः स्वकान्तानयनोत्पलेषु।।"

*Ācārya*s say the 'borrowing of three words or less (insequence) which do not have double meaning is not *appropriation*'.

Thus —

May Lord Viṣṇu who bears the white and bright moon in his locks like a beautiful swan resting on a heap of stalks of blue lotuses in the winter season, bless and protcct you.

And also

In the battle between gods and demons, the demons (who have yet to be vanquished) look into the dark kohlless and lotus like eyes of their wives and are reminded of Lord Viṣṇu which induces terror in them. May this same God bless and protect you.[5]

'न' इति यायावरीयः। उल्लेखवान्पदसन्दर्भः परिहरणीयो नाप्रत्यभिज्ञायातः पादोऽपि। तस्यापि साम्येन किञ्चन दुष्टं स्यात्।

यथा —

"इत्युक्तवानुक्तिविशेषरम्यं
मनः समाधाय जयोपपत्तौ।
उदारचेता गिरमित्युदारां
द्वैपायनेनाभिदधे नरेन्द्रः।।"

यथा च —

"इत्युक्तवानुक्तिविशेषरम्यं
रामानुजन्मा विरराम मानी।

5. Here the three words *sa, patu* and *va* are borrowed from the first verse but according to the *ācāryas*, this is not appropriation.

सङ्क्षिप्तमाप्तावसरं च वाक्यं
सेवाविधिज्ञैः पुरतः प्रभूणाम्।।"

Yāyāvarīya (Rājaśekhara) disagrees with the opinion of *ācāryas* and says — the composition where the poet's genius (*pratibhā*) is evident should not be appropriated. Well-known (where the composer at once comes to mind) words as well as lines can be borrowed.

Thus —

When the large hearted king Yudhiṣṭhira with a collected mind and in extremely moving words rendered prayers to Veda-Vyāsa, he in turn spoke out in heart-felt and resounding words.

And also —

Lakṣmaṇa, Rāma's brother, expressed himself in extremely moving words and became quiet because a dutiful person in the presence of a revered superior expresses himself in the briefest possible manner.[6]

उल्लेखवान्यथा —

"नमः संसारनिर्वाणविषामृतविधायिने।
सप्तलोकोर्म्मिभङ्गाय शङ्करक्षीरसिन्धवे।।"

यथा च —

"प्रसरद्बिन्दुनादाय शुद्धामृतमयात्मने।
नमोऽनन्तप्रकाशाय शङ्करक्षीरसिन्धवे।।"

Appropriation of an allusive description —

Obeisance to 'Śiva like sea of milk' who created this 'world like poison' and 'salvation like nectar' and is beautified by the 'seven world like waves'.

And also

Obeisance to 'Śiva like sea of milk' (*kṣīrasāgara*) in which spread the 'echoing sound like water-droplets', who has a pure 'nectar

6. The second verse borrows *ityaktavanuktiviśeṣarabhyam* but this cannot be called appropriation because here there is no evidence of the poet's genius.

like soul' and who helps to spread light everywhere.[7]

'पाद एवान्यथात्वकरणकारणं न हरणम्, अपि तु स्वीकरणम्' इति आचार्याः।

यथा —

"त्यागाधिकाः स्वर्गमुपाश्रयन्ते
त्यागेन हीना नरकं व्रजन्ति।
न त्यागिनां किञ्चिदसाध्यमस्ति
त्यागो हि सर्वव्यसनानि हन्ति।।"

यथा च —

"त्यागो हि सर्वव्यसनानि हन्ती-
त्यलीकमेतद् भुवि सम्प्रतीतम्।
जातानि सर्वव्यसनानि तस्या-
स्त्यागेन मे मुग्धविलोचनायाः।।"

*Ācārya*s say that if 'a quarter of an earlier stanza is borrowed by a later poet, with a view to conveying an opposite idea, it should be called not appropriation but adoption.

Thus —

Those superior people who indulge in supreme sacrifice obtain Heaven whereas those who do not sacrifice go to Hell. Nothing is out of reach for those who make a sacrifice. It helps in alleviating all suffering.

And also —

Someone has said that, sacrifice alleviates all suffering. This has been proved a falsehood in reality. It is because of having sacrificed my beloved with the beautiful eyes that I am experiencing suffering.[8]

---

7. In the two verses quoted above the figure of speech known as *rūpaka* (a figure of speech corresponding to the English metaphor, in which the *upameya* is represented as being identical with the *upamāna*) applies to both Śaṅkara (Śiva) and *kṣīrasindhu* which have several adjectives each with two meanings. This is distinctive use of *pratibhā* (suggestive power of words/genius) due to the innate faculty of a poet. Thus, though only one word, *śaṅkara kṣīrasindhave* is borrowed in the second verse, this is considered to be a case of appropriation.

8. Here it has been acknowledged in the second verse that 'sacrifice alleviates suffering' is spoken by someone. Thus this is acceptance and not appropriation.

तदिदं स्वीकरणापरनामधेयं हरणमेव। तद्वदर्द्धप्रयोगेऽपि। यथा —

"पादस्ते नरवर दक्षिणे समुद्रे
पादोऽन्यो हिमवति हेमकूटलग्ने।
आक्रामत्यलघु महीतलं त्वयीत्थं
भूपालाः प्रणतिमपास्य किन्नु कुर्युः।।"

Yāyāvarīya (Rājaśekhara) says that the above adaptation is also appropriation. Likewise borrowing of half a verse (or of one quarter from one half and of another from the other half) also constitutes appropriation.

Thus —

(O, Emperor!) With one foot in the southern ocean and the other on Hemkūṭa near the Himālayas, you have completely won over this vast earth and have left no choice to the other kings but to fall at your feet.

यथा चोत्तरार्द्धे —

"इत्थं ते विधृतपदद्वयस्य राज-
न्नाश्चर्यं कथमिव सीवनी न भिन्ना।।"

एवं व्यस्तार्द्धप्रयोगेऽपि। यथा —

"तत्तावदेव शशिनः स्फुरितं महीयो
यावन्न तिग्मरुचिमण्डलमभ्युदेति।
अभ्युद्गते सकलधामनिधौ तु तस्मि-
न्निन्दोः सिताभ्रशकलस्य च को विशेषः।।"

यथा च —

"तत्तावदेव शशिनः स्फुरितं महीयो
यावन्न किञ्चिदपि गौरतरा हसन्ति।
ताभिः पुनर्विहसिताननपङ्कजाभि-
रिन्दोः सिताभ्रशकलस्य च को विशेषः।।"

And also —

It is very surprising that in spite of placing your feet on two different mountains the seams (connecting your joints) have not burst.

An adaptation of apparently unconnected words/lines is also appropriation. As in —

> The silvery moon in the sky remains of consequence only so long as the Sun does not come up and spread its shiny web of rays. With the dawn of the shining sun there remains no difference between the moon and a bright piece of cloud.

And also —

> The silvery sheen of moonshine is of consequence only till the fair and beautiful maidens do not exhibit laughter. When the laugher will spread across their beautiful lotus faces then there will remain no difference between the moon and a bright piece of cloud.[9]

पाद एवान्यथात्वकरणं न स्वीकरणं पादापहरणं वा। यथा —

> **"अरण्ये निर्जने रात्रावन्तर्वेश्मनि साहसे।**
> **न्यासापह्नवने चैव दिव्या सम्भवति क्रिया।।"**

यथा चोत्तरार्द्धे —

> **"तन्वङ्गी यदि लभ्येत दिव्या सम्भवति क्रिया।"**

यथा वा —

> **"यस्य केशेषु जीमूता नद्यः सर्वाङ्गसन्धिषु।**
> **कुक्षौ समुद्राश्चत्वारस्तस्मै तोयात्मने नमः।।"**

When only one quarter is changed and the rest of the verse (three-quarters) is carried over in a similar fashion, it is not adaptation but appropriation.

As in —

> In the forests, in lonely places, at night, in the interiors of houses, during moments of daring and when someone hides goods it could be due to the intervention of supernatural powers.

Thus also in —

9. Here the first and the fourth line have been appropriated in the second verse from the first.

In all such opportune moments, if one gets a beautiful maiden, then it could be due to the intervention of divine powers.

Another example —

Obeisance to the lord of waters who bears clouds in his hair, rivers flow through whose limbs and whose womb has the four seas in it.

यथा चोत्तरार्द्धे —

"कुक्षौ समुद्राश्चत्वारः स सहेत स्मरानलम्।।"

भिन्नार्थानां तु पादानामेकेन पादेनान्वयनं कवित्वमेव। यथा —

"किमिह किमपि दृष्टं स्थानमस्ति श्रुतं वा
व्रजति दिनकरोऽयं तत्र नास्तं कदाचित्।
भ्रमति विहगसार्थानित्थमापृच्छमानो
रजनिविरहभीतश्चक्रवाको वराकः।।"

And also —

The one who is the lord of waters can bear the fire of passion.

When three quarters (having different meanings) that are apparently unconnected are appropriately connected with one quarter, it cannot be called an appropriation since it involves the creativity of the poet.

As in —

Petrified at the thought of separation at night the poor *cakravāka*[10] in desperation asks other birds if there be any place seen or heard of on this earth where the sun does not set.

यथा च —

"जयति सितविलोलव्यालयज्ञोपवीती
घनकपिलजटान्तर्भ्रान्तगङ्गाजलौघः।
अविदितमृगचिह्नामिन्दुलेखां दधानः
परिणतशितिकण्ठश्यामकण्ठः पिनाकी।।"

And also —

Glory to the Lord Śaṅkara, who bears on his pure and bright chest

10. Conventionally the bird who faces throes of separation with nightfall.

a sacrificial thread made of serpents, the web of whose thick matted hair has the sacred river Gaṅgā flowing through it, who bears a streak of the moon which does not have any mark of a deer (unmarked) on his head, whose blue throat has given him the epithet of Nīlakaṇṭha and who bears a trident and so is called Pinākī.

यथा च —

"कुमुदवनमपश्रि श्रीमदम्भोजखण्डं
त्यजति मुदमुलूकः प्रीतिमांश्चक्रवाकः।
उदयमहिमरश्मिर्याति शीतांशुरस्तं
हतविधिलसितानां ही विचित्रो विपाकः।।"

And also —

During early morning when forests of water lilies wither and loose their beauty, the forests of water-lotuses open out in all their glory. The owls become unhappy and try to enter their dark nests. The *cakravāka* pair becomes intoxicated with joy at the thought of union after the night long separation. The rays of the rising sun are on the ascent and the cool moon is on the descent. It is surprising that men have to bear the fruits of their own actions.

यथा च —

"किमिह किमपि दृष्टं स्थानमस्ति श्रुतं वा
घनकपिलजटान्तर्भ्रान्तिगङ्गाजलौघः।
निवसति स पिनाकी यत्र यायात्तदस्मिन्
हतविधिलसितानां ही विचित्रो विपाकः।।"

And also —

Has anyone seen or heard of the place on this earth wherein resides Lord Śaṅkara with his yellow thick matted hair in the webs of which he bears the river Ganges. I would also like to go there. It is surprising that men have to bear the fruits of their own actions.[11]

---

11. In this verse, we find that the first line has been taken from the first verse, the second from the second, the third has been added and the fourth taken from the third verse. This cannot be called appropriation. Rājaśekhara's stand here seems to be peculiar as there is observed blatant borrowing here from three different sources unless combining sources in a new whole is considered a kind of creativity.

पादोनवत्कतिपयपदप्रयोगोऽपि। यथा —

> "या व्यापारवती रसान् रसयितुं काचित्कवीनां नवा
> दृष्टिर्या परिनिष्ठितार्थविषयोन्मेषा च वैपश्चिती।
> ते द्वे अप्यवलम्ब्य विश्वमनिशं निर्वर्णयन्तो वयं
> श्रान्ता नैव च लब्धमब्धिशयन त्वद्भक्तितुल्यं सुखम्।।"

Taking a few words from a line and using them may be neither appropriation nor acceptance.

As in —

> The world may be described from two points of view. The first from the point of view of new aesthetic poets who use *abhidhā*, *lakṣaṇā* and *vyañjanā*. On the other hand we have the philosophical scholars who justify the theory of meaning on the basis of reality. O God! We are tired of these worldly descriptions from both view-points, the happiness we get in your devotion is inaccessible elsewhere.

यथा च चतुर्थपादे —

> "श्रान्ता नैव च लब्धमुत्पलदृशां प्रेम्णः समानं सुखम्।।"

पादैकदेशग्रहणमपि पदैकदेशोपलक्षणपरम्। यथा —

> "असकलहसितत्वात्क्षालितानीव कान्त्या
> मुकुलितनयनत्वाद्व्यक्तकर्णोत्पलानि।
> पिबति मधुसुगन्धीन्याननानि प्रियाणां
> त्वयि विनिहितभारः कुन्तलानामधीशः।।"

Another example —

> We are tired of these worldly descriptions from both view-points but the happiness obtained from the love of lotus-eyed maidens is inaccessible elsewhere.

To change a part of a word cannot be called appropriation or acceptance.

As in —

> Someone said to the Minister of Kuntala.[12] O, Minister! The king

12. Name of a place. Cf. Appendix II.

of Kuntala has left the entire burden of the kingdom on your shoulders and is busy in partaking of the pleasures of honey sweet faces of the beloved maidens. There are half smiles on the faces of these maidens and the eyes are half-open which make the lotuses in their ears clearly visible.

यथा चोत्तरार्धे —

"पिबतु मधुसुगन्धीन्याननानि प्रियाणां
मयि विनिहितभारः कुन्तलानामधीशः।।"

वाक्यस्यान्यथाव्याख्यानमपि न स्वीकरणं हरणं वा। यथा —

"सुभ्रु त्वं कुपितेत्यपास्तमशनं त्यक्ता कथा योषितां
दूरादेव मयोज्झिताः सुरभयः स्रग्दामधूषादयः।
कोपं रागिणि मुञ्च मय्यवनते दृष्टे प्रसीदाधुना
सद्यस्त्वद्विरहाद्भवन्ति दयिते सर्वा ममान्धा दिशः।।"

एतच्च कान्ताप्रसादनपरं वाक्यं कुपितदृष्टिपरतया व्याख्यातं न स्वीकृतं हृतं वा।

यत्तु परकीयं स्वीयमिति प्रोक्तानामन्यतमेन कारणेन विलपन्ति, तत्र केवलं हरणम्, अपि तु दोषोदाहरणम्। मुक्तकप्रबन्धविषयं तत्।

मूल्यक्रयोऽपि हरणमेव। वरमप्राप्तिर्यशसो न पुनर्दुर्यशः।

(The Minister answers) Kuntaleśvara (king of Kuntala); Leave the burden of the entire kingdom on my shoulders and indulge yourself in partaking of the pleasures of beloved maidens.[13]

Similarly taking an entire line from a verse but using it in a different context is also neither appropriation nor acceptance.

(O maiden!) with the beautiful brows. You are angry with me. So I have left food and I no longer talk of other women. I have stopped using perfumed garlands, flowers, incense, perfumes, etc. Don't be angry with me. You should be happy with your lover at your feet. All directions are dark and empty for me in your separation.[14]

---

13. This is neither a case of appropriation nor acceptance. Here from the third line of the first verse is taken a word *pibatu* instead of *pibati* and instead of *tvayi* from the fourth line there is the use of *asmad* in *mayi*.

14. This, verse is to appease the angry beloved. Yet if the word *dṛṣṭe* is taken as an →

If a later poet interprets a verse of a former poet in an altogether different way or claims on the basis of one or the other circumstance that a particular stanza or a poem is his own then it is not a case of mere appropriation but a fault of the highest order. This applies to both a *muktaka* (a detatched stanza, the meaning of which is complete in itself) and a *prabandha* (a literary work).

If one gets work written for money and passes it off as his own, that too is nothing but appropriation. It is better if one fails to win fame than to incur ignominy.

'तद्वदुक्तिहरणम्' इति आचार्याः।

यथा —

"ऊरुद्वन्द्वं सरसकदलीकाण्डसब्रह्मचारि।"

यथा च —

"ऊरुद्वयं कदलकन्दलयोः सदंशं
श्रोणिः शिलाफलकसोदरसन्निवेशा।
वक्षः स्तनद्वितयताडितकुम्भशोभं
सब्रह्मचारि शशिनश्च मुखं मृगाक्ष्याः।।"

*Ācārya*s say, 'Borrowing of *ukti*s (epigrammatic expressions) is also appropriation.'

As in —

The pair of thighs (of a damsel) resemble the juicy trunks of a plantain tree.

And also —

The thighs of that doe-eyed (maiden) resemble the juicy trunks of a plantain tree, her hips are like the smooth stone-slab, her chest with expansive breasts resembles the water pitchers and her face is like the moon.

"उक्तयो ह्यर्थान्तरसङ्क्रान्ता न प्रत्यभिज्ञायन्ते, स्वदन्ते च; तदर्थास्तु हरणादपि हरणं स्युः" इति यायावरीयः।

→ address then this verse becomes an appeasement of an angry glance and the address *subhru* will become an adjective of the glance.

"नास्त्यचौरः कविजनो नास्त्यचौरा वणिग्जनः।
स नन्दति विना वाच्यं यो जानाति निगूहितुम्।।"

"उत्पादकः कविः कश्चित्कश्चिच्च परिवर्त्तकः।
आच्छादकस्तथा चान्यस्तथा संवर्गकोऽपरः।।"

"शब्दार्थोक्तिषु यः पश्येदिह किञ्चन नूतनम्।
उल्लिखेत्किञ्चन प्राच्यं मान्यतां स महाकविः।।"

Yāyāvarīya (Rājaśekhara) says that —

Expressions (of other poets) which convey a different sense are not treated as borrowings but are to be appreciated. If they are, on the contrary, used in the same sense, they deserve to be condemned as the worst kind of appropriation.

There is no poet who is not a thief, no merchant who does not cheat but the one who knows how to hidc his theft flourishes.

One poet is a *creator* (*utpādaka* — creative), another an *adapter* (*parivartaka* — given to emendation), still others are *concealers* (*ācchādaka* — those who can conceal his improvisation) and then the *collectors* (*saṁvargaka* — one who utilises more than one source).

The one who comprehends something novel in a word, phrase or an idea and has the innate faculty (*pratibhā*) to use the suggestive power of words to create can be called a poet of *eminence* (*mahākavi* — with flashes of originality).

।। इति राजशेखरकृतौ काव्यमीमांसायां कविरहस्ये प्रथमेऽधिकरणे एकादशोऽध्यायः शब्दहरणानि।।

12

शब्दार्थहरणेषु कविप्रभेदाः प्रतिबिम्बकल्पविकल्पस्य च समीक्षा

Arthaharaṇam

(Appropriation of Meanings)

'पुराणकविक्षुण्णे वर्त्मनि दुरापमस्पृष्टं वस्तु, ततश्च तदेव संस्कर्त्तु प्रयतेत' इति आचार्याः।

'न' इति वाक्पतिराजः।

"आसंसारमुदारैः कविभिः प्रतिदिनगृहीतसारोऽपि।
अद्याऽप्यभिन्नमुद्रो विभाति वाचां परिस्यन्दः।।"

Ācāryas say that,

> In the poet's province there is hardly anything left untouched by ancient poets. A modern poet should, therefore endeavour to improve on what the ancients have said.

Vākpatirāja disagrees with this,

> This source of speech is endless and everlasting. There have been innumerable poetic geniuses who have dipped into its vast reservoir since the beginning of creation but this endless source continues to flow on endlessly.

तत्प्रतिभासाय च परप्रबन्धेष्ववदधीत।

'तदवगाहने हि तदेकयोनयोऽर्थाः पृथक्पृथक् प्रथन्ते' इत्येके।

'तत्रत्यानामर्थानां छायया परिवृत्तिः फलम्' इत्यपरे।

'महात्मनां हि संवादिन्यो बुद्धय एकमेवार्थमुपस्थापयन्ति, तत्परित्यागाय तानाद्रियेत' इति च केचित्।

'न' इति यायावरीयः। सारस्वतं चक्षुरवाङ्मनसगोचरेण प्रणिधानेन दृष्टमदृष्टं चार्थजातं स्वयं विभजति।

> To obtain this rare capacity one should endeavour a close study of the ancient and modern poets.

Some say that

> with a critical study of the compositions of different poets one learns to express similar thoughts in different forms.

Others say,

> with a close critical observation of compositions by other poets one can get ideas for one's own poetic-compositions.

Still others say —

> Eminent poets have similarities of poetic genius and temper and present identical thoughts. Thus to avoid such resemblances and gain new insights a poet should study the words of other poets also.

Yāyāvarīya (Rājeśekhara) does not agree with all these opinions. According to him one possessed of literary eye intuitively knows the division between the meaningful and meaningless.

तदाहुः —

सुप्तस्यापि महाकवेः शब्दार्थौ सरस्वती दर्शयति तदितरस्य तत्र जाग्रतोऽप्यन्धं चक्षुः। अन्यदृष्टचरे ह्यर्थे महाकवयो जात्यन्धास्तद्विपरीते तु दिव्यदृशः। न तत् त्र्यक्षः सहस्राक्षो वा यच्चर्मचक्षुषोऽपि कवयः पश्यन्ति। मतिदर्पणे कवीनां विश्वं प्रतिफलति। कथं नु वयं दृश्यामह इति महात्मनामहंपूर्विकयैव शब्दार्थाः पुरो धावन्ति। यत्सिद्धप्रणिधाना योगिनः पश्यन्ति, तत्र वाचा विचरन्ति कवय इत्यनन्ताम हाकविषु सूक्तयः।

'समस्तमस्ति' इति यायावरीयः। किन्तु त्रिपथमर्थमध्यगीष्महि यदुतान्ययोनि-र्निह्नुतयोनिरयोनिश्च।

तत्रान्ययोनिर्द्विधा प्रतिबिम्बकल्प आलेख्यप्रख्यश्च। निह्नुतयोनिरपि द्विधा तुल्यदेहितुल्यः

परपुरप्रवेशसदृशश्च। अयोनिः पुनरेक एव। तत्र —

Sarasvatī (goddess of wisdom and learning) makes words and senses flash on the mind of great poets even in their sleep. An inferior poet remains blind to them even when wide awake. Great poets may be blind to the merits and demerits of other poets but as regards novel and original ideas which have been unobserved by their predecessors, they have a divine vision. What poets can see with their nakea eye even the three-eyed god Śiva or the thousand-eyed Indra cannot see. In the mirror of the poet's intellect, the whole universe is, as it were reflected. Words and their senses, of their own accord and with eagerness accumulate near good poets. Poets' speech easily sees what *yogins*, who have mastered the power of concentration can see.

Yāyāvarīya (Rājaśekhara) says that 'all this is true'. *Artha* (idea or matter) is threefold. The first is *anyayoni* (its source is in the work of other poets). The second is *nihynutyoni* (its source is not definite) and the third is *ayoni* (its source is the poet himself).

Further *anyayoni*[1] *artha* is of two kinds — (1) *pratibimbakalpa* and (2) *ālekhyaprakhya*. *Nihynutyoni artha* is also of two kinds — (1) *tulyadehitulya* and (2) *parapurapraveśapratimā* (*sadṛśa*). *Ayoni artha* is only of one kind.

अर्थः स एव सर्वो वाक्यान्तरविरचनापरं यत्र।
तदपरमार्थविभेदं काव्यं प्रतिबिम्बकल्पं स्यात्।।

यथा —

"ते पान्तु वः पशुपतेरलिनीलभासः
कण्ठप्रदेशघटिताः फणिनः स्फुरन्तः।
चन्द्रामृताम्बुकणसेकसुखप्ररूढै-
र्यैरङ्कुरैरिव विराजति कालकूटः।।"

1.

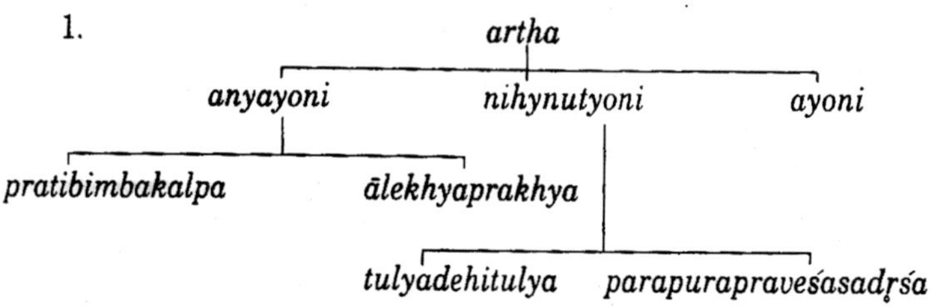

The composition in which the sense is almost the same (as in an earlier poem) but the expressions used are different, is called *pratibimbakalpa kāvya*.

Thus —

May the black serpents coiled around the neck of Lord Paśupatī Śaṅkara (Śiva) like bumble bees, which appear to come out of the blue throat and are fed upon the nectar like rays of the moon and sprout like small seeds of poison (churned out of the ocean and drunk by Śiva) bless and protect you.

यथा च —

"जयन्ति नीलकण्ठस्य नीलाः कण्ठे महाहयः।
गलद्गङ्गाम्बुसंसिक्तकालकूटाङ्कुरा इव।।

कियताऽपि यत्र संस्कारकर्मणा वस्तु भिन्नवद्भाति।
तत्कथितमर्थचतुरैरालेख्यप्रख्यमिति काव्यम्।।

And also —

Glory to the dark serpents hanging from the vast matted locks of Lord Paśupati (Śiva) which appear to sprout like seeds of poison due to continuously being fed by drops of water from the river Gaṅgā.[2]

When some polish (or garnishing) is given to the old idea with the result that the subject appears as though it is a different one, then clever people call it *ālekhyaprakhya*.

तत्रैवार्थे यथा —

"जयन्ति धवलव्यालाः शम्भोर्जूटावलम्बिनः।
गलद्गङ्गाम्बुसंसिक्तचन्द्रकन्दाङ्कुरा इव।।"

विषयस्य यत्र भेदेऽप्यभेदबुद्धिर्नितान्तसादृश्यात्।
तत्तुल्यदेहितुल्यं काव्यं बध्नन्ति सुधियोऽपि।।

Thus —

Glory to the white serpents present in the matted locks of the lord

2. Here the second verse is a *pratibiṁbakalpa* of the first one, where the sense is the same entirely but the expressions used are different.

(Śiva) which appear moon like white buds of *kunda* fed with the continuous flow of the Gaṅgā.[3]

When despite difference of matter identity is apprehended through extreme resemblance, that poem due to *'corporeal equivalence'* is (composed by clever men) an instance of *tulyadehitulya*.[4]

यथा —

"अवीनादौ कृत्वा भवति तुरगो यावदवधिः
पशुर्धन्यस्तावत्प्रतिवसति यो जीवति सुखम्।
अमीषां निर्माणं किमपि तदभूद्दग्धकरिणां
वनं वा क्षोणीभृद्भुवनमथवा येन शरणम्।।"

Thus —

The house, which gives refuge to other animals (goats and sheep, etc.) and lives a contented life is worthy. And these elephants are a burden because they can only stay in a forest or the stables of a palace.

अत्रार्थे —

"प्रतिगृहमुपलानामेक एव प्रकारो
मुहुरुपकरणत्वादर्घिताः पूजिताश्च।
स्फुरति हतमणीनां किन्तु तद्धाम येन
क्षितिपतिभवने वा स्वाकरे वा निवासः।।"

मूलैक्यं यत्र भवेत्परिकरबन्धस्तु दूरतोऽनेकः।
तत्परपुरप्रवेशप्रतिमं काव्यं सुकविभाव्यम्।।

The simple stones found in every house and being of frequent use are respected and worshipped but the bright lustre of the jewel resides either in a palace or in a mine.[5]

3. Here in the verse taken to represent *pratibiṁbakalpa* variety there have been made slight variations in the details of serpents (instead of comparing it to poison, it has been compared to *kunda*) and this is called *ālekhyaprakhya*.

4. This is the third way to borrow or imitate and consists in having different subjects or senses expressed in a similar phraseology or word-construction.

5. In the two examples given above the ideas or objects of description differ but the method of description is similar for example the ordinary use of horses and simple stones and the extraordinary use of elephants and rubies has been described in a similar fashion.

Where there is substantial identity, but the manner of presentation is entirely different it is called *parapurapraveśasadṛśa*. Even excellent poets adopt this mode (of appropriation).

यथा —

"यस्यारातिनितम्बिनीभिरभितो वीक्ष्याम्बरं प्रावृषि
स्फूर्जद्गर्जितनिर्जिताम्बुधिरवस्फाराभ्रवृन्दाकुलम्।
उत्सृष्टप्रसभाभिषेणनभयस्पष्टप्रमोदाश्रुभिः
किञ्चित्कुञ्चितलोचनाभिरसकृद् घ्राताः कदम्बानिलाः।।"

Thus —

The wives of the enemies of a certain king (with the advent of rainy season and) on witnessing the thick rain clouds filled sky thundering over the roar of the sea were thereby relieved of the fear of their husbands' leaving for battle, wept with tears of joy and screwing up their eyes inhaled the *kadamba*-blossom scented breeze.

अत्रार्थे —

"आच्छिद्य प्रियतः कदम्बकुसुमं यस्यारिदारैर्नवं
यात्राभङ्गविधायिनो जलमुचां कालस्य चिह्नं महत्।
हृष्यद्भिः परिचुम्बितं नयनयोर्न्यस्तं हृदि स्थापितं
सीमन्ते निहितं कथञ्चन ततः कर्णावतंसीकृतम्।।"

The wives of his foes made their husbands pluck the *kadamba* blossoms which signify the advent of rainy season due to which the procession to the battle has stopped. Overwhelmed with joy (the wives) kissed it (the *kadamba* blossoms), placed it on the eyes, laid it on the heart and then made it into an ear-ornament.[6]

तदेतच्चतुष्टयनिबन्धनाश्च कवीनां द्वात्रिंशद्धरणोपायाः। अमीषां चार्थानामन्वर्था अयस्कान्तवच्चत्वारः कवयः, पञ्चमश्चादृष्टचरार्थदर्शी। तदाहुः —

6. Thus the poets of these two different verses have based their poetic idea on the same principle that is, kings do not undertake war-campaigns during the rainy season — and this has been described as an occasion of unprecedented joy for the wives of the enemies of a certain king. In these two cases the manner of presentation is entirely different because the second verse is superior in excellence to the first.

In this way on the basis of these four kinds of appropriation of meanings, poets can use thirty two different means of appropriation. In accordance with the above four there are four kinds of poets and the fifth is called *cintāmaṇi* or the one who is entirely original.

"भ्रामकश्चुम्बकः किञ्च कर्षको द्रावकश्च सः।
स कविर्लौकिकोऽन्यस्तु चिन्तामणिरलौकिकः।।
तन्वानोऽनन्यदृष्टत्वं पुराणस्यापि वस्तुनः।
योऽप्रसिद्ध्यादिभिर्भ्राम्यत्यसौ स्याद्भ्रामकः कविः।।
यश्चुम्बति परस्यार्थं वाक्येन स्वेन हारिणा।
स्तोकार्पितनवच्छायं चुम्बकः स कविर्मतः।।
परवाक्यार्थमाकृष्य यः स्ववाचि निवेशयेत्।
समुल्लेखेन केनापि स स्मृतः कर्षकः कविः।।
अप्रत्यभिज्ञेयतया स्ववाक्ये नवतां नयेत्।
यो द्रावयित्वा मूलार्थं द्रावकः स भवेत्कविः।।
चिन्तासमं यस्य रसैकसूतिरुदेति चित्राकृतिरर्थसार्थः।
अदृष्टपूर्वो निपुणैः पुराणैः कविः स चिन्तामणिरद्वितीयः।।"

Laukika (worldly or terrestrial) poets are of four kinds (1) *bhrāmaka*, (2) *cuṁbaka*, (3) *karṣaka*, and (4) *drāvaka*. The fifth poet is an *alaukika* (other-worldly) poet who is called *cintāmaṇi*.

The poet who can give a new twist even to the old familiar material and prove it as his own composition, thereby creating confusion in the minds of the people is called a *bhrāmaka*.

The poet who softly retouches the old material but adds his own beauty is called a *cuṁbaka*.

The poet who uses his own originality and puts old ideas into a novel framework is called a *karṣaka*.

The poet who can transform the original so much that it cannot be recognised at all in his work is called a *drāvaka*.

The poet whose compositions are imbued with imagination and originality of a kind never before exhibited is a poet-*par-excellence* and is called a *cintāmaṇi*.

तस्य चायोनिरर्थः। स च त्रिधा लौकिकालौकिकभेदेन, तयोर्मिश्रत्वेन च। तत्र लौकिकः —

"मा कोशकारलतिके वह वर्णगर्वं
किं डम्बरेण चणिके तव कौसुमेन।
पुण्ड्रेक्षुयष्टिरियमेकतरा चकास्तु
या स्यन्दते रसमृतेऽपि हि यन्त्रयोगात्।।"

The matter of the *cintāmaṇi* poet is *ayoni* that is, it is entirely original. It is three-fold — *laukika*, *alaukika* and *miśra*.

Example of *laukika* (meaning) —

O, Sugarcane! Don't be proud of your shining colour. On shrubs of chick-pea, don't be proud of your flowers. This thick sugarcane is better than you which lets its juice like nectar be extracted even without the use of any implement.

अलौकिकः —

"देवी पुत्रमसूत नृत्यत गणाः किं तिष्ठतेत्युद्भुजे
हर्षाद्भृङ्गिरिटावुदाहृतगिरा चामुण्डयालिङ्गिते।
पायाद्वो जितदेवदुन्दुभिघनध्वानप्रवृत्तिस्तयो-
रन्योन्याङ्कनिपातजर्जरजरत्स्थूलास्थिजन्मा रवः।।"

Alaukika artha (meaning) —

On the birth of Kārttikeya, Bhṛṅgriti[7] was seen coming from one side happily exclaiming to the people, "Why are you sitting?" Pārvatī has given birth to a son. Sing and dance." Cāmuṇḍā[8] was coming from the other end. They both met and started dancing together. The garlands of dry bones around their necks made terrible sounds which drowned the deafening sound of the drums of gods.

मिश्रः —

"स्थिते कुक्षेरन्तर्मुरजयिनि निःश्वासमरुतो

7. Bhṛṅgiriti is the name of an attendant of Śiva.

8. Cāmuṇḍā is the terrific form of Durgā which drowned the deafening sounds of the drums of the gods. In this example the matter relates to gods and goddesses and thus is *alaukika* but it is also original.

जनन्यास्तन्नाभीसरसिजपरागोत्करमुचः।
निपीताः सानन्दं रचितफणचक्रेण हलिना
समन्तादस्यासुः प्रतिदिवसमेनांसि भवतः।।"

Miśra —

When God Kr̥ṣṇa was in his mother's (Devakī's) womb, the exhaled air of Devakī contained the aroma of Lord Viṣṇu (incarnate as Kr̥ṣṇa) residing in her womb. This aromatic air was inhaled by Baladeva (an incarnation of Śeṣa-nāga, elder brother of Lord Kr̥ṣṇa) by spreading out his hoods. May this air protect you from all evils.[9]

तेषां च चतुर्णामर्थानाम् —

चत्वार एते कथिता मयैव
येऽर्था कवीनां हरणोपदेशे।
प्रत्येकमष्टत्ववशाद्भवन्ति
द्वात्रिंशता तेऽनुगताः प्रभेदैः।।

Anyayoni has two types of appropriation (*pratibimbakalpa* and *ālekhyaprakhya*). *Nihynutayoni* also has two types of imitation under it (*tulyadehitulya* and *parapurapraveśasadr̥śa*). These four kinds of imitation are further divisible into eight kinds each and thus altogether there are thirtytwo divisions.

तत्र प्रतिबिम्बकल्पविकल्पाः।

स एवार्थः पौर्वापर्यविपर्यासाद् व्यस्तकः।

यथा —

"दृष्ट्वान्येभं छेदमुत्पाद्य रज्ज्वा
यन्तुर्वाचं मन्यमानस्तृणाय।
गच्छन्दध्रे नागराजः करिण्या
प्रेम्णा तुल्यं बन्धनं नास्ति जन्तोः।।"

अत्रार्थे —

"निर्विवेकमनसोऽपि हि जन्तोः

9. This verse has a depiction of both earthly and divine (celestial) characters and thus is a mixture of *laukika* and *alaukika* and so it is called *miśra*.

प्रेमबन्धनमाशृङ्खलदाम।
यत्प्रति प्रतिगजं गजराजः
प्रस्थितश्चिरमधारि करिण्या।।"

Out of these *pratibimbakalpa* has eight divisions.

The first is *vyastaka* (when the *bhāva* of the source is retained) it is signified by changing the former meaning into the latter and the latter into former.

Thus —

When the elephant saw his arch-rivals he broke loose from the ropes binding him, paid no heed to the words of the mahout and rushed to attack him but he was stopped by the she-elephant. It is true that for a living (being) there is no bond stronger than love.

Another example with the same meaning —

It is true that even for a non-discriminative living thing (an animal) love remains the strongest bond because even when attacking another elephant, the Gajarāja (elephant) was stopped for a long time by a she-elephant after engaging him in love.[10]

बृहतोऽर्थस्यार्द्धप्रणयनं खण्डम्।

यथा —

"पुरा पाण्डुप्रायं तदनु कपिशिम्ना कृतपदं
ततः पाकोद्रेकादरुणगुणसंवर्गितवपुः।
शनैः शोपारम्भे स्थपुटनिजविष्कम्भविषमं
वने वीतामोदं बदरमरसत्वं कलयति।।"

In a poetic composition if the vast meaning is broken into parts and partially recreated, it is called *khaṇḍam*.

Thus —

On ripening, the berry fruit, at first has a yellow colour, then it becomes light brown and on further ripening, it acquires a

10. The second verse is an example of *vyastaka* because here the sequence of ideas has interchanged places with reference to the first verse.

reddish tinge. On drying it shrivels up. Thus, slowly it loses colour, shape, dries up and falls in the forest.

अत्रार्थे —

"पाकक्रियापरिचयप्रगुणीकृतेन
संवर्गितारुणगुणं वपुषा निजेन।
आपादितस्थपुटसंस्थितिशोषपोषा-
देतद्वने विरसतां बदरं बिभर्त्ति।।"

Another example with the same meaning —

When the berry fruit ripens it swells into a blackish red colour. When it shrivels up it loses colour and falls into the forest.[11]

संक्षिप्तार्थविस्तरेण तैलविन्दुः।

यथा —

"यस्य तन्त्रभराक्रान्त्या पातालतलगामिनी।
महावराहदंष्ट्राया भूयः सस्मार मेदिनी।।"

अत्रार्थे —

"यत्तन्त्राक्रान्तिमज्जत्पृथुलमणिशिलाशल्यवेल्लत्फणान्ते
क्लान्ते पत्यावहीनां चलदचलमहास्तम्भसम्भारसीमा।।
सस्मार स्फारचन्द्रद्युति पुनरवनिस्तद्धिरण्याक्षवक्षः-
स्थूलास्थिश्रेणिशाणानिकषणसितमप्याशु दंष्ट्राग्रमुग्रम्।।"

To describe something which has been given in short in a verse in detail in one's own composition is called *telbindu*.

Thus —

That earth which was going under *pātāla* due to the pressure of the king's army brought the tusks of Mahāvarāha[12] to mind (the Primordial Boar who bore the earth on its tusks).

Another example with the same meaning —

---

11. In the first verse the entire process of ripening of a fruit of a berry has been described but in the second verse only a part of it has been described.

12. Mahāvarāha is an epithet of Viṣṇu in his third or boar incarnation. See Bhide, *op. cit.*, p. 866.

The Śeṣa-nāgas were put to grief due to the pain in the tips of their hoods induced by the pointed nail-like rubies pressing down due to the burden of the king's army. The earth afraid of losing the dignity of bearing the mammoth pillar like mountains also remembered the tusks of the Mahāvarāha (Primordial Boar) which due to being rubbed on the broad chest of Hiraṇyākṣa[13] became sharp, bright and with a brilliant shine like the moon.[14]

अन्यतमभाषानिबद्धं भाषान्तरेण परिवर्त्यत इति नटनेपथ्यम्।

यथा —

"नेच्छइ पासासंकी काओ दिण्णं पि पहिअघरिणीए।
ओहत्तकरयलोग्गलियवलयमज्झट्ठिअं पिण्डं।"

अत्रार्थे —

"दत्तं पिण्डं नयनसलिलक्षालनाधौतगण्डं
द्वारोपान्ते कथमपि तया सङ्गमाशानुबन्धात्।
वक्रग्रीवश्चलनतशिराः पार्श्वसञ्चारिचक्षुः
पाशाशङ्की गलितवलयं नैनमश्नाति काकः।।"

Translating the essence of a poem from one language to another is called *naṭnepathyam*.

Thus —

The traveller's bride gives a morsel to the crow. While thus giving when her hand is bent low, the bracelet from her hand also falls off which to the crow's eye appears to be a trap. Thus in spite of repeated efforts the crow does not come near it.

Another example with the same meaning —

With the hope of the husband's arrival and her face awash with tears the languishing maiden waits to provide a morsel to the crow. The crow, with a bent neck and dancing eyes goes to and fro but on also seeing the round bracelet which has fallen off from the

---

13. Hiraṇyākṣa is the name of a celebrated demon (*rākṣasa*), twin brother of Hiraṇyakaśipu. See Bhide, *op. cit*, p. 1195.

14. In the second verse there is greater detail in the description, thus it is an instance of *telbindu*.

maiden's wrist and assuming it to be a trap, does not go near the morsel.[15]

छन्दसा परिवृत्तिश्छन्दोविनिमयः।

यथा —

"कान्ते तल्पमुपागते विगलिता नीवी स्वयं बन्धनात्
तद्वासः श्लथमेखलागुणधृतं किञ्चिन्नितम्बे स्थितम्।
एतावत्सखि वेद्मि केवलमहं तस्याङ्गसङ्गे पुनः
कोऽसौ कास्मि रतं नु किं कथमपि स्वल्पापि मे न स्मृतिः।।"

If the same meaning or essence of a verse is expressed in a different metre, it is called *chandovinimayaḥ*.

Thus —

(O, friend!) As soon as I reached my lover's bed the knot tying my lower garment opened by itself and a part of the cloth which remained in the girdle was left on the hips. I remember this, but after that with the touch of his body, I forgot my own self in the ecstasy of his love making.

अत्रार्थे —

"धन्यास्तु याः कथयथ प्रियसङ्गमेऽपि
विश्रब्धचाटुकशतानि रतान्तरेषु।
नीवीं प्रति प्रणिहितश्च करः प्रियेण
सख्यः शपामि यदि किञ्चिदपि स्मरामि।।"

Another example with the same meaning —

(O, friends!) You are indeed blessed that in spite of the beloved's proximity, you can utter and hear love sayings in between love making. But I can vow that once my lover opens my knotted garment, I forget the entire world.[16]

---

15. The first verse is in Prākṛta while the second one is in Sanskrit. Thus it is an example of Naṭnepathyam.

16. The first verse has been said in the *Śārdūla-vikrīḍita* metre while the second one is in *Vasanta-tilaka* metre.

Śārdūla-vikrīḍita (the metre with) the feet of nineteen syllables of which the first three, the sixth, eighth, the twelfth, the thirteenth, the fourteenth, the →

कारणपरावृत्त्या हेतुव्यत्ययः।

यथा —

"ततोऽरुणपरिस्पन्दमन्दीकृतरुचिः शशी।
दध्रे कामपरीक्षामकामिनीगण्डपाण्डुताम्।।"

अत्रार्थे —

"समं कुसुमचापेन गर्भिणीगण्डपाण्डुना।
उदयाद्रिशिरःसीम्नि निहितं पदमिन्दुना।।"

When the same meaning is expressed but due to a different reason, it is called *hetuvyaṭyayaḥ*.

Thus —

In the early morning when the sun-chariot dawns in the east, the moon loses its brilliance. At that time the moon becomes yellow like the cheeks of the love-lorn thin and languished maiden.

Another example with the same meaning —

During the evening, like the cheeks of the pregnant woman; the pale moon along with Kāmadeva placed its feet on the mountain-top[17] the rays of the moon spread all over.

दृष्टस्य वस्तुनोऽन्यत्र सङ्क्रमितिः सङ्क्रान्तकम्।

यथा —

"स्नानार्द्रार्द्रैर्विधुतकबरीबन्धलोलैरिदानीं

→ sixteenth, the seventeenth and the last are heavy (and the rest light), is called *Śārdūla-vikrīḍita*.

See Bharata-Muni's *The Nāṭyaśāstra*, Vol. 1 (chapter I-XXVII) by Manomohan Ghosh, Manisha Granthalaya Private Limited, Calcutta, 1967, rev 2nd, edn., p. 283.

Vasanta-tilaka (the metre with) the feet of fourteen syllables of which the first two, the fourth, the eighth and the eleventh and the thirteenth and the last are heavy (and the rest light) See Bharata's *Nāṭyaśāstra*, *ibid*., p. 277.

17. In the first verse, the paleness of the moon is compared to the cheeks of the languished maiden and is the cause of the moon's decline; while in the second verse the same paleness is compared to the cheeks of a pregnant maiden and is the cause of the rise of the moon. Thus the second verse is an example of *hetuvyatyayaḥ*.

श्रोणीभारः कृतपरिचयः पल्लवैः कुन्तलानाम्।
अप्येतेभ्यो नभसि पततः पङ्क्तिशो वारिबिन्दून्
स्थित्वोद्ग्रीवं कुवलयदृशां केलिहंसाः पिबन्ति।।"

The transference of a thing mentioned in one verse into another with reference to some other context is called *saṁkrāntakam*.

Thus —

> After the maidens' bath their wet and loose (with the opening of plaits) hair has fallen down to their waist and the swans belonging to these maidens raise their necks and drink the droplets falling from their wet hair.

अत्रार्थे —

"सद्यःस्नातजपत्तपोधनजटाप्रान्तस्रुताः प्रोन्मुखैः
पीयन्तेऽम्बुकणाः कुरङ्गशिशुभिस्तृष्णाव्यथाविक्लवैः।
एतां प्रेमभरालसां च सहसा शुष्यन्मुखीमाकुलः
श्लिष्यन् रक्षति पक्षसम्पुटकृतच्छायः शकुन्तः प्रियाम्।।"

Another example with the same meaning —

> The intensely thirsty young deers with raised mouths drink the water-drops falling from the tips of the matted locks of recently bathed and meditating sages and the thirsty bird looking at the love-sick and thirst-parched face of his beloved mate hides her in the shadowy embrace of its wings thus protecting it from the heat.[18]

उभयवाक्यार्थोपादानं सम्पुटः।

यथा —

"विन्ध्यस्याद्रेः परिसरनदी नर्मदा सुभ्रु सैषा
यादोभर्त्तुः प्रथमगृहिणीं यां विदुः पश्चिमस्य।
यस्यामन्तः स्फुरितशफरत्रासहासाकुलाक्षी
स्वैरं स्वैरं कथमपि मया तीरमुत्तारितासि।।"

When the essence of two different verses is combined in a concise manner together in one verse, it is called *samputaḥ*.

---

18. In the second verse, the context has been changed, so it is an example of *saṅkrāntakam*.

Thus —

(O maiden with beautiful brows!) This is the Narmadā river which flows at the base of the Vindhyā mountain and which people know as the wife of the western ocean (Arabian ocean) and the same one in which the touch of jumping fishes induced fear and laughter in you and caused you to close your eyes when I slowly helped you to cross the river.

यथा च —

"नाभीगुहाबिलविशच्चलवीचिजात-
मञ्जुध्वनिश्रुतिकणत्कलकुक्कुभानि।
रेवाजलान्यविरलं ग्रहिलीक्रियन्ते
लाटाङ्गनाभिरपराह्णनिमज्जनेषु।।"

And also —

The maidens of Lāṭa-deśa, during their post-midday bath and on hearing the sound of forest peacocks (which is) induced by the sweet sound of the dashing waves of the river Narmadā, dirty these waters.

अत्रार्थे —

"यद्वग्र्याभिर्जगाहे गुरुशकुलकुलास्फालनत्रासहास-
व्यस्तोरुस्तम्भिकाभिर्दिशि दिशि सरितां दिग्जयप्रक्रमेषु।
अम्भो गम्भीरनाभीकुहरकवलनोन्मुक्तिपर्यायलोल-
त्कल्लोलाबद्धमुग्धध्वनिचकितरणत्कुक्कुभं कामिनीभिः।।"

सोऽयं कवेरकवित्वदायी सर्वथा प्रतिबिम्बकल्पः परिहरणीयः।

यतः —

पृथक्त्वेन न गृह्णन्ति वस्तु काव्यान्तरस्थितम्।
पृथक्त्वेन न गृह्णन्ति स्ववपुः प्रतिबिम्बितम्।।

During the victory march of the king, the maidens from the army, frolicked in different water-reservoirs. During their frolicks, the big fishes jumped and touched them thereby tiring their legs due to fear and laughter and the waves dashing against the deep water-reservoirs created sweet sounds which amazed and caused the peacocks in the forests to create shrill sounds.

Pratibiṁbakalpa should be avoided at all costs as it is unpoetical.

Thus —

In poetry if the same content/meaning is found in a different poem, it is not looked upon as different just as in ordinary life the reflection of one's body in a mirror is not regarded as different from one's body.

।। इति राजशेखरकृतौ काव्यमीमांसायां कविरहस्ये प्रथमेऽधिकरणेषु शब्दार्थहरणेषु कविप्रभेदाः प्रतिबिम्बकल्पविकल्पस्य समीक्षा द्वादशोऽध्यायः।।

13

अर्थहरणेष्वालेख्यप्रख्यादिभेदाः

Arthaharaṇeṣvālekhyaprakhyādibhedaḥ

(Different kinds of Appropriation)

आलेख्यप्रख्यपरिसङ्ख्याः।

THE sub-divisions of *ālekhyaprakhya*.

सदृशसञ्चारणं समक्रमः।

यथा —

"अस्ताद्रिवेश्मनि दिशो वरुणप्रियाया-
स्तिर्यक्कथञ्चिदपयन्त्रणमास्थितायाः।
गण्डैकपार्श्वमिव कुङ्कुमपङ्कचुम्बि
बिम्बं रुचामधिपतेररुणं रराज।।"

यथा च —

"प्राग्दिशः प्रतिकलं विलसन्त्याः
कुङ्कुमारुणकपोलतलेन।
साम्यमेति कलितोदयरागः
पश्य सुन्दरि तुषारमयूखः।।"

When there is a transference of similar description to another verse, it is called *saṁkramaḥ*.

Thus —

Like the saffron pasted cheek of a love-sick maiden, sitting at an angle in the western direction in the morning, the setting moon which is part dark and part light is shining in the room.

And also —

(O maiden!) Look, the rising moon with its brilliance is like the saffron-pasted cheeks of the maiden in the western direction.[1]

अलङ्कृतमनलङ्कृत्याभिधीयत इति विभूषणमोषः।

यथा —

"कुवलयसिति मूले बालचन्द्राङ्कुराभं
तदनु खलु ततोऽग्रे पाकपीताम्रपीतम्।
अभिनवरविरोचिर्धूमधूम्रं शिखाया-
मिति विविधविकारं दिद्युते दैषमर्चिः।।"

Reproducing the same description after stripping it off of its embellishments is called *vibhuṣaṇamosāḥ*.

Thus —

The flame of the lamp was shining with brilliant colours — in the beginning it was blue like the blue-lotus then it became red like the newly risen moon, gradually it became yellow like a ripe mango, the inside of which was orange like the young sun and the top was grey like smoke.

अत्रार्थे —

"मनाङ् मूले नीलं तदनु कपिशोन्मेषमुदरे
ततः पाण्डु स्तोकं स्फुरदरुणलेखं च तदनु।
शिखायामाधूम्रं धृतविविधवर्णक्रममिति
क्षणादर्चिर्दैपं दलयति तमः पुञ्जितमपि।।"

Another example with the same meaning —

Black at the root, grey in the centre, then yellow with a red line in the centre and smoky at the top, the glowing flame of the lamp with its various colours destroys the darkness instantaneously.[2]

क्रमेणाभिहितस्यार्थस्य विपरीताभिधानं व्युत्क्रमः।

---

1. In the first verse the setting moon has been described but in the next verse it is the rising moon.
2. In the second example the similis are missing.

यथा तत्रैव —

> "श्यामं शिखाभुवि मनागरुणं ततोऽधः
> स्तोकावपाण्डुरघनं च ततोऽप्यधस्तात्।
> आपिञ्जरं तदनु तस्य तले च नील-
> मन्धं तमःपटलमर्दति दैपमर्चिः।।"

When there is an inversion of the order in which a particular thing is described, it is called *vyutkramaḥ*.

Blue at the top and red below it, followed by yellow with whitish yellow inside and black at the end, the flame of the lamp helps in destroying the dense darkness.[3]

सामान्यनिबन्धे विशेषाभिधानं विशेषोक्तिः।

यथा —

> "इत्युद्गते शशिनि पेशलकान्तदूती-
> संलापसञ्चलितलोचनमानसाभिः।
> अग्राहि मण्डनविधिर्विपरीतभूषा-
> विन्यासहासितसखीजनमङ्गनाभिः।।"

अत्रार्थे —

> "चकार काचित्सितचन्दनाङ्के
> काञ्चीकलापं स्तनभारपृष्ठे।
> प्रियं प्रति प्रेषितचित्तवृत्ति-
> र्नितम्बबिम्बे च बबन्ध हारम्।।"

When a description which is general is described in specific detail, it is called *viśeṣoktiḥ*.

Thus —

With the rising moon, the heroines in their pleasant camaraderie with the messenger of the beloved and with elated eyes and in an excited state of mind appeared dazed and in their confusion

3. In this verse, unlike the prior verses where the colours of the flame have been described from top to the bottom the order has been reversed in that the coloured flame has been described from bottom to the top.

interchanged their ornaments thereby being reduced to a laughing stock amongst other friends.

Another example with the same meaning —

> A particular heroine in her longing to meet her beloved, while adorning herself wore a waist band on the chest heavy with the weight of her white sandal pasted breasts and tied a pearl necklace on her hips.[4]

उपसर्जनस्यार्थस्य प्रधानतायामुत्तंसः।

यथा —

> "दीपयन्नथ नभः किरणौघैः
> कुङ्कुमारुणपयोधरगौरः।
> हेमकुम्भ इव पूर्वपयोधे-
> रुन्ममज्ज शनकैस्तुहिनांशुः।।"

अत्रार्थे —

> "ततस्तमः श्यामलपट्टकञ्चुकं
> विपाटयत्किञ्चिददृश्यतान्तरा।
> निशातरुण्याः स्थितशेषकुङ्कुम-
> स्तनाभिरामं शकलं कलावतः।।"

Adopting the secondary meaning as the main or principal meaning is called *uttaṁśaḥ*.

> After the setting of the sun, the spreading rays of the moonlight brighten up the sky, the shining brilliant moon, which appears like the saffron pasted breasts and the golden earthen pot coming out of the western sea, is rising slowly.

Another example with the same meaning —

> With approaching nightfall the night like a beautiful maiden and the darkness like the black clothes of the maiden are being shed

---

4. In the second verse, a specific instance of a particular maiden has been described unlike the first verse where only a general description of maidens has been given, thus this is an instance of *viśeṣoktiḥ*.

by a segment of the moon which appears as beautiful as the saffron pasted breasts of the night like beautiful maiden.[5]

तदेव वस्तूक्तिवशादन्यथा क्रियत इति नटनेपथ्यम्।

यथा —

"आननेन्दुशशलक्ष्म कपोले
सादरं विरचितं तिलकं यत्।
तत्प्रिये विरचितावधिभङ्गे
धौतमीक्षणजलैस्तरलाक्ष्याः।।"

अत्रार्थे —

"शोकाश्रुभिर्वासरखण्डितानां
सिक्ताः कपोलेषु विलासिनीनाम्।
कान्तेषु कालात्ययमाचरत्सु
स्वल्पायुषः पत्रलता बभूवुः।।"

Giving the same meaning a new expression by adopting a new style is called *naṭnepathyam*.

Thus —

The beloved had applied a dark spot on the cheek of the maiden but the vivacious maiden washed off the black mark with her tears when her lover did not reach her at the fixed time.

Another example with the same meaning —

The intricately designed patterns on the cheeks of the maiden appeared to be fed by the tears of the maiden thus giving them an independent existence (washing them away) when her beloved could not reach her at the fixed hour.

परिकरसाम्ये सत्यपि परिकार्यस्यान्यथात्वादेकपरिकार्यः।

"अव्याद् गजेन्द्रवदनः स इमां त्रिलोकीं
यस्योद्गतेन गगने महता करेण।
मूलावलग्नसितदन्तबिसाङ्कुरेण

5. In the first verse the moon is of importance and not its comparatives whereas in the latter verse moon has become less important. Thus it is an example of *uttaṁsaḥ*.

नालायितं तपनबिम्बसरोरुहस्य।।"

अत्रार्थे —

सरलकरदण्डनालं गजवपुषः पुष्करं विभोर्जयति।
मूलबिसकाण्डभूमौ यत्राभूदेकदंष्ट्रैव।।

When the same rhetorical figure is adopted but the object of description is different, it is called *ekaparikāryaḥ*.

> May the Lord Gaṇapati, who with a long trunk lifted to the sky giving the appearance of a stalk of a lotus like the sun mirrored in the sky and whose white tusk at the end of the trunk appears to be like the root of the lotus, protect the three worlds.

Another example with the same meaning —

> Glory to the lotus which resides at the tip of the trunk of Lord Gaṇapati, whose stalk is like the uplifted trunk and the tusk at the base is like the new root of the lotus.

विकृतेः प्रकृतिप्रापणं प्रत्यापत्तिः।

यथा —

"रविसङ्क्रान्तसौभाग्यस्तुषाराविलमण्डलः।
निःश्वासान्ध इवादर्शश्चन्द्रमा न प्रकाशते।।"

अत्रार्थे —

"तस्याः प्रतिद्वन्द्विभवाद्विषादा-
त्सद्यो विमुक्तं मुखमाबभासे।
निःश्वासबाष्पापगमे प्रपन्नः
प्रसादमात्मीयमिवात्मदर्शः।।"

When the deformed (or changed) meaning is transformed into the natural (innate) state it is called *pratyāpattiḥ*.

Thus —

> The sun with its passage from one zodiacal sign to another and the moon misted over by the dense fog was like the invisible mirror due to a collection of exhaled air on it.

Another example with the same meaning —

Free from the lamentations, Indumatī's face was aglow like a mirror to which its natural shine is restored when the moisture from the breath collected on it is wiped off.[6]

ता इमा आलेख्यप्रख्यस्य भिदाः। सोऽयमनुग्राह्यो मार्गः। आहुश्च —

"सोऽयं भणितिवैचित्र्यात्समस्तो वस्तुविस्तरः।
नटवद्वर्णिकायोगादन्यथात्वमिवार्च्छति।।"

Thus *ālekhyaprakhya* has eight sub-divisions which should be acceptable to a poet in the making.

Thus as has been said —

The entire content (of poetry) when expressed in a fresh light using varied striking expressions acquires a new look like an actor whose appearance changes with every new character that he depicts.

अथ तुल्यदेहितुल्यस्य भिदाः।

तस्यैव वस्तुनो विषयान्तरयोजनादन्यरूपापत्तिर्विषयपरिवर्त्तः।

यथा —

"ये सीमन्तितगात्रभस्मरजसो ये कुम्भकद्वेषिणो
ये लीढाः श्रवणाश्रयेण फणिना ये चन्द्रशैत्यद्रुहः।
ते कुप्यद्गिरिजाविभक्तवपुषश्चित्तव्यथासाक्षिणः
स्थाणोर्दक्षिणनासिकापुटभुवः श्वासानिलाः पान्तु वः।।"

अत्रार्थे —

"ये कीर्णक्वथितोदराब्जमधवो ये म्लापितोरःस्रजो
ये तापात्तरलेन तल्पफणिना पीतप्रतीपोज्झिताः।
ते राधास्मृतिसाक्षिणः कमलया सासूयमाकर्णिता
गाढान्तर्दवथोः प्रतप्तसरलाः श्वासा हरेः पान्तु वः।।"

Now come the sub-divisions of *tulyadehitulya*.

When the same idea expressed (by an earlier poet) with reference to

---

6. In the first example the mirror is shown to be invisible and without a shine which is the deformed meaning, whereas in the second verse the innate characteristic shine of the mirror is brought out thereby exhibiting *pratyāpattiḥ*.

one object of description is connected (by a later poet) to another object of description, it acquires a new appearance. This is called *viṣayaparivartāḥ*.

> On separation from his beloved Pārvatī, (Ardhanārīśvara) Śiva's breath is issuing out in short forceful gusts from his right nostril. May these powerful breathings protect you, which seem to be leaving behind a line of partition on his ash-swept body, which are in opposition to a form of a Yogi-exercise (*kumbhaka*), which are being inhaled by the serpents hanging from the ears, which are in opposition to the coolness of the moon and which are an indication of his heart in a state of longing (brought due to separation from Pārvatī).

Another example with the same meaning —

> The lord's heart is heavy with the burden of longing and filled with grief due to his beloved Rādhā's separation. May the hot and long breaths of Lord Kṛṣṇa protect you. This exhaled air seems to enter the lotuses in the Lord's hands and scatters the pollen in the air, it also seems to be withering the garlands around his neck though it is being inhaled by the Śeṣanāga (Lord of the Nāgas, on whom the Lord rests) yet the heat makes the Nāga exhale the air which appears to bring Rādhā's memory back to the Lord's mind and the loud sound of the breath is being heard by Lakṣmī enviously (because Kṛṣṇa longs for Rādhā).[7]

द्विरूपस्य वस्तुनोऽन्यतमरूपोपादानं द्वन्द्वविच्छित्तिः।

यथा —

> **"उत्क्लेशं केशबन्धः कुसुमशररिपोः कल्मषं वः स मुष्या-**
> **द्यत्रेन्दुं वीक्ष्य गङ्गाजलभरलुलितं बालभावादभूताम्।**
> **क्रौञ्चारातिश्च फाण्टस्फुरितशफरिकामोहलोलेक्षणश्रीः**
> **सद्यः प्रोद्यन्मृणालीग्रहणरसलसत्पुष्करश्च द्विपास्यः।।"**

अत्रार्थे —

> **"दिश्याद्धूर्जटिजूटकोटिसरिति ज्योत्स्नालवोद्भासिनी**

7. Here the subject in the first verse is the separation of Śiva-Pārvatī while in the second one it is Kṛṣṇa-Rādhā. Thus this is an instance of *viṣayaparivartāḥ*.

शाशाङ्की कलिका जलभ्रमिवशाद् द्रागदृष्टनष्ठा सुखम्।
यां चञ्चत्शफरीभ्रमेण मुकुलीकुर्वन्फणालीं मुहु-
र्मुह्यल्लक्ष्यमहिर्जिघृक्षतितमामाकुञ्चनप्राञ्चनैः।।"

When there is appropriation of only one of the two aspects of a thing described (by an earlier poet) thereby giving it one fixed direction, it is called *dvandvaviccittiḥ*.

May the matted locks of Śiva (a God of the Hindu Trinity) free you of your sins. The locks in which the digit of the moon appears to be moving with the flowing waters of the river Gaṅgā (flowing through his locks) thereby creating the delusion of a fish jumping in and out in the young and playful mind of Kārttikeya (the son of Śiva and Pārvatī) who is staring at it with rapt attention. It also appears to delude Gajānan who thinks it is a young and tender lotus root and is thus ready to devour it with his swaying trunk.

Another example with the same meaning —

May the brilliant white digit of the moon shining in the moonlit waters of the Gaṅgā river flowing through the matted locks of Lord Śiva protect you which the serpent belonging to Lord Śiva believes is a fish dancing in the water and tries to trap it by expanding and contracting its hood.[8]

पूर्वार्थानामर्थान्तरैरन्तरणं रत्नमाला।

यथा च —

"कपाले मार्जारः पय इति करांल्लेढि शशिनः
तरुच्छिद्रप्रोतान्बिसमिति करेणुः कलयति।
रतान्ते तल्पस्थान्हरति वनिताप्यंशुकमिति
प्रभामत्तश्चन्द्रो जगदिदमहो विभ्रमयति।।"

8. In the first verse the digit of the moon in the shining water of the river flowing through the matted locks of Śiva has been picturised as the fibrous stalk of a lotus and a fish but in the second verse its comparison has been restricted to a fish, thus it is an example of *dvandvavicittiḥ*.

अत्रार्थे —

"ज्योत्स्नार्चिर्दुग्धबुद्ध्या कवलितमसकृद्भाजने राजहंसैः
स्वांसे कर्पूरपांसुच्छुरणरभसतः सम्भृतं सुन्दरीभिः।
पुम्भिर्व्यस्तं स्तनान्तात्सिचयमिति रहःसम्भ्रमे वल्लभानां
लीढं द्राक्सिन्धुवारेष्वभिनवसुमनोलम्पटैः षट्पदैश्च।।"

When the ideas of an earlier poet are interwoven with new ones, the variety is called *Ratnamālā*.

Thus —

It is a matter of wonder that the moon intoxicated with moonlight is putting the world under a confusion. The cat appears to lick the white moonlight in an empty bowl under the pretext of its being full of milk. Then the she- elephant attempts to grasp the rays of moonlight which have filtered through the leaves of trees under the delusion of their being fibrous roots. After passionate love-making the beautiful maiden seems to be pulling the pale-moonlight falling across the bed around her under the confusion of its being a sheet.

Another example with the same meaning —

The swan is repeatedly using its beak to drink milk from an empty bowl filled with moonlight. The beautiful maidens are confusedly rubbing the moonlight falling on their shoulders under the impression of its being camphor. Men alone and united with their beloveds appear to be removing the moonlight from the exposed breasts of maidens under the impression of their being covered with clothes and bumble bees are attracted to the *sindhuvāra* trees in the confusion of their being new blooms of flowers.

सङ्ख्यावैषम्येणार्थप्रणयनं सङ्ख्योल्लेखः।

यथा —

"नमन्नारायणच्छायाच्छुरिताः पादयोर्नखाः।
त्वच्चन्द्रमिव सेवन्ते रुद्र रुद्रेन्दवो दश।।"

अत्रार्थे —

> "उमैकपादाम्बुरुहे स्फुरन्नखे
> कृतागसो यस्य शिरःसमागमे।
> षडात्मतामाश्रयतीव चन्द्रमाः
> स नीलकण्ठः प्रियमातनोतु वः।।"

When there is a striking difference in the numbers expressed in two different verses, it is called *saṁkhyollekhaḥ.*

> (O Rudra![9]) On Nārāyaṇa's bending down in obeisance to you, your form is reflected in his ten nails and appears to be like a collection of ten half-moons on the forehead of the other ten Rudras which seem to have collected together to pay respects to the half-moon on your forehead.

Another example with the same meaning —

> Lord Śiva who himself has bent low in Umā's (Parvatī's) lotus feet with shining nails and the moon on whose forehead appears divided into six parts. May the same Śiva bless and protect you.[10]

सममभिधायाधिकस्योपन्यासश्चूलिका। द्विधा च सा संवादिनी विसंवादिनी च।

तयोः प्रथमा यथा —

> "अङ्गणे शशिमरीचिलेपने
> सुप्तमिन्दुकरपुञ्जसन्निभम्।
> राजहंसमसमीक्ष्य कातरा
> रौति हंसवनिताश्रुगद्गदम्।।"

अत्रार्थे —

> "चन्द्रप्रभाप्रसरहासिनि सौधपृष्ठे
> दुर्लक्षपक्षतिपुटां न विवेद जायाम्।
> मूढश्रुतिर्मुखरनूपुरनिःस्वनेन
> व्याहारिणीमपि पुरो गृहराजहंसः।।"

---

9. Rudra is the name of a group of Gods (eleven in number) supposed to be lesser manifestations of Śiva. See Bhide, *op. cit.*, p. 922.
10. In the second verse the half-moon on Śiva's forehead divides itself into six parts which is in direct contrast to the description of ten half moons on the foreheads of the ten Rudras described in the first verse.

द्वितीया तत्रैवार्थे यथा —

"ज्योत्स्नाजलस्नायिनि सौधपृष्ठे
विविक्तमुक्ताफलपुञ्जगौरम्।
विवेद हंसी दयितं कथञ्चि-
च्चलत्तुलाकोटिकलैर्निनादैः।।"

Cūlikā is when the idea of an earlier poet is made more striking by adding a new dimension to it. *Cūlikā*, again is two-fold: *saṁvādinī* (in correspondence with) or *visaṁvādinī* (not in correspondence with) the original idea.

Thus an example of the first (*saṁvādinī cūlikā*) —

On not seeing the swan which looks like a cluster of moonshine gathered together and sleeping in a corner of a yard bright with the rays of moonlight, the she-swan laments and cries piteously.

Another example with the same meaning —

The swan deafened by the sound of the laughter and the pealing bells of the anklets of the beautiful maidens on the moonlit balcony did not recognise the moonlight like white wings of the she-swan coming from upfront.

An example of *visaṁvādinī cūlikā* —

The she-swan seated on the moonlight like water washed balcony, saw and recognised a white swan which looked like a cluster of white pearls and heard the melodious sound of the swan which was like the sound of anklets.[11]

निषेधस्य विधिना निबन्धो विधानापहारः।

यथा —

"कुरबक कुचाघातक्रीडारसेन वियुज्यसे
बकुलविटपिन् स्मर्त्तव्यं ते मुखासवसेचनम्।
चरणघटनाशून्यो यास्यस्यशोक सशोकता-
मिति निजपुरत्यागे यस्य द्विषां जगदुः स्त्रियः।।"

11. The meaning of this verse is in opposition to the other two verses. Thus it is an example of *visaṁvādinī cūlikā*.

अत्रार्थे —

"मुखमदिरया पादन्यासैर्विलासविलोकितै-
र्बकुलविटपी रक्ताशोकस्तथा तिलकद्रुमः।
जलनिधितटीकान्ताराणां क्रमात्ककुभां जये
झगिति गमिता यद्वर्ग्याभिर्विकासमहोत्सवम्।।

When a negative statement is presented affirmatively it is called *vidhānāpahāraḥ*.

Thus —

The beautiful women of the king's enemy on leaving the city, address the trees and plants in their garden thus — 'O, ***kurbak***! (a species of *Amarnath*). Now you will not be able to get the pleasure of being injured by our chests.''O, *bakula*![12] Our mouthfuls of wine which was used for sprinkling you will now become a thing of the memory' and 'O, *aśoka* (a kind of tree). You will become full of grief on being deprived of the kicks from our feet.

Another example with the same meaning —

Due to the series of victories of the kings' located in forests near the sea-shore, the maidens of the kings' forces used mouthfuls of wine, kicks of their feet and sidelong glances to help the *bakula*, *aśoka* and *tilaka* trees to blossom.

बहूनामर्थानामेकत्रोपसंहारो माणिक्यपुञ्जः।

यथा —

"शैलच्छलेन स्वं दीर्घं भुजमुत्तभ्य भूवधूः।
निशासख्याः करोतीव शशाङ्कतिलकं मुखे।।"

यथा च —

"फुल्लातिमुक्तकुसुमस्तबकाभिराम-
दूरोल्लसत्किरणकेसरमिन्दुसिंहम्।
दृष्ट्वोदयाद्रिशिखरस्थितमन्धकार-
दुर्वारवारणघटा व्यघटन्त सद्यः।।"

---

12. *Bakula* is a kind of tree said to put forth blossoms when sprinkled by young women with mouthfuls of wine.

यथा च —

"संविधातुमभिषेकमुदासे
मन्मथस्य लसदंशुजलौघः।
यामिनीवनितया ततचिह्नः
सोत्पलो रजतकुम्भ इवेन्दुः।।

यथा च —

"उदयति पश्य कृशोदरि दलितत्वक्क्षीरकरणिभिः किरणैः।
उदयाचलचूडामणिरेष पुरो रोहिणीरमणः।।"

When different ideas scattered in various verses are collected together in a concise manner it is called *Māṇikyapuñjaḥ*.

Thus —

The earth is like a bride with its high mountains and gives a semblance of uplifted arms for applying a *tilaka* (mark of respect on the forehead) in the form of the moon on the forehead of her friend, the night.

And also —

The moon which looks beautiful like a bunch of newly blossomed *vāsantī* flowers and shines from afar like a lion is on the rise thus reducing the darkness which is like a herd of elephants.

Thus —

The moon (to consecrate Lord Kāmadeva) appears to be like a metal-pitcher decorated with a *svastika*[13] mark by the night like beautiful maiden and filled with the water like moon-rays to consecrate the Lord Kāmadeva.

And thus —

---

13. *Svastika* is a kind of mystical mark on persons or things denoting good luck. See Bhide, *op. cit.*, p. 1182. Sanskrit lends itself to very effective evocative compounding. For example *aṁśujala* and *yāminīvanitayā*. In English this will have to be paraphrased into "*X* like *Y*" construction which disperses the effect so what we have done is to employ "*Y* like *X*" construction to capture the unity of the Sanskrit compound.

O, Kṛśodari (Pārvatī). Look at the beautiful moon brightened by the white rays of moonlight which is like the milk oozing out of the fresh bark of trees and which is on the rise like a crest-jewel.

यथा च —

"उदयति नवनीतपिण्डपाण्डुः कुमुदवनान्यवघट्टयन्कराग्रैः।
उदयगिरितटस्फुटाट्टहासो रजनिवधूमुखदर्पणः शशाङ्कः।।"

यथा च —

"प्रोषितैकेन्दुहंसेऽस्मिन्सस्नाविव तमोऽम्बुभिः।
नभस्तडागे मदनस्ताराकुमुदहासिनि।।"

अत्रार्थे —

"रजनिपुरन्ध्रिरोध्रतिलकस्तिमिरद्विपयूथकेसरी
रजतमयोऽभिषेककलशः कुसुमायुधमेदिनीपतेः।
अयमुदयाचलैकचूडामणिरभिनवदर्पणो दिश-
मुदयति गगनसरसि हंसस्य हसन्निव विभ्रमं शशी।।"

And thus —

The moon which is white like a ball of fresh butter, with rays which appear to be like a forest of flowers, like the boisterous laughter accumulating on Udayagiri[14] and shining brightly like the mirror of the night-bride, is on the rise.

And thus —

Kāmadeva (Cupid, God of Love), like the moon is devoid of a swan but blessed with flowers like stars and constellations and in the pond like sky seems to be bathing with water like darkness.

Another example with the same meaning —

The moon which is on the rise is like the *tilaka* (a red mark) on the foreheads of night maidens, like a lion for the dark elephants, a metal pitcher for the consecration of Lord Kāmadeva, the crest-jewel atop the Udayācala mountain, a brilliant mirror for the

14. Udayagiri is the eastern mountain behind which the sun and moon are supposed to rise. See Bhide, *op. cit.*, p. 265.

wives of enemies and laughing at the swan's amorous sports in the pond like sky.[15]

कन्दभूतोऽर्थः कन्दलायमानैर्विशेषैरभिधीयत इति कन्दः।

यथा —

"विशिखामुखेषु विसरति पुञ्जीभवतीव सौधशिखरेषु।
कुमुदाकरेषु विकसति शशिकलशपरिस्रुता ज्योत्स्ना।।"

अत्रार्थे —

"वियति विसर्पतीव कुमुदेषु बहूभवतीव योषितां
प्रतिफलतीव जरठशरकाण्डपाण्डुषु गण्डभित्तिषु।
अम्भसि विकसतीव लसतीव सुधाधवलेषु धामसु
ध्वजपटपल्लवेषु ललतीव समीरचलेषु चन्द्रिका।।

To express the basic idea in its various forms can be called a *kandaḥ*.

Thus —

The moonlight falling out from the moon like pitcher is spreading in the lanes, collecting on the palatial-mansion tops and enveloping the ponds filled with flowers.

Another example with the same meaning —

The moonlight is spreading across the sky, is filling up the flowers, falling upon a portion of the dry yellow cheeks of maidens (like the dry reeds) is growing upon the water, is being reflected from the white cemented mansions and is playing upon the flags moving with the breeze.

स्फटिकमणिघट इवेन्दुस्तस्यामपिधानमाननमिवाङ्कः।
क्षरति चिरं तेन यथा ज्योत्स्ना घनसारधूलिरिव।।

"सितमणिकलशादिन्दोर्हरिणहरित्तृणपिधानतो गलितैः।
रजनिभुजिष्या सिञ्चति नभोऽङ्गणं चन्द्रिकाम्भोभिः।।"

"संविधातुमभिषेकमुदासे
मन्मथस्य लसदंशुजलौघः।

15. In this verse the meanings have been collected and condensed from all the previous verses and since it is like a collection of rubies, it is called *māṇikyapuñjaḥ*.

यामिनीवनितया ततचिह्नः
सोत्पलो रजतकुम्भ इवेन्दुः।।"

On the day of *Śarad-pūrṇimā*,[16] the bright moon shining in the sky looks like a pitcher of crystalline rubies and the dark spot on the moon appears to be like the open mouth of a pitcher and the camphor powder which seems to be falling out from it like white and bright moonlight.

And also —

And the night like a common serving girl is sprinkling the yard with moonlight like water which is flowing out from crystalline ruby pitcher like moon with its mouth closed with green leaves.

The moon (to consecrate Lord Kāmadeva, Cupid, God of Love) appears to be like a metal pitcher decorated with the *svastika* mark by the night like beautiful maiden and filled with water like moon rays to consecrate the Lord Kāmadeva.[17]

ता इमास्तुल्यदेहितुल्यस्य परिसंख्याः। 'सोऽयमुल्लेखवाननुग्राह्यो मार्गः' इति सुरानन्दः।

तदाह —

"सरस्वती सा जयति प्रकामं
देवी श्रुतिःस्वस्त्ययनं कवीनाम्।
अनर्घतामानयति स्वभङ्ग्या
योल्लिख्य यत्किञ्चिदिहार्थरत्नम्।।"

Thus the *tulyadehitulya*, a kind of appropriation has eight divisions which have been described.

Surānanda approves of this kind of borrowing as 'it reveals some kind of originality on the part of the borrowers.'

Thus —

Glory to that goddess Sarasvatī who is a source of inspiration to the poets and induces in them the capacity to present in a striking

16. *Pūrṇimā* stands for the full moon night and *Śarad* is the season.

17. In the above verses the meaning of the first verse has been expressed subsequently in a variety of ways and thus it is an example of *kandaḥ*.

expression an ordinary jewel of *artha* and transform it into something highly precious.

अथ परपुरप्रवेशसदृशस्य भिदाः।

उपनिबद्धस्य वस्तुनो युक्तिमती परिवृत्तिर्हुडुयुद्धम्।

यथा —

"कथमसौ न भजत्यशरीरतां
हतविवेकपदो हतमन्मथः।
प्रहरतः कदलीदलकोमले
भवति यस्य दया न वधूजने।।"

अत्रार्थे —

"कथमसौ मदनो न नमस्यतां
स्थितविवेकपदो मकरध्वजः।
मृगदृशां कदलीललितं वपु-
र्यदभिहन्ति शरैः कुसुमोद्भवैः"।।

Now the sub-divisions of *parapurapraveśa sadṛśa* have been described.

Transformation of a verse of an ancient poet by using counterbalanced reasoning is called *huduyuddhaṁ*.

Thus —

Why should the cruel and indiscriminating Kāmadeva (Cupid)[18] not become bodiless for he did not show the slightest pity before attacking the brideswoman soft like the leaves of plantain plant?

Another example with the same meaning —

Why shouldn't one offer one's prayers to the discriminating Lord Kāmadeva (Cupid, God of Love) who uses his flowered arrows to attack the plantain like soft and beautiful eyed women.[19]

18. Cupid, the bodiless one so-called from his having been reduced to ashes by Śiva with the fire of his third eye when he tried to seduce the god's mind towards Pārvatī for the birth of a deliverer of the gods from Tāraka. See Apte, *op. cit.*, p. 51.

19. In the prior verse the same act of Lord Kāmadeva has been called indiscriminative and it has been faulted while in the second verse it has been praised.

प्रकारान्तरेण विसदृशं यद्वस्तु तस्य निबन्धः प्रतिकञ्चुकम्।

यथा —

"माद्यच्चकोरक्षणतुल्यधाम्नो
धारां दधाना मधुनः पतन्तीम्।
चञ्च्वग्रदष्टोत्पलनालहृद्या
हंसीव रेजे शशिरत्नपारी।।"

अत्रार्थे —

"मसारपारेण बभौ ददाना
काचित्सुरां विद्रुमनालकेन।
वल्लूरवल्लीं दधतेव चञ्च्वा
केलीशुकेनाञ्जलिना धृतेन।।"

When an idea present in a verse appears different due to a different mode of expression it is called *pratikañcukam*.

Thus —

The falling red coloured wine like the intoxicated red eyes of the *cakora* (partridge) held in the moonlight made earthen pitcher look like a beautiful swan with a lotus-stalk hanging in its beak.

Another example with the same meaning —

A beautiful maiden has an emerald studded earthen pitcher with corals set in its neck and wine pouring out from it which gives it the appearance of a parrot with a piece of flesh hanging in its mouth and held in the hand of that maiden.[20]

उपमानस्योपमानान्तरपरिवृत्तिर्वस्तुसंचारः।

यथा —

"अविरलमिव दाम्ना पौण्डरीकेण बद्धः
स्नपित इव च दुग्धस्रोतसा निर्भरेण।
कवलित इव कृत्स्नश्चक्षुषा स्फारितेन
प्रसभममृतमेघेनेव सान्द्रेण सिक्तः।।"

---

20. In both the verses the point of comparison is the pitcher used for pouring wine. In the first verse, it being made of lightning is compared to a swan while in the second it is compared to a parrot.

अत्रार्थे —

"मुक्तानामिव रज्जवो हिमरुचेर्माला: कलानामिव
क्षीराब्धेरिव वीचय: क्लममुष: पीयूषधारा इव।
दीर्घापाङ्गनदीं विलङ्घ्य सहसा लीलानुभावस्थिता:
सद्य: प्रेमभरोल्लसा मृगदृशो मामभ्यषिञ्चन्दृश:।।

When the standard of comparison used in the original verse is changed and other standards are used it is called *vastusañcāraḥ*.

[Mādhava (to himself) Ah!, I am blessed, since by her, with her eyes brightened at my unexpected sight, I am] —

> Closely bound as if with a garland of lotuses, bathed as if with an overflowing stream of milk, as if wholly swallowed up with her expanded eyes and sprinkled over perforce, as it were, by a dense nectar-laden cloud.[21]

Another example with the same meaning —

> The woman with the beautiful eyes (*mṛgalocana*) bestows sidelong glances filled with love which appear bound as if with a garland of jasmines or like a garland of the rays of the moon, or like the waves of the sea water or like a stream of nectar and these love-lorn looks seem to cut across the wide river to fill me with ecstasy.[22]

शब्दालङ्कारस्यार्थालङ्कारेणान्यथात्वं धातुवाद:।

यथा —

"जयन्ति बाणासुरमौलिलालिता:
दशास्यचूडामणिचक्रचुम्बिन:।
सुरासुराधीशशिखान्तशायिनो
भवच्छिदस्त्र्यम्बकपादपांसव:।"

---

21. See Bhavabhūti's *Mālatīmādhava* with the commentary of Jagaddhara edited with a literal English translation, Notes and Introduction by M.R. Kale, Motilal Banarsidass, Delhi, 1967, 3rd edn., rpt. 1983, Act II. 16, p. 34.
22. In both the verses the comparison is of eyes but in the first verse the point of comparison is with lotuses, etc., while in the second it is with jasmines.

अत्रार्थे —

"सन्मार्गालोकनप्रौढिनिरजीकृतजन्तवः।
जयन्त्यपूर्वव्यापाराः पुरारेः पादपांसवः।।"

Transformation of a *śabdālaṁkāra* (figure of speech related to word) into an *arthālaṁkāra* (figure of speech related to sense) is called *dhātuvādaḥ*.

Thus —

Triumphant are the particles of dust sticking to the feet of Tryambaka, the cutters of the bonds of worldly existence, which were joyfully borne on his head (or crown) by the demon Bāṇa, which kissed (fell on) the circle of the crest jewels of Rāvaṇa, and which lie on the points of the crests of the lords of the gods and the demons.[23]

Praise to the dust of Lord Śiva's feet which is a means towards the right path and helps to alleviate the mental darkness (*rajo-guṇa*).[24]

तस्यैव वस्तुन उत्कर्षेणान्यथाकरणं सत्कारः।

यथा —

"स्नानार्द्रार्द्रैर्विधुतकबरीबन्धलोलैरिदानीं
श्रोणीभारः कृतपरिचयः पल्लवैः कुन्तलानम्।

---

23. See Bāṇa's *Kādambarī* (Pūrvabhāga Complete) ed. with new Sanskrit Commentary *Tattvaprakāśikā*, Introduction, Notes and a literal English Translation by late M.R. Kale, Motilal Banarsidass, Delhi, 1968, pp. 2-3.

This is in praise of god Śiva, a deity of destruction. He is generally known to be fair. It was owing to this that many cunning demons like Rāvaṇa, Bāṇa took advantage of his disposition and obtained from him boons which made them all powerful in the world. The verb *jayantī* which literally means 'conquer' conveys by implication the meaning of a salutation, which is generally accompanied by good wishes for the person bowed to. The word Bāṇāsura, though apparently the name of a demon suggests another meaning by *śabdaśleṣa* or similarity of sound. It may be explained as those who gave life to Bāṇa, i.e., his forefathers. That Bāṇa was a worshipper of Śiva is clear from his salutation to that deity before Viṣṇu.

24. *Rajo-guṇa* is the second of the three *guṇas* or constituent qualities of all material substances (the other two being *sattva* and *tamaṣ*).

अप्येतेभ्यो नभसि पततः पङ्क्तिशो वारिबिन्दून्
स्थित्वोद्ग्रीवं कुवलयदृशां केलिहंसाः पिबन्ति।।"

अत्रार्थे —

"लक्ष्म्याः क्षीरनिधेरुदक्तवपुषो वेणीलताग्रच्युता
ये मुक्ताग्रथनामसूत्रसुभगाः प्राप्ताः पयोबिन्दवः।
ते वः पान्तु विशेषसस्पृहदृशा दृष्टाश्चिरं शार्ङ्गिणा
हेलोद्ग्रीवजलेशहंसवनितालीढाः सुधास्वादवः।।"

Using elevated and extraordinary expression for common place things is called *satkāraḥ*.

Thus —

After the maidens' bath, their wet and loose (with the opening of plaits) hair has fallen down to their waist and the swans belonging to these maidens raise their necks and drink the droplets of water falling from their wet hair.

Another example with the same meaning —

May the nectar like drops of water which are falling from the wet hair of goddess Lakṣmī and which appear to be like loose beads of a necklace, which are looked at with longing by Lord Viṣṇu and are sipped by the uplifted beaks of the she-swans by the banks of the river, protect you.

पूर्वं सदृशः पश्चाद्भिन्नो जीवञ्जीवकः।

यथा —

"नयनोदरयोः कपोलभागे
रुचिमद्रत्नगणेषु भूषणेषु।
सकलप्रतिबिम्बितेन्दुबिम्बा
शतचन्द्राभरणैव काचिदासीत्।।"

अत्रार्थे —

"भास्वत्कपोलतलकुण्डलपारिहार्य-
सन्मेखलामणिगणप्रतिबिम्बितेन।
चन्द्रेण भाति रमणी रमणीयवक्त्र-
शोभाभिभूतवपुषेव निषेव्यमाणा।।"

When the first half of the verse is similar but the latter half is unlike the original, we get the sub-division called *jivañjīvakaḥ*.

Thus —

Reflected in her eyes, her bosom, her cheeks and her bejewelled body the maiden seemed to be ornamented with innumerable moons.

Another example with the same meaning —

The reflected moon seen in the shining cheeks, earrings, bracelets and in the gems studded in the waist belt appeared to have lost out to the maidens' beautiful face and was thus serving her completely.

प्राक्तनवाक्याभिप्रायनिबन्धो भावमुद्रा।

यथा —

"ताम्बूलवल्लीपरिणद्धपूगा-
स्वेलालतालिङ्गितचन्दनासु।
तमालपत्रास्तरणासु रन्तुं
प्रसीद शश्वन्मलयस्थलीषु।।"

अत्रार्थे —

"निश्चेतनानामपि युक्तयोगदो
नूनं स एनं मदनोऽधितिष्ठति।
एला यदाश्लिष्टवतीह चन्दनं
पूगद्रुमं नागलताधिरोहति।।"

When the sentences or ideas of earlier poets are incorporated into later creations we get the variety called *bhāvamudrā*.

Be pleased, O princess, to sport oftentimes in the dales of the Malaya mountain, over-spread with *tamāla* leaves, where the sandle (*sic*) trees are encircled (literally embraced) with cardamom creepers and where the betel trees are enclosed within a ring of *tāmbūla* creepers.[25]

---

25. See *Raghuvaṁśa-Kālidāsa* by Gopal Raghunath Nandargikar *op. cit.*, p. 181 (canto 6 *śloka* 64).

Another example with the same meaning —

> On watching the embracing cardamom creepers with the betel (areca-nut) climbers it appears that Kāmadeva (Cupid, God of Love) appears to reside even in rooted plants in the spring season.[26]

पूर्वार्थपरिपन्थिनी वस्तुरचना तद्विरोधी।

यथा—

"हारो वक्षसि दन्तपत्रविशदं कर्णे दलं कौमुदं
माला मूर्ध्नि दुकूलिनी तनुलता कर्पूरशुक्लौ स्तनौ।
वक्त्रे चन्दनबिन्दुरिन्दुधवलं बालं मृणालं करे
वेषः किं सित एष सुन्दरि शरच्चन्द्रात्त्वया शिक्षितः।।"

अत्रार्थे —

"मूर्तिर्नीलदुकूलिनी मृगमदैः प्रत्यङ्गपत्रक्रिया
बाहू मेचकरत्नकङ्कणभृतौ कण्ठे मसारावली।
व्यालम्बालकवल्लरीकमलिकं कान्ताभिसारोत्सवे
यत्सत्यं तमसा मृगाक्षि विहितं वेषे तवाचार्यकम्।।"

इत्यर्थहरणोपाया द्वात्रिंशदुपदर्शिताः।
हानोपादानविज्ञाने कवित्वं तत्र मां प्रति।।

किं चैते हरणोपाया ज्ञेयाः सप्रतियोगिनः।
अर्थस्य वैपरीत्येन विज्ञेया प्रतियोगिता।।

किञ्च —

शब्दार्थशासनविदः कति नो कवन्ते
यद्वाङ्मयं श्रुतिधनस्य चकास्ति चक्षुः।
किन्त्वस्ति यद्वचसि वस्तु नवं सदुक्ति-
सन्दर्भिणां स धुरि तस्य गिरः पवित्राः।।

Similarly when ideas expressed by former poets are opposed by the latter ones, there arises the variety called *tadvirodhī*.

---

26. The second verse expresses the idea found in the first verse of Kālidāsa, thus it is an instance of *bhāvamudrā*.

Thus —

(O beautiful maiden!) Have you learnt to ornament yourself from the moon of the *śarad* season with a bright necklace of white flowers which look like ivory, a garland of (white) flowers on the forehead, a bright cloth over the body, camphor pasted breasts, (white) sandal mark on the face and bright bracelets made of lotus roots in the wrists.

Another example with the same meaning —

(O maiden with beautiful eyes!) Your ornamentation and attire appears to have been acquired from the darkness. With your blue-coloured *sārī* and cloth, each part of your body decorated with musk patterns, wearing blue precious stones studded bracelets in your arms, a blue emerald necklace in the neck and long and curly hair falling over the shoulders.

Thus in all, thirty-two means of appropriation have been shown. In my (Rājaśekhara's) opinion poetical skill lies in the exact knowledge of the ways either to be given up or adopted from among these thirty-two kinds.

All these means of appropriation of meanings can be opposed by contradicting the meaning of each one.

There are numerous grammarians, Mīmāṃsakas and Nayāyikas who have a profound knowledge of words and meanings. Yet, it is the learned scholars in whom the eyes are the entire discourse of literature (*vāṅgmaya*) and speech is original and presents novel insights who become the most eminent of poets. It is these eminent poets whose words are honoured.

।। इति राजशेखरकृतौ काव्यमीमांसायां कविरहस्ये प्रथमेऽधिकरणे अर्थहरणेष्वालेख्यप्रख्यादिभेदास्त्रयोदशोऽध्याय: ।।

14

जातिद्रव्यक्रियासमयस्थापना

Kavi-Samaya
(Conventions of a Poet)

अशास्त्रीयमलौकिकं च परम्परायातं यमर्थमुपनिबध्नन्ति कवयः स कविसमयः।

STATEMENT of such meanings as are part of the tradition of poetic-expression (but) contrary to what is known to happen in the world and contrary to the *śāstras* (texts of knowledge) comes under poetic convention.

'नन्वेष दोषः कथङ्कारं पुनरुपनिबन्धनार्हः?' इति आचार्याः। 'कविमार्गानुग्राही कथमेष दोषः?' इति यायावरीयः। 'निमित्तं तर्हि वाच्यम्' इति आचार्याः। 'इदमभिधीयते' इति यायावरीयः।

*Ācārya*s say — 'description of things contrary to what is known to exist in the world and contrary to *śāstric* knowledge is a fault'. Then how can it be correct for poets to describe thus.

Yāyāvarīya (Rājaśekhara) says that these descriptions are beneficial to the poet and these light up the poetic path. Thus how can they be faults? The *ācārya*s say — if this be so, then tell us the reason? Yāyāvarīya says —

It has been said —

"पूर्वे हि विद्वांसः सहस्रशाखं साङ्गं च वेदमवगाह्य, शास्त्राणि चावबुध्य, देशान्तराणि द्वीपान्तराणि च परिभ्रम्य, यानर्थानुपलभ्य प्रणीतवन्तस्तेषां देशकालान्तरवशेन अन्यथात्वेऽपि तथात्वेनोपनिबन्धो यः स कविसमयः। कविसमयशब्दश्चायं मूलमप श्यद्भिः प्रयोगमात्रदर्शिभिः प्रयुक्तो रूढश्च।"

The ancient scholars described things after a deep study of various branches and parts of the Vedas, factual knowledge of the *śāstras* and after travelling different countries and islands. Poetic-convention is thus to describe things in their previous unchanged and ancient form even though time or space may have brought about a difference or opposition in them. The use of the word *kavi-samaya* (poetic convention) was made prevalent by some people who failed to understand its basis or origin and so it (acquired currency) came to be used conventionally.

"तत्र कश्चिदाद्यत्वेन व्यवस्थितः कविसमयेनार्थः, कश्चित्परस्परोपक्रमार्थं स्वार्थाय धूर्तैः प्रवर्त्तितः।"

"स च त्रिधा स्वर्ग्यो भौमः पातालीयश्च। स्वर्ग्यपातालीययोर्भौमः प्रधानः। स हि महाविषयः। स च चतुर्द्धा जातिद्रव्यगुणक्रियारूपार्थतया। तेऽपि प्रत्येकं त्रिधा, असतो निबन्धनात्, सतोऽप्यनिबन्धनात्, नियमतश्च।"

तत्र सामान्यस्याऽसतो निबन्धनं यथा। नदीषु पद्मोत्पलादीनि, जलाशयमात्रेऽपि हंसादयो। यत्र तत्र पर्वतेषु सुवर्णरत्नादिकं च।

Some of these things are well-known since former times as poetic-conventions yet certain things have been made popular by mischievous people out of competitive jealousy or for selfish ends.

Kavi-samaya is of three types — *svargya* (celestial), *bhaumya* (terrestrial) and *pātālīya* (of the nether world). Of these, poetic conventions about terrestrial things are of greater importance for the simple reason that their province is far wider. This variety of terrestrial things (*bhauma*) has four sub-varieties depending upon (1) *jāti* (*sāmānya*-class), (2) *dravya* (substance or particular things), (3) *guṇa* (quality) and, (4) *kriyā* (action). Everyone of these four sub-varieties has its own threefold sub-divisions — (i) *asatonibandhanam* (description of unreal things which are not actually found in a particular place), (ii) *satopi anibandhanam* (non-mention of things), (iii) *niyamataḥ* (restriction or laying down part of the truth).[1]

The description of *asatonibandhanam* in *jātirūpa* —

The description of lotuses of different kinds in all rivers, presence of swans and water-birds in all water-reservoirs, presence of gold and mines of precious stones in all mountains.[2]

नदीपद्मानि यथा —

> "दीर्घीकुर्वन्पटुमदकलं कूजितं सारसानां
> प्रत्यूषेषु स्फुटितकमलामोदमैत्रीकषायः।
> यत्र स्त्रीणां हरति सुरतग्लानिमङ्गानुकूलः
> शिप्रावातः प्रियतम इव प्रार्थनाचाटुकारः।।"

At daybreak in Ujjayinī, Śiprā's cool breeze scented with the fragrance of lotuses comes prolonging the piercing cries of lover-maddened *sāras*-cranes and is refreshing to the tired limbs of women.

---

1. Divisions of *kavi-samaya* : Poetic conventions (*kavi-samaya*)

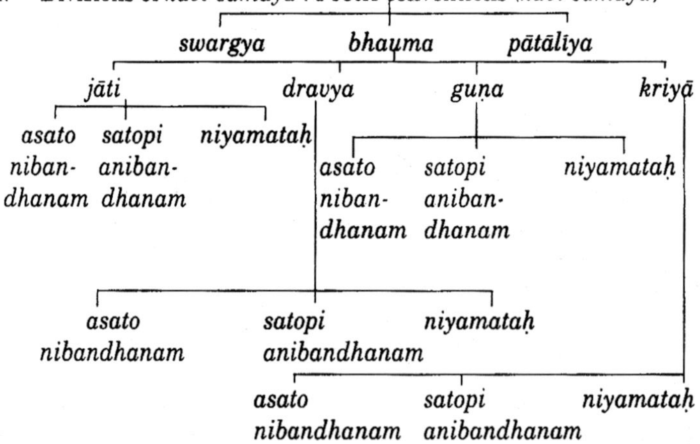

2. In these lines, these sweeping statements are contrary to facts though they are taken for granted. The poetic convention in the sense of regulation of meaning is evident when the hare and the deer seen in the moon are considered as identical, the moon as born of the ocean is the same as that born of the sage Attri, all the twelve Ādityas are identical, Nārāyaṇa, Mādhava, Viṣṇu, Dāmodara, the Lord's incarnation as a tortoise, etc., refer to the self-same Lord, the goddess of wealth and the goddess of beauty are identical, cobras and serpents, the milky ocean and the saline ocean, the seas and the oceans and the demons known as *daitayas*, *dānavas* and *asuras* are all identical.

After passion's ecstatic play, it removes their langour like an artful lover, plying his love with amorous entreaties.[3]

नदीनीलोत्पलानि —

"गगनगमनलीलालम्भितान्स्वेदबिन्दून्
मृदुभिरनिलवारैः खेचराणां हरन्तीम्।
कुवलयवनकान्त्या जाह्नवींसोऽभ्यपश्यत्
दिनपतिसुतयेव व्यक्तदत्ताङ्कपालीम्।।

Description of blue-lotuses in rivers —

While desiring to travel the sky like the birds and thus producing beads of sweat which evaporated with the gentle gusts of cool wind, that king beheld a forest of blue lotuses in the midst of the river Gaṅgā who appeared to play in the folds of Yamunā's lap.

एवं नदीकुमुदाद्यपि।

सलिलमात्रे हंसा यथा —

"आसीदस्ति भविष्यतीह स जनो धन्यो धनी धार्मिकः
यः श्रीकेशववत्करिष्यति पुनः श्रीमत्कुडुङ्गेश्वरम्।
हेलान्दोलितहंससारसकुलक्रेङ्कारसम्मूर्च्छितै-
रित्याघोषयतीव तन्नवनदी यच्चेष्टितं वारिभिः।।"

Similarly, there is the description of flowers in rivers.

The description of swans in water-reservoirs —

Swaying with the waves the collective sound of swans and herons echoing in the water seemed to pronounce that the supreme Lord of Kuduṅga region who is rich and religious and will remain so appears to be like Lord Kṛṣṇa.

पर्वतमात्रे सुवर्णं यथा —

"नागावासश्चित्रपोताभिरामः
स्वर्णस्फीतिव्याप्तदिक्चक्रवालः।
साम्यात्सख्यं जग्मिवानम्बुराशे-
रेष ख्यातस्तेन जीमूतभर्त्ता।।"

3. See Kālidāsa's *Meghadūtam*, *op. cit.*, (I.33), pp. 144-5.

The description of gold in mountains —

> The mountain, Jimūtabharatā visible before us is similar to the ocean and has acquired its friendship. The ocean is an abode of serpents and water-elephants and the mountain also houses serpents and elephants. The ocean is filled with beautiful ships and the mountain with animals. The ocean is known for its treasures and the mountain for its gold mines.[4]

रत्नानि यथा —

> "नीलाश्मरश्मिपटलानि महेभमुक्त-
> सूत्कारसीकरविसृञ्चि तटान्तरेषु।
> आलोकयन्ति सरलीकृतकण्ठनालाः
> सानन्दमम्बुदधियाऽत्र मयूरनार्यः"

Description of precious stones in mountains —

> At the foot of the mountains the pea-hens arch their long necks towards the sky and watch the blue sapphire like meshed water-drops giving the illusion of clouds due to the water-droplets being thrown up by the trunks of snorting elephants.

एवमन्यदपि।

सतोऽप्यनिबन्धनं। तद्यथा न मालती वसन्ते, न पुष्पफलं चन्दनद्रुमेषु, न फलमशोकेषु।

Similarly other examples depicting presence of non-existent objects with their classes are seen in poetic-compositions.

Next comes the examples of *non-mention of a class*. Such as the *mālatī* flowers not being described in spring, the sandal tree being described as without flowers and the *aśoka* tree as devoid of fruits.

तत्र प्रथमः —

> "मालतीविमुखश्चैत्रो विकासी पुष्पसम्पदाम्।
> आश्चर्यं जातिहीनस्य कथं सुमनसः प्रियाः।।"

---

4. In this verse, double entendre is used where we have two meanings. Thus *nāga* refers to serpents or elephants, *chitrapota* to young animals or boats, *svarṇa* to water or gold and *jimūtabhartā* to feeder of clouds or bearer of clouds. All these words with their double meanings apply to both the ocean and the mountain.

द्वितीयः —

"यद्यपि चन्दनविटपी विधिना फलकुसुमवर्जितो विहितः।
निजवपुषैव परेषां तथापि सन्तापमपहरति।।"

तृतीयः —

"दैवायत्ते हि फले किं क्रियतामेतदत्र तु वदामः।
नाशोकस्य किसलयैर्वृक्षान्तरपल्लवास्तुल्याः।।"

Thus the first example —

> Though the spring season causes bloom all around yet it is known to be devoid of *mālatī* flowers. It is surprising how this spring season (devoid of *mālatī*) can be filled with flowers or how this brāhmaṇa (devoid of class) can be near to God.[5]

The second example —

> Though nature has created the sandal tree devoid of flowers and fruits yet it serves others by relieving their weariness by its own body (application).

The third example —

> Fruits are the gifts of god so nothing can be said about them but this is undebatable that the leaves of the *aśoka* tree are like no other tree.

अनेकत्र प्रवृत्तवृत्तीनामेकत्राचरणं नियमस्तद्यथा। समुद्रेष्वेव मकराः, ताम्रपर्ण्यामेव मौक्तिकानि।

तयोः प्रथमः —

"गोत्राग्रहारं नयतो गृहत्वं
स्वनाममुद्राङ्कितमम्बुराशिम्।
दायादवर्गेषु परिस्फुरत्सु
दंष्ट्रावलेपो मकरस्य वन्द्यः।।"

The restriction (*niyama*) pertaining to class means the use of regulations prevalent in many parts by restricting them to a particular region or

5. In this verse again double entendre is used where *jāti* and *sumanas* have two meanings each. The former stands for *mālatī* blossoms and a brāhmaṇa (or birth) while the latter denotes flowers and God.

place for example the restriction of crocodiles to the ocean only and of pearls to the river Tāmraparṇī alone.

Thus the first example —

> The pride of the crocodile is laudable because it resides in this vast ocean which encircles the earth and gives it the name *makrālaya* and thus the crocodile proudly shows its teeth to its mates in the ocean.

द्वितीयः —

> "कामं भवन्तु सरितो भुवि सप्रतिष्ठाः
> स्वादूनि सन्तु सलिलानि च शुक्तयश्च।
> एतां विहाय वरवर्णिनी ताम्रपर्णी
> नान्यत्र सम्भवति मौक्तिककामधेनुः।।"

The second example —

> Though the world may have many well-known rivers filled with pearls, yet the (mythical) river Tāmraparṇī is a veritable wish-fulfilling cow (Kāmadhenu) in respect of pearls.

असतोऽपि द्रव्यस्य निबन्धनम् तद्यथा। मुष्टिग्राह्यत्वं सूचीभेद्यत्वं च तमसः, कुम्भापवाह्यत्वं च ज्योत्स्नायाः।

तत्र प्रथमम् —

> "तनुलग्ना इव ककुभः भूवलयं चरणचारमात्रमिव।
> दिवमिव चालिकदघ्नीं मुष्टिग्राह्यं तमः कुरुते।।"

यथा च —

> "पिहिते कारागारे तमसि च सूचीमुखाग्रनिर्भेद्ये।
> मयि च निमीलितनयने तथापि कान्ताननं व्यक्तम्।।"

द्वितीयम् —

> "यन्त्रद्रावितकेतकोदरदलस्रोतःश्रियं बिभ्रती
> येयं मौक्तिकदामगुम्फनविधेर्योग्यच्छविः प्रागभूत्।
>
> उत्सेच्या कलशोर्मिरञ्जलिपुटैर्ग्राह्या मृणालाङ्कुरैः
> पातव्या च शशिन्यमुग्धविभवे सा वर्त्तते चन्द्रिका।।"

Next comes the mention of a thing with respect to a substance (*dravyāgat*) as for example darkness is said to be capable of being held in the palm of the hand or as being pierced by a needle or the moonlight being measurable by filling it in earthen pots, etc.

Thus the first example —

> The power of intense darkness, held in a palm makes, as it were, the quarters stick to our frame (of the body) the entire globe of the earth as traversable by foot and the heaven as though carried on our heads.

And also —

> Though the prison walls are closed on all sides, there is dense darkness all around and my eyes are weak yet the beloved's face is clearly visible.

Thus the second example —

> The moonlight which on earlier occasion appeared as charming as the juice obtained by mechanically crushing the petals of a *ketaka* plant and possessed the beauty of the weaving of a pearl necklace, today, when the moon shines in its full glory, it has become fit to be collected in an earthen pitcher, in the cavity of the folded hands and to be drunk by lotus-stalks.

द्रव्यस्य सतोऽनिबन्धनं तद्यथा। कृष्णपक्षे सत्या अपि ज्योत्स्नायाः, शुक्लपक्षे त्वन्धकारस्य।

तयोः प्रथमम् —

> **"ददृशाते जनैस्तत्र यात्रायां सकुतूहलैः।**
> **बलभद्रप्रलम्बघ्नौ पक्षाविव सितासितौ।।"**

द्वितीयम् —

> **"मासि मासि समा ज्योत्स्ना पक्षयोः शुक्लकृष्णयोः।**
> **तत्रैकः शुक्लतां यातो यशः पुण्यैरवाप्यते।।"**

A particular thing may be actually in existence but it is not described to exist at a particular time. For example, moonlight exists in the dark half of the month as well as the bright half or darkness exists in the bright half of the month.[6]

6. Poetic convention, however, describes that moonlight exists in the bright fortnight (only) and darkness in the dark fortnight.

Thus —

The anxious onlookers compared Balarāma[7] and Kṛṣṇa who were travelling through Mathurā to the bright half and the dark half of the month respectively.

The second example —

Though every month has moonlight equally present in both the bright and the dark halves of the month, yet only one fortnight is called the bright fortnight (*śukla-pakṣa*). Similarly renown is obtained only after innumerable good turns.

द्रव्यनियमस्तद्यथा। मलय एव चन्दनस्थानं, हिमवानेव भूर्जोत्पत्तिस्थानम्।

तत्र प्रथमः —

"तापापहारचतुरो नागावासः सुरप्रियः।
नाऽन्यत्र मलयादद्रेर्दृश्यते चन्दनद्रुमः।।"

द्वितीयः —

"न्यस्ताक्षरा धातुरसेन यत्र
भूर्जत्वचः कुञ्जरबिन्दुशोणाः।
व्रजन्ति विद्याधरसुन्दरीणा-
मनङ्गलेखक्रिययोपयोगम्।।"

Restriction of substances (*dravyāgat niyama*) is evidenced in the sandal tree growing only on the Malaya mountain and the birch leaf (writing paper) being found on the Himālayas alone.

The first example —

The sandal tree which is known for its unique heat-relieving capacity is an abode of serpents and is dear to the gods. It cannot be found anywhere except the Malaya mountain.

Second example —

Where the barks of the birch trees, having characters written on them with mineral fluid, and so resembling the red spots on (the

7. Balarāma is elder brother of Kṛṣṇa. For more details, see John Dowson, *op. cit.*, pp. 40-1.

bodies of full grown) elephants become useful to the Vidyādhara damsels for amatory correspondence.[8]

प्रकीर्णकद्रव्यकविसमयस्तु तद्यथा। क्षीरक्षारसमुद्रयोरैक्यं, सागरमहासमुद्रयोश्च।

तयोः प्रथमः —

"शेतां हरिर्भवतु रत्नमनन्तमन्त-
र्लक्ष्मीप्रसूतिरिति नो विविदामहे हे।
हा दूरदूरसपया'स्तृषितस्य जन्तोः
किं त्वत्र कूपपयसः स मरोर्जघन्यः।।"

द्वितीयः —

"रङ्गत्तरङ्गभ्रूभङ्गैस्तर्जयन्तीमिवापगाः ।
स ददर्श पुरो गङ्गां सप्तसागरवल्लभाम्।।"

Kavi-samaya (poetic-convention) is also applicable to certain miscellaneous substances — for example, the oneness of sea of milk (*kṣīra-samudra*) and sea of salt (*kṣāra-samudra*) and that of the sea and the ocean.

The first example —

Though Lord Viṣṇu may reside in the sea of milk (*kṣīra-samudra*) and it may be a reservoir of precious stones, even goddess of wealth (Lakṣmī) may arise from it, yet for a person dying of thirst, this ocean (*kṣāra-samudra* — sea of salt) is worse than the desert land (since it cannot quench his thirst).[9]

The second example —

The king while travelling witnessed the bright and sparkling waters of the river Gaṅgā, the beloved of the seven seas.[10]

---

8. See Kālidāsa's *Kumārasambhava*, Cantos I-VIII edited with the commentary of Mallinātha a Literal English Translation, Notes and Introduction by M.R. Kale, Motilal Banarsidass, Delhi, 7th edn., 1981, p. 1 (of English translation).
9. Though the sea of milk is famous as the abode of Lord Viṣṇu and the origin of Goddess Lakṣmī and not the sea of salt yet the two become one according to poetic convention.
10. In this verse again, the poet seems to point to the oneness of the seven-seas according to poetic convention as the river Gaṅgā falls into one sea and not seven.

असतोऽपि क्रियार्थस्य निबन्धनम् यथा। चक्रवाकमिथुनस्य निशि भिन्नतटाश्रयणं, चकोराणां चन्द्रिकापानं च।

तत्र प्रथमः —

> "संक्षिपता यामवतीस्तटिनीनां तनयता पयःपूरान्।
> रथचरणाह्वयवयसां किं नोपकृतं निदाघेन।।"

द्वितीयः —

> "एतास्ता मलयोपकण्ठसरितामेणाक्षि रोधोभुव-
> श्चापाभ्यासनिकेतनं भगवतः प्रेयो मनोजन्मनः।
> यासु श्यामनिशासु पीततमसो मुक्तामयीश्चन्द्रिकाः
> पीयन्ते विवृतोर्ध्वचञ्चु विचलत्कण्ठं चकोराङ्गनाः।।"

Next comes the mention of a non-existing thing relating to action (*asat-kriyāgat*) for example the proverbial drinking of the moonlight by the *cakora* bird and the conventional separation of the *cakravāka* birds on the two banks of water reservoirs at night.

The first example —

> The summer by shortening the nights and drying up the water of the river has favourably acted towards the pair of *cakravāka* birds.

The second example —

> This is the region on the river banks of the Malaya mountain where Cupid practices archery and where the *cakora* drink the pearl like moonlight with their open beaks and long throats in the dark fortnight.

सतोऽपि क्रियार्थस्यानिबन्धनम् तद्यथा। दिवा नीलोत्पलानामविकासो, निशानिमित्तश्च शेफालिकाकुसुमानामविस्रंसः।

तत्र प्रथमः —

> "आलिख्य पत्रमसितागुरुणाभिरामं
> रामामुखे क्षणसभाजितचन्द्रबिम्बे।
> जातः पुनर्विकसनावसरोऽयमस्ये-
> त्युक्त्वा सखी कुवलयं श्रवणे चकार।।"

द्वितीयः —

> "त्वद्विप्रयोगे किरणैस्तथोग्रै-
> र्दग्धाऽस्मि कृत्स्नं दिवसं सवित्रा।
> इतीव दुःखं शशिने गदन्ती
> शेफालिका रोदिति पुष्पवाष्पैः।।"

Next comes the absence of action, thought it is present in a thing for example the not-blooming of blue-lotuses in the day time and not falling off of *śefālikā* flowers in the night.

The first example —

A girl friend of the heroine, very fondly made up the face of the heroine, which resembled the evening moon in beauty and thereafter she painted a blue-lotus as she whispered in the heroine's ears that "the time for the blooming of this (lotus) has arrived".

The second example —

The *śefālikā* flower seems to address her beloved, the moon, emitting sighs of vapour (tears), as if crying to describe her pain arising from being scorched by the fierce rays of the sun during the day.

नियमस्तु तद्यथा। ग्रीष्मादौ सम्भवतोऽपि कोकिलानां विरुतस्य वसन्त एव, मयूराणां वर्षास्वेव विरुतस्य नृत्तस्य च निबन्धः।

तयोः प्रथमः —

> "वसन्ते शीतभीतेन कोकिलेन वने रुतम्।
> अन्तर्जलगताः पद्माः श्रोतुकामा इवोत्थिताः।।"

द्वितीयः —

> "मण्डलीकृत्य बर्हाणि कण्ठैर्मधुरगीतिभिः।
> कलापिनः प्रनृत्यन्ति काले जीमूतमालिनि।।"
> कवीनां समयः सोऽयं जातिद्रव्यक्रियागतः।
> गुणस्थैष ततः स्वर्ग्यः पातालीयश्च कथ्यते।।

Restriction (*niyama*) of the action of warbling by cuckoos in spring, though it occurs in the summer as well and the dancing and singing of the peacocks only in monsoon though it is present in other seasons as well are also poetic conventions.

Thus the first example —

> When the cuckoo out of sheer cold in the spring season started warbling in the forests, then the lotuses hidden in the water reservoirs appeared to raise their heads as if to hear the notes (of the cuckoo).

The second example —

> Spreading their plumage in a circle these feathery-peacocks with their throats full of sweet songs are dancing in (this) season that gathers clouds.[11]

In this way this chapter has described the poetic conventions relating to class (*jāti*), substance (*dravya*) and action (*kriyā*). The following chapters will take up the description of qualities, celestial and nether-worldly poetic-conventions.

।। इति राजशेखरकृतौ काव्यमीमांसायां कविरहस्ये प्रथमेऽधिकरणे जातिद्रव्यक्रियासमयस्थापना चतुर्दशोऽध्यायः ।।

---

11. See S.K. Belvalkar (tr.), *Kāvyādarśa of Daṇḍin*, The Oriental Book Supplying Agency, Poona, 1924, 1.70, .9 (of English translation).

15

गुणसमयस्थापना

Guṇa-Samaya-Sthāpanā

(Poetic Conventions)

असतो गुणस्य निबन्धनं यथा, यशोहासप्रभृतेः शौक्ल्यम्, अयशसः पापप्रभृतेश्च कार्ष्ण्यं, क्रोधानुरागप्रभृतेश्च रक्तत्वम्।

तत्र यशःशौक्ल्यम् —

"स्तेमः स्तोकोऽपि नाङ्गे श्वसितमविकलं चक्षुषां सैव वृत्ति-
र्मध्येक्षीराब्धि मग्नाः स्फुटमथ च वयं कोऽयमीदृक्प्रकारः।
इत्थं दिग्भित्तिरोधःक्षतविसरतया मांसलैस्त्वद्यशोभिः
स्तोकावस्थानदुःस्थैस्त्रिजगति धवले विस्मयन्ते मृगाक्ष्यः।।"

हासशौक्ल्यम् —

"अट्टहासच्छलेनास्याद्यस्य फेनौघपाण्डुराः।
जगत्क्षय इवापीताः क्षरन्ति क्षीरसागराः।।"

अयशःकृष्णत्वम् —

"प्रसरन्ति कीर्त्तयस्ते तव च रिपूणामकीर्त्तयो युगपत्।
कुवलयदलसंवलिताः प्रतिदिनमिव मालतीमालाः।।"

THE manifestation of incorporeal qualities is depicted by white, blue and yellow colours in *kavi-samaya* (poetic-conventions), for example fame and laughter have no manifest form. According to poetic-conventions they are denoted by the white colour. Similarly ignominy, evil is symbolised by black and love and anger by red colour!

As in —

O king! Your renown has spread in all the four directions of the earth, but after having rebounded from the walls (of directions) collected in large amounts and entered the centre of the ocean, but in spite of that neither did its body get wet, not did its breath stop and nor did its eyes close. Thus after changing the ocean to white when it still lacked space, it started to whiten the sky. Thus, your *renown* has made *white*[1] three worlds and this is a cause of amazement for beautiful maidens.

White laughter —

The echoing white laughter of Śivaji (a Hindu God) seems to be overflowing from his mouth, fancied, due to the sea of milk (*kṣīra-sāgara*) swallowed by him and it appears whiter due to the frothy foam.

Blue Ignominy —

(O, King!) Like a garland of *white* jasmines and *blue* lotuses interspersed together, your *renown* and your enemies *infamy* appear to spread everyday in the world.

पापकार्ष्ण्यम् —

"उत्खातनिर्मलमयूखकृपाणलेखा-
श्यामायिता तनुरभूद्धयकन्धरस्य।
सद्यः प्रकोपकृतकेशववंशनाश-
सङ्कल्पसंजनितपापमलीमसेव।।"

क्रोधरक्तता —

"आस्थानकुट्टिमतलप्रतिबिम्बितेन
कोपप्रभाप्रसरपाटलविग्रहेण।
भौमेन मूर्च्छितरसातलकुक्षिभाजा
भूमिश्चचाल चलतोदरवर्त्तिनेव।"

Hayagrīva, a demon who had committed the sin of vowing to destroy the race of Keśava (Kṛṣṇa)[2] lost the lustre of his body

1. Here the renown or glory is represented by the white colour.
2. Viṣṇu in his eighth incarnation was born as Kṛṣṇa, the son of Vāsudeva and Devakī. See Bhide, p. 384.

which became *black* like the blades of a drawn sword as if through his *sinful* intention.[3]

The body of the dreadful demon, Bhāmāsura[4] who stays in the womb of fire in the netherworld like the digestive fire in the stomach, has acquired *red colour* due to increased anger and is mirrored in the jewel-studded surface of the pavilion. When the demon is ready (to move out to battle) he is accompanied by the shaking of the entire earth.

अनुरागरक्तता यथा —

"गुणानुरागमिश्रेण यशसा तव सर्पता।
दिग्वधूनां मुखे जातमकस्मादर्द्धकुङ्कुमम्।।"

सतोऽपि गुणस्यानिबन्धनम्। कुन्दकुड्मलानां कामिदन्तानां च रक्तत्वं, कमलमुकुलप्रभृतेश्च हरितत्वं, प्रियङ्गुपुष्पाणां च पीतत्वम्।

The excellent virtues and the everspreading renown of the king in all directions is like the brides on whose forehead suddenly appears a half saffron mark.

Now begin the examples of excellences prevalent in the world which have not been described in accordance with poetic conventions as for example jasmine buds and teeth of passionate women as red in colour, lotus buds as green and flowers of *priyaṅgū*[5] are yellow in accordance with their existence in the world but in poetic-compositions according to poetic-conventions they have been described as white and blue in colour.

कुन्दकुड्मलाद्यरक्तता —

"द्योतितान्तःसभैः कुन्दकुड्मलाग्रदतः स्मितैः।
स्नपितेवाभवत्तस्य शुद्धवर्णा सरस्वती।।"

पद्ममुकुलाहरितत्वम् —

"उद्दण्डोदरपुण्डरीकमुकुलभ्रान्तिस्पृशा दंष्ट्रया

---

3. The poet here uses the popular convention that sin is black.
4. An epithet of the demon *naraka*. See Bhide, p. 838.
5. Name of a creeper said to put forth blossoms when touched by women, Bhide, *op. cit.*, p. 781.

मग्नां लावणसैन्धवेऽम्भसि महीमुद्यच्छतो हेलया।
तत्कालाकुलदेवदानवकुलैरुत्तालकोलाहलं
शौरेरादिवराहलीलमवतादभ्रंलिहाग्रं वपुः।।"

Lack of red colour of jasmines —

Kṛṣṇa's white jasmine-buds like teeth lit up the entire assembly with his smile which now looked as pure and white as Sarasvatī (goddess of learning and wisdom) after a bath.

White colour of lotus bud —

The earth which lay sunk under the waters of *lavaṇa-sāgara* (sea of salt) was held up with the tusks of the *primordial boar*[6] which is fancied as a slender stalk of a white lotus bud. May this massive form of the Primordial Boar (*ādivarāḥ*) rising from the waters amidst the noisy violence between gods and demons protect us.

प्रियङ्गुपुष्पापीतत्वम् —

"प्रियङ्गुश्याममम्भोधिरान्ध्रीणां स्तनमण्डलम्।
अलङ्कर्तुमिव स्वच्छाः सूते मौक्तिकसम्पदः।।"

गुणनियमस्तु तद्यथा, सामान्योपादाने माणिक्यानां शोणता, पुष्पाणां शुक्लता, मेघानां कृष्णता च।

The darkness of Priyaṇgū flowers —

The Southern ocean produces the wealth of transparent pearls to beautify the circular breasts, dark like the *priyaṇgū*[7] blossom, of the *āndhra* damsels.

Now comes the description of qualities. In poetic-compositions rubies are described as red, flowers as white and clouds as dark in colour.

तत्र प्रथमः —

"सांयात्रिकैरविरतोपहृतानि कूटैः
श्यामासु तीरघनराजिषु सम्भृतानि।

6. Viṣṇu, God of the Hindu Pantheon, in his third incarnation. See Bhide, *op. cit.*, p. 214.

7. Though *priyaṅgū* flowers are yellow, here they have been described as dark.

रत्नानि ते दधति कश्चिदिहायताक्षि
मेघोदरोदितदिनाधिपबिम्बशङ्काम्।।"

The first example —

A flower set down on a young leaf
Or a pearl lying on the finest coral,
Only they can echo the dancing
Of her white smile and her red lips[8]

पुष्पशुक्लता —

"पुष्पं प्रवालोपहितं यदि स्या-
न्मुक्ताफलं वा स्फुटविद्रुमस्थम्।
ततोऽनुकुर्याद्विशदस्य तस्या-
स्ताम्रौष्ठपर्यस्तरुचः स्मितस्य।।"

Whiteness of flowers —

If *white flowers* were present on new leaves and pearls in the creepers then they could be used in a simile white describing the pure and beautiful smile which spreads on the *red lips* of Pārvatī.

मेघकार्ष्ण्यम् —

"मेघश्यामेन रामेण पूतवेदिर्विमानराट्।
मध्ये महेन्द्रनीलेन रत्नराशिरिवाबभौ।।"

कृष्णनीलयोः, कृष्णहरितयोः, कृष्णश्यामयोः, पीतरक्तयोः शुक्लगौरयोरेकत्वेन निबन्धनं च कविसमयः।

The darkness of clouds —

The *puṣpaka* air-plane with Rāma, dark like a cloud sitting in it appeared as beautiful as a sapphire in the midst of a heap of precious stones.

According to poetic-conventions, the colours black and blue, black and green, black and dark, yellow and red and white and fair can be used in place of each other.

---

8. See Kālidāsa' *Kumārasambhava*, *The Origin of the Young God*, Hank Heifetz, *op. cit.*, 1.44, p. 28.

कृष्णनीलयोरैक्यम् —

"नदीं तूर्णं कर्णोऽप्यनुसृतपुलिनां दाक्षिणात्यङ्गनाभिः
समुत्तीर्णो वर्णामुभयतटबलाबद्धवानीरहाराम्।
तटे सह्यस्योच्चैः स्वसलिलनिवहो भाति नीलः स यस्याः
प्रियस्यांशे पीने लुलित इव घनः केशपाशः सुकेश्याः।।"

The similarity of black and blue[9] —

King Karṇa also crossed the Varṇā river which is inhabited by the southern women who wear garlands made of bamboos which grow on either side of the river. The *blue* waterfall which falls from the mountain-top into this river appears to be like the dark mass of *black* hair of the beloved falling on the shoulders of her lover.

कृष्णहरितयोरैक्यम् —

"मरकतसदृशं च यामुनं
स्फटिकशिलाविमलं च जाह्नवम्।
तदुभयमुदकं पुनातु वो
हरिहरयोरिव सङ्गतं वपुः।।"

The similarity of black and green colours —

The *blue* sapphire like water of river Yamunā and the green crystal like waters of the river Gaṅgā mingle like Kṛṣṇa and Śiva. May these two Gods purify you!

कृष्णश्यामलयोरैक्यम् —

"एतत्सुन्दरि नन्दनं शशिमणिस्निग्धालवालद्रुमं
मन्दाकिन्यभिषिक्तमौक्तिकशिले मेरोस्तटे नन्दति।
यत्र श्यामनिशासु मुञ्चति मिलन्मन्दप्रदोषानिला-
मुद्दामामरयोषितामभिरतं कल्पद्रुमश्चन्द्रिकाम्।।"

पीतरक्तयोरैक्यम् —

"लेखया विमलविद्रुमभासा सन्ततं तिमिरमिन्दुरुदासे।

9. Here *nīla* (blue) and *kṛṣṇa* (black) colours are identical.

दंष्ट्रया कनकभङ्गपिशङ्ग्या मण्डलं भुव इवादिवराहः।।"

शुक्लगौरयोरैक्यम् —

"कैलासगौरं वृषमारुरुक्षोः
पादार्पणानुग्रहपूतपृष्ठम्।
अवेहि मां किङ्करमष्टमूर्तेः
कुम्भोदरं नाम निकुम्भपुत्रम्।।"

एवं वर्णान्तरेष्वपि। चक्षुरादेरनेकवर्णोपवर्णनम्।

The similarity of black (*kṛṣṇa*) and dark (*śyāma*) colours —

> O beautiful maiden! This forest is filled with brilliant precious stones in the base of trees and is situated at the foot of the Sumeru mountain which is rich with pearls washed ashore by the Mandākinī river. In the *dark* night, the *kalpavṛkṣa*[10] trees provide a soft breeze and moonlight to the goddesses according to their desires.

The similarity of yellow and red colours —

> The moon with its softly shining moonshine overthrows the darkness just like the *Primordial Boar* who with his shining yellow tusks bore the earth out of water.[11]

The non-discrimination between white and fair shades of colour —

> Know me to be the servant of Śiva of eight forms when the God wanted to mount his bull as *white* as Kailāsa he sanctified my back by deigning to set his foot on it. My name is Kumbhodara, the friend of Nikumbha.[12]

Similarly, one should see the similarity in mixed colours. The eyes have also been described in various colours by poets.

---

10. See Chapter 9, Reference 9, p. 129.
11. Here the *red* tusks of the Primordial Boar (*ādivarāḥ*) are described as possessing a yellow lustre.
12. See Kālidāsa's *Raghuvaṁśa, The Dynasty of Raghu*. Translated from the Sanskrit by Robert Antoine, A Writer's Workshop Publication, Calcutta, 1972, II.35, p. 28.

तत्र चक्षुषः शुक्लता —

"तिष्ठन्त्या जनसङ्कुलेऽपि सुदृशा सायं गृहप्राङ्गणे
तद्द्वारं मयि निःसहालसतनौ वीक्ष्यामृदु प्रेङ्खति।

ह्रीनम्राननयैव लोलसरलं निःश्वस्य तत्रान्तरे
प्रेमार्द्राः शशिखण्डपाण्डिममुषो मुक्ताः कटाक्षच्छटाः।।"

Thus the description of whiteness of eyes —

During the evening the girl with beautiful eyes was standing in the yard filled with people. On seeing me gesturing to her with tired and languishing limbs while going to my room, she bashfully and with bent head took a long and deep breath and gave me a sidelong love lorn look which appeared to steal the *white* brightness of moonshine.[13]

श्यामता —

"अथ पथि गमयित्वा रम्यक्लृप्तोपकार्ये
कतिचिदवनिपालः शर्वरीः शर्वकल्पः।
पुनरविशदयोध्यां मैथिलीदर्शिनीनां
कुवलयितगवाक्षां लोचनैरङ्गनानाम्।।"

Dark colour of eyes —

The lord of the earth, who looked like Śiva, spent a few nights on the way along which lovely tents had been erected. Then he entered the city of Ayodhyā. All the windows were full of (*dark*) lotus like lattices in the form of the eyes of the ladies eager to see the princesses of Mithilā.[14]

कृष्णता —

"पादन्यासक्वणितरशनास्तत्र लीलावधूतै-
रत्नच्छायाखचितबलिभिश्चामरैः क्लान्तहस्ताः।
वेश्यास्त्वत्तो नखपदसुखान्प्राप्य वर्षाग्रबिन्दू-

13. Here the description is of the beauty of the sidelong glances of a damsel surpassing the *whiteness* of the moon. Thus the whiteness of the glances reveals the whiteness of the eyes.

14. See Kālidāsa's *Raghuvaṁśa*, Robert Antoine, *ibid.*, XI.93, p. 134. Here the eyes of the ladies are compared to blue or dark lotuses.

नामोक्ष्यन्ते त्वयि मधुकरश्रेणिदीर्घान्कटाक्षान्।।"

Black colour of eyes —

With jewelled bells tinkling as they move with measured steps,
temple-dancers whose hands tire, gracefully waving,
Chowries with glittering gem-studded handless,
Will taste from the first rain-drops you shed,
pleasure as from a lover's nail-marks and shower on you,
(dark) sidelong glances streaming like a line of (black)
honey-bees.[15]

मिश्रवर्णता —

"तामुत्तीर्य व्रज परिचितभ्रूलताविभ्रमाणां
पक्ष्मोत्क्षेपादुपरि विलसत्कृष्णशारप्रभाणाम्।
कुन्दक्षेपानुगमधुकरश्रीमुषामात्मबिम्बं
पात्रीकुर्वन्दशपुरवधूनेत्रकौतूहलानाम्।।"

Mixed colour of eyes —

Crossing that river go onwards making yourself the target for the
eager eyes,
Of Daśapura's women accomplished
in the graceful play of curving eye-brows,
their eyes (with dark pupils) with upturned lashes flashing
With the beauty of gazelles leaping up,
And for surpassing the grace of honey (black) bees,
On white jasmines swaying.[16]

।। इति राजशेखरकृतौ काव्यमीमांसायां कविरहस्ये प्रथमेऽधिकरणे गुणसमयस्थापना पञ्चदशोऽध्यायः।।

---

15. See Kālidāsa's *Meghadūtam*, *The Loom of Time*, A Selection of His Plays and Poems. Translated from the Sanskrit and Prākṛt with an introduction by Chandra Rajan, Penguin Books, New Delhi, 1989, I.37, pp. 145-6.

    The words dark and black in parentheses have been added by me and are not present in the translation.

16. See Kālidāsa's, *Meghadūtam*, Chandra Rajan, *ibid.*, (I.49) p. 148.

    The words in the parentheses have been added by me since they appear in the original text of Rājaśekhara but are not a part of the translation cited above.

16

स्वर्ग्यपातालीयकविरहस्यस्थापना

Svargya-Pātālīya-Kavi-Rahasya-Sthāpanā
(Poetic Conventions Relating to Celestial and Nether Worlds)

भौमवत्स्वर्ग्योऽपि कविसमयः। विशेषस्तु चन्द्रमसि शशहरिणयोरैक्यम्।

यथा —

"मा भैः शशाङ्क मम सीधुनि नास्ति राहुः
खे रोहिणी वसति कातर किं बिभेषि।
प्रायो विदग्धवनितानवसङ्गमेषु
पुंसां मनः प्रचलतीति किमत्र चित्रम्।।"

यथा च —

अङ्काधिरोपितमृगश्चन्द्रमा मृगलाञ्छनः।
केसरी निष्ठुराक्षिप्तमृगयूथो मृगाधिपः।।"

JUST as terrestrial *kavi-samaya* has been described so also is the celestial *kavi-samaya* such as the union of the rabbit and the deer in the moon.

Thus —

Do not thou fear, O Moon! Rāhu (the Eclipser) is not present in my wine: as for Rohiṇī (thy wife) she is in the sky — why then shouldst thou be afraid of her? As a rule whenever young men meet clever women for the first time, their minds are fickle, what wonder then that thou art behaving thus[1]?

1. See Vāmana's, *Kāvyālaṁkāra-Sūtra-Vṛtti*, *op. cit.*, 3-2-8, p. 50.

Also

> The moon which holds the deer in its lap is called *mṛgalāñcana* whereas the lion who ruthlessly destroys a group of deer is called a *mṛgarāja*.

कामकेतने मकरमत्स्ययोरैक्यं यथा —

"चापं पुष्पमयं गृहाण मकरः केतुः समुच्छ्रीयतां
चेतालक्ष्यभिदश्च पञ्च विशिखाः पाणौ पुनः सन्तु ते।
दग्धा कापि तवाकृतेः प्रतिकृतिः कामोऽसि किं गूहसे
रूपं दर्शय नाऽत्र शङ्करभयं सर्वे वयं वैष्णवाः।।"

यथा च —

"मीनध्वजस्त्वमसि नो न च पुष्पधन्वा
केलिप्रकाश तव मन्मथता तथापि।
इत्थं त्वया विरहितस्य मयोपलब्धाः
कान्ताजनस्य जननाथ चिरं विलापाः।।"

यथा वा —

"आपातमारुतविलोडितसिन्धुनाथो
हात्कारभीतपरिवर्त्तितमत्स्यचिह्नाम्।
उल्लङ्घ्य यादवमहोदधिभीमवेलां
द्रोणाचलं पवनसूनुरिवोद्धरामि।।"

Similarly the emblem of Kāmadeva (Cupid, God of Love) is sometimes signified by a *makara*[2] while at others by a fish but for a poet they both should be considered one.

> O, Kāmadeva! Lift your flowery bow string, unfurl your *makara* banner, take the five arrows which will pierce their respective target in your land. Mahādeva (Lord Śiva) must have incinerated some other body which resembled yours. You are Kāma. Why are you hiding? Come out in your true form! Here there is no fear of Śaṅkara (Śiva). We are all Vaiṣṇavas.[3]

---

2. *Makara* is a kind of sea animal resembling a crocodile and is regarded as the emblem of God of love. See Bhide, *op. cit.*, p. 841.

3. *Vaiṣṇavas* are worshippers of Viṣṇu, one of the three important, modern Hindu sects, the other two being Śaiva and Śākta sects.

Also —

> O Jananāth! Maidens are seen lamenting for long in separation. Though you are not a *mīnadhvaj* (an emblem of a fish) nor a *puspadhānva* (flowered bow-string) yet you who are present in the art of amorous sport are surely God of Love.

Thus —

> Just as Māruta (a name of Hanumān) to acquire medicinal drugs, crossed an ocean full of animals and came back with a mountain so also I with my strong winds will inundate Sindunātha, cross over the mighty shores of Yādava ocean and carry back the mountain Droṇācala.

अत्रिनेत्रसमुद्रोत्पन्नचन्द्रयोरैक्यम् —

> "वन्द्या विश्वसृजो युगादिगुरवः स्वायम्भुवाः सप्त ये
> तत्रात्रिर्दिवि सन्दधे नयनजं ज्योतिः स चन्द्रोऽभवत्।
> एका यस्य शिखण्डमण्डनमणिर्देवस्य शम्भोः कला
> शेषाभ्योऽमृतमाप्नुवन्ति च सदा स्वाहास्वधाजीविनः।।"

According to tradition the origin of the moon is attributed to either the eye of the sage Attrī or the ocean. But (according to poetic-convention) they both are one.

Thus —

> Obeisance is paid to the Lord of Creation's progeny (Brahmā) and creators of the entire world the *saptarṣis*.[4] Of them the sage Attrī has concentrated the light of the eye in the sky, which has come to be known as the Moon. One digit of this moon has become the ornament of the matted locks of Śambhu (Śiva) and from the remaining digits[5] of the moon. May the Svāhājīvī[6] Gods and

---

4. The *Saptarṣis* or the seven *ṛṣis* are the holiest of the human ascetics who have become divine through their mental and physical *tapas*. They are the stars in the constellation of the Great Bear. See Hank Heifetz (tr.), *The Origin of the Young God*, *op. cit.*, Notes. 1.16, p. 137.

5. Total digits of the moon are sixteen.

6. *Svāhā* is an oblation or offering made to all Gods indiscriminately.

Svadhājīvī[7] ancestors forever obtain *amṛta* (nectar, drink of Gods).

बहुकालजन्मनोरपि शिवचन्द्रमसोर्बालत्वम्।

यथा —

"मालायमानामरसिन्धुहंसः
कोटीरवल्लीकुसुमं भवस्य।
दाक्षायणीविभ्रमदर्पणश्रि
बालेन्दुखण्डं भवतः पुनीतात् ।।"

कामस्य मूर्त्तत्वं च यथा —

"अयं स भुवनत्रयप्रथितसंयमः शङ्करो
बिभर्त्ति वपुषाधुना विरहकातरः कामिनीम्।
अनेन किल निर्जिता वयमिति प्रियायाः करं
करेण परिताडयन् जयति जातहासः स्मरः।।"

यथा च —

"धनुर्माला मौर्वी क्वणदलिकुलं लक्ष्यमबला
मनोभेद्यं शब्दप्रभृति य इमे पञ्च विशिखाः।
इयान् जेतुं यस्य त्रिभुवनमनङ्गस्य विभवः
स वः कामः कामान्दिशतु दयितापाङ्गवसतिः।।"

Though of ancient origin the half-moon on Śiva's forehead is always described in the form of a young boy.

Thus —

May the pearl necklace like Mandākinī flowing though the matted hair of Śiva with the swans by its side, the white flower like creepers in his tangled locks and the mirror or fragment of the child-moon for Pārvatī's ornamentation bless and purify you.

Poets have described Passion Incarnate thus —

This is the same Śaṅkara (Śiva) whose self-restraint is famous in all the three worlds. Today he in the longing borne of separation

7. *Svadhā* is the oblation of food offered to the *pitṛ*s of ancestors.

is sitting with a beautiful woman in half his body. "Did he ever win me over". Thus saying and playfully patting his beloved's hand (Rati the wife of Kāmadeva) laughs Kāmadeva. Glory to the God of Love!

Also —

For the one who has a bow of flowers, a buzzing-bees like bow-string, for whom gentle maidens are the ends and words and the five subjects to pierce the heart are the arrows. For this same one who has this abundance of means to win over the three worlds and who resides in the side glances of beloved maidens — May Lord Kāmadeva (God of Love) grant success to all your desires.

द्वादशानामप्यादित्यानामैक्यम् —

"यस्याधोऽधस्तथोपर्युपरि निरवधि भ्राम्यतो विश्वमश्वै-
रावृत्तालातलीलां रचयति रयतो मण्डलं चण्डधाम्नः।
सोऽव्यादुत्तप्तकार्त्तस्वरसरलशरस्पर्द्धिभिर्द्धामदण्डै-
रुद्दण्डैः प्रापयन्वः प्रचुरतमतमःस्तोममस्तं समस्तम्।।"

नारायणमाधवयोश्च यथा —

"येन ध्वस्तमनोभवेन बलिजित्कायः पुरास्त्रीकृतो
यो गङ्गां च दधेऽन्धकक्षयकरो यो बर्हिपत्रप्रियः।
यस्याहुः शशिमच्छिरोहर इति स्तुत्यं च नामामराः
सोऽव्यादिष्टभुजङ्गहारवलयस्त्वां सर्वदो माधवः।।"

Though the Purāṇas mention twelve suns for poetic-compositions there should be considered only one —

In this world moving by means of horses down below and the swift winds above, the shining rays of the disc like sun appears to be like the burning and rotating wind swept ball of fire. May this shining orb, by means of the heated gold rod like rays which destroy the dense darkness protect you.

Thus also Nārāyaṇa (epithet of Viṣṇu) and Mādhava (name of Indra) are one.

The one who slew Śakṭāsura,[8] who transformed the Vāmana[9] body of Bālī's victor into that of a woman, the one who in Kr̥ṣṇa's form (Viṣṇu's incarnation) bore the Govardhana mountain and in Kūrma's[10] incarnate form bore the earth, the one who vanquished Andhak,[11] he who has a fondness for peacock feathers, who is known by other Gods as 'the one who had slain the moon's enemy or Rāhu and the one who slew a snake — May the same Lord Mādhava protect you'.

Śiva or the one who destroyed Kāmadeva, who used Nārāyaṇa's body (epithet of Viṣṇu) as a weapon while killing Tripurāsura,[12] the one who destroyed Andhakāsura (name of a demon), the one who is loved by Kārttikeya, the one who bears a half moon on the forehead, the one who is fondly addressed as 'Har' by other Gods and the one who wears bracelets and garlands of snakes. May the same Śiva, beloved of Umā always protect you.

एवं दामोदरशेषकूर्मादेः, कमलासम्पदोश्च। यथा —

"दोर्मन्दीरित मन्दरेण जलधेरुत्थापिता या स्वयं
यां भूत्वा कमठः पुराणककुदन्यरतागुदस्तम्भयत्।
तां लक्ष्मीं पुरुषोत्तमः पुनरसौ लीलाञ्चितभ्रूलता-
निर्देशैः समवीविशत्प्रणयिनां गेहेषु दोष्णि क्षितिम्।।"

भौमस्वर्ग्यवत्पातालीयोऽपि कविसमयः।

तत्र नागसर्पयोरैक्यम् —

"हे नागराज बहुमस्य नितम्बभागं
भोगेन गाढमभिवेष्टय मन्दराद्रेः।

8. Name of a demon slain by Kr̥ṣṇa when quite a boy. See Chaturvedi, *op. cit.*, p. 1033.

9. Viṣṇu in his fifth incarnation. See Bhide, *op. cit.*, p. 967.

10. Kūrma is a tortoise, Viṣṇu is his second incarnation. See Bhide, *op. cit.*, p. 379.

11. Andhaka is the name of a demon killed by God Śaṅkara, See Bhide, *op. cit.*, p. 86.

12. Name of a demon presiding over these cities — a collection of three cities of gold, silver and iron in the sky, air and earth built for demons by Maya. See Bhide, *op. cit.*, p. 524.

सोढाविषह्यवृषवाहनयोगलीला-
पर्यङ्कबन्धनविधेस्तव कोऽतिभारः।।"

Similarly Dāmodara, Śeṣa, Kūrma Kamala (an epithet of Lakṣmī) and Sampadā (wealth) should also be treated as one.

Thus —

Lord Viṣṇu has by means of his own hands while churning the ocean created Lakṣmī (goddess of wealth) and in the incarnate form of Kūrma stabilised the earth on his back and then the same Supreme Power with only a shaking of Lakṣmī's eyebrow established her in the hearts of the devotees and taken the earth in his own arms.

Just as terrestrial and celestial so also is time of the nether world for poets.

Though the king of Nāgas is Śeṣa (a mythical Nāga) and that of snakes is Vāsuki,[13] for poets, they should be treated as one.

Thus —

For churning the ocean the Mandāra mountain was used as the stick and Vāsuki as the rope and here the poet addresses Vāsuki.

O Nāgarāja! With your body, hold the sides of the Mandāra mountain tightly. For you to bear this weight is nothing compared to the posture[14] adopted in meditation for Lord Śiva.

दैत्यदानवासुराणामैक्यम्, यथा तत्र हिरण्याक्षहिरण्यकशिपुप्रह्लादविरोचनबलिबाणादयो दैत्याः, विप्रचित्तिशम्बरनमुचिपुलोमप्रभृतयो दानवाः, बलवृत्रविक्षुरस्त वृषपर्वादयोऽसुराः।

तेषामैक्यं यथा —

"जयन्ति बाणासुरमौलिलालिता
दशास्यचूडामणिचक्रचुम्बिनः।
सुरासुराधीशशिखान्तशायिनो

13. Name of a celebrated serpent, king of snakes.

14. Paryaṅka is a particular kind of posture adopted in meditation. It requires sitting on the hams with a cloth girt around the back, loins and knees. See Bhide, *op. cit.*, p. 672.

भवच्छिदस्त्र्यम्बकपादपांसवः।।"

Thus *daityas*[15], *dānavas*[16] and *asura*[17] are the different kinds of demons residing in *pātāla* (the nether world) and are different, for example, Hiraṇyākṣa, Hiraṇyakaśipu, Prahlāda, Virocana, Bāli, Bāṇa, etc., are *daityas*. Vipracitti Sambara, Namuci, Puloma, etc., are *dānavas* and Bāla, Vṛtra, Vṛṣaparva are *asuras*.

Thus —

Caressing the forehead of Bāṇasūra, kissing the rubies in the round crown of Rāvaṇa and with a place on the foreheads of gods and demons alike, glory be to the dust off Śiva's feet.

यथा च —

"तं शम्बरासुरशराशनिशल्यसारं
केयूररत्नकिरणारुणबाहुदण्डम्।
पीनांसलग्नदयिताकुचपत्रभङ्गं
मीनध्वजं जितजगत्त्रितयं जयेत्कः।।"

यथा च —

"अस्ति दैत्यो हयग्रीवः सुहृद्वेश्मसु यस्य ताः।
प्रथयन्ति बलं बाह्वोः सितच्छत्रस्मिताः श्रियः।।"

यथा च हयग्रीवं प्रति —

"दानवाधिपते भूयो भुजोऽयं किं न नीयते।
सहायतां कृतान्तस्य क्षयाभिप्रायसिद्धिषु।।"

यथा च —

"महासुरसमाजेऽस्मिन् न चैकोऽप्यस्ति सोऽसुरः।
यस्य नाशनिनिष्पेषनीराजितमुरःस्थलम्।।"

---

15. *Daitya* is 'the son of Diti' — a *rākṣasa*, epithets of Śukra, the preceptor of the *asuras*. See Bhide, *op. cit.*, p. 557.
16. *Dānava* most probably a term for an ethnic group.
17. *Asura* is an ethnic group.

However these differences between *daityas*, *dānavas* and *asuras* are dissolved in case of poetic-conventions. *Dānava*, *daityas* and *asuras* are terms for ethnic groups that have racial affinity with Indian Āryans but do not subscribe to the Vedic culture.

एवमन्येपि भेदाः —

सोऽयं कवीनां समयः काव्ये सुप्त इव स्थितः।
स साम्प्रतमिहास्माभिर्यथाबुद्धिविबोधितः।।

Thus —

Who can vanquish Kāmadeva (cupid, God of Love), vanquisher of the three worlds who is strong like the weapons or bow-string of Śambrāsura, arms wearing amulets tinged with the earth and bearing a bosom marked by the words imprinted on his beloved Rati's breasts?

Thus —

Hayagrīva is the *daitya*, from whose friends' homes sitting under a bright umbrella the gently smiling Lakṣmī appears to give an indication of his muscular strength.

And also the same Hayagrīva is addressed as a *dānava*.

O *dānava rāja*! Why don't you use time and your muscular strength to achieve the intended desire of universal destruction (of your enemies).

Also —

In this entire community of *mahāsuras* there is not a single *asura*, whose chest is free of imprints occasioned by the attack of Indra's weapon.

Similarly poets should imagine the other differences themselves. Thus *kavi-samaya* which seemed to be in a state of sleep in poetic compositions has been reawakened according to our intellect.

।। इति रजशेखरकृतौ काव्यमीमांसायां कविरहस्ये प्रथमेऽधिकरणे स्वर्ग्यपातालीयकविरहस्यस्थापना षोडशोऽध्यायः।।

17

देशविभागः

Deśa-Vibhāgaḥ

(Geographical Regions and its Divisions)

देशं कालं च विभजमानः कविर्नार्थदर्शनदिशि दरिद्राति।

जगज्जगदेकदेशाश्च देशः। द्यावापृथिव्यात्मकमेकं जगदित्येके।

तदाहुः —

"हलमगु बलस्यैकोऽनड्वान्हरस्य न लाङ्गलं
क्रमपरिमिता भूमिर्विष्णोर्नगौर्न च लाङ्गलम्।
प्रवहति कृषिर्नाद्याप्येषां द्वितीयगवं विना
जगति सकले नेदृग्दृष्टं दरिद्रकुटुम्बकम्।।"

"दिवस्पृथिव्यौ द्वे जगती" इत्यपरे।

A POET who learns the division of region, space and time does not remain devoid of the ability to see or understand meanings.

Deśa[1] refers to the world or anyone of its geographical regions.

As in —

Balarāma (elder brother of Lord Kṛṣṇa), the ploughman has a plough but not a bull. Śiva (a god of the Hindu Pantheon), has a bull but not a plough. Viṣṇu (a God of the Hindu Trinity) has a foot measure of land obtained in alms but does not possess a plough or a bull. If the three of them together wish to farm it would be

---

1. *Deśa* is a country, land, native-home, region space. See Chaturvedi, *op. cit.*, p. 328. Here the word *deśa* is restricted to space, region or land.

impossible without another bull. Such a poor family is unseen and unheard of in the entire world.

Others say that the earth and the sky constitute the two worlds.

तदाहुः —

"रुणद्धि रोदसी वास्य यावत्कीर्त्तिरनश्वरी।
तावत्किलायमध्यास्ते सुकृती वैबुधं पदम्।।"

"स्वर्ग्यमर्त्यपातालभेदास्त्रीणि जगन्ति" इत्येके।

यदाहुः —

"त्वमेव देव पातालमाशानां त्वं निबन्धनम्।
त्वं चामरमरुद्भूमिरेको लोकत्रयायसे।।"
"तान्येव भूर्भुवःस्वः" इत्यन्ये।

तदाहुः —

"नमस्त्रिभुवनाभोगभृतिखेदभरादिव।
नागनाथाङ्गपर्यङ्कशायिने शार्ङ्गधन्वने।।"

'महर्जनस्तपः सत्यमित्येतैः सह सप्त' इत्यपरे।

तदाहुः —

"संस्तम्भिनी पृथुनितम्बतटैर्धरित्र्याः
संवाहिनी जलमुचां चलकेतुहस्तैः।
हर्षस्य सप्तभुवनप्रथितोरुकीर्तेः
प्रासादपङ्क्तिरियमुच्छिखरा विभाति।।"

'तानि सप्तभिर्वायुस्कन्धैः सह चतुर्दश' इति केचित्।

तदाहुः —

"निरवधि च निराश्रयं च यस्य
स्थितमनुवर्त्तितकौतुकप्रपञ्चम्।
प्रथम इह भवान्स कूर्ममूर्त्ति-
र्जयति चतुर्द्दशलोकवल्लिकन्दः।।"

Thus also —

And as long as this everlasting fame of an author encircles the *sky and the earth*, so long does the privileged one surely continue to hold a place among the gods.[2]

Others say that, 'there are three worlds, heaven (*svarga*), earth or human world (*mṛtya loka*) and the nether world (*pātāla*).'

As in —

O King! Thou art the nether world, thou art the basis of all directions found in this world and thou art the land of gods and sea-breezes. You alone are the *three worlds*.

Some posit that these three worlds are denoted as *bhūr*, *bhuvar* and *svar*.[3]

Obeisance is paid to Lord Viṣṇu bearer of the Śārṅga bow and reclining on the Śeṣa-nāga (the lord of Nāgas), to rid himself of the weariness born of the burden of sustaining the vast *three worlds.*

Others say that including *mahar*, *janas*, *tapas* and *satya* there are seven worlds.

Thus —

Shining in splendour, these rows of palatial mansions with high elevated towers, solid foundations holding back the earth, flying pennant like waving arms flowing with the clouds, belong to Emperor Harṣa whose renown fills the seven worlds.

Some say that, 'these seven worlds alone with seven divisions of winds together from *fourteen worlds*'.

As in —

Your operations being endless and independent you are like the Primeval tortoise being the very root of the creeper of the *fourteen worlds.*[4]

---

2. See Bhāmaha's *Kāvyālaṁkāra*, *op. cit.* (I.7).
3. In the Śruti texts, these terms it is said denote the three worlds.
4. Rājaśekhara quotes this from Vāmana's *Kāvyālaṁkāra-Sūtra-vṛtti*, *op. cit.*, IV.3.31, p. 88. Here the metaphor contained in the phrase 'root of the creeper of the worlds' is based upon the simile contained in the rest of the verse between the king and the tortoise-shaped Viṣṇu.

'तानि सप्तभिः पातालैः सहैकविंशतिः' इति केचित्।

तदाहुः —

"हरहासहरावासहरहारनिभप्रभाः।
कीर्त्तयस्तव लिम्पन्तु भुवनान्येकविंशतिम्।।"

'सर्वमुपपन्नम्' इति यायावरीयः। अविशेषविवक्षा यदेकयति, विशेषविवक्षात्वनेकयति। तेषु भूर्लोकः पृथिवी। तत्र सप्त महाद्वीपाः। यथा —

"जम्बूद्वीपः सर्वमध्ये ततश्च प्लक्षो नाम्ना शाल्मलोऽतः कुशोऽतः।
क्रौञ्चः शाकः पुष्करश्चेत्यथैषां बाह्या बाह्या संस्थितिर्मण्डलीभिः।।
लावणो रसमयः सुरोदकः सार्पिषो दधिजलः पयःपयाः।
स्वादुवारिरुदधिश्च सप्तमस्तान्परीत्य त इमे व्यवस्थिताः।।"

'एक एवायं लावणः समुद्रः' इत्येके।

In yet another opinion 'these fourteen worlds along with seven nether worlds (*pātāla*) makes *twenty-one worlds*'.

As in —

May your renown radiant like the laughter of the Lord (Śiva), the abode of Śiva (Kailāsa) and the garlands of Śiva (of serpents) light up all the twenty one worlds.

Yāyāvarīya (Rājaśekhara) says 'All the opinions mentioned above are correct.' When plainly stated an object may be described and conceptualised as one but when extraordinarily conceptualised it becomes manifested in many forms. So though there is one world the earth, it has seven island continents (*mahādvīpas*).

Jambudvīpa is in the centre of all islands. It comprises serially the islands of Plākṣa, Śālmalī, Kuśa, Krauñca, Śāka and Puṣkara. The position of these islands is outer and circular (concentric).[5]

There are seven oceans of salt water (*lavaṇa*), sugarcane juice (*ikṣu-rasa*), wine (*surā*), ghee (*sarpi*), curd (*dadhi*), milk (*kṣīra*) and water (*jala*) which surround these islands.

5. The modern equivalents of places are given at the end in Appendix II.

Some say that, 'salt and water together form one ocean only.'

तदाहुः —

"द्वीपान्यष्टादशात्र क्षितिरपि नवभिर्विस्तृता स्वाङ्गखण्डै-
रेकोऽम्भोधिर्दिगन्तप्रविसृतसलिलः प्राज्यमेतत्सुराज्यम्।
कस्मिन्नप्याजिकेलिव्यतिकरविजयोपार्जिते वीरवर्ये
चक्रे पुञ्जेन दातुं तदिदमिति धिया वेधसे यश्चुकोप।।"

'त्रयः' इत्यन्ये।

तदाहुः —

"आकम्पितक्षितिभृता महता निकामं
हेलाभिभूतजलधित्रितयेन यस्य।
वीर्येण संहतिभिदा विहतोन्नतेन
कल्पान्तकालविसृतः पवनोऽनुचक्रे।।"

Thus —

This world has eighteen islands, the earth has nine divisions. The great warrior (probably) Paraśurāma became dissatisfied with Brahmā because he thought that all these eighteen islands, earth with its nine sub-divisions, one mighty ocean and the fertile country all around, acquired by him through his prowess in battles seemed to him to be insufficient.[6]

Some people posit '*the existence of three oceans*'.

As in —

A mighty warrior, the king's skill in breaking through the enemies squad was like the destructive and violent mind which made mountains and other kings tremble in fear and put the three oceans in tumult.

यथा वा —

"मातङ्गानामभावे मदमलिनमुखैः प्राप्तमाशाकरीन्द्रैः
जाते रत्नापहारे दिशि दिशि ततयो भान्ति चिन्तामणीनाम्।
छिन्नेषूद्यानवापीतरुषु विरचिताः कल्पवृक्षा रिपूणां

6. See Dalal, *op. cit.*, p. 240.

यस्योदञ्चत्त्रिवेलावलयफलभुजां मानसी सिद्धिरासीत्।।"

'चत्वारः' इत्यपरे।

तदाहुः —

"चतुःसमुद्रवेलोर्मिरचितैकावलीलतम्।
मेरुमप्यद्रिमुल्लङ्घ्य यस्य क्वापि गतं यशः।।"

The enemies of a king were defeated and driven out to the shores of the *three oceans*, where also they found riches of a king in the form of elephants *cintāmaṇi*[7] jewels and *kalpavṛksa*[8] trees although they had lost their own elephants, jewels and gardens.

Some people say there exist 'four oceans'

Thus —

The king's glory is like the garland made from the waves of the sea-shores of the *four oceans* and seems to have reached far and wide much beyond the Sumeru[9] mountain.

'भिन्नाभिप्रायतया सर्वमुपपन्नम्' इति यायावरीयः। सप्तसमुद्रीवादिनस्तु शास्त्रादनपेता एव।

तदाहुः —

"आगस्त्यचुलुकोच्छिष्टसप्तवारिधिवारिणि।
मुहूर्तं केशवेनाऽपि तदन्तः पूतरायितम्।।

मध्ये जम्बूद्वीपमाद्यो गिरीणां
मेरुर्नाम्ना काञ्चनः शैलराजः।
यो मूर्त्तानामौषधीनां निधानं
यश्चावासः सर्ववृन्दारकाणाम्।।

Yāyāvarīya (Rājaśekhara) says that, 'different poets have different interpretations and thus all opinions are valid'. Those who believe in the existence of seven seas are also not non-technical, their belief also has a scientific (*śāstric*) basis.

---

7. *Cintāmaṇi* is a fabulous mythological gem supposed to grant all desires. See Chaturvedi, *op. cit.*, p. 207.

8. *Kalpavṛkṣa* is a mythological tree or plant that is supposed to grant all desires. See Chaturvedi, *op. cit.*, p. 124.

9. Sumerū is a mythological mountain made of gold. See Chaturvedi, *op. cit.*, p. 823.

Thus —

Keśava (Viṣṇu) also appeared to be momentarily like a piece of straw in the hands of Agastya when he commenced drinking the water of the seven oceans.

In the centre of Jambudvīpa is the king of mountains, the goldern Meru mountain which is an incarnate reservoir of medicinal drugs and an abode for all the Gods.

तमेनमवधीकृत्य देवेनाम्बुजजन्मना।
तिर्यगूर्ध्वमधस्ताच्च विश्वस्य रचना कृता।।

स भगवान्मेरुराद्यो वर्षपर्वतः। तस्य चतुर्दिशमिलावृतं वर्षम्। तस्योत्तरेण त्रयो वर्षगिरयः, नीलः श्वेतः शृङ्गवांश्च। रम्यकं, हिरण्मयम्, उत्तराः कुरव इति च क्रमेण त्रीणि तेषां वर्षाणि। दक्षिणेनापि त्रय एव निषधो हेमकूटो हिमवांश्च। हरिवर्षं, किंपुरुषं, भारतमिति च त्रीणि वर्षाणि। तत्रेदं भारतं वर्षमस्य। च नव भेदाः। इन्द्रद्वीपः, कसेरुमान्, ताम्रपर्णो, गभस्तिमान्, नागद्वीपः, सौम्यो, गन्धर्वो, वरुणः, कुमारीद्वीपश्चायं नवमः।

पञ्चशतानि जलं, पञ्च स्थलमिति विभागेन प्रत्येकं योजनसहस्रावधयो दक्षिणात्समुद्रादद्रिराजं हिमवन्तं यावत्परस्परमगम्यास्ते।

तान्येतानि यो जयति स सम्राडित्युच्यते। कुमारीपुरात्प्रभृति बिन्दुसरोऽवधि योजनानां दशशती चक्रवर्त्तिक्षेत्रम्। तां विजयमानश्चक्रवर्त्ती भवति।

चक्रवर्त्तिचिह्नानि तु —

"चक्रं रथो मणिर्भार्या निधिरश्वो गजस्तथा।
प्रोक्तानि सप्त रत्नानि सर्वेषां चक्रवर्त्तिनाम्।।"

With the Sumeru mountain as centre point, Brahmā has created the world above, below and sideways from it.

Bhagvān Mount Meru is the first mount in the centre. Around it are the Ilāvṛta Varṣa Mount. In the north of Jambū- dvīpa are the Nīla, Śveta and Śṛṅgavān Varṣa mounts and the geographical divisions (*deśa*) are the Ramyaka, Hiranmaya and Uttara-Kuru. To the south are Niṣādha, Hemakūṭa and Himavān Varṣa Mounts and Harivarṣa, Kiṁpuruṣa and Bhārata are the three *varṣas*. This is Bhārata-varṣa. It has nine divisions. These are Indradvīpa, Kaserumān, Tāmraparṇa, Gabhastimān, Nāga-dvīpa, Saumya, Gandharva, Varuṇa-dvīpa and Kumārī-dvīpa.

Of these nine islands, the five-hundredth part is water and fifth part is land. The measurement of each island is one thousand *yojanas*.[10]

These islands are spread from the ocean in the south to the Himālayas in the north and are mutually inaccessible.

The one who gains victory over these islands is called a *samrāṭ*. The area between Kumārī-dvīpa and Bindusāra is one thousand *yojanas* and is called a Cakravartīkṣetra. The king who gains victory on this entire area is called a Cakravartī.

Signs of a Cakravartī —

Disc, carriages, ruby, wife, treasure, horses and elephants are the seven signs of Cakravatīs.

Jambū-Dvīpa

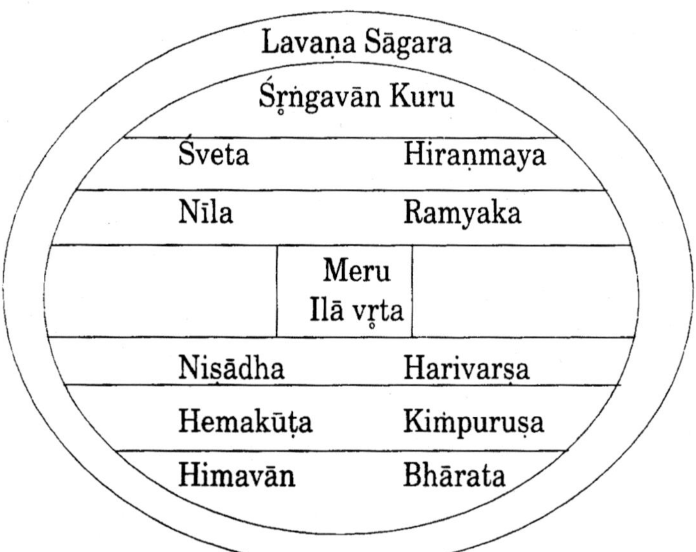

Diagram 1: See M.R. Singh, *Geographical Data in the Early Puranas: A Critical Study*, 1972, p. 3, Diagram No. 1.

अत्र च कुमारीद्वीपे —

10. *Yojana* is a measure of distance roughly equal to eight miles. See Chaturvedi and Tiwari, *op. cit.*, p. 533.

"विन्ध्यश्च पारियात्रश्च शुक्तिमानृक्षपर्वतः।
महेन्द्रसह्यमलयाः सप्तैते कुलपर्वताः।।"

तत्र विन्ध्यादयः प्रतीतस्वरूपा मलयविशेषास्तु चत्वारः।

तेषु प्रथमः —

"आ मूलयष्टेः फणिवेष्टितानां
सच्चन्दनानां जननन्दनानाम्।
कक्कोलकैलामरिचैर्युतानां
जातीतरूणां च स जन्मभूमिः।।"

Kumārī-dvīpa has seven Kula mounts. These are Vindhyas, Pāriyātra, Śuktimān, Ṛkṣa, Mahendra, Sahay and Malaya.

Out of these the Vindhyas and five other mounts are well-known. The Malaya mount has four divisions.

Thus the first Malaya —

This Malaya mount is covered with trees which have coiled serpents from the roots to the tips and it is the birthplace of sandalwood, cardamom, nutmeg (*Myristica moschata*) and black pepper trees.

द्वितीयः —

"यस्योत्तमां मौक्तिककामधेनुरुपत्यकामर्चति ताम्रपर्णी।
रत्नेश्वरो रत्नमहानिधानं कुम्भोद्भवस्तं मलयं पुनाति।।
तत्र द्रुमा विद्रुमनामधेया वंशेषु मुक्ताफलजन्म तत्र।
मदोत्कटैः केसरिकण्ठनादैः स्फुटन्ति तस्मिन्घनसारवृक्षाः।।"

The second Malaya —

In the low-lying areas of this Malaya mount there flows the Muktā-Kāmadhenu (producer of pearls) or Tāmraparṇī river. This river is a mine of pearls and is made pure by the *āśrama* of the sage Agastya near it. The *vidrum* trees (*coral* tree) grow on the Malaya. The bamboos produce pearls and when the intoxicated lions roar the *karpūra* trees blossom forth.

तृतीयः —

"विलासभूमिः सकलामराणां

पदं नृणां गौर्मुनिपुङ्गवस्य।
सदाफलैः पुष्पलताप्रवालै-
राश्चर्यमूलं मलयः स तत्र।।"

The third Malaya —

> This Mount of Malaya is the sporting ground for the Gods. For men it is a holy place and the abode of the sage Agastya. There are fruit laden trees and creepers filled with flowers and leaves.

चतुर्थः —

"सा तत्र चामीकररत्नचित्रैः
प्रासादमालावलभीविटङ्कैः।
द्वारार्गलाबद्धसुरेश्वराङ्का
लङ्केति या रावणराजधानी।।
प्रवर्त्तते कोकिलनादहेतुः
पुष्पप्रसूः पञ्चमजन्मदायी।
तेभ्यश्चतुर्भ्योऽपि वसन्तमित्र-
मुदङ्मुखो दक्षिणमातरिश्वा।।"

The fourth Malaya —

> In this Malaya there are rows of precious stone-studded golden palatial mansions which bear on their top parts cages of pigeons through which can be seen the gleaming capital city of Rāvaṇa called Laṅkā (Ceylon). The main entrance gate to the city has an emblem of God Indra present on it.

In all these four mounts there blows the southern wind moving towards north and blessing the cuckoos with a sweet sound, helping to produce new flowers, originating the *pañcaṁ* musical note and a friend of the spring season.

पूर्वापरयोः समुद्रयोर्हिमवद्विन्ध्ययोश्चान्तरमार्यावर्त्तः। तस्मिंश्चातुर्वर्ण्यं चातुराश्रम्यं च। तन्मूलश्च सदाचारः। तत्रत्यो व्यवहारः प्रायेण कवीनाम्।

तत्र वाराणस्याः पुरतः पूर्वदेशः। यत्राङ्गकलिङ्गकोसलतोसलोत्कलमगधो-मुद्गरविदेहनेमपालपुण्ड्रप्राग्ज्योतिषतामलिप्तक मलदमल्लवर्त्तकसुह्मब्रह्मोत्तरप्रभृतयो जनपदाः। बृहद्गृहलोहितगिरिचकोरदर्दुरनेपालकामरूपादयः पर्वताः। शोणलौहित्यौ नदौ। गङ्गाकरतोयाक-

पिशाद्याश्च नद्यः। लवलीग्रन्थिपर्णकागुरुद्राक्षाकस्तूरिकादीनामुत्पादः।

Between the eastern and western oceans and in the centre of Himālayas and the Vindhyas there is the Āryāvartta. There are (*varṇas*) four classes and four stages (*āśrama*) of people prevalent in Āryāvartta. This forms the basis for society. The poets also follow the tradition prevalent in Āryāvartta in their descriptions.

In Āryāvartta, east of Vārāṇasī are the *janapadas* of Aṅga, Vaṅga, Kaliṅga, Kośala, Toṣala, Utkala, Magadha, Mudgara, Videha, Nepāla, Puṇḍra, Prāgjyotiṣa, Tāmraliptaka, (or Tāmaliptaka), Malada, Mallavarttaka, Suhay and Brahmottara, Bṛhadgraha, Lohitgiri, Cakora, Dadur, Nepāla, and Kāmarūpa are the mountains. Śoṇa, Lauhitya, Gaṅgā, Kartoyā and Kapiśā are the rivers. Lovely, Kasturī, Granthiparṇaka, Agurū and *drākṣā* (grapes) are the plants produced here.

माहिष्मत्याः परतो दक्षिणापथः। यत्र महाराष्ट्रमाहिष काश्मकविदर्भ-कुन्तलक्रथकैशिकसूर्पारक काञ्चीकेरलकावेरमुरलवानवासकसिंहलचोडदण्डक-पाण्ड्यपल्लवगाङ्गनाशिक्य कौङ्कणकोल्लगिरिवल्लरप्रभृतयो जनपदाः। विन्ध्य-दक्षिणपादमहेन्द्रमलयमेकलपालमञ्जरसह्यश्रीपर्वतादयः पर्वताः। नर्मदातापीपयोष्णी-गोदावरीकावेरीभैमरथीवेणाकृष्णवेणावञ्जुरातुङ्गभद्राताम्रमण्युत्पलावतीरावणगङ्गाद्या नद्यः। तदुत्पत्तिर्मलयोत्पत्त्या व्याख्याता।

After Mahiṣmatī is the south which has the following *janapadas* — Mahārāṣṭra, Māhiṣaka, Aśmaka, Vidarbha, Kuntala, Krathkaiśika, Sūrpāraka, Kāñcī, Kerala, Kāvera, Murala, Vanvāsaka, Siṁhala, Cola, Daṇḍaka, Pāṇḍya, Pallava, Gāṅga, Nāśikya, Koṅkaṇa, Kollagiri and Vallara.

In the south of Vindhyas are the Mahendra, Malaya, Meṅkala, Pāla, Mañjara, Sahāy and Śrīparvat mountains. Narmadā, Tāpī, Payoṣṇī, Godāvarī, Kāverī, Bhīmrathī, Venā, Kṛṣṇa, Vañjurā, Tuṅgabhadrā, Tāmraparṇī, Utplāvatī and Rāvaṇagaṅgā are the rivers. The substances obtained in Malaya are similar to those found in Dakṣiṇāpath (sandal, cardamom, black-pepper, camphor, pearls, etc).

देवसभायाः परतः पश्चाद्देशः। तत्र देवसभसुराष्ट्रदशेरकत्रवणभृगुकच्छ-कच्छीयानर्त्तार्बुदब्राह्मणवाहयवनप्रभृतयो जनपदाः। गोवर्धनगिरिनगरदेवसभ-

माल्यशिखरार्बुदादयश्च पर्वताः। सरस्वतीश्वभ्रवतीवार्तघ्नीमहीहिडिम्बाद्या नद्यः। करीरपीलुगुग्गुलुखर्जूरकरभदीनामुत्पादः।

After Devasabhā comes the western region. Here Devasabhā, Surāṣṭra, Daśeraka, Travaṇa, Bhṛgukaccha, Kacchīya, Ānartta, Arbudā, Brāhmaṇavāha and Yavana are the *janapadas*. Govardhana, Girinagar, Devasabhā, Mālyaśikhara and Arbudā are the mountains. Sarasvatī, Śvabhravatī, Vārttaghnī, Mahī and Hiḍimbā are the rivers. Bamboo, *pīlu*-tree, gum resin, dates and camels are the plants and animals found in this region.

पृथूदकात्परतः उत्तरापथः। यत्र शककेकयवोक्काणहूणबाणायुजकाम्बोजवाह्लीकवह्लवलिम्पाककुलूतकीरतङ्गणतुषारतुरुष्कबर्बरहरहूरवहुहुकसहुडहंसमार्गरमठकरकण्ठप्रभृतयो जनपदाः। हिमालयकलिन्देन्द्रकीलचन्द्राचलादयः पर्वताः। गङ्गासिन्धुसरस्वतीशतद्रुचन्द्रभागायमुनेरावतीवितस्ताविपाशाकुहूदेविकाद्या नद्यः। सरलदेवदारुद्राक्षाकुङ्कुमचमराजिनसौवीरस्रोतोञ्जनसैन्धववैदूर्यतुरङ्गाणामुत्पादः।

After Pṛthudaka comes the Uttarāpatha. It has Śaka, Kekaya, Bokkāṇa, Hūṇa, Bāṇāyuja, Kāmboja, Vāhlīka, Bahlava, Lipāka, Kulūta, Kīra, Taṅgaṇa, Tuṣāra, Turūṣka, Barbar, Harhūrava, Huhuka, Sahuda, Haṁsamārga, Ramaṭha and Karkaṇṭha are the *janapadas*. Himālaya, Kalinda, Indrākila and Candrācala are the mountains. Gaṅgā, Sindhu, Sarasvatī, Śatadru, Candrabhāgā, Yamunā, Irāvatī, Vitastā, Vipāśā, Kuhū and Devikā are the rivers. The things obtained from these *janapadas* are *sarala* (pine), *devadāru* (pine), *drākṣā* (grapes), *aśoka* tree, the *jujube* tree, *vaidūrya* (lapis lazuli) and horses.

तेषां मध्ये मध्यदेश इति कविव्यवहारः। न चाऽयं नानुगन्ता शास्त्रार्थस्य।

यदाहुः —

"हिमवद्विन्ध्ययोर्मध्यं यत्प्राग्विनशनादपि।
प्रत्यगेव प्रयागाच्च मध्यदेशः प्रकीर्त्तितः।।"

तत्र च ये देशाः पर्वताः सरितो द्रव्याणामुत्पादश्च तत्प्रसिद्धिसिद्धमिति न निर्दिष्टम्।

द्वीपान्तराणां ये देशाः पर्वताः सरितस्तथा।
नातिप्रयोज्याः कविभिरिति गाढं न चिन्तिताः।।

In between these regions lies the Madhya-deśa according to the practice of poets. This is not only according to poetic convention but also in accordance with *śāstric* tenets. Thus

> In between Himālayas and Vindhyācala extending from Vinśana in the east and Prayāga in the west is called Madhya-deśa.

The *janapadas*, mountains, rivers and substances obtained in Madhya-deśa are too well-known so they have not been listed.

Besides these the regions of other islands and their *janapadas*, mountains and rivers have not been listed as they are not of much interest to poets.

'विनशनप्रयागयोर्गङ्गायमुनयोश्चान्तरमन्तर्वेदी। तदपेक्षयादिशो विभजेत' इति आचार्याः। तत्रापि महोदयं मूलमवधीकृत्यं इति यायावरीयः।

'अनियतत्वाद्दिशामनिश्चितो दिग्विभाग' इत्येके। तथा हि यो वामनस्वामिनः पूर्वः स ब्रह्मशिलायाः पश्चिमः, यो गाधिपुरस्य दक्षिणः स कालप्रियस्योत्तर इति।

'अवधिनिबन्धनमिदं रूपगितरत्त्वनियतगेव' इति यायावरीयः।

'प्राच्यबाचीप्रतीच्युदीच्यः चतस्रो दिशः' इत्येके।

तदाहुः —

"चतसृष्वपि दिक्षु रणे द्विषतः प्रति येन चित्रचरितेन।
विहितमपूर्वमदक्षिणमपश्चिममनुत्तरं कर्म।।"

> The region between Vinśana and Prayāga and between Gaṅgā and Yamunā is called *antarvedī*. Ācāryas state that the division of direction should be taken from *antarvedī*. Rājaśekhara says that, in *antarvedī*, *mahodaya* (or Kanauja) should be used for division of direction.

Some people state that, 'directions are indefinite so their divisions are also uncertain'. Thus a region east of Vāmanasvāmī is west of Brahmaśilā and a region south of Kanauja is north of Kālapariya.

Yayāvarīya (Rājaśekhara) states that, 'the above division of directions has been established after fixing a certain place as Avadhī though of course directions are indefinite'.

'East, south, west and north are the four directions', according to some people.

As —

The extraordinary king who in the battlefield showed prowess against his enemies in all the *four directions* (*pūrva*, *dakṣiṇa*, *paścima*, *uttara*) and thus was described as *apūrva*,[11] (one who has never achieved similar feats prior to this), *adakṣiṇa* (cruel), *apaścima* (feats which cannot be achieved in future) and *anuttara* (incomparable).

'ऐन्द्री, आग्नेयी, याम्या, नैर्ऋती, वारुणी, वायव्या, कौबेरी, ऐशानी चाष्टौ दिशः' इत्येके।

तदाहुः —

"एकं ज्योतिर्दृशौ द्वे त्रिजगति गदितान्यब्जजास्यैश्चतुर्भि
र्भूतानां पञ्चमं यान्यलमृतुषु तथा षट्सु नानाविधानि।
युष्माकं तानि सप्त, त्रिदशमुनिनुतान्यष्टदिग्भाञ्जि भानो-
र्यान्ति प्राह्णे नवत्वं दश दधतु शिवं दीधितीनां शतानि।।"

Some scholars state there are eight directions like eastern, south-eastern, south, south-western, west, north-west, northern and north-eastern.

Thus —

The light of the three worlds — Viṣṇu with his two eyes and the fifth element or the Sun paid obeisance to by (the four mouths of) Brahmā, and manifested in different forms in the six seasons, prayed to by the seven sages (Marici, Attri, Aṅgirasa, Pulastya, Pulaha, R̥tu and Vasiṣṭha) spread over in all directions and ever new in each dawn — May these ten thousand rays protect you.

'ब्राह्मी नागीया च द्वे ताभ्यां सह दशैताः' इत्यपरे।

तदाहुः —

"दशदिक्कटपर्यन्तसीमसङ्कटभूमिके।

---

11. The literal translation from Sanskrit to English would have robbed the effect made by the addition of the letter '*a*' which is the first letter of the Sanskrit alphabet and among others is used to denote 'absence', 'negation', 'want' or 'privation'. See Bhide, *op. cit.*, p. 1.

    The four directions are denoted by the prefix '*a*' and also the qualifies assigned thereof.

विषमा स्थूललक्ष्यस्य ब्रह्माण्डग्रामके स्थितिः।।"

सर्वमस्तु, विवक्षापरतन्त्रा हि दिशामियत्ता। तत्र चित्रास्वात्यन्तरे प्राची, तदनुसारेण प्रतीची, ध्रुवेणोदीची, तदनुसारेणावाची, अन्तरेषु विदिशः, ऊर्ध्वं ब्राह्मी, अधस्तान्नागीयेति।

द्विविधो व्यवहारः कवीनां प्राक्सिद्धो विशिष्टस्थानावधिसाध्यश्च। तत्र प्राक्सिद्धे प्राची —

"द्वित्रैर्व्योम्नि पुराणमौक्तिकमणिच्छायैः स्थितं तारकै-
ज्योत्स्नापानभरालसेन वपुषा सुप्ताश्चकोराङ्गनाः।
यातोऽस्ताचलचूलमुद्वसमधुच्छत्रच्छविश्छन्द्रमाः
प्राची बालबिडाललोचनरुचां जाता च पात्रं ककुप्।।"

According to another opinion in addition to these eight *nagīyā* (lower *paṭala*) and Brāhma (upper-heavenly) are also directions so altogether there are ten directions.

Thus —

For an extremely charitable and generous person it is difficult to live in this insignificant though universal region closely contracted within the borders of the ten directions.

Therefore, directions whether they are four, eight or ten, there remains no difference because the number of directions is within the control of the narrator or the poet. The direction between the Citrā[12] and Svāti[13] constellations is east and in front of it is west. The direction towards the Dhruva[14] star is northern and that opposite is southern. The mid-point of the four centre-points of directions is called Vidiśā.[15] Above it is the sky

---

12. Citrā (a) Name of the fourteenth lunar mansion consisting of one star. See Bhide, *op. cit.*, p. 464. (b) The *nakṣatra* or *Azimech*. See *Advanced Hindi-English Dictionary*, Dr. Hardev Bahri, Vani Prakashan, New Delhi, 1991, 2nd edn., p. 106.

13. Swātī is the fifteenth of the twenty-seven traditional *nakṣatras*. See Chaturvedi, *op. cit.*, p. 714.

14. Dhruva — the polar star, the distance of a planet from the beginning of the real Zodiac, polar longitude.

15. Vidiśā means an intermediate point of the compass. See Bhide, *op. cit.*, p. 981.

or is Brāhmī direction and below it is Pātāla[16] or Nāgīyā direction.

On the subject of directions, poets have two conventions. The former as stated above is according to previous practice and the latter is by taking a specific place as centre-point (*avadhi*).

An example of eastern direction according to the former practice is thus —

> In the sky are two to three stars lacking lustre like old pearls. Partridges (*cakora*) are languishing in sleep due to spending the night in partaking of moonlight. The dark moon like the honeyless and dry beehives has gone stop the western mountain (behind which the sun is supposed to set) and the eastern direction is brilliant with light like the eyes of a kitten.

दक्षिणा —

> "दक्षिणो दक्षिणामाशां यियासुः सोऽधिकं बभौ।
> जिहासुर्दक्षिणामाशां भगवानिव भास्करः।।"

पश्चिमा —

> "पश्य पश्चिमदिगन्तलम्बिना
> निर्मितं मितकथे विवस्वता।
> दीर्घया प्रतिमया सरोम्भस-
> स्तापनीयमिव सेतुबन्धनम्।।

Southern direction —

> That large-hearted king proceeding to the southern direction increases in grandeur just as the Lord Bhāskara desirous of leaving the southern direction increases in brilliance.

Western-direction —

> Look, the sun hanging on the border of the western direction seems to have constructed a golden bridge in the mirrored waters

16. *Pātāla* is the last of the seven regions or worlds under the earth said to be peopled by *nāgas*. The seven regions are *atala*, *vitala*, *sutala*, *rasātala*, *talātala*, *mahātala* and *pātāla*. It also stands for the lower world in general. In Astronomy it stands for the fourth house or sign in which the Sun is present. See Bhide, *op. cit.*, p. 682.

of lakes by means of its red rays.

उत्तरा —

"अस्त्युत्तरस्यां दिशि देवतात्मा
हिमालयो नाम नगाधिराजः।
पूर्वापरौ तोयनिधी वगाह्य
स्थितः पृथिव्या इव मानदण्डः।।"

विशिष्टस्थानावधौ तु दिग्विभागे पूर्वपश्चिमौ यथा —

"यादांसि हे चरत सङ्गतगोत्रतन्त्रं
पूर्वेण चन्दनगिरेरुत पश्चिमेन।
नो चेन्निरन्तरधराधरसेतुसूति-
राकल्पमेष न विरंस्यति वो वियोगः।।

Northern direction

In thc northern direction is the famous mountain, the Himālayas, which enters the eastern and western oceans and is a signpost of the earth.

Taking a specific place as the limit the description of eastern and western directions is as follows —

O creatures of the animal world! Wander in either the eastern or the western parts of Malaya (Candangiri) mountains otherwise these mountains which form bridges across each other will never put an end to your separate existence from each other.

दक्षिणोत्तरौ यथा —

"काञ्च्याः पुरो दक्षिणदिग्विभागे
तथोत्तरस्यां दिशि वारिराशेः।
कर्णान्तचक्रीकृतचारुचापो
रत्या समं साधु वसत्यनङ्गः।।"

उत्तरादावप्युत्तरदिगभिधानं, अनुत्तरादावपि उत्तरदिगभिधानम्।

तयोः प्रथमम् —

"तत्रागारं धनपतिगृहादुत्तरेणास्मदीयं
दूराल्लक्ष्यं सुरपतिधनुश्चारुणा तोरणेन।

यस्योद्याने कृतकतनयः कान्तया वर्द्धितो मे
हस्तप्राप्यः स्तबकविनतो बालमन्दारवृक्षः।।"

द्वितीयम् —

"सह्याद्रेरुत्तरे भागे यत्र गोदावरी नदी।
पृथिव्यामिह कृत्स्नायां स प्रदेशो मनोरमः।।"

The southern and northern directions is described thus —

In the southern part of Kāñcī city and in the northern part of the ocean, with a strung and beautiful bow Kāmadeva (Cupid, God of Love) stays in bliss with Rati (his wife).

The northern direction is described in the north and also while describing other directions.

Thus —

O cloud! In this place Alkāpurī, to the north of the rich Kubera's (God of riches and wealth) house lies my home which can be seen from afar due to its distinctive bow-shaped main entrance. The garden of my house has a flower laden small and beautiful Mandāra[17] tree, which has been nurtured like a son by my wife.

Second example —

The Sahaya mountain, to the north of which lies the Godāvarī river, is the most beautiful region on this earth.

एवं दिगन्तरेष्वपि। तत्र देशपर्वतनद्यादीनां दिशां च यः क्रमस्तं तथैव निबध्नीयात्। साधारणं तूभयत्र लोकप्रसिद्धितश्च।

तद्वद्वर्णनियमः। तत्र पौरस्त्यानां श्यामो वर्णः, दाक्षिणात्यानां कृष्णः, पाश्चात्यानां पाण्डुः, उदीच्यानां गौरः, मध्यदेश्यानां कृष्णः श्यामो गौरश्च।

पौरस्त्यश्यामता —

"श्यामेष्वङ्गेषु गौडीनां सूत्रहारैकहारिषु।
चक्रीकृत्य धनुः पौष्पमनङ्गो वल्गु वल्गति।।"

Similarly the other directions also exhibit their own features. A poet

17. *Mandāra* is the coral tree, one of the five trees in Indra's paradise. See Bhide, *op. cit.*, p. 857.

should follow the description of mountains, rivers and directions specific to particular regions in his own compositions. The ordinary descriptions should follow *śāstra* and popular practice.

Similarly different directions and regions also have different colour distinctions. People residing in the east are black or dark coloured. Southerners have a dark bluish colour. Westerners are yellowish white while people residing in the north are white in colour. Those staying in the centre (Madhya-deśa) are a mixture of dark, black and white colours.

Dark colour of easterners —

> Kāmadeva (Cupid, God of Love) armed with a flower-laden bow directs his arrows towards the dark limbs of the beautiful Gauḍīya maidens made more attractive by stringed garlands.

दाक्षिणात्यकृष्णता —

> "इदं भासां भर्त्तुर्द्रुतकनकगोलप्रतिकृति
> क्रमान्मन्दज्योतिर्गलति नभसो बिम्बवलयम्।
> अथैष प्राचीनः सरति मुरलीगण्डमलिन-
> स्तरुच्छायाचक्रैः स्तबकित इव ध्वान्तविसरः।।"

Darkish blue colour of southerners —

> The shadow of the sun with its decreasing luminosity and which appears like a ring of molten gold is travelling downwards from the sky in the eastern direction. Like the dark cheeks of Muraladeśa the darkness of the shadows of trees is widening out.

पाश्चात्यपाण्डुता —

> "शाखास्मेरं मधुकवलनाकेलिलोलेक्षणानां
> भृङ्गस्त्रीणां बकुलमुकुलं कुन्तलीभावमेति।
> किं चेदानीं यवनतरुणीपाण्डुगण्डस्थलीभ्यः
> कान्तिः स्तोकं रचयति पदं नागवल्लिच्छदेषु।।"

Yellowish white colour of westerners —

The hair of the nimble-eyed beautiful Bhṛṅga maidens is like the buds of Bakula flowering on the branches ready for the sporting of bees and the beautiful sheen of the yellowish white cheeks of Yavaṇa maidens finds a place on the leaves of *pāna* (a kind of plant).

उदीच्यगौरता —

"पुष्पैः सम्प्रति काञ्चनारतरवः प्रत्यङ्गमालिङ्गिताः
वाह्लीकीदशनव्रणारुणतरैः पत्रैरशोकोऽञ्चितः।
जातं चम्पकमप्युदीच्यललनालावण्यचौर्यक्षमं
माञ्जिष्ठैर्मुकुलैश्च पाटलतरोरन्यैव काचिल्लिपिः।।"

यथा वा —

"काश्मीरीगात्रलेखासु लोलल्लावण्यवीचिषु।
द्रावयित्वेव विन्यस्तं स्वर्णं षोडशवर्णकम्।।"

White colour of the northerners —

In the spring season at this time the flowers of the *kacnāra* tree have tightly embraced all parts of the *aśoka* tree and it is covered with red coloured leaves like the gums of maidens from Vāhlīka. The *campā* appears to steel the charm and grace of the northern maidens and the red buds of roses are a sight to be seen.

Thus —

Adorned with a tremulous grace, the bodies of maidens from Kāśmīra appears to be covered with a paste of molten gold.

मध्यदेश्यकृष्णता यथा —

"युधिष्ठिरक्रोधवह्नेः कुरुवंशैकदाहिनः।
पाञ्चालीं ददृशुः सर्वे कृष्णां धूमशिखामिव।।"

तद्वन्मध्यदेश्यश्यामता। न च कविमार्गे श्यामकृष्णयोः पाण्डुगौरयोर्वा महान्विशेष इति कविसमयेष्ववोचाम।

मध्यदेश्यगौरता —

"तव नवनवनीतपिण्डगौरे प्रतिफलदुत्तरकोसलेन्द्रपुत्र्याः।
अवगतमलिके मृगाङ्कबिम्बं मृगमदपत्रनिभेन लाञ्छनेन।।"

विशेषस्तु पूर्वदेशे राजपुत्र्यादीनां गौरः पाण्डुर्वा वर्णः। एवं दक्षिणदेशेऽपि।

The dark colour of Madhya-deśa is thus —

For everyone in the assembly the dark Pāñcālī (Draupadī) appeared to be like a spiral of smoke emanating from the fire of

Yudhiṣṭhira's anger which was the sole destroyer of the Kuru race.

Similarly the people of Madhya-deśa are also bluish black. In the world of poets there is not much difference between black and dark and yellow and white as was made clear during the description of poetic-conventions.

The white colour of Madhya-deśa —

O daughter of the northern Kauśalendra! Your fresh and butter like body and white forehead mirrors the moon and is recognised by a mark similar to the mark on the moon.

In the east region also the ladies of the court and other prominent people should be described as fair or yellowish white. Similarly in the southern region.

तत्र प्रथमः —

"कपोले जानक्याः करिकलभदन्तद्युतिमुषि
स्मरस्मेरः स्फारोड्डमरपुलके वक्त्रकमलम्।
मुहुः पश्यञ्छृण्वन्रजनिचरसेनाकलकलं
जटाजूटग्रन्थिं द्रढयति रघूणां परिवृढः।।"

Thus —

Smooth and shiny like elephant tusks and radiant with passion, the cheeks of the young maiden act as a mirror for Rāma, who on hearing the commotion in the army of *rākṣasas* ties his mass of twisted hair into a tight knot.

द्वितीयः —

"तासां माधवपत्नीनां सर्वासां चन्द्रवर्चसाम्।
शब्दविद्येव विद्यानां मध्ये जज्वाल रुक्मिणी।।"

एवमन्यदपि यथासम्भवमभ्यूह्यम्।
निगदितनयविपरीतं देशविरुद्धं वदन्ति विद्वांसः।
तत्परिहार्यं यत्नात्तदुदाहृतयस्तु दोषेषु।।

इत्थं देशविभागो मुद्रामात्रेण सूत्रितः सुधियाम्।
यस्तु जिगीषत्यधिकं पश्यतु मद्भुवनकोशमसौ।।

Amongst all the moon like bright wives of Kṛṣṇa, Rukmiṇī shone out like the study of words amongst all sciences.

Similarly poets should use their own imagination for other descriptions.

As opposed to the regional divisions already given and called by other scholars as Deśa-virudha should be abandoned because these appear as faults in poetic compositions.

Thus far we have only given a bare outline of divisions of regions. Those interested in details should study the Bhuvankośa composed by us.

।। इति राजशेखरकृतौ काव्यमीमांसायां कविरहस्ये प्रथमेऽधिकरणे देशविभागः सप्तदशोऽध्यायः।।

18

कालविभागः

Kāla-Vibhāgaḥ

(Divisions based on Time)

कालः काष्ठादिभेदाभिन्नः। तथा च —

काष्ठा निमेषा दश पञ्च चैव त्रिंशच्च काष्ठाः कथिताः कलेति।
त्रिंशत्कलश्चैव भवेन्मुहूर्त्तस्तैस्त्रिंशता रात्र्यहनी समेतौ।।

15 NIMEṢAS[1] make one *kāṣṭhā*,[2] 30 *kāṣṭhā*s one *kalā*,[3] 30 *kalā*s one *muhūrta*[4] and 30 *muhūrtas*[5] a day and night. In the two months of Caitra and Aśvin the days and nights are equal that is fifteen *muhūrta*s for days and fifteen *muhūrtas* for nights.

ते च चैत्राश्वयुजमासयोर्भवतः। चैत्रात्परं प्रतिमासं मौहूर्त्तिकी दिवसवृद्धिः निशाहानिश्च त्रिमास्याः; ततः परं मौहूर्त्तिकी निशावृद्धिः दिवसहानिश्च। आश्वयुजात्परतः पुनरेतदेव विपरीतम्।

---

1. *Nimeṣa* forms the lowest unit in the measurement of time. The time required by a *nimeṣa* is equal to that taken in pronouncing the shortest letter (*akṣara*) 57. 3-4. See Devendra Kumar Rajaram Patil, *Cultural History from the Vāyu Purāṇa*, Motilal Banarsidass, Delhi, rpt. 1973, p. 72, 15 *nimeṣas* — *kāṣṭhā*; 30 *kāṣṭhās* — *kalā*; 30 *kalās* — *muhūrta*; 30 *muhūrtas* — day and night.
2. See 38.213, 38.214, 38.215 and 38.216 respectively of G.P Bhatt, ed., tr. by A Board of Scholars, *Ancient Indian Tradition and Mythology*, vol. 38 and *The Vāyu-Purāṇa*, Part II, tr. and annotated by G.V. Tagare, Motilal Banarsidass, Delhi, 1988, p. 843.
3. *Ibid.*
4. *Ibid.*
5. *Ibid.*

After Caitra (in Vaiśākha) for three months there is an increase of one *muhūrta* each for everyday and month. Correspondingly the night gets shorter. After this the night gets longer and the day gets shorter. In Āśvin the day and night becomes equal and after this for the next three months the opposite cycle starts. The nights get longer and the days shorter.

राशितो राश्यन्तरसङ्क्रमणमुष्णभासो मासः, वर्षादि दक्षिणायनं शिशिराद्युत्तरायणं द्व्ययनः संवत्सर इति सौरं मानम्।

The entry of the sun from one sign of the zodiac into the other is called a month. The six-month period following the rainy season is *dakṣiṇāyaṇa* and the six months following the winter season is *uttarāyaṇa*. Two *ayaṇa*s make a *saṁvatasara* (solar-year). This measurement of time has been done by solar measurement.

पञ्चदशाहोरात्रः पक्षः। वर्द्धमानसोमः शुक्लो, वर्द्धमानकृष्णिमा कृष्ण इति पित्र्य मासमानम्। अमुना च वेदोदितः कृत्स्नोऽपि क्रियाकल्पः।

Fifteen days and nights constitute a *pakṣa* (fortnight). The fortnight in which the moon increases in *śukla-pakṣa* and when darkness increases it is called *kṛṣṇa-pakṣa*. The Vedic rituals and *yajña*s are conducted according to this division.

पित्र्यमेव व्यत्ययितपक्षं चान्द्रमसम्। इदमार्यावर्त्तवासिनश्च कवयश्च मानमाश्रिताः। एवं च द्वौ पक्षौ मासः। द्वौ मासावृतुः। षण्णामृतूनां परिवर्त्तः संवत्सरः। स च चैत्रादिरिति दैवज्ञाः, श्रावणादिरिति लोकयात्राविदः।

According to ancestral measurement *kṛṣṇa-pakṣa* followed by *śukla-pakṣa* makes a lunar month (*candramāsa*). The poets and Āryāvarttas use this lunar month as their basis.

तत्र नभा नभस्यश्च वर्षाः, इष ऊर्जश्च शरत्, सहः सहस्यश्च हेमन्तः, तपस्तपस्यश्च शिशिरः, मधुर्माधवश्च वसन्तः, शुक्रः शुचिश्च ग्रीष्मः।

Two months make one *ṛtu* (season) and six seasons make a lunar year. *Jyotiṣa* scholars believe that the lunar year starts with Caitra. The popular belief, is that Śrāvaṇa starts the lunar year. In this Śrāvaṇa and Bhādra comprise the rainy season. Āśvin and Kārttika comprise *śarad* (autumn), Māragaśīrṣa and Pauṣa comprise *hemanta* (winter), Māgha and Phālguna comprise *śiṣir* (cold winter), Caitra and Vaiśākha comprise *vasanta* (spring) and Jyeṣṭha and Āṣāḍha comprise *grīṣma* (summer).

तत्र "वर्षासु पूर्वो वायुः" इति कवयः। 'पाश्चात्यः, पौरस्त्यस्तु प्रतिहन्ता' इत्याचार्याः। तदाहुः — 'पुरोवाता हता प्रावृद् पश्चाद्वाता हता शरत्' इति।

'In the rainy season the eastern wind flows' according to poets. *Ācārya*s posit that 'western winds bring rain and eastern winds oppose it'.

Thus

Eastern winds impede rains and western winds impede autumn.

तदाहुः —

"प्रावृष्यम्भोभृताम्भोदाभरनिर्भरमम्बरम्।
कादम्बकुसुमामोदा वायवो वान्ति वारुणाः।।"

During the rains the sky is overcast with thundering clouds and the western wind (Varuṇa)[6] is filled with the fragrance of *kadamba*[7] flowers.

'वस्तुवृत्तिरतन्त्रं, कविसमयः प्रमाणम्' इति यायावरीयः।

Rājaśekhara states that, 'The natural state cannot be taken as evidence. In poetic expression the poets' words alone are the evidence.'

तदाहुः —

"पौरस्त्यस्तोयदर्त्तोः पवन इव पतन्पावकस्येव धूमो
विश्वस्येवादिसर्गः प्रणव इव परं पावनं वेदराशेः।
सन्ध्यानृत्तोत्सवेच्छोरिव मदनरिपोर्नन्दिनान्दीनिनादः
सौरस्याग्रे सुखं वो वितरतु विनतानन्दनः स्यन्दनस्य।।"

Thus —

Just as eastern winds signify rains, smoke signifies fire, the ultimate holy sacred and mystical syllable *oṁ* signifies the God Almighty and creation so also the benedictory verses in praise of Śiva signify the commencement of the *tāṇḍava*.[8] May the dawn

6. Vāruṇa is also the God for the western wind.

7. *Kadamba* (Nauclea Cadamba), A kind of tree said to put forth buds at the roaring of thunder clouds.

8. *Tāṇḍava* — The dance of Śiva with his consort, Pārvatī.

personified as the charioteer of the Sun bless You!

शरद्यनियतदिक्को वायुर्यथा —

"उषःसु ववुराकृष्टजडावश्यायशीकराः।
शेफालीकलिकाकोशकषायामोदिनोऽनिलाः।।"

The wind in *śarad* season —

The direction of wind during *śarad* season is not fixed for example:

In the early morning dawn during *śarad* season the wind touched by the dew-drops and the buds of *śefālikā*[9] is astringent.

'हेमन्ते पाश्चात्यो वायुः' इत्येके। 'उदीच्य' इत्यपरे। 'उभयमपि' इति यायावरीयः।

तयोः पाश्चात्यः —

"भञ्जन्भूर्जद्रुमालीस्तुहिनगिरितटेषूद्गतास्त्वक्कराला:।
रेवाम्भःस्थूलवीचीचयचकितचलच्चातकान् व्याधुनानः।
पाश्चात्यो वाति वेगाद्द्रुततुहिनशिलाशीकारासारवर्षी
मातङ्गक्षुण्णसान्द्रस्नुतसरलतरत्सारसारी समीरः।।"

Some people feel that, 'western winds blow during the *hemanta* season'. Others say that, 'northern winds blow during this season.' Rājaśekhara feels that 'both kinds of winds blow during the *hemanta* season'.

An example of western winds —

Arising out of the Himālayas, breaking through the rows of birch trees with thick barks, billowing playfully among the high waves of the river Revā[10] and the restless *cātaka* birds, bringing down tiny drops of melted snow and smelling of the juice extract of the pine trees, the bark of which has been peeled off by elephants, the western wind blows with a certain velocity.

उदीच्यः —

"लम्पाकीनां किरन्तश्चिकुरविरचनां रल्लकांल्लासयन्तः
चुम्बन्तश्चन्द्रभागासलिलमविकलं भूर्जकाण्डैकचण्डाः।
एते कस्तूरिकैणप्रणयसुरभयो वल्लभा वाह्लवीनां

---

9. *Śafālikā*, a kind of plant, *Vitex negundo*. See, *op. cit.*, p. 633.
10. Revā, name of the river Narmadā which arises in Vindhyas.

कौलूतीकेलिकाराः परिचयितहिमं वायवो वान्त्युदीच्याः।।"

Example of northern winds —

Playing with the tresses of the beautiful maidens of Lampāka,[11] inducing deers to dance happily, kissing the cool waters of Candrabhāgā[12] river, murmuring through the branches of birch trees, smelling of the musk-deer, loved by the maidens of Valhava[13] and playing with the beautiful maidens of Kulūta,[14] the northern wind blows.

शिशिरेऽपि हेमन्तवदुदीच्यः पाश्चात्यो वा। वसन्ते दक्षिणः। तदुक्तम् —

"धुन्वंल्लङ्कावनालीर्मुहुरलकलता लासयन्केरलीना-
मन्ध्रीधम्मिल्लबन्धान्सपदि शिथिलयन्वेल्लयन्नागवल्लीः
उद्दामं दाक्षिणात्यो मलितमलयजः सारथिर्मीनकेतोः
प्राप्तः सीमन्तिनीनां मधुसमयसुहृन्मानचौरः समीरः।।"

In the *śiśira* season also like *hemanta*, the direction of wind is both northern and western. In the *vasanta* season the direction of the wind is southern.

Thus —

Waving through the rows of plants in the gardens of Laṅkā, dancing through the curly locks of Kerala maidens, loosening the hair knots of maidens from Āndhra, making restless the creeper vines of Nāgavalli, producing sandal from the sandalwood trees in Malaya mountains, indicative of the victory of Kāmadeva (Cupid, God of Love), welcomed by the maidens, a bosom friend of the *vasanta* season, the southern wind blows.

'अनियतदिक्को वायुर्ग्रीष्मे' इत्येके। 'नैर्ऋतः' इत्यपरे। 'उभयमपि' इति यायावरीयः। तत्र प्रथमः —

"वात्याचक्रकचुम्बिताम्बरभुवः स्थूला रजोदण्डकाः

11. Lampāka, name of a place, see Appendix II.
12. Chandrabhāgā, name of a river, see Appendix II.
13. Valhava, name of a place, see Appendix II.
14. Kulūta, name of a place, see appendix II.

संग्रथ्नन्ति भविष्यदभ्रपटलस्थूणावितर्कं नभः।
किं चान्यन्मृगतृष्णिकाम्बुविसरैः पात्राणि वीतार्णसां
सिन्धूनामिह सूत्रयन्ति दिवसेष्वागामिनीं सम्पदम्।।"

'The direction of wind is not fixed in the *grīṣma* season' according to some people. Some people feel that, 'the south-western directed wind' should be described. Yāyāvarīya (Rājaśekhara) feels that both are right.

Thus —

In the *grīṣma* season, due to whirlwinds there arise great spiralling towers of dust between the earth and the sky, producing a delusion of rain clouds, the wide expanse of waterless rivers add to the mirage like effect and point to rains in the near future.

द्वितीयः — "सोऽयं करैस्तपति वह्निमयैरिवार्कः
साङ्गारविस्तरभरेव धरा समग्रा।
वायुः कुकूलमिक वर्षति नैर्ऋतश्च
कार्शानवैरिव शरैर्मदनश्च हन्ति।।"

Second example —

The Sun heats the earth with its rays of fire. The entire earth seems to be full of burning embers. The south-western winds seem to be producing fire from burnt chaff of corn and Kāmadeva appears to incinerate the world with his arrows of fire.

किञ्च —

"गर्भान्बलाकासु निवेशयन्तः वंशाङ्कुरान्स्वैर्निनदैः सृजन्तः।
रजोऽम्बुदाः प्रावृषि मुद्रयन्तो यात्रोद्यमं भूमिभृतां हरन्ति।।"

"स सल्लकीसालशिलीन्ध्रयूथीप्रसूनदः पुष्पितलाङ्गलीकः।
दग्धोर्वरासुन्दरगन्धबन्धुरर्घत्ययं वारिमुचामनेहा।।"

"वनानि नीलीदलमेचकानि धाराम्बुधौता गिरयः स्फुरन्ति।
पूराम्भसा भिन्नतटास्तटिन्यः सान्द्रेन्द्रगोपानि च शाद्वलानि।।

"चकोरहर्षी यतिचारचौरो वियोगिनीवीक्षितनाथवर्त्मा।
गृहान्प्रति प्रस्थितपान्थसार्थः कालोऽयमाध्मातनभाः पयोदैः।।

"या केलियात्रा करिकामिनीभिर्या तुङ्गहर्म्याग्रविलासशय्या।
चतुःसमं यन्मृगनाभिगर्भं सा वारिदर्त्तोः प्रथमातिथेयी।।

The clouds in the rainy season induce conception in the *balākās*[15] (cranes), growth of new shoots in bamboo plants, settle the dust in the atmosphere and postpone the King's intention to travel.

During the rains the *sāl* tree, the plantain tree and jasmine bring forth new leaves and the coconut tree produces flowers. The first drops of rain on the dry and parched earth produces a sweet aroma. The rainy days are very pleasant.

The forests appear blue in colour due to the coloured leaves of the indigo plant. The rain washed mountains are attractive and beautiful. Overflowing rivers cut through the banks due to their swift current. The smooth green plains are soothing.

The rainy season brings happiness to the partridge (*cakora*) and stops the preaching of widows and ascetics. During this season separated wives wait anxiously for the return of their husbands. Groups of wayfarers are in a hurry to reach their destinations and the sky is continuously overcast with rain clouds.

During this season the most appropriate mode of travel is atop the she-elephants. In the terraces of high palatial mansions beds are laid for amorous sport. It is also the appropriate time to partake of the musk (*catuḥ : sam*)[16] obtained from musk-deer.

"चलच्चटुलचातकः कृतकुरङ्गरागोदयः
सदर्दुररवोद्यमो मदभरप्रगल्भोरगः।
शिखण्डिकुलताण्डवामुदितमद्गुकङ्काह्वयो
वियोगिषु घनागमः स्मरविषं विषं मुञ्चति।।

"दलत्कुटजकुड्मलः स्फुटितनीपपुष्पोत्करो
धवप्रसवबान्धवः प्रचितमञ्जरीकार्जुनः।

15. Balākās, a crane, see Apte, *op. cit.*, p. 695.
16. *Catuḥ sam* — It is a technical term found in the *Ṛgveda* — a mixture of *keśar* (saffron), *kastūrī* (musk), *candana* (sandal) and *kapūr* (agallochum) makes *catuḥ sam*.

कदम्बकलुषाम्बरः कलितकेतकीकोरक-
श्लथ्निचुलसञ्चयो हरति हन्त घर्मात्ययः।। वर्षाः ।"

Playful *cātakas* (birds) are seen on all sides in forests. Love is induced in deers, the sound of frogs is heard everywhere, snakes are intoxicated, groups of peacocks dance in abandon and birds and animals are filled with happiness. But this arrival of rain-clouds induces lustful poison and brings down rain (like poison) in the hearts of separated lovers.

During the rains the flower buds blossom, the group of *kadamba* trees sprout into flower, *keśar* (or saffron) grows, there is a new cluster of flowers in the *arjuna* trees, new blossoms choke the sky, the screw-pines bring forth new buds and cranes move about with the water-current. Here ends the description of the rainy season.

"द्रागगर्जयन्ती विमदान्मयूरान्प्रगल्भयन्ती कुररद्विरेफान्।
शरत्समभ्येति विकाश्य पद्मानुन्मीलयन्ती कुमुदोत्पलानि।।

"सा भाति पुष्पाणि निवेशयन्ती बन्धूकबाणासनकुङ्कुमेषु।
शेफालिकासप्तपलाशकाशभाण्डीरसौगन्धिकमालतीषु।।

"सखञ्जरीटा सपयःप्रसादा सा कस्य नो मानसमाच्छिनत्ति।
कादम्बकारण्डवचक्रवाकससारसक्रौञ्चकुलानुयाता।।

"उपानयन्ती कलहंसयूथमगस्त्यदृष्ट्या पुनती पयांसि।
मुक्तासु शुभ्रं दधती च गर्भं शरद्विचित्रैश्चरितैश्चकास्ति।।

"क्षितिं खनन्तो वृषभाः खुराग्रै रोधो विषाणैर्द्विरदा रदन्तः।
शृङ्गं त्यजन्तो रुरवश्च जीर्णं कुर्वन्ति लोकानवलोकनोत्कान्।।

"अत्रावदातद्युति चन्द्रिकाम्बु नीलावभासं च नभः समन्तात्।
सुरेभवीथीदिवसावतारो जीर्णाभ्रखण्डानि च पाण्डुराणि।।

"महानवम्यां निखिलास्त्रपूजा नीराजना वाजिभटद्विपानाम्।
दीपालिकायां विविधा विलासा यात्रोन्मुखैरत्र नृपैर्विधेयाः।।

"व्योम्नि तारतरतारकोत्करः स्यन्दनप्रचरणक्षमा मही।
भास्करः शरदि दीप्रदीधितिर्बुध्यते च सह माधवः सुरैः।।

"केदार एव कलमाः परिणामरम्याः
प्राचीनमामलकमर्घति पाकनीलम्।

Śarad season produces lack of intoxication in peacocks, enthuses the pewits and beetles and helps the lotuses and other flowers to grow.

In the *śarad* season, *bandhūk* (a kind of tree), *bāṇa* (a kind of tree), *asan* (a kind of tree), *keśar* (bakula tree), *śefālikā* (a kind of plant), *saptaparṇa* (white water lily or the blue lotus), jasmine and *campā* blossoms flower, and it becomes very pleasant.

During *śarad* season can be seen wagtails among birds. The water in rivers, lakes and ponds becomes clear and on the banks can be seen a wide array of swans, ducks, geese, cranes and herons.

Śarad season pleases the mind with its variety. Groups of ducks return from lakes to their own ponds, the water reservoirs become clear and raindrops help to conceive radiant pearls in oyster shells.

In this season, intoxicated bulls dig up the earth with their hooves, joyous elephants uproot the banks of rivers with their tusks, deers drop off their old horns and are a source of frolic, fun and curiosity for people.

In this season, the white and bright moonlight, the clear and wide expanse of the sky, the milky way with its stars shining appear bright even at night and the blue sky filled with wandering dark clouds presents a beautiful picture.

On the day of *Vijayadaśamī*,[17] the victorious kings perform a religious ceremony of arms, warfare, horses and soldiers light lamps on *Dīwālī* and the kings involved in a variety of tasks intent upon their victory march, collectively present a pleasing picture.

Elaborate star clusters in the sky, earth — a fit pathway for chariots,

17. *Vijayadaśamī* is one of the auspicious days according to Indian tradition. It is the tenth day of the bright half of Āśvina (*Dussehrā*).

Sun with its bright and shiny rays and the awakening of Kṛṣṇa (Mādhava) are the covetable pictures of the *śarad* season.

During this season the fields filled with ripening yellow paddy look attractive. The fruits of *āmalā*[18] hanging from the trees are a pleasing sight.

एर्वारुकं स्फुटननिर्गतगर्भगन्ध-
मम्लीभवन्ति च जरत्त्रपुसीफलानि।।

"गेहाजिरेषु नवशालिकणावपात-
गन्धानुभावसुभगेषु कृषीवलानाम्।
आनन्दयन्ति मुसलोल्लसनावधूत-
पाणिस्खलद्वलयपद्धतयो वधूट्यः।।

"तीक्ष्णं रविस्तपति नीच इवाचिराढ्यः
शृङ्गं रुरुस्त्यजति मित्रमिवाकृतज्ञः।
तोयं प्रसीदति मुनेरिव धर्मचिन्ता
कामी दरिद्र इव शोषमुपैति पङ्कम्।।

"नद्यो वहन्ति कुटिलक्रमयुक्तशुक्ति-
रेखाङ्कबालपुलिनोदरसुप्तकूर्माः।
अस्यां तरङ्गिततनुतोयपलायमान-
मीनानुसारिबकदन्तकरालफालाः।।

"अपङ्किलतटावटः शफरफाण्टफालोज्ज्वलः
पतत्कुररकातरभ्रमदद्भ्रमीनार्भकः।
लुठत्कमठसैकतश्चलबकोटवाचाटितः
सरित्सलिलसञ्चः शरदि मेदुरः सीदति।। शरत् ।"

Ripe cucumbers burst open to produce a sweet fragrance and the fruits of old tamarind become ripe and sour.

The aroma of new sheafs of paddy fresh from the fields fills the yards of farmers and it becomes a store-house of pleasure because the new paddy which is being beaten by the village-brides makes the bracelets on their hands quiver with every beat of the pestle.

---

18. *Āmlā*, the tree *Emblic myrobalan*, see Mahendra and Chaturvedi, *op. cit.*, p. 51.

In the *śarad* season the Sun penetrates with heat just as a petty man due to a fortunate chance becomes rich and thus proud. A deer sheds his horns like an ungrateful person who leaves his friend after his ends have been met. Water becomes clear just like the clear contemplation of a sage and the sludge dries up just as a pauper dries up due to anxiety and worry.

In this season the water dries up in small rivers. The sandy banks become visible in which can be seen the wavy lines and marks of oyster shells. On this sandy beach the turtles come out of water to rest and herons can be seen chasing and attacking fishes in the shallow and clear water.

In the *śarad* season, there is pleasure in watching the clear and dense water in rivers, the sludge along the bank dries up, the antics of fishes appear pleasing, the baby fishes can be seen running around due to fear of attack from ospreys, at places on the sandy banks can be seen turtles and at other places can be heard the screeching of herons. The accumulated treasure of rain water in rivers becomes impaired in the *śarad* season. Heare ends the description of the *śarad* season.

> "द्वित्रिमुचुकुन्दकलिकस्त्रिचतुरमुकुलः क्रमेण लवलीषु।
> पञ्चषफलिनीकुसुमो जयति हिमर्त्तुर्नवावतरः।।
>
> "पुन्नागरोध्रप्रसवावतंसा वामभ्रुवः कञ्चुककुञ्चिताङ्गयः।
> वक्रोल्लसत्कुङ्कुमसिक्थकाङ्काः सुगन्धतैलाः कबरीर्वहन्ति।।
>
> "यथा यथा पुष्यति शीतकालस्तुषारचूर्णोत्करकीर्णवातः।
> तथा तथा यौवनशालिनीनां कवोष्णतामत्र कुचा लभन्ते।।
>
> "वराहवर्ध्राणि नवोदनानि दधीनि सन्नद्धशराणि चाऽत्र।
> सुकोमलाः सर्षपकन्दलीश्च भुक्त्वा जनो निन्दति वैद्यविद्याम्।।

With the advent of *hemanta* season can be seen two or three buds of *mucukunda*,[19] three-four buds in the *lovely*[20] creepers and five-

19. *Mucukunda* — name of a tree. See Vamana Apte, *op. cit.*, p. 765.
20. *Lovely* — a kind of creeper. See Vamana Apte, *op. cit.*, p. 814.

six flowers appear in *priyaṅgulatā*.[21] May the passage of *hemanta* be glorious.

During the days of *hemanta* season, the ornamental flowers of *nāgkesara*[22] and *laudhra*[23] are worn by the women of Vakrabhrū who wear tight bodices, rub wax mixed saffron paste on themselves and use perfumed oil to set their hair. During this time, the wind spreads the snow particles and thereby increases the cold, so also the heat in the breasts of women increases in the same degree.

During these days the new rice cooked with the flesh of forest pigs, thick creamy curd and a thick paste of the slender stalks of mustard leaves is eaten by people and thus they disregard the Āyurvedic physicians.

"अत्रोपचारः सलिलैः कवोष्णैर्यत्किञ्चिदत्र स्वदतेऽन्नपानम्।
सुदुर्भगामत्र निपीड्य शेते स्वस्त्यस्तु नित्यं तुहिनर्त्तवेऽस्मै।।

"विमुक्तबर्हा विमदा मयूराः प्ररूढगोधूमयवा च सीमा।
व्याघ्रीप्रसूतिः सलिलं सबाष्पं हेमन्तलिङ्गानि जयन्त्यमूनि।।

During these days, a bath should be taken with luke warm water and food and drink tastes delicious. During this season the longing of neglected maidens also increases.

During *hemanta* the peacocks lack intoxication and they shed their feathers, the borders of villages appear beautiful with the fields of wheat and barley, lionesses deliver babies and in the morning one can see vapour rising from the water — these signify the *hemanta* season.

"सशमीधान्यपाकानि क्षेत्राण्यत्र जयन्ति च।
त्रिशङ्कुतिलका रात्र्यः पच्यन्ते लवणानि च।।

During this season, one can see peas, black gram and lentils

21. *Priyaṅgulatā* — name of a creeper said to put forth blossoms at the touch of women. See Vamana Apte, p. 684.
22. *Nāgakesara* — name of a tree with fragrant flowers, *Hesna roxburghii*. See Vamana Atpe, *op. cit.*, p. 540.
23. *Laudhra* — name of a tree with red or white flowers.

waving in the fields. One can also see the star Triśaṅku in the night and during these days turmeric and salt is made.

"उद्यानानां मूकपुंस्कोकिलत्वं भृङ्गस्त्रीणां मौनमुद्रा मुखेषु।
मन्दोद्योगा पत्रिणां व्योमयात्रा हेमन्ते स्यात्सर्पदर्पक्षयश्च।।

"कर्कन्धूनां नागरङ्गीफलानां पाकोद्रेकः खाण्डवोप्याविरस्ति।
कृष्णेक्षूणां पुण्ड्रकाणां च गर्भे माधुर्ये श्रीर्जायते चाप्यपूर्वा।।

येषां मध्येमन्दिरं तल्पसम्पत् पार्श्वे दाराः सफारतारुण्यताराः।
लीलावह्निर्निह्नुतोद्दामधूमस्ते हेमन्तं ग्रीष्मशेषं विदन्ति।।"

इति हेमन्तः।

हेमन्तधर्माशिशिरः।

During the *hemanta* season, in the parks the cuckoo becomes quiet, the maidens of *bhṛṅga* present a mute countenance, birds in flight lose their enthusiasm and snakes also become sullen.

Berries, oranges and other fruits begin to ripen and sweeten and in thick and black sugarcanes is manifest an indescribable sweetness.

Inside houses in the bedrooms are beautiful beds besides which sit young maidens intoxicated with the wine of their youth near smoke filled embers in burning stoves. These resources being easily available to some people they think of *hemanta* season as the last part of summer. Thus ends the description of *hemanta*.

The descriptive subjects of *śiśira* are similar to *hemanta*.

विशेषस्तु —

"रात्रिर्विचित्रसुरतोचितयामदैर्घ्या
चण्डो मरुद्वहति कुङ्कुमपङ्कसाध्यः।
तल्पस्थितिर्द्विगुणतूलपटा किमन्य-
दर्घन्ति चात्र विततागुरुधूपधूमाः।।

"आश्लेषिणः पृथुरतक्लमपीतशीत-
मायामिनीं घनमुदो रजनीं युवानः।
ऊर्वोर्मुहुर्वलनबन्धनसंधिलोल-

पादान्तसंवलिततूलपटाः स्वपन्ति।।

"पानेऽम्भसोः सुरसनीरसयोर्न भाति
स्पर्शक्रियासु तुहिनानलयोर्न चाऽत्र।
नो दुर्भगासुभगयोः परिरम्भणे च
नो सेवने च शशिभास्करयोर्विशेषः।।

The main are —

The nights of *śiśira* season being long are suitable for various kinds of amorous love-sport. During these days due to the excessively violent and impetuous winds winter sets in during which it is desirable to partake of *keśar* (saffron), *kastūrī* (camphor), etc. Cotton filled quilts are used for covering and lying on and coals and embers are used to heat rooms and bed-rooms.

During the long nights of *śiśira* season, trying to overcome the fatigue due to love play, the extremely happy youths embrace the maidens and due to repeatedly changing sides loosen the stitches in their quilts so that the cotton in quilts collects together, so they push the quilts under their feet and sleep.

In this season due to the intense cold, one cannot distinguish between tasty and tasteless water, and in the touch of snow and fire, one cannot perceive the difference between heat and cold, in embracing one cannot distinguish between a beautiful and plain maiden and one cannot also differentiate between the sun and the moon.

"पुष्पक्रिया मरुबके जलकेलिनिन्दा
कुन्दान्यशेषकुसुमेषु धुरि स्थितानि।
सौभाग्यमेणतिलकाद्व्रजतेऽर्कबिम्बं
काले तुषारिणि दहन्ति च चन्दनानि।।

"सिद्धार्थयष्टिषु यथोत्तरहीयमान-
सन्तानभिन्नघनसूचिपरम्परासु।
द्वित्रावशेषकुसुमासु जनिक्रमेण
पाकक्रमः कपिशिमानमुपादधाति।।

"उदीच्यचण्डानिलताडितासु
सुलीनमीनासु जलस्य मूले।
नालावशेषाब्जलतास्विदानीं
विलासवापीषु न याति दृष्टिः।।

"माद्यन्मतङ्गः पृषतैकतोषी
पुष्यद्वराहो धृतिमञ्जुलायः।
दरिद्रनिन्द्यः सधनैकवन्द्यः
स एष कालाः शिशिरः करालः।।

Mārjoram puts forth flowers, water sports are all but forgotten, flowers of jasmines are everywhere, the musk mark on the forehead mirrors the sun and during this season the application of sandal paste burns the body.

During the *śiśira*, season the thick hairy tendrils of the mustard plant ripen and are shed off, two to three yellow flowers can be seen and gradually the plants start changing colour from yellow to brown.

During this season, there is no desire to even look at water reservoirs. The water in them seems to quiver due to the northern cold and violent winds, fishes hide themselves in the surface of the reservoir and only the dry stalks of the lotus plants are visible.

In the *śiśira* season, elephants get intoxicated, contented deer are seen to move around. Hogs thrive in this season and bulls are also intoxicated. The poor due to lack of resources disapprove of this season whereas the rich and resourceful approve of this season. This is the uneven *śiśira* season.

"अभिनववधूरोषस्वादुः करीषतनूनपा-
दसरलजनाश्लेषक्रूरस्तुषारसमीरणः।
गलितविभवस्याज्ञेवाऽद्य द्युतिर्मसृणा रवे-
र्विरहिवनितावक्त्रौपम्यं बिभर्त्ति निशाकरः।।

"स्त्रियः प्रकृतिपित्तलाः क्वथितकुङ्कुमालेपनै-
र्नितम्बफलकस्तनस्थलसुजोरुमूलादिभिः।

इहाभिनवयौवनाः सकलरात्रिसंश्लेषितै-
र्हरन्ति शिशिरज्वराररतिमतीव पृथ्वीमपि।। शिशिरः ।"

During this season the smoke emanating from the burning of dried cow-dung and *ghī* (clarified butter) is sweet like the wrath of a newly-wed bride. Icy winds induce discomfort as does the proximity to an evil person. The heat of the sun appears useless like the orders given by a poor person and the moon appears sullied and dark like the face of a separated mistress.

Naturally of a bilious temperament the young and beautiful maidens apply boiled saffron paste on their hips, breasts, arms and legs, the essence of which provides heat in addition to the heat provided by an embrace which lasts the entire night long. Thus they are able to reduce the terrible aspect of winter. Here ends the description of *śiśira* season.

"चैत्रे मदर्द्धिः शुकसारिकाणां
हारीतदात्यूहमधुव्रतानाम्।
पुंस्कोकिलानां सहकारबन्धुः
मदस्य कालः पुनरेष एव।।

In the month of Caitra, the birds like pigeons, parrots, black bees and *cātakas* become intoxicated. The season also helps to obtain the pollen of the mango plant and to increase the intoxication in cuckoos.

"मनोऽधिकं चात्र विलासलास्ये
प्रेङ्खासु दोलासु च सुन्दरीणाम्।
गीते च गौरीचरितावतंसे
पूजा प्रपञ्चे च मनोभवस्य।।

"पुंस्कोकिलः कूजति पञ्चमेन
बलाद्विलासा युवतौ स्फुरन्ति।
स्मरो वसन्तेऽत्र नवैः प्रसूनैः
स्वचापयष्टेर्घटनां करोति।।

During this season, the minds of women are busy with playful sport, dance, sing and swing, so they crib in praying to Gaurī[24] and Kāmadeva.[25] This month is marked by several fasts and festivals like *Gaurī-pūjan*,[26] *Navrātras*,[27] *Śrīpañcamī*,[28] *Madan-mahotsava*,[29] etc.

In *vasanta* (spring) the male cuckoo sings in the *pañcam rāga*.[30] It possibly induces lustful passion in maidens and Kāmadeva creates an arc with the flowers of spring.

"पिनद्धमाहारजनांशुकानां
सीमन्तसिन्दूरजुषां वसन्ते।
स्मरीकृते प्रेयसि भक्तिभाजां
विशेषवेषः स्वदते वधूनाम्।।

"अयं प्रसूनोद्धुरकर्णिकारः
पुष्पप्रपञ्चाञ्चितकाञ्चनारः।
विजृम्भणाकोविदकोविदारः
कालो विकाशोद्यतसिन्दुवारः।।

"रोहीतकाम्रातककिङ्किराता
मधूकमोचाः सह माधवीभिः।
जयन्ति शोभाञ्जनकश्च शाखी
सकेसरः पुष्पभरैर्वसन्ते।।

During *vasanta* (spring) wives devoted to their husbands with

24. Gaurī — Consort of Lord Śiva.
25. Kāmadeva — God of Love, Cupid.
26. *Gaurī-pūjan* — For worship of the goddess *Navamīvrata* is observed. See Vettam Mani, *op. cit.*, p. 536.
27. *Navrātras* or *Navarātripūjā* (nine day's worship) is in praise of goddess Durgā. It is conducted by undertaking fasts for nine days (or the ninth night of bright lunar fortnight in month of *tulam*) to worship goddess Gaurī. See Vettam Mani, pp. 536-7.
28. *Śrī-pañcamī* — the fifth day of the bright half of Māgha. See Apte, *op. cit.*, p. 931.
29. *Madan-Mahotsava* is a festival celebrated in honour of Kāmadeva (Cupid, God of Love). See Apte, *op. cit.*, p. 736.
30. *Pañcam rāga* — Name of a musical mode or *rāga* which is an organised sequence of musical notes in the Indian tradition of Music. See Apte, *op. cit.*, p. 579.

hair-partings marked with *sindūr*[31] (red-vermilion), wearing saffron coloured thin clothes look very attractive.

During this season the *karṇikāra*[32] tree gets loaded with flowers, the *kacanāra*[33] is filled with flowers, the *kovidāra*[34] trees get rich with foliage and *sinduvāra*[35] trees are on the point of growth.

During *vasanta* (spring), the trees of *rohiḍā*,[36] *āmlā*,[37] *mahuā*,[38] banana, *mādhvaī-latā*[39] and *sahajan*[40] are filled with buds and blossoms. These saffron filled trees appear very attractive.

"यो माधवीमुकुलदृष्टिषु वेणिबन्धो
यः कोकिलाकलरुते कथने च लाभः।
पूजाविधिर्दमनकेन च यः स्मरस्य
तस्मिन्मधुः स भगवान्गुरुरङ्गनानाम्।।

The Caitra month is the preceptor of fortunate women because they use flowers of *mādhavī-latā* to adorn their hair, emulate the sweet notes of the cuckoo and use the offerings from the Daune[41] for their prayers to Kamadeva.[42]

"नालिङ्गितः कुरबकस्तिलको न दृष्टो

---

31. *Sindūr* — Red pigment used by married Indian women in the parting of the hair as an auspicious mark.
32. *Karṇikāra* is a kind of tree. See Bhide, *op. cit.*, p. 336.
33. *Kacanāra* is a kind of tree, *Bauhinia variegata,* the buds are used as vegetable and its flowers are used in medical prescriptions. See Chaturvedi and Tiwari, *op. cit.*, p. 97.
34. *Kovidāra* is a kind of tree.
35. *Sinduvāra* is a kind of tree.
36. *Rohiḍā* is a kind of tree.
37. *Āmlā*. See, *op. cit.*, p. 8 of the same chapter.
38. *Mahuā*, a tree, *Bassia latifolia* bearing sweet flowers used for preparing liquor, See Chaturvedi and Tiwari, p. 496.
39. *Mādhavī-latā*, *Gaertnera racemosa* is a creeper which yields fragrant flowers. See Chaturvedi and Tiwari, p. 498.
40. *Sahajan*, a kind of tree.
41. *Daune*, a kind of tree.
42. Kāmadeva is God of Love, Cupid.

नो ताडितश्च चरणैः सुदृशामशोकः।
सिक्तो न वक्त्रमधुना बकुलश्च चैत्रे
चित्रं तथापि भवति प्रसवावकीर्णः।।

It is amazing that *kurbak*[43] tree flowers without a maiden's embrace, the *tilaka*[44] tree flowers without a maiden's beautiful sight, the *aśoka*[45] flowers without a maiden's kick and the *bakula*[46] tree flowers without the nectar like sweetness of their faces in this season.

"चैत्रे चित्रौ रक्तनीलावशोकौ
स्वर्णाशोकस्तत्तृतीयश्च पीतः।
जैत्रं तन्त्रं तत्प्रसूनान्तरेभ्यः
चेतोयोनेः भूर्भुवःस्वस्त्रयेऽपि।।

"गूवाकानां नालिकेरद्रुमाणां
हिन्तालानां पाटलीकिंशुकानाम्।
खर्जूराणां ताडताडीतरूणां
पुष्पापीडन्यासहेतुर्वसन्तः।। वसन्तः ।"

Even more amazing is the fact that the red *aśoka*, the blue *aśoka* and the golden *aśoka*, all three are used as Cupid's (Kāmadeva) arrows in place of other weapons to gain victory over the three worlds.

The *vasanta* season (spring) is also the cause for the blossoming of the betelnut tree, coconut tree, rose and date-palms.

This is the description of the *vasanta* season.

"विकाशकारी नवमल्लिकानां
दलच्छिरीषप्रसवाभिरामः।

---

43. *Kurbak* is a species of *Amaranth*. According to convention of poets it does not put forth flowers without a maiden's embrace. See Apte, *op. cit.*, p. 364.

44. *Tilaka* is sesamum.

45. *Aśoka* — Name of a tree with red flowers, *Jonesia Aśoka Roxb*. (said according to convention of poets to put forth flowers when it is struck by young and beautiful ladies with the foot decked with jingling anklets.) See Apte, *op. cit.*, p. 181.

46. *Bakula*, a kind of tree. See *Apte, op. cit.*, p. 698.

पुष्पप्रदः काञ्चनकेतकीनां
ग्रीष्मोऽयमुल्लासितधातकीकः।।

The *grīṣma* season causes the jasmine to flower, looks beautiful with the flowers of *śiriṣa*, the *campaka* and *ketakī* plants to blossom and the flowers of the plant *dhāya* to grow.

"खर्जूरजम्बूपनसाम्रमोचा
प्रियालपूगीफलनालिकेरैः।
द्वन्द्वानि खेदालसतामुपास्य
रतानुसन्धानमिहाद्रियन्ते।।

"स्रोतांस्यनम्भांसि सकूपकानि
प्रपाः कठोरेऽहनि पान्थपूर्णाः।
शुचौ समभ्यर्थितसक्तुपाने
प्रगे च सायं च वहन्ति मार्गाः।।

"यत्कायमानेषु दिनार्द्धनिद्रा
यत्स्नानकेलिर्दिवसावसाने।
यद्रात्रिशेषे सुरतावतारः
स मुष्टियोगो घनघर्ममाथी।।

In the *grīṣma* season, couples use dates, fruit of the rose-apple tree, jackfruit, mangoes, bananas, betel nuts and coconut to remove their weariness and sloth and indulge in amorous past-time.

In the days of *grīṣma* the sources of water supply and wells dry up. During the hot noons travellers crowd around cisterns or wells, a drink made of barley water (*sattū*)[47] is pleasing and travellers travel by morning or evening.

A restful and short sleep in the huts during noon, bathing in the evenings and amorous love-making in the night are some of the means to get rid of the dreadful heat.

"या चन्द्रिका चन्दनपङ्कहृद्या
या जालमार्गानिलवीचिमाला।

47. *Sattū* — flour of barley, first fried and then grond.

या तालवृन्तैरुदबिन्दुवृष्टि-
र्जलाञ्जलिं सा शुचये ददाति।।

"कर्पूरचूर्णं सहकारभङ्ग-
स्ताम्बूलमार्द्रक्रमुकोपक्लृप्तम्।
हाराश्च तारास्तनुवस्त्रमेत-
न्महारहस्यं शिशिरक्रियायाः।।

"मुक्तालताश्चन्दनपङ्कदिग्धा
मृणालहारानुसृता जलार्द्राः।
स्रजश्च मौलौ स्मितचम्पकानां
ग्रीष्मेऽपि सोऽयं शिशिरावतारः।।"

The cool sandalpaste akin to the clear moonlight, the waft of breeze coming in through the windows and the drops of water which scatter due to movement of the fans are the offerings of the *grīṣma* season.

The friction caused on the body due to rubbing of dust or camphor, a cooling drink made from mashed mangoes (*pannā*),[48] *pāna*[49] made from wet betel nuts, garlands of pure pearls and thin clothes are the secrcts for acquiring a cool sensation in summers.

Pearl necklaces soaked in sandalpaste, neck garlands made of fresh and wet lotus talks and garlands made of *campaka* blossoms for the head help in the incarnation of *śiśira* (winters) even in *grīṣma* (summers).

अत्र हि —

"पच्यन्त इव भूतानि ताप्यन्त इव पांसवः।
क्वथ्यन्त इव तोयानि ध्मायन्त इव चाद्रयः।।

"एणाः स्थलीषु मृगतृष्णिकया ह्रियन्ते
स्रोतस्तनुत्वजनिता जलवेणिबन्धाः।
ताम्यत्तिमीनि च सरांसि जलस्य शोषा-
दुद्धारघट्टघटिकावलयाश्च कूपाः।।

48. *Pannā* is a cooling drink used for warding off the ill effects of heat.

49. *Pāna* is a kind of betel-leaf, folded, seasoned ready to be chewed. See Apte, *op. cit.*, p. 441.

"करभाः शरभाः सरासभा
मदमायान्ति भजन्ति विक्रियाम्।
करवीरकरीरपुष्पिणीः
स्थलभूमीरधिरुह्य चासते।।

"सहकाररसार्चिता रसाला
जलभक्तं फलपानकानि मन्थाः।
मृगलावरसाः सृतं च दुग्धं
स्मरसञ्जीवनमौषधं निदाघे।।

In the *grīṣma* season, living beings appear to be ripening, the dust appears to be heated, water appears to be boiled and mountains become hot.

Deer are deluded by the illusion (or mirage) in the deserts, due to emaciation of water resources the water in the rivers is reduced to a trickle, due to drying up of water the living creatures in the ponds appear desperate and Persian wheels are used in wells to draw water out from the low levels.

Baby elephants, pigs and donkeys become perverse and intoxicated and climb up to higher places where there are trees of *kaner*[50] and *karīl*.[51]

The delicious and juicy drink obtained from mangoes, wet boiled rice, juices of different fruits, a drink of barley, soup or broth made from the flesh of lamb and boiled milk — these are the drug like medicines to bring alive the God of Love (Kāmadeva).

"जडचन्दनचारवस्तरुण्यः
सजलार्द्राः सहतारहारमालाः।
कदलीदलतल्पकल्पनस्थाः
स्मरमाहूय निवेशयन्ति पार्श्वे।।

"ग्रीष्मे चीरीनादवन्तो वनान्ताः
पङ्काभ्यक्ताः सैरिभाः सेभकोलाः।

50. *Kaner* — The plant oleander, see Chaturvedi and Tiwari, p. 100.

51. *Karīl* — A thorny leafless shrub, *capparis aphylla,* shoot of a bamboo. See Chaturvedi and Tiwari, p. 104.

लोलज्जिह्वाः सर्पसारङ्गवर्गा
मूलस्रस्तैः पत्रिणश्चांसदेशैः।।

"हर्म्यं रम्यं चन्द्रिकाधौतपृष्ठं
कान्तोच्छिष्टा वारुणी वारिमिश्रा।
मालाः कण्ठे पाटला मल्लिकानां
सद्यो ग्रीष्मं हन्त हेमन्तयन्ति।। ग्रीष्मः ।"

During the *grīṣma* season, attractive due to sandalpaste, wet with water, adorned with long pearl garlands and sitting on beds of banana leaves these beautiful maidens appear to have called Kāmadeva (God of Love) to sit next to them.

During this time one can hear the musical sounds of crickets in jungles. The young one of bulls, elephants and pigs are seen coated with slush, snakes and deers are seen with their tongues moving in and out and the feathers of birds loosen up.

On the moonlit washed ceilings of palatial mansions, the remnants of a mixture of water and liquor and necks adorned with garlands of pink jasmines make *hemanta* out of the *grīṣma* season.

Thus ends the description of grīṣma.

चतुरवस्थश्च ऋतुरूपनिबन्धनीयः। तद्यथा — सन्धिः, शैशवं, प्रौढिः, अनुवृत्तिश्च। ऋतुद्वयमध्यं सन्धिः। शिशिरवसन्तसन्धिर्यथा —

"च्युतसुमनसः कुन्दाः पुष्पोद्गमेष्वलसा द्रुमा
मनसि च गिरं गृह्णन्तीमे गिरन्ति न कोकिलाः।
अथ च सवितुः शीतोल्लासं लुनन्ति मरीचयो
न च जरठतामालम्बन्ते क्लमोदयदायिनीम्।।"

A poet while describing seasons should describe the four stages of the season—(a) *ṛtusandhi* (conjunction), (b) *ṛtuśaiśava* (infancy), (c) *ṛtupraudi* (maturity), and (d) *ṛtuanuvṛtti* (compliance). The compliance of *śiśira* and *vasanta* is exemplified thus —

Flowers fall off from the *kunda* trees. Other trees appear to be slow in putting forth new leaves. Cuckoos appear to be singing mutely as the notes do not venture forth. The rays of the sun appear to destroy the effects of cold but are not yet really hot.

वसन्तशैशवम् —

"गर्भग्रन्थिषु वीरुधां सुमनसो मध्येऽङ्कुरं पल्लवा
वाञ्छामात्रपरिग्रहः पिकवधूकण्ठोदरे पञ्चमः।
किं च त्रीणि जगन्ति जिष्णु दिवसैर्द्वित्रैर्मनोजन्मनो
देवस्यापि चिरोज्झितं यदि भवेदभ्यासवश्यं धनुः।।"

Description of *vasanta* in its infancy —

The secret nodes of creepers are now alive with flowers. New leaves can be seen amidst new shoots. The throat of the cuckoo is rustling with the notes of the *pañcam-rāga*.[52] If the long forsaken bow of Kāmadeva (Cupid, God of Love) is brought under control with practice, then it could gain victory over the three worlds in a short span of two to three days.

वसन्तप्रौढिः —

"साम्यं सम्प्रति सेवते विचकिलं षाण्मासिकैर्मौक्तिकैः
कान्तिं कर्षति काञ्चनारकुसुमं मञ्जिष्ठधौतात्पटात्।
हूणीनां कुरुते मधूकमुकुलं लावण्यलुण्ठाकतां
लाटीनाभिनिभं चकास्ति च पतद्वृन्ताग्रतः केसरम्।।"

अतिक्रान्तर्त्तुलिङ्गं यत्कुसुमाद्यनुवर्त्तते।
लिङ्गानुवृत्तिं तामाहुः सा ज्ञेया काव्यलोकतः।।

Description of the maturity of *vasanta* —

During this time the jasmine flowers appear like pearls, *kacanāra*[53] flowers appear like clothes dyed with *mañjhīṭha*.[54] Buds of *mahuā*[55] are vying with the grace and charm of women from Hūṇa[56] and saffron dripping from the tip of a stalk looks like the

52. *Pañcam rāga*. See the same chapter, Note 30.

53. *Kacanāra* — The tree *Bauhinia variegata* — its buds are used as vegetable and its flowers in medical prescriptions. See Chaturvedi and Tiwari, p. 91.

54. *Mañjhīṭha* — the colour of the Indian Madder. See Bhide, p. 843.

55. *Mahuā* (*Bassia latifolia*) — a tree bearing sweet flowers that are used for preparing liquor. See Chaturvedi and Tiwari, p. 496.

56. Hūṇa — name of a country and its people. See Bhide, p. 119, also see Appendix II.

navel of beautiful maidens from Lāṭa.[57]

When the signs, flowers, etc., of the season gone by are visible in the present one, it is known as *ṛtuanuvṛtti* (compliance) and this can be learnt from the world of poets.

वर्षासु ग्रीष्मलिङ्गाब्जविकासानुवृत्तिः।

यथा —

"खं वस्ते कलविङ्ककण्ठमलिनं कादम्बिनीकम्बलं
चर्चां पारयतीव दर्दुरकुलं कोलाहलैरुन्मदम्।
गन्धं मुञ्चति सिक्तलाजसदृशं वर्षेण दग्धा स्थली
दुर्लक्ष्योऽपि विभाव्यते कमलिनीहासेन भासां पतिः।।"

Growth of lotuses symbolic of *grīṣma* season is being described in the rainy season as —

The sky has covered itself with a blanket of accumulated dark clouds like the neck of a hen-sparrow. Intoxicated frogs in an uproar seem to be praying and chanting incantations. The heat scorched earth is sending out an aroma of the parched paddy after it receives the first drops of rain and the sun in spite of being partially obscured by the clouds makes its presence felt by the growth of lotuses.

एवमन्येऽपि।

किञ्च —

ग्रैष्मिकसमयविकासी कथितो धूलीकदम्ब इति लोके।
जलधरसमयप्राप्तौ स एव धाराकदम्बः स्यात्।।

यथा —

"धूलिकदम्बपरिधूसरदिङ्मुखस्य
रक्तच्छटासुरशरासनमण्डनस्य।
दीप्तायुधाशनिमुचो ननु नीलकण्ठ
नोत्कण्ठसे समरवारिधरागमस्य।।"

Thus the other seasons may also be understood.

---

57. Lāṭa — name of a country. See Appendix II.

According to popular belief, though similar *kadamba*[58] flowers in *grīṣma* are called *dhūli-kadamba* whereas in the rainy season they are called *dhāra-kadamba.*

Thus —

O! blue-throated one (peacock)! Are you not eager to welcome the war like advent of rains? In this tumultuous advent of the rainy season dust fills the atmosphere in all directions, the rainbow can be seen in the sky and brilliant lightning falls from it.

जलसमयजायमानां जातिं यां कार्द्दमीति निगदन्ति।
सा शरदि महोत्सविनी गन्धान्वितषट्पदा भवति।।

The species of flowers which might be useless for the rainy season appear pleasing, attractive perfumed and are filled with bumble bees during the autumn season.

यथा —

"स्थूलावश्यायबिन्दुद्युतिदलितबृहत्कोरकग्रन्थिभाजो
जात्या जालं लतानां जरठपरिमलप्लावितानां जजृम्भे।
नानाहंसोपधानं सपदि जलनिधेश्चोत्ससर्पापरस्य
ज्योत्स्नाशुक्लोपधानं शयनमिव शशी नागभोगाङ्कमम्भः।। "

Thus —

In the *śarad* season bunches of laden buds are like dew-drops and groups of pollen filled ripe flowers of *mālatī*[59] are seen waving. The moon with its clear moonlight filled with various swan like excellences appears to be going down from the sky to sleep on the snake like water-bed of the western sea.

स्तोकानुवृत्तिं केतक्या अपि केचिदिच्छन्ति।

यथा —

"असूच्यत शरत्कालः केतकीधूलिधूसरैः।

---

58. *Kadamba* tree — a kind of tree said to put forth buds at the roaring of thunder clouds.

59. *Mālatī* is a kind of creeper that yields very sweet smelling flowers. See Chaturvedi and Tiwari, *op. cit.*, p. 502.

पङ्काताम्रैर्नवायातश्चरणैरिव वासरैः।।"

शरद्भवानामनुवृत्तिरत्र
बाणासनानां सकुरुण्टकानाम्।
हेमन्तवक्त्रे यदि दृश्यतेऽपि
न दृश्यते बन्धविधिः कवीनाम्।।

Some poets describe the *ketakī*[60] flowers prevalent in the rainy season in the *śarad* season also.

Thus —

> Coming from afar, therefore with red and dusty feet, a guest's arrival can be inferred from a distance. Similarly dusty days with the dust of *ketakī* and red with red-lotuses are an indication of the advent of *śarad* season.
>
> The flowers of such trees as *bandhūka*,[61] *karnīkārā* tree and *bānjh* are also visible in the beginning of *hemanta* season but no poet has described them in the conjunction of *hemanta* and *śarad* seasons. Therefore future poets should also not describe them thus.

हेमन्तशिशिरयोरैक्ये सर्वलिङ्गानुवृत्तिरेव। उक्तञ्च। 'द्वादशमासः संवत्सर, पञ्चर्तवो हेमन्तशिशिरयोः समासेन'।

मरुबकदमनकपुन्नागपुष्पलिङ्गानुवृत्तिभिः सुरभिः।
रचनीयश्चित्रश्रीः किञ्चित्कुन्दानुवृत्त्या च।।

"गेहे वाहीकयूनां वहति दमनको मञ्जरीकर्णपूरा-
नुन्मादः पामरीणां मरुति मरुबकामोदिनि व्यक्तिमेति।

Hemanta and *śiśira* seasons being alike the nature description of both is similar. It has been stated:

> Twelve months make a solar year and in a solar year there are only five seasons because *hemanta* and *śiśira* are basically one.

While describing the *śiśira* season, a poet should describe some of the

---

60. *Ketakī* — *Pandanus*, screw-pine. See Chaturvedi and Tiwari, *op. cit.*, p. 126.
61. *Bandhūka* — name of a tree. See Bhide, *op. cit.*, p. 531.

plants found in the *hemanta* season like the *damnaka*,[62] *marūbaka*[63] and *puññāga.*[64] He should also describe *kunda*[65] flowers. Thus —

सद्योभङ्गानुसारस्नुतसुरभिशिराः शीकरः साहकारः
सर्पत्रम्भः शरावे रचयति च रसो रेचकीचन्द्रकाणि।।"

During the *śarad* season, the youth of Vāhīka[66] have a cluster of *kunda* flowers hanging behind their ears, the fragrant breeze due to clusters of *marūbaka* intoxicates the maidens of Pāmardeśa and in an earthen vessel the drops of mango-juice become moon-shaped.

"कुन्दे मन्दस्तमाले मुकुलिनि विकलः कातरः किङ्किराते
रक्ताशोके सशोकश्चिरमतिविकचे चम्पके कुञ्चिताक्षः।
पान्थः खेदालसोऽपि श्रवणकटुरटच्चक्रमभ्येति धुन्वन्
सोत्कण्ठः षट्पदानां नवमधुपटलीलम्पटं कर्पटेन।।

यथा वा —

"धुनानः कावेरीपरिसरभुवश्चन्दनतरून्
मरुन्मन्दः कुन्दप्रकरमकरन्दानवकिरन्।
प्रियक्रीडाकर्षच्युतकुसुममामूलसरलं
ललाटे लाटीनां लुठितमलकं ताण्डवयति।।"

एवमन्याऽप्यनुवृत्तिः।

"विचकिलकेसरपाटलिचम्पकपुष्पानुवृत्तयो ग्रीष्मे।
तत्र च तुहिनर्त्तुभवं मरुबकमपि केचिदिच्छन्ति।।

During the *śiśira* season, the travellers look at *kunda* flowers with indifference, at the buds of *tamāla*[67] with alarm, at the tender buds of the *aśoka* tree with a timid look, at the red *aśoka* tree with grief and turn away from the blossoming *campaka* flowers. Though tired and lazy he yet waves away with a cloth the

62. *Damnaka* — the *kunda* plant. See Bhide *op. cit.*, p. 531.
63. *Marūbaka* — name of a plant. See Vamana Apte, *op. cit.*, p. 771.
64. *Puññāga nāgakeśar* — name of a flower.
65. *Kunda* — name of a tree with fragrant flowers. See Bhide, *op. cit.*, p. 593.
66. Vāhīka — name of a place. See Appendix II.
67. *Tamāla* — name of a tree with a very dark bark.

cluster of greedy bumble bees buzzing around the juicy flowers.

Thus —

The gentle breeze waves through the sandalwood trees on the banks of Kāverī (name of a river) spreads the honey of *kunda* flowers and dances amongst the locks of loose and flower less hair on the forehead of the maidens of Lāṭa country.

In this way the other seasons should also be described.

In the *grīṣma* season, *camelī*, *keśar* (saffron), rose and *campā* flowers should be described. These grow in *vasanta* but blossom completely only in *grīṣma*. Some poets also describe the winter time *marūbak* flowers in *grīṣma*.

यथा —

"कर्णे स्मेरं शिरीषं शिरसि विचकिलस्रग्लताः पाटलिन्यः
कण्ठे मार्णालहारो वलयितमसिताम्भोजनालं कलाच्योः।
सामोदं चन्दनाम्भः स्तनभुवि नयने म्लानमाञ्जिष्ठपृष्ठे
गात्रं लोलज्जलार्द्रं जयति मृगदृशां ग्रैष्मिको वेष एषः।।"

यथा च —

"अभिनवकुशसूचिस्पर्द्धि कर्णे शिरीषं
मरुबकपरिवारं पाटलादाम कण्ठे।
स तु सरसजलार्द्रोन्मीलितः सुन्दरीणां
दिनपरिणतिजन्मा कोऽपि वेषश्चकास्ति।।"

Wearing a blossom of the *śiriṣa*[68] tree in the ear, a garland made out of *camelī* and roses on the head, bracelets made out of stalks of blue lotus in the wrists, breasts covered with a paste of camphor and sandal, eyes shaded with dull red colour and the body dripping with water is the attractive and pleasing summer attire of beautiful maidens.

Thus —

Wearing the novel, sharp, *śiriṣa* flowers which have pointed

68. *Śiriṣa* — name of a tree. See Bhide, p. 1053.

inner ends in the ears, a garland made of a cluster of *marūbak* and rose flowers in the neck and dripping wet body is the attractive and graceful attire of beautiful maidens in the *grīṣma* season.

एवमुदाहरणान्तराणि।

ऋतुभववृत्त्यनुवृत्ती दिङ्मात्रेणाऽत्र सूचिते सन्तः।
शेषं स्वधिया पश्यत नामग्राहं कियद् ब्रूमः।।

देशेषु पदार्थानां व्यत्यासो दृश्यते स्वरूपस्य।
तत्र तथा बध्नीयात्कविबद्धमिह प्रमाणं नः।।

शोभान्धोगन्धरसैः फलार्चनाभ्यां च पुष्पमुपयोगि।
षोढा दर्शितमेतत्स्यात्सप्तममनुपयोगि।।

Similar are other examples —

The flowers and fruits prevalent in different seasons and in compliance with the following seasons have been described in detail. Remaining can be gathered by a poet himself. After all, how many names can be described?

With the change in geographical regions objects may also differ. But a poet must describe in accordance with poetic conventions and not according to geographical regions. For a poet the only evidence is the description given by ancient poets of eminence.

Decoration, food, aroma, sap, fruit and worship are the six beneficial uses of flowers. Besides these the seventh is useless and not worth description.

यथा —

यत्प्राचि मासे कुसुमं निबद्धं
तदुत्तरे बालफलं विधेयम्।
तदग्रिमे प्रौढिधरं च कार्यं
तदग्रिमे पाकपरिष्कृतं च।।

द्रुमोद्भवानां विधिरेप दृष्टो
वल्लीफलानां न महाननेहा।
तेषां द्विमासावधिरेव कार्यः

पुष्पे फले पाकविधौ च कालः।।

अन्तर्व्याजं बहिर्व्याजं बाह्यान्तर्व्याजमेव च।
सर्वव्याजं बहुव्याजं निर्व्याजं च तथा फलम् ।।

Thus —

If in a particular month the origin of the flower is being described, then in the next month its fruit bearing should be described, in the third month its maturity and in the fourth its ripening and refining should be described. This four-monthly sequence is applicable only to fruits and flowers of trees. In creepers the entire span of flowering, fruition and ripening is only two months.

Fruits are of six kinds — (1) *antarvyāja*[69] (useless on the insdie), (2) *bahirvyāja* (useless outside), (3) *bāhyāntarvyāja* (useless both inside and outside), (4) *sarvavyāja* (useless all throughout), (5) *bahuvyāja*, and (6) *nirvyāja* (without any useless part).

लकुचाद्यन्तर्व्याजं तथा बहिर्व्याजमत्र मोचादि।
आम्राद्युभयव्याजं सर्वव्याजं च ककुभादि।।

पनसादि बहुव्याजं नीलकपित्थादि भवति निर्व्याजम्।
सकलफलानां षोढा ज्ञातव्यः कविभिरिति भेदः।।

एकद्वित्र्यादिभेदेन सामस्त्येनाथवा ऋतून्।
प्रबन्धेषु निबध्नीयात्क्रमेण व्युत्क्रमेण वा ।।

न च व्युत्क्रमदोषोऽस्ति कवेरर्थपथस्पृशः।
तथा कथा कापि भवेद् व्युत्क्रमो भूषणं यथा।।

अनुसन्धानशून्यस्य भूषणं दूषणायते।
सावधानस्य च कवेर्दूषणं भूषणायते।।

इति कालविभागस्य दर्शिता वृत्तिरीदृशी।
कवेरिह महान्मोह इह सिद्धो महाकविः।।

इति राजशेखरकृतौ काव्यमीमांसायां

---

69. The word *vyāja* here means pretence. In every fruit the kernel is hidden in the useless and rough skin and this is what is known as pretence.

Baḍhara fruits are *antarvyāja*, bananas belong to *bahirvyāja*, mangoes are *ubhayvyāja* and *kakubh* fruits are *sarvavyāja*.

Jackfruit is *bahuvyāja* and *nīl-kaith* is *nirvyāja*. In this way all fruits can be classified under these six groups.

A poet should describe in simple language one, two, three or all the season sequentially or in the opposing order in his poetic composition.

To describe the seasons in the opposing order is not a defect for the poet. But the context of the narrative should be such that the reciprocation should appear like an excellence.

For a poet who lacks in research, even excellences appear as flaws and for a careful poet flaws become ornaments.

Thus, in the last chapter has been described the division of time for the poet for they are sometimes negligent in this sphere. Those poets who are entirely acquainted with these subjects are *mahākavis* (poets of eminence).[70]

।। कविरहस्ये प्रथमेऽधिकरणे कालविभागो नाम अष्टादशोऽध्यायः ।।
समाप्तमिदं प्रथममधिकरणं कविरहस्यं काव्यमीमांसायाम्।

70. **In this chapter, Rājaśekhara gives information about time and seasons and the seasons' activities, a knolwedge that poets must possess. This suggests a requirment on composers to be faithful to facts and to be logical (for example, describing fruition after flowering *vide* lines 339-48).**

Appendix I

THE names of important persons mentioned in *Kāvyamīmāṁsā* have been listed here. (Adapted and abridged from the Hindi translation by Pt. Kedarnath Sharma Sarasvat).

Ācāryas — They have been quoted eighteen times in the *Kāvyamīmāṁsā*, probably used for Sanskrit critics like Bhāmaha, Vāmana, Daṇḍin, etc.

Amara — Composer of the Sanskrit dictionary. *Amarakośa*, was one of the nine jewels of Vikramāditya's court.

Ānanda — Probably Ānandavardhana, composer of *Dhvanyāloka*, a poet of Kaśmīra.

Āparājiti — Son of Āparājita, probably the commentator, *Bhaṭṭalollaṭa* of Bharata's *Nāṭyaśāstra*.

Aumeyi — Daughter of Umā (wife of Śiva) also known as Sāhitya-vidyā-vadhū.

Aupkāyana — One of the eighteen disciples of Kāvya-puruṣa.

Auśanas — Political follower of Uśanas.

Avantīsundarī — A learned poetess critic, wife of Rājaśekhara, has been quoted thrice in the *Kāvyamīmāṁsā*.

Bārhaspatya — An *ācārya* who is known to be a follower of Bṛhaspati.

Bharata — Bharata *muni* is the well-known composer of *Nāṭyaśāstra*, a treatise on dramaturgy.

Bhāravi — An eminent poet of the Sanskrit language known for his Epic, *Kirātārjunīya*.

Bhavānī — Another name of Pārvatī, the creator of Sāhitya-vidyā-vadhū.

Candragupta — A number of kings with the same name are part of Indian history, this one particularly refers to Samudragupta's son and Skandagupta's father, the famous Candragupta II.

Citraśikha — King of Vidyādhara (as mentioned in the Purāṇas).

Citrāsundarī — Wife of Citraśikha.

Citrāṅgadā — One of the eighteen disciples of Kāvya-puruṣa.

Dhiṣaṇa — One of the eighteen disciples of Kāvya-puruṣa.

Dhruvsvāminī — Rāmagupta's (Samudragupta's elder brother) wife, whom ultimately Samudragupta married.

Drauhiṇī — Son of Brahmā, another name for Bharata, author of *Nāṭyaśāstra*.

Dvaipāyana — Name of the famous sage Vyāsa or Veda-vyāsa, creator of the Epic *Mahābhārata*, *Brahmasūtras*, etc.

Gaurī — Another name for Pārvatī, wife of Śiva, daughter of Himālaya, gave birth to Sāhitya-vidyā-vadhū.

Gondārdīya — Another name for Patañjali, author of *Mahābhāṣya*.

Haricandra — An ancient poet known for his work in prose called *Prabandharāja*.

Harṣa — Patron of Bāṇabhaṭṭa, king Harṣavardhana was also a renowned poet.

Kālidāsa — One of the greatest writers of Sanskrit, has a number of Epics to his credit like *Raghuvaṁśa*, *Abhijñānaśākuntala*, *Kumārasambhava*.

Kāmadeva — One of the eighteen disciples of Kāvya-puruṣa.

Karṇa — One of the kings of the southern geographical regions.

Kauṭilya — Also known as Cāṇakya, chief-minister during the reign of Candragupta Maurya, creator of the *Arthaśāstra*.

Kāvya-puruṣa — Legendary son of Sarasvatī (goddess of learning and wisdom) and propagator of *kāvya-vidyā*.

Khasadhipati — Mentioned in the eighth chapter of *Kāvyamīmāṁsā*, defeated Candragupta II's (Samudra-gupta's son) elder brother Rāmgupta and asked for a part of his kingdom and beautiful wife Dhruvsvāminī (or Dhruvadevī) in truce. Annoyed at this Candragupta II in the disguise of Dhruvasvāminī took his revenge on Khasadhipati, killed him and also his unworthy brother Rāmagupta. Consequently he himself married Dhruvasvāminī and took the reigns of the kingdom in his own hands.

Kubera — One of the eighteen disciples of Kāvya-puruṣa, created an *adhikaraṇa* on *ubhaya alaṁkāra*.

Kucumāra — One of the eighteen disciples of Kāvya-puruṣa.

Kuduṅgeśvara — Probably one of kings of Ujjayinī, a famous city of learning.

Kumāradāsa — A great poet born blind, probably of eighth century AD, known for his Epic *Jānakīharaṇa*.

Kuvinda — King of Mathurā who advocated the disuse of rough words like *ṭaṅkāra*, etc.

Mānavāḥ — *Ācāryas* known to be followers of Manu.

Maṅgala — An *ācārya* who has been cited at four different places in the *Kāvyamīmāṁsā*. Nothing much is known about him.

Medhāvirudra — A poet blind by birth, known for his work on rhetorics.

Meṇṭha or Bhattra-meṇṭha — An eminent poet probably belonging to Kaśmīra, known for his *mahākāvya*, *Hayagrīvavadha*.

Nandikeśvara or Nandi — One of the eighteen disciples of Kāvya-puruṣa.

Pālyakīrti — A well-known *ācārya* belonging to the Jain community, composer of a work on grammar called *Śabdānuśāsana*.

Pāṇinīyaḥ — *Ācārya* of Pāṇini and a great scholar.

Pāṇini — The famous grammarian, also known as Dākṣīputra.

Parameṣṭhi or Brahmā — One of the sixty-four disciples of Lord Śiva.

Parāśara — One of the eighteen disciples of Kāvya-puruṣa, has composed a treatise on *atiśayokti*.

Patañjali — According to Rājaśekhara, Patañjali and Gonardīya are the same person but this is also a matter of dispute.

Pracetā — One of the eighteen disciples of Kāvya-puruṣa known for his work on *anuprāsa*.

Pulastya — One of the eighteen disciples of Kāvya-puruṣa, known for his composition on *svabhāvokti*.

Piṅgala — Probably a younger relation of Pāṇini known for his work on metrics.

Prācetasa — Another name of the sage Mitrāvaruṇa.

Rājaśekhara — A poet, critic and dramatist belonging to the Yāyāvara family.

Rudraṭa—A poet critic from Kaśmīra, known for his work, *Kāvyālaṁkāra*.

Rūpa — An ancient poet about whom nothing can be said with certainty.

Sāhasāṅka — Name of Vikramāditya or a poet.

Sahasrākṣa — One of the eighteen disciples of Kāvya-puruṣa who is supposed to have composed the first *adhikaraṇa*, *Kavirahasya*.

Sāhitya-vidyā-vadhū — In the legend concerning Kāvya-puruṣa, she is the wife acquired for him by Pārvatī.

Sarasvateya — Son of Brahmā and Sarasvatī, the Kāvyaputra. There is also a reference to this legend in Bāṇabhaṭṭa's *Harṣacarita* and *Vāyu Purāṇa*.

Sarasvatī — Wife of Prajāpati and mother of Kāvya-puruṣa Goddess of wisdom and learning.

Sātavāhana — A famous poet of the Sanskrit world. He was also the king of Kuntala.

Śeṣa — One of the eighteen disciples of Kāvya-puruṣa, known for his *adhikaraṇa* on *Śabdaśleṣa*.

Siśunāga — A king, probably of Vārāṇasī.

Śrīkaṇṭha — Another name for Śiva who first instructed Vaikuṇṭha and 64 other disciples in the discipline of *Kāvya-vidyā*.

Śriśarmagupta — He was the eldest son of Samudragupta and elder brother of Candragupta II.

Śūdraka—A famous king and dramatist known for the play *Mṛcchakaṭika*.

Sūra — One of the ancient poets belonging to Buddhist community. Has composed the *Jātakamālā*.

Surananda — One of the ancestral poets of Rājaśekhara, born in the Yāyāvara family of which Rājaśekhara was a descendant.

Suvarṇanābha — One of the eighteen disciples of Kāvya-puruṣa.

Śyāmadeva— Probably a contemporary of Rājaśekhara. This opinion has been stated thrice in the *Kāvyamīmāṁsā*.

Udbhaṭa—A rhetorician critic from Kaśmīra known to have lived during the reign of king Jayapada.

Uktigarbhā — One of the disciples of the legendary Kāvya-puruṣa, supposed to have composed a treatise on *ukti*.

Upamanyu — One of the eighteen disciples of Kāvya-puruṣa.

Upavarṣa — Believed to be the teacher (*guru*) of the grammarian Pāṇini.

Uśanas — Son of sage Bhṛgu, known to be the first *ācārya* of *Nītiśāstra*.

Utathya — Son of the sage Angīrā elder brother of Bṛhaspati after obtaining instructions from Kāvya-puruṣa. Composed a treatise on *Arthaśleṣa*.

Vaikuṇṭha — Another name for Viṣṇu, one of the sixtyfour disciples of Śrīkaṇṭha.

Vākpatirāja — An eminent poet of the Prākṛta language known for his Prākṛta *mahākāvya, Gauḍavaho*.

Vālmiki — Another name for Prācetasa.

Vāmaṇiya — An ancient poet belonging to Kaśmīra, known for his *Kāvyālaṁkārasūtra*.

Vararūci — A number of literary men with this name occur in history, but the one referred to by Rājaśekhara is probably a grammarian.

Varṣa — An *ācārya* of grammar and prior to Pāṇini.

Vāsudeva — Two well-known kings who flourished at different times during history. It cannot be ascertained as to whom Rājaśekhara refers to in his *Kāvyamīmāṁsā*.

Vyāḍi — A famous grammarian known for his work on grammar called *Saṁgraha*.

Yāyāvarīya — The family name of the poet Rājaśekhara, the composer of *Kāvyamīmaṁsā*.

Appendix II

IDENTIFICATION of geographical names occurring in the *Kāvyamīmāṁsā* (based on and abbreviated from C.D. Dalal).

Ānarta — Includes northern Gujarat and portions of the Mālwā country.

Āndhra — The Country lying between the river Godāvarī in the north and the Kṛṣṇa in the south.

Aṅga — The country lying between Bhāgalpur and Monghyr.

Antarvedī — The tract of country between Gaṅgā in the north and the Yamunā in the south.

Arbudā — Mount Ābu in the Arāvallī range now included in the Rajasthan.

Āryāvartta — The northern part of India lying between the Himālayas in the north and the Vindhya range in the south.

Aśmaka — Rājaśekhara mentions this among the countries of south India.

Avantī — The country of which Ujjain was the capital.

Ayodhyā — Situated on the river Sarayū in the United Provinces.

Bālhaveya — Rājaśekhara locates this country in northern India. This may be the same as Bhāṭiā near Multān.

Bālhīka — See Vāhīka.

Barbara — It is mentioned as one of the countries in northern India.

Bhādānaka — People of Bhādānaka talked a language which had an admixture of Apabhraṁśa like the people of Maru and the Takkas.

Bhaimarathī — The river Bhīmā in the Dakṣiṇāpatha which joins with the Kṛṣṇā.

Bhāratavarṣa — This is one of the *varṣas* in the Jambūdvīpa or Asia with the Himālayas as the Varṣaparvata.

Bhṛgukaccha — Broach and its surrouding parts.

Bindusaras — A sacred spot in the Himālayas two miles south of Gaṅgotrī.

Brahma — A country in the eastern India, presumably the modern Burma.

Brahmaśilā — Brahmaśilā formed the eastern boundary of the city of Kannauj.

Brāhmaṇavāha — It is one of the countries in western India. Brāhmaṇavāha seems to be the Hindu name of the city which the Muhammedans afterwards called Brāhmanābād.

Brahmottara — A country in eastern India, the northern portion of the Brahma country or the Upper Burma.

Bṛhadgṛha — Rājaśekhara calls it a mountain in eastern India. This may represent the Mount Everest in the eastern range of the Himālayas.

Cakora — A mountain in eastern India, it may be identified as Caraṇādri or Cunār, the hill-fort in the district of Mirzāpur, which was built by the Pāla Kings.

Cakravartīkṣetra — Rājaśekhara designates the whole country of India from Cape Comorin in the south to the Bindusaras in the Himālayas in the north, as the Cakravartīkṣetra. This land consists of 1,000 *yojanas*. One who conquers and rules over the whole of this land is called a Cakravartin. This seems to be the same as the Kumārīdvīpa, one of the nine parts of the Bhāratavarṣa, India, that is to say, India proper along with her eight colonies, Indradvīpa, etc. These colonies are bounded by the southern sea or the Indian ocean and the Himālayan range and are separated from one another by oceans.

Candanagiri — Malayagiri or the southern portion of the westerṅ Ghāṭs.

Candarabhāgā — The river Cenāb, a tributary of the river Indus.

Candrācala —A peak of the Himālayas whereform the river Candrabhāgā rises.

Coḍa — Coḍa country is represented by the districts of Tanjore and south Arcoṭ in the Madras Presidency.

Dakṣiṇadeśa — Southern India bounded by the Narmadā in the north and the Cape Comorin in the south.

Dakṣiṇāpatha — Same as Dakṣiṇadeśa.

Daṇḍaka — Situated in south India between the countries of Cola and Kāñcī, may be identified with Daṇḍaka.

Dardura — Mount Dardura, thus, can be with little difficulty identified with the Nīlgiris in the Madras Presidency.

Draviḍa —The words Dramila and Draviḍa are mentioned by Rājaśekhara to denote the inhabitants of southern India, and not the name of the country.

Daśapura — Mandasor in Mālwā.

Dāśerka — Mālwā.

Devasabhā — Devasabhā is also the name of a mountain in western India, and as such this may be identified with the mountainous parts of either the Dewās state or Udaipur where the Dhebar lake is situated.

Devikā — It is a river in northern India, and may be identified with the present river, the Deeg, which is a tributary of the Rāvī.

Dramila — Same as Draviḍa.

Droṇācala — The Doonagiri mountain in Kumaun.

Gabhastimān — One of the nine parts of the Bhāratavarṣa.

Gādhipura — A suburb of Kanauj, and situated on the northern side of the city.

Gandharva — One of the nine parts of the Bhāratavarṣa.

Gaṅgā — The river Ganges. Rājaśekhara mentions Gaṅgā in the list of rivers of the northern and western India, probably because the Ganges flows through both.

Gaṅgā — This country located in the Daksiṇāpatha may be identified as the Kongu country of the southern India which comprises the districts of Coimbatore and Sālem.

Gauḍa — The Gauḍas are a people inhabiting the whole tract of country lying between Benāres and the Bay of Bengal.

Girinagara — Girnār. Rājaśekhara places this hill in western India.

Godāvarī — A river in south India.

Govardhana — Mount Govardhana, eighteen miles from Vṛndāvana in the district of Mathurā.

Harahūrava — The country lying between the Indus and the Jhelum.

Harivarṣa — This is the first *varṣa* on the southern side of the Mahāmeru.

Hastināpura — The capital of the Kurus, north-west of Delhi. It was situated on the right bank of the Ganges at a distance of 22 miles north-west of Meerut.

Hemakūṭa — This is a Varṣa Parvata, being the second from the Mahāmerū on the southern side, is the principal mountain range of the Kimpuruṣavarṣa, and is situated on the northern side of the Himavān and the Bhāratavarṣa.

Hiḍimbā — A river in western India, according to Rājaśekhara identified with Cambal or Carmaṇavati which rises from the Vindhyas, flows through western India and meets with the Yamunā.

Himavān — The Himālayan range which is the principal mountain of the Bhāratavarṣa.

Himālaya — Same as Himavān.

Hiṁsamārga — This is also called as Krauñcarandhra or Haṁsadvāra, in the Himālayas identified with the Niti- pāss, in the district of Kumāun, connecting Tibet with India.

Hiraṇmayavarṣa — This is one of the seven *varṣas* constituting the

Jambūdvīpa or Asia.

Huhūka — One of the countries in nothern India. It may be identified with northern Kāśmīra.

Hūṇa — One of the countries in north India.

Ilāvṛtavarṣa — The country surrounding the Mahāmerū, or the mountain situated in the middle of the Jambūdvīpa. The Merū is said to have three *varṣas* in the north and three more in the south with Bhāratvarṣa being the third to the south.

Indrakīla — One of the peaks in the interior of the Himālayas.

Indradvīpa — One of the nine parts of the Bhāratavarṣa.

Irāvatī — This may be identified with the river Rāvī on the banks of which Lahore is situated.

Jambūdvīpa — One of the seven *dvīpas* of the world, situated in the middle, with the three *dvīpas* on both sides. The mountain Mahāmerū is situated in the middle of the Jambudvīpa and the *dvīpa* may be identified with the Asia of the present day. The Bhāratavarṣa is the southern-most *varṣa* or country in the Jambudvīpa and includes within its boundary the mighty Himālayas.

Jānhavī — The river Gaṅgā.

Kacchīya — Cutch.

Kālapriya — Kālapriyanātha is the name of the Mahādeva worshipped in a temple situated in the sourthern part of the city Kānyakubja or Kanuaj.

Kalinda — A part of the Himālayas known by this name. It is the source of the river Yamunā which is called Kālindī in consequence.

Kaliṅga — The northern Circārs, country lying between Orissā in the north and Āndhra in the south and bordering on the sea.

Kāmarūpa — Assam.

Kāmboja — Afghanistan, or at least its northern part.

Kanei — Kāñcīpura or Conjeevaram, the capital of the Draviḍa or the

Cola country on the river Palār, situated at a distance of forty-three miles south-west of Madras.

Kapiśā — The river Suvarṇarekhā in Singhbhūm and Orissā.

Karakaṇṭha — One of the countries in the Uttarāpatha.

Karatoyā — A sacred river flowing through the districts of Raṅgpur, Dīnājpur and Bogrā in Bengāl and joining the river Brahmaputra near the Gangetic delta.

Karṇāṭas — People living in the Karnāṭadeśa which includes the Mysore state, Coorg and part of the Ceded districts.

Kārttikeyanagara — Baijanātha or Vaidyanātha in the district of Kumāun about eighty miles from Almorā.

Kaserumān — One of the nine parts of the Bhāratavarṣa.

Kāśmīra — Kashmir.

Kāvera — Some districts of the Draviḍadeśa on the banks of the Kāverī.

Kāverī — River Kāverī in the southern India.

Kekaya — The country lying between the Biās and the Sutlej in the Punjāb.

Kerala — The Mālābār coast or the Cera country comprising Mālābār, Travancore and Cochin states.

Kimpuruṣavarṣa — This *varṣa* is situated immediately to the north of the Himālayas encircling the Hemakūṭa Parvata.

Kīra — Baijnātha or Kīrāgrāma in the Punjāb. But Rājaśekhara includes this amongst the countries of the Uttarāpatha. It is, therefore, possible to locate this country in South Afghanistan to the north of the Kīrthār range.

Kollagiri — Coorg which is now included in the Mysore state.

Koṅkaṇa — Paraśurāmakṣetra or the tract of land lying between the western Ghāṭs and the Arabian sea.

Kośala — The southern part of the kingdom of Oudh. Kośala was divided into two kingdoms called Uttarakośala and Kośala.

Krathakaiśika — The country of Vidarbha is called the land of Krathakaiśikas. But Rājaśekhara mentions these two countries separately in the Dakṣiṇāpatha.

Kumārīdvīpa — One of the nine parts of the Bhāratavarṣa. According to Rājaśekhara's conception, this *dvīpa* seems to represent India, situated between the Himālayas in the north and the Cape Comorin in the south.

Krauñcadvīpa — One of the seven *dvīpas* of the world. It is said to be encircled by the Dadhi ocean.

Kṛṣṇaveṇā — The Kṛṣṇā river which flows through the Dakṣiṇāpatha or the southern India.

Kuhū — A river in the Uttarāpatha.

Kulūta — This country is situated in the northern India or Uttarāpatha, refers to the modern Kulu in the Kāngrā district.

Kuśadvīpa — One of the seven *dvīpas* of the world, and this is said to be surrounded by the Sarpi-samudra.

Kumārīpuram — Cape Comorin, also known as Kanyākumārī.

Kuntala — Rājaśekhara locates Kuntala in the southern India with Sātavāhanas as its rulers.

Laṅkā — This Laṅkā seems to be situated in southernmost parts of the Indian peninsula, as an island somewhere in the Indian ocean. The island of Laṅkā is situated on the western side of the peninsula beyond Travancore, while Siṁhala or Ceylon is on the eastern side of it.

Lāṭa — Southern Gujarāt including Khāndeśa or the tract of territory situated between the river Māhī and the lower Narmadā.

Lauhitya — The river Brahmaputra.

Limpāka — Rājaśekhara places this country in north India.

Lohitagiri — One of the mountains of eastern India.

Madhyadeśa — The country bounded by the river Sarasvatī in Kurukṣetra, Allāhābād, the Himālayas and the Vindhyas.

Magadha — The province of Bihar or South Bihar.

Mahārāṣṭra — The Marāṭhā country or the country watered by the upper Godāvarī, or the land lying between this river and the Kṛṣṇā.

Mahendra — Rājaśekhara mentions Mahendra among the mountains of south India.

Mahī — The river Mahī which springs in Mālavā and falls into the gulf of Cāmbay.

Māhiṣaka — This is a country on the lower Narmadā with Māhiṣmatī as its capital.

Māhiṣmatī — Maheśvara or Maheśa on the right bank of the Narmadā forty miles to the south of Indore.

Mahodaya — Kanauj or Kānyakubja.

Māladā — A portion of the district of Śāhābād in Bihār.

Mālavā — Mālwā or Avantī.

Mallavartaka — One of the eastern countries.

Mālvā — The southern ranges of the western Ghāṭs.

Mālyaśikhara — It is a mountain in western India.

Mañjara — See Pāla.

Māru — Rājapūtānā or Mārwār.

Mekala — It is a part of the Vindhya range called Amarakaṇṭaka wherefrom the river Narmadā rises.

Merū — Mahāmerū, or the mountain situated in the middle of the Jambūdvīpa.

Mudgara — The country of Mudgara is identified with Monghyr in Bihār.

Murala — Rājaśekhara locates this country in south India.

Nāgadvīpa — One of the nine parts of the Bhrāratavarṣa.

Narmadā — Rājaśekhara includes this amongst the rivers of south India.

Nāsikya — Nāsik. Same as Pañcavaṭī.

Nepāla — Nepal.

Nīlagiri — One of the Varṣa mountains of Jambūdvīpa or Asia.

Niṣādha — This is mentioned as a mountain in the Jambūdvīpa or Asia, and as situated immediately to the south of the Mahāmerū.

Orissā — The northern part of the Kaliṅga country.

Pāla — The words Pāla and Mañjara occur in two places in this work, and in both the places they appear joined together, and are said to be the *janapadas* as well as mountains situated in the Dakṣiṇāpatha. These two, therefore, may be taken as one word and identified with Pāla near Mahād.

Pallava — This name often denotes a dynasty which ruled over the southern India from the fifth to the ninth century AD with the capital at Kāñcī. The country surrounding Kāñcī very probably was known as the Pallava country.

Pāñcāla — The Pāñcāla country is located in the central India or Madhyadeśa which is extended from the foot of Himālayas to the Yamunā and between Vinaśana and Prayāga.

Pāṇḍya — The modern districts of Tinnevelly and Madurai in the Madras presidency.

Pāriyātra — One of the Kulparvatas in the Kumārīdvīpa. This may be identified with the north-western part of the Vindhya range.

Paścāddeśa — Western India. This comprises Sindh, Western Rājapūtānā, Cutch, Gujarāt and a portion of the adjoining coast on the lower course of the Narmadā.

Pāṭaliputra — Paṭnā, the capital of Magadha.

Payoṣṇi — A river in southern India and may be identified with the Pūrṇā, a tributary of the river Tāpī.

Plakṣadvīpa — One of the seven *dvīpas* constituting the world. This is the first *dvīpa* from Jambū which is in the middle of the earth.

Prāgjyotiṣa — Kāmarūpa or Kāmākhyā in Assam.

Prayāga — Allāhābād. This is the eastern boundary of the Madhyadeśa or central India which is bounded by the Himālayas, the Vindhyas and the Vinaśana.

Pṛthūdaka — Pehoa in the Karnāl district of the Punjab on the river Sarasvatī.

Puṇḍra — Puṇḍravardhana. The district of Māldā in East Bengal.

Pūrvadeśa — Eastern India, includes within it Assam and Burma.

Puṣkaradvīpa — One of the seven *dvīpas* of the world. Jambūdvīpa is situated in the middle, while the Puṣkara is the third from Jambū.

Ramatha—This country is situated according to Rājaśekhara in northern India.

Ramyakavarṣa — This is the first *varṣa* to the north of the Mahāmerū which is situated in the middle of the Jambūdvīpa.

Ratnāvalī — A city on the southern ranges of the Malaya mountain.

Rāvaṇagaṅgā — This is a river in south India.

Ṛkṣaparvata — This is one of the Kulaparvatas of the Kumārīdvīpa of India. This mountain forms a part of the eastern range of the Vindhyas extending from the Bay of Bengal to the source of the Narmadā.

Sahuda — Rājaśekhara includes this among the countries in north India, representing western Afghanistan where the present Safadkoh and Sabzawar are situated.

Sahya—The northern portion of the western Ghāṭs situated between the river Kāverī in the south and the Godāvarī in the north.

Śaka — Śakasthān where the Śakas first settled after coming to India. Śākala or Siālkoṭ in the Lahore division, Punjab, may be identified with this Śaka of Rājaśekhara.

Śālmalidvīpa — One of the seven *dvīpas* constituting the world. This is said to be surrounded by the ocean of Surā.

Sarasvatī—Rājaśekhara mentions two rivers of the same name Sarasvatī; one, he places in northern India, while the other is in the west.

Sarayū — A river in the United Provinces. The town of Ayodhyā is situated on the bank of this river and it meets the Gaṅgā near Chāprā.

Śatadru — The river Sutlej.

Saumya — One of the nine parts of the Bhāratavarṣa. Saumya seems to be a country situated in the north-west direction of India.

Siṁhala — Ceylon different from the Laṅkā.

Sindhu — The river Indus in north India.

Śiprā — A river on which Ujjayinī is situated.

Śoṇa — Rājaśekhara mentions Śoṇa as a Nadī in eastern India which meets the Gaṅgā near Paṭnā.

Śrīparvata — Rājaśekhara locates this mountain in south India. Śrīśaila which is situated near Kurnool and at a distance of 50 miles from the Kṛṣṇā station of the G.I.P. Railway appears to be the same Śrīparvata.

Śṛṅgavāḥ — This is said to be the third mountain to the north of the Mahāmerū which is situated in the middle of the Jambūdvīpa.

Śuktimān — The portion of the Vindhya range which connects the Prāriyātra and the Ṛkṣaparvata.

Suṁha — Rājaśekhara mentions this as one of the eastern countries.

Sūrpāraka — This is a country in south India according to Rājaśekhara identified with Śopārā in the district of Thānā, 37 miles north of Bombay and 4 miles north-west of Bassein.

Surāṣṭra — Kāṭhiāwāḍ and other portions of northernmost Gujarāt.

Śūrasena — Śūrasena is one of the countries in north India.

Śvabharavatī — A river in western India identified with the river Sābaramatī in North Gujrāt which flows into the gulf of Cāmbay.

Śvetagiri — This is said to be the second mountain to the north of the Mahāmerū which is situated in the middle of the Jambūdvīpa.

Takka — The country lying between the two rivers, the Vipāśā and the

Sindhu.

Tāmraliptaka — Tāmluk, situated on the western bank of the Rūpanārāyaṇa in the district of Midnāpur in Bengal.

Tāmraparṇa — One of the nine parts of the Bhāratavarṣa. It is identified with Ceylon.

Tāmraparṇī — The river Tāmraparṇī which rises from the Agastikūṭa on the Malaya hills and flows through the district of Tinnevelly in the Madras Presidency.

Taṅgaṇa — This is a country in the Uttarāpatha.

Tāpī — The river Tapatī or Tāptī.

Toṣala — It is identified with Dakṣiṇakośala, as Toṣali is mentioned in the Aśoka inscription at Dhauli.

Travaṇa — This country is located in western India.

Tuṅgabhadrā — A tributary of the Kṛṣṇā river.

Turuṣka — Eastern Turkistan.

Tuṣāra — This is a country in northern India.

Tuṣāragiri — A peak of the Himālayas near Gaṅgotrī.

Ujjayinī — Modern Ujjain.

Utpalāvatī — This is a river in the Tinnevelly district in southern India. The river runs parallel to the Tāmraparṇī.

Uttarakośala — The kingdom of Oudh had two divisions, Uttarakośala and Kośala.

Uttarakuru — The Purāṇas consider this to be a *varṣa* surrounding the Varṣa Parvata Śṛṅgavān which is the third mountain range from the Mahāmerū in the north.

Uttarāpatha — The country to the north of Pṛthūdaka is called Uttarāpatha.

Vāhika — Same as Vālhīka.

Vaidiśā — Vidiśā. Bhilsā in Mālwā in the kingdom of Bhopāl on the river

Betwā or Vetravatī 26 miles to the north-east of Bhopal.

Valhava — One of the countries in northern India. It may be identified with the Vallapura (Ballawar) one of the hill states mentioned in the *Rājataraṅgiṇī*.

Vālhika — The country between Bias and Sutlej north of Kekaya.

Vallāra — The country ruled by the Vallāla dynasty in south India seems to be called Vallāra. It represents the country near Veṅkaṭagiri including Chittoor and Vellore in the Madras Presidency.

Vāmanasvāmi — This is a temple of Vāmana situated in the western part of the city of Kanauj.

Vānavāsaka — North Kanārā was known by this name.

Vāṇāyuja — A country in the north, generally identified with Arabia.

Vaṅga — The name Vaṅga is applied to the eastern portion of the delta of the Gaṅgā on the coast of the Bay of Bengal.

Vañjurā — Known also as Bañjulā or Mañjulā, a tributary of the Godāvarī.

Vārāṇasī — Benares.

Varṇā — This is a river in south India, identified either with the river Kṛṣṇā or Beṇā which is a branch of the Kṛṣṇā and rises from the western Ghāṭs.

Vārtaghnī — A river in western India, identified with the river Vātrak a tributary of the Sābarmatī.

Varuṇa — One of the nine divisions of the Bhāratavarṣa.

Vatsagulma — Vatsagulma is a city in the country of Vidarbha.

Veṇā — A tributary of the river Kṛṣṇā (see Varṇā).

Vidarbha — In ancient days, the country of Vidarbha comprised the whole of Berār, Khāndeśa and portions of the Nizam's territory and Central Provinces.

Videha — Tirhut or Tīrabhukti.

Vinaśana — The spot where the Sarasvatī disappears in the desert after taking a westerly course from the Thāneśvar located in Sirhind (Paṭiālā State).

Vindhya — The Vindhya range or Vindhyadakṣiṇapāda or the Satpurā hills between the Tāpī and Narmadā.

Vipāśā — The Biās or Beās, a tributary of Sutlej.

Viśālā — The city of Ujjain, the capital of Avantī.

Vitastā — The river Jhelum.

Vokkāṇa — Rājaśekhara mentions this as one of the countries in north India.

Yamunā — The river Jumnā.

Yavana — It is a country in western India. The Yavanas were foreigners and they were originally living in countries beyond the Indus.

Bibliography

(A) Primary Texts

Ānandvardhana, *Dhavanyāloka*, ed. with an introduction, English translation and notes by K. Krishonamoorthy. Karnatak University, Dharwar, 1975.

——, *Dhvanyāloka of Ānandvardhana*, Udyotas I, II. ed. with an English exposition by Bishnupada Bhattacharya, 2 Vols, Firma K.L. Mukhopadhyaya, Calcutta, 1956-72.

Bāṇa, *Harṣa-Carita*, tr. by E.B. Cowell and F.W. Thomas, Motilal Banarsidass, Delhi, 1968.

Bhāmaha, *Kāvyālamkara* of Bhāmaha, ed. with an English translation and notes by P.V. Naganatha Sastri, Motilal Banarsidass, Delhi, 1970.

Bharata, *The Nāṭyaśāstra*, chapters 1-27. Edited with translation by Manmohan Ghosh, 2 Vols, Manisha Granthalaya, Calcutta, 1967.

——, *The Nāṭyaśāstra*, tr. by A Board of Scholars, Delhi, Sri Satguru Publications, New Delhi.

Bhoja, *Śṛṅgāra Prakāśa*, tr. by V. Raghavan, Punarvasu, Madras, 1963.

Daṇḍin, *Kāvyādarśa*, ed. with commentary by Pandit Rangacharya Raddi Shastri, 2nd edn., Bhandarkar Oriental Research Institute, Poona, 1970.

——, *Kāvyādarśa*, Sanskrit Text and English Translation S.K. Belvalkar. The Oriental Book Supplying Agency, Poona, 1924.

Hemacandra, *Kāvyānuśāsanam*. Kāvyamālā, 2nd edn., Niranyasagar Press, Bombay, 1934.

Jagannātha, *Rasagaṅgādhara*, with 'Marmaprakāśa' by Nāgeśa. Edited with Sanskrit Commentary and Hindi translation by Madhusudana Shastri, 3 Vols, Banaras Hindu University (BHU), Varanasi, 1964-70.

Jaimini, *Mīmāṁsādarśanam*, with *Sābarabhāṣya* and *Tantravārttika*, 6 pts., Anandasram, Poona, 1970-74.

——, *Mīmāṁsā Sūtras of Jaimini*. tr. by Mohan Lal Sandal. 2 Vols., 1923-5, reprint, Motilal Banarsidass, Delhi, 1980.

Kālidāsa, *Raghuvaṁśa*, A study by Padma Ranganathan, The Gondals Press, New Delhi, 1964.

——, *Raghuvaṁśa. The Dynasty of Raghu*. Translated from the Sanskrit by Robert Antoine. A Writer's Workshop Publication, Calcutta, 1972.

——, *The Raghuvaṁśa of Kālidāsa* by Gopal Raghunath Nandargikar, Motilal Banarsidass, Delhi, 4th edn., 1971.

——, *Kumārasaṁbhava. The Origin of the Young God*. Translated with Annotation and an Introduction by Hank Heifetz, University of California Press, London, 1985.

——, *Kumārasambhava* (Cantos I-VIII), ed. with the commentary of Mallinatha, a Literal English Translation, Notes and Introduction by M.R. Kale, Motilal Banarsidass, Delhi, 7th edn., 1981.

——, *Meghadūtam. The Loom of Time: A Selection of His Plays and Poems*. Translated from the Sanskrit and Prākṛt with an introduction by Chandra Rajan, Penguin Books, New Delhi, 1989.

——, *Tales from Kālidāsa* by Suna. K. Surveyor, Jaico Publishing House, Delhi, 1951.

——, *Works of Kālidāsa*, Vol.1 and 2, tr. and ed. by C.R. Devadhar, Motilal Banarsidass, Delhi, 1986, rpt. 1986.

Kumārila, *Ślokavārttika*, tr. by Ganganath Jha, 2 Vols. 1924, Reprint, Sri Satguru Publications, Delhi, 1983.

——, *Ślokavārttikam*, Tara Publications,Varanasi, 1978.

——, *Tantravārttika*, tr. by Ganganath Jha, 2 Vols. 1924. Reprint, Sri Satguru Publications, Delhi, 1983.

Kuntaka, *The Vakrokti Jīvita*, ed. by Sushil Kumar De., 3rd edn., rev, Firma K.L. Mukhopadhyay, Calcutta, 1961.

——, *Vakrokti Jīvita of Kuntaka*, ed. and tr. by K. Krishnamoorthy, Karnatak University, Dharwar, 1977.

Mahimabhatta, *Vyaktiviveka* with Ruyyaka's Commentary. Edited with Hindi translation, by Rewaprasada Dwivedi. Chowkhamba Sanskrit Series, Varanasi, 1964.

Mammaṭa, *The Kāvyaprakāśa of Mammata with English Translation*, rev. edn. ed. by Ganganath Jha, Bhartiya Vidya Prakashan, Varanasi, 1967.

——, *Kāvya Prakāśa or The Poetic Light* with translation and Vidyacakravartin's commentary, Ed. by R.C. Dwivedi, 2 Vols, Motilal Banarsidass, Delhi, 1966-70.

——, *Kāvyaprakāśa*, tr. by Ganganath Jha, The Indian Press, Allahabad, 1925.

Nanda Chidbhava Swami (tr.), *The Bhagavad Gītā*, Sri Ramakrishna Tapuvanan, Madras, 1970.

Nikhilananda, Swami, *The Upaniṣads. A Second Selection, Śvetāśvātāra. Praśna and Māṇḍūkya with Gauḍapāda's Kārikā*. Phoenix House Limited, London, 1954 rpt. 1951.

Rājaśekhara, *Kāvyamīmāṁsā*, ed. by C.D. Dalal and K.S. Ramaswami Sastri, Oriental Institute, Baroda, 1934.

——, *Kāvyamīmāṁsā*, tr. in Hindi by Kedarnath Sharma Saraswat, Bihar Rastrabhasa Parishad, Patna, 1965.

——, *Bālarāmāyaṇa* ed. by Pt. Govinda Deva Sastri, the Medical Hall Press, Benares, 1869.

——, *Karpūra-Mañjarī*, ed. by Sten Konow, tr. by Charles Rockwell Lanman, Motilal Banarsidass, Delhi, 1963.

Rudraṭa, *Kāvyālaṁkāra*, ed. with commentary of Namisadhu by Durgaprasad and V.L. Sastri. Nirnayasagar Press, Bombay, 1928.

Śabara, *Śābara-Bhāṣya*, tr by Ganganath Jha, 3 Vols. 1933. Oriental Institute, Baroda, rpt. 1973.

Tagare, G.V., tr. and annotated, *The Vāyu Purāṇa*, Part II, Motilal Banarsidass, Delhi, 1988.

Viśvanātha, *Sāhityadarpaṇa*, tr. by Kumudranjan Ray, Calcutta, 1957.

Vāmana, *Kāvyālaṁkāra-Sūtra-Vṛtti*, tr. by Ganganath Jha, 2nd edn., Oriental Book Agency, Poona, 1928.

Vālmīki, *Rāmāyaṇa*, tr. by Ralph TH Griffith, Chowkhambha Sanskrit Series Office, Varanasi, 1963.

———, tr. by Hari Prasad Shastri, 3 Vols, London, Shanti Sadan, 1962.

(B) Secondary Sources

Bhattacharya, Bishnupada, *A Study in Language and Meaning: a Critical Examination of Some Aspects of Indian Semantics*, Calcutta, Progressive Publishers, 1962.

Dhayagude, S.K., *Western and Indian Poetics: A Comparative Study*, Bhandarkar Oriental Research Institute, Pune, 1981.

Butcher, S.H., *Aristotle's Theory of Poetry and Fine Arts*; Kalyani Publishers, Delhi, 1987.

Bhatt, G.P. (ed.), *Ancient Indian Tradition and Mythology*, Vol. 38, tr. by a Board of Scholars, Motilal Banarsidass, Delhi, 1988.

Chaitanya, Krishna, *Sanskrit Poetics, A Critical and Comparative Study*, Asis Publishing House, Bombay, 1965.

Chakrabarti, Tarapada, *Indian Aesthetics and the Science of Language*, Sanskrit Pustak Bhandar, Calcutta, 1971.

Chari, V.K., *Sanskrit Criticism*, Motilal Banarsidass Publishers, Delhi, 1993.

Coomaraswamy, Ananda K., *The Dance of Śiva*, Indian edn. rev., Sagar Publications, New Delhi, 1982.

Copeland, Rita, *Academic Traditions and Vernacular Texts: Rhetorics, Hermeneutic and Translation in the Middle Ages*, Cambridge University Press, 1991.

Culler, Jonathan, *Structuralist Poetics: Structuralism Linguistics and the Study of Literature*, Routledge and Kegan Paul, London, 1980.

———, *On Deconstruction: Theory and Criticism after Structuralism*. Ithaca, N.Y., Cornell University Press, 1982.

Dasgupta, S.N. and S. K. De., *History of Sanskrit Literature* University of Calcutta, Calcutta, 1947.

De, S.K., *Some Problems of Sanskrit Poetics*, Firma K.L. Mukhopadhyay, Calcutta, 1959.

———, *History of Sanskrit Poetics*, 2nd edn., rev. 2 Vols. in 1, Firma K.L. Mukhopadhyay, Calcutta, 1960.

———, *Sanskrit Poetics as a Study of Aesthetics*, University of California Press, Berkeley, 1963.

Dwivedi, R.C. (ed.), *Principles of Literary Criticism in Sanskrit*, Motilal Banarsidass, Delhi, 1969.

Fowler, Roger, *The Languages of Literature: Some Linguistic Contributions to Criticism*, Routledge & Kegan Paul, London, 1971.

———, (ed)., *Essays on Style and Language: Linguisitc and Critical Approaches to Literary Style*, Humanities, New York, 1966.

Gerow, Edwin, *A Glossary of Indian Figures of Speech*, The Hague, Mouton, 1971.

———, *Indian Poetics*, Vol. 5, fasc. 3 of *A History of Indian Literature*, ed. by Jan Gonda, Wiesbaden, Otto Harrassowitz, 1977.

Gupta, D.K., *A Critical Study of Daṇḍin and his Works*, Meharchand Lachmandas, Delhi, 1970.

Hewson Lance and Jacky Martin, *Redefining Translation: The Variational Approach*, Routledge, London & New York, 1991.

Inglis, Fred, *Media Theory: An Introduction*, Oxford, Basil Blackwell, 1990, rpt. 1991.

Jacob, Col. G.A., *Laukikanyāyāñjalī, A Second Handful of Popular Maxims Current in Sanskrit Literature*, The 'Nirnaya Sagar' Press, Bombay, 1925.

Kane, P.V., *History of Sanskrit Poetics*, 2nd edn., Motilal Banarsidass, Delhi, 1961.

Kapoor, Kapil, "Metaphor in Sanskrit and English Criticism", *Journal of Literary Criticism*, Delhi, 1985.

———, "Some Reflections on the Interpretation of Texts in the Indian Tradition", in *Structures of Signification*, Vol. I ed. by H.S. Gill, Delhi, JNU, 1990.

———, *Integration of Texts in the Tradition*, MLDB, forthcoming.

———, *Language, Linguistics and Literature: An Indian Perspective*, Academic Foundation, Delhi, 1994.

———, *Sylvia Plath's 'Daddy' in the Other Tradition: An Example Analysis in Rājaśekhara's Model*, unpublished paper.

———, "Vyākaraṇa aur Jñāna Mīmāṁsā", *Abhrānta*, Year 1, Issue 1, Patna, 1994.

———, (mimeod papers)

1. "The Cognising Self and the Experience of Poetry", *Indian Poetics and Modern Texts* (eds.), P.K. Rajan and Swapana Daniel, S. Chand & Company, Delhi, 1998.
2. "The Concept of *Padārtha* in Philosophy and Language", *The 200 Years, William Jones Memorial Volume*, Deccan College, Pune, 1997.
3. "Structure of Knowledge in Keats's Ode to Nightingale." (1995).
4. "Forms in the ocean: The Indian Conception of Language and

Reality." (1989).

5. "*Vivarta* and *Pariṇāma*: Bhartṛhari's Theories of Language." (1996).

6. "Cultural Determination of Literary Theories." (1995).

7. "Linguistic Meaning and Referential Reality." (1991).

Keith, A. Berriedale, *A History of Sanskrit Literature*, 1920, Reprint, Oxford University Press, London, 1966.

Krishnamachariar, M., *History of Classical Sanskrit Literature*. Reprint, Motilal Banarsidass, Delhi, 1970.

Kushwaha, M.S., *Indian Poetics and Western Thought*, Argo Publishing House, Lucknow, 1988.

———, (ed.), *New Perspectives on Indian Poetics*. Argo Publishing House, Lucknow, 1991.

Krishna, Daya, *India's Intellectual Traditions*, Motilal Banarsidass, Delhi, 1987.

Krishnamoorthy, K., *Essays in Sanskrit Criticism*. Karnatak University Press, Dharwar, 1964.

———, *Studies in Indian Aesthetics and Criticism*, Mysore, 1979.

———, *Indian Literary Theories: A Reappraisal*, Meharchand Lacchmandas, Delhi, 1985.

Kunjunni Raja, K., *Indian Theories of Meaning*, The Adyar Library and Research Centre, Madras, 1963.

Lahiri, P.C., *Concepts of Rīti and Guṇa in Sanskrit Poetics*, V.K. Publishing House, Delhi, 1987.

Lawrence, Venuti, *Rethinking Translation: Discourse Subjectivity, Ideology*, London & N.Y. Routledge, 1992.

Matilal, Bimal Krishna, *Epistemology, Logic and Grammar in Indian Philosophical Analysis*, The Hague, Mouton, 1971.

———, *Logic, Language and Reality: An Introduction to Indian Philosophical Studies*, Motilal Banarsidass, Delhi, 1985.

Nagendra, *Literary Criticism in India*, Sarita Prakashan, Meerut, 1976.

Patil Rajaram Devendra Kumar, *Cultural History from the Vāyu Purāṇa*, Motilal Banarsidass, Delhi, 1964, rpt. 1973.

Raghavan, V., *Studies on Some Concepts of the Alaṁkāra Śāstra*, 2nd. rev. edn., Adyar Library and Research Centre, Madras, 1973.

Rayan, Krishna, *Suggestion and Statement in Poetry*, Athlone Press, London, 1972.

——, *Text and Sub-text: Suggestion in Literature*, Arnold Heinemann, Delhi, 1987.

Śāstri, Kuppuswami, *Highways and Byways of Literary Criticism in Sanskrit*, Kuppuswami Sastri Research Institute, Madras, 1945.

Śāstri, Subrahmanya, *Lectures on Patañjali's Mahābhāṣya*, Vol. I, Annamalainagar, 1944.

Sebeok, Thomas A. (ed.), *Style in Language*, Technology Press of MIT/ Wiley, New York, 1960.

Singh, M.R., *Geographical Data in the Early Purāṇas: A Critical Study*, Punthi Pustak, Calcutta, 1972.

Staal, J.F. (ed.), *A Reader on Sanskrit Grammarians*, Mass: MIT Press, Cambridge, 1972; Motilal Banarsidass, Delhi, 1985.

Tiwary, R.S., *A Critical Approach to Classical Indian Poetics*, Chowkhamba Orientalia, Delhi and Varanasi, 1984.

Verma, Dr. Shyama, *Acarya Rājaśekhara*, in Hindi, Madhya Pradesh Hindi Granth Akadami, Bhopal, 1971.

Warder, A.K., *Indian Kavya Literature* (Vols. I-V), Motilal Banarsidass, Delhi, 1972-83.

——, *The Science of Criticism in India*, The Adyar Library and Research Centre, Madras, 1978.

(C) Dictionaries and other Reference Books

Abhyankar, Kashinath Vasudev, *A Dictionary of Sanskrit Grammar*,

Geakwad Oriental Series, Baroda, Oriental Institute, 1961.

Apte, Vaman Sivarama, *The Practical Sanskrit-English Dictionary*, Motilal Banarsidass, Delhi, rpt., 1985.

———, *Sanskrit Hindi Kosh*, Motilal Banarsidass, Delhi, 1966, ed., rpt. 1973.

———, *The Student's Sanskrit English Dictionary*, Motilal Banarsidass, Delhi, 1988.

Bhide, Vidhyadhar Vaman, *A Concise Sanskrit English Dictionary*, Gian Publishing House, Delhi, 1986.

Bahri, Hardev, *Advanced Hindi English Dictionary*, Vani Prakashan, 2nd edn., New Delhi, 1991.

Chaturvedi, Mahendra and Tiwari B.N., *A Practical Hindi-English Dictionary*, National Publishing House, Delhi, 1970.

Dowson, John, *A Classical Dictionary of Hindu Mythology and Religion: Geography, History and Literature*, in 2 Vols. Munshiram Manoharlal Publishers Pvt. Ltd., New Delhi, 1973.

Garg, Dr. Ganga Ram, *Encyclopaedia of the Hindu World*, Vol. 3, Ar-Az, Concept Publishing Company, New Delhi, 1992.

Mani, Vettam, *Purāṇic Encyclopaedia: A Comprehensive Dictionary with Special Reference to the Epic and Purāṇic Literature*, Motilal Banarsidass, Delhi, 1975.

Nagendra, *A Dictionary of Sanskrit Poetics*, B.R. Publishing Corporation, Delhi, 1987.

Sebeok, T.A. (ed.), *Encyclopaedic Dictionary of Semiotics*. Tome 2. Berlin, N.Y.; Mouton de gruyter, 1986.

Vaidya, Lakshman Ramchandra, *The Standard Sanskrit, English Dictionary*, M/s. Radhabai Amaram Sagoon Booksellers and Publishers, Kalka Devi Road, Bombay, 1889.

Walker, Benjamin, *Hindu World: An Encyclopedic Survey of Hindusism*, in two vols., George Allen and Unwin Ltd. London, 1968.